D1297371

# CELTIC MYTH
## AND
## ARTHURIAN ROMANCE

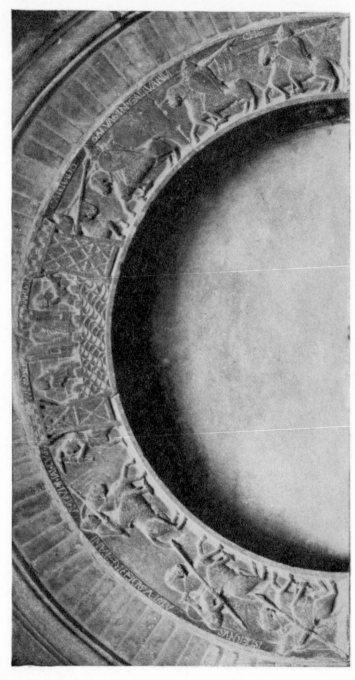

SCULPTURED ARCHIVOLT AT MODENA CATHEDRAL
Attack by Gawain and Arthur on Castle of Mardoc, Lord of Hades

# CELTIC MYTH
# AND
# ARTHURIAN ROMANCE

Roger Sherman Loomis

Constable · London

This edition published 1993
by Constable and Company Limited
3 The Lanchesters, 162 Fulham Palace Road
London W6 9ER
ISBN 0 09 472800 3
First edition published 1926
by Columbia University Press
Printed in Great Britain by
St Edmundsbury Press Limited
Bury St Edmunds, Suffolk

A CIP catalogue record for this book
is available from the British Library

# TABLE OF CONTENTS

## BOOK IV. BRIDES OF THE SUN

## BOOK V. FROM IRISH AND WELSH GODS TO A BRITISH CHIEFTAIN

# BOOK ONE

## FROM KNIGHTS OF THE ROUND TABLE
## TO IRISH GODS

# CHAPTER I

To think of Medieval Romance is to gaze through magic casements opening on the foam of perilous seas in faery lands forlorn: it is to dream of faery damsels met in forest wide by knights of Logres or of Lyones, Lancelot or Pelleas or Pellenore; it brings near the island valley of Avilion, deep-meadowed, happy, fair with orchard lawns and bowery hollows crowned with summer sea; we behold Bors, Perceval, and Galahad sailing in Solomon's magic bark for the Land of Sarras; with Parsifal we listen bewildered to the haunting music of the Grail and witness that strange agonized ritual with a mute wonder.

In short, Medieval Romance is dominated by the legends of Arthur and the Table Round. It is they which during the twelfth century placed their enchantment upon Europe. In Sicily, Spain, Iceland, and the Kingdom of Jerusalem, the names of Gawain and Morgan le Fay came to be as well known as they were in England or France. So powerful was the spell of Arthurian legend that its great rival, the Carolingian epic, took over, as the *Pélerinage Charlemagne* indicates, much of its supernatural machinery. Arthurian legend borrowed little from the *chansons de geste*, but the "epics" of Ogier and Huon de Bordeaux incorporate masses of Arthurian material. Quite properly, then, is our conception of Medieval Romance filled with the strange pageantry, charged with the mysterious glamour that distinguishes the Matter of Britain from other medieval cycles.

This strangeness, this mystery lies not simply in the common magical elements of folklore, — the sudden metamorphoses and vanishings, the enchanted weapons and barges, the giants, dwarfs, and monsters. It lies also in the tantalizing suggestion which must occur at times to every sensitive reader that more is meant than meets the ear. It is not only Matthew Arnold who in reading the tales of the *Mabinogion* suspects that "the medieval story-teller is pillaging an antiquity of which he does not fully possess the secret; . . . he builds, but what he builds is full of materials of which he knows not the history, or knows by a glimmering tradition merely, stones 'not of this building,'

3

but of an older architecture, greater, cunninger, more majestical.''

But so scattered, so battered are the relics of that older architecture that there are scholars who deny altogether that Arthurian romance is constructed out of the ruins of a pagan Pantheon. There are others, however, who have pointed out that Gawain, whose strength waxed and waned with the mounting and sinking of the sun in the heavens, must have been a solar hero; others have seen in the Grail legend the survival of a long forgotten initiation ceremony into a cult of fertility; others have traced the enchanter Mabon back through the Welsh Mabon son of Modron to Apollo Maponos, worshiped in Gaul and Britain. But there has been only one comprehensive attempt to discover the mythological concepts and figures which, like gigantic shadows thrown on a hillside, loom up behind the mail-clad knights and trimly girdled ladies of Camelot.

Sir John Rhys did not, however, work out the Celtic mythological system from the evidence of the Irish and Welsh legends themselves, but tried to fit them into the scheme which Max Müller had constructed largely from Sanscrit sources. Rhys further weakened his case by his patent ignorance of any but the Welsh and English versions of the Arthurian cycle.[1] He not only failed, in spite of the great value of many of his suggestions, to impress the learned world; he himself abandoned and led others to abandon the attempt to interpret the Matter of Britain as a faded mythology. So, although medieval authors themselves referred to Morgan le Fay as ''dea quaedam phantastica,'' spoke of Gawain and Lunete as the sun and moon, and testified that the common folk in old times regarded Merlin as a god,[2] modern scholars have been much warier. An influential body of them consider the vast literature of the Round Table cycle as mainly springing from the imaginations of French authors of the twelfth and thirteenth centuries.[3] The old practise of claiming as

---

[1] *Hibbert Lectures*, 1888; *Studies in the Arthurian Legend*, 1891. It is to Rhys's credit that from the outset he spoke of the certainty that his more ambitious theories might prove untenable. Noteworthy partial attempts to discover mythological connections are Cook's in *Folklore*, XVII, 308, 427, XVIII, 184; Macculoch's in *Mythology of All Races*, III, 184; Squire's in his *Mythology of the British Islands*, 354; Anwyl's in Hastings' *Encyclopedia of Religion*, II, 1.

[2] Giraldus Cambrensis, *Opera*, ed. Brewer, IV, 48 f; Crestien de Troyes, *Yvain*, ll. 2395–414; Sommer, *Vulgate Version*, III, 19.

[3] W. Foerster and W. Golther in Germany, E. Faral in France, W. W.

authority the tales of the "Bretons" they consider mere convention; the romances, broadly speaking, a late invention.

Without accepting Rhys's particular mythological identifications, it seems possible none the less to accept his basic theory and to agree whole-heartedly in the belief that most of the British and Armoric knights that encircle Uther's son were once gods or deified men. The fundamental stories about their births, their deaths, their combats, their loves, are, once understood, as good mythology as any that exists.

How and where shall we find our entrance from the world of romance into that Other World of the gods? A number of facts scattered about in books on archaeology, history, and literature, when brought together and correlated, enable us to imagine with fair accuracy a scene where knightly adventure and mythical significances seem clearly mingled in the tale of a Breton minstrel.

In November 1096 along the white road, bordered with grey-green olive orchards, leading into the city of Bari, far down in the heel of Italy, a long cavalcade of knights on jaded horses was riding. Their ringed hauberks were rusty, but their shields and fluttering pennons were gay with indigo, green, and cinnabar. It was a long journey they had come, for here were the Duke of Brittany, Alan Fergant, and his vassals, Riou de Loheac, Ralph de Gael, Conan de Lamballe, and Alan, steward of the Archbishop of Dol.[4] And on every knight's arms was the sign of the cross, for they were all vowed to win back the Holy Sepulchre from the Turk. Presently the battlemented walls of Bari loomed up before them; their horses drummed across the drawbridge and clattered through the cobbled streets. Here they were destined to stay for four months, since the Apulian mariners would not risk a winter crossing to Greece. The Breton nobles had to wile away many a long hour. Doubtless they visited the newly built church of Saint Nicholas, and prostrated themselves before the hallowed bones of its patron. But they had other resources. If we enter the great banqueting hall of the Norman Count of Apulia, Roger Bursa, we may find help in our quest. There he sits on the dais with his guests, Robert Curthose, the warrior Duke of Normandy, and the aged Alan

---

Newell and J. D. Bruce in the U. S. are the chief exponents of this view. It may be noted that none of them possessed or possesses any special competence in Celtic languages or literatures.

[4] C. W. David, *Robert Curthose*, 94, 221.

Fergant, Duke of Brittany. Squires pass frequently, filling the great drinking-horns with wine. In the middle of the hall the logs blaze. Robert of Normandy, known as a liberal patron of minstrels, calls for a tale. There arises, as we may surmise, a famous Breton *conteur*. He stands before the dais, and in a loud clear voice, tells his story, impersonating the various characters in gesture, thrust and blow, and intonation. What the story was that he told we shall never know precisely, but its general outline we may by strange chance guess. If we follow the road north from Bari along the coast as far as the Po Valley and turn north-west to Modena, we come to the famous cathedral, on which in 1099 a group of sculptors from Bari began work.[5] On the archivolt of the north portal there is carved a scene which we shall presently recognize as an Arthurian story with Bretonized names.[6] The only explanation for its existence is the one already suggested — that it was a story told by a Breton *conteur* in the presence of Crusaders and craftsmen gathered at Bari in 1096, a story so memorable and so graphic that it was at last fixed in marble at Modena. To this day it still bears witness to the power of that ancient tale. (See frontispiece.)

In the center is a castle surrounded by waters. On the keep hang a shield and spear. Two persons are within, a woman named Winlogee and a man named Mardoc, both much perturbed. The castle has two opposite entrances defended by wooden barbicans. Before the left barbican stands a churl labeled Burmaltus, brandishing a pick-like weapon called a *baston cornu*. Against him ride three knights, Artus de Bretania, Isdernus, and an unnamed knight. It is noteworthy that Isdernus wears neither helmet nor hauberk. From the other barbican gallops forth a knight, Carrado, striking with his lance the first of three attacking knights, — Galvaginus, Galvariun, and Che.

Practically all archaeologists agree that the sculpture is to be

---

[5] The demonstration of their presence at Bari is due to A. K. Porter. *Cf.* his *Romanesque Sculpture of the Pilgrimage Roads*, I, 66 f; also *Art Studies*, I, 12; *Burlington Magazine*, XLIII, 63.

[6] On this sculpture see A. K. Porter, *Lombard Architecture*, I, 280: III, 44; B. Colfi, *Di una recente interpretazione data alle sculture* etc. (extract from *Atti e memorie del R. deputazione di storia patria per le provincie modenesi*, ser. IV, vol. 9, 133); *Memorie della regia accademia di scienze, lettere, ed arti in Modena*, ser. III, vol. 8, 167; my article in *Medieval Studies in Memory of Gertrude Schoepperle Loomis; RR*, XV, 266.

dated early in the twelfth century. An account of the building of the cathedral, the *Relatio Translationis Corporis Sancti Geminiani*, speaks of sculptural activity between the commencement of the work in 1099 and the consecration in 1106. "The marbles are dug out, and the scenes carved and polished with marvelous art." [7] That the Arthurian sculpture belongs among these earliest works is proved by the fact that five of the helmets depicted are conical, forming in outline an isosceles triangle, — a fashion which by the year 1109 was being supplanted by a form which showed a curved or longer line in the back and of which no later twelfth century example can be found. [8] The knights of the Modena sculpture, then, mirror for us the champions of the first Crusade. Such in appearance were Bohemund, Tancred, and Godfrey de Bouillon.

This carving was first brought directly to the attention of students of medieval romance by Foerster in 1898. [9] He detected a curious resemblance between the sculptured scene and the story of Carado of the Dolorous Tower in the *Vulgate Lancelot*, which related the carrying off of Gawain by a gigantic knight named Carado; the imprisonment of Gawain in a castle with two perilous entrances, at one of which stood a churl; the pursuit of Carado by Galeschin, Ivain, Arthur, and Keu; and the final deliverance of Gawain by Lancelot, who slays Carado with his own sword, placed by a maiden whom Carado had abducted within Lancelot's reach. Foerster pointed out that in this episode were the castle with two entrances, the churl standing before the gate, the lord of the castle Carado fighting against Arthur and his knights, Keu and Galeschin, who correspond to Che and Galvariun on the sculpture.

Foerster had the puzzle half solved, but he failed to identify the key personage of the sculpture, — the lady Winlogee. To be sure, back in the year 1845 Borghi had proposed that we had here a version of the encounter between Arthur and Modred for the possession of Guinevere, [10] but no one had taken the suggestion seriously enough to proceed on the assumption that Winlogee was Guinevere. But certain facts make that assumption secure. Winlogee is a form of the Breton name Winlowen or Wenlowen, meaning "white and joyous." [11] In the *De Ortu*

[7] G. Bertoni, *Atlante storico-paleografico del duomo di Modena*, 88.

[8] *Medieval Studies in Memory of Gertrude Schoepperle Loomis*.

[9] *ZrP*, XXII, 243, 526.          [10] C. Borghi, *Il Duomo*, 68 ff.

[11] J. Loth, *Chrestomathie bretonne*, 147.

*Walwanii* Arthur's queen is called Gwendoloena.[12] In the romance of *Yder* the hero is represented as the lover of a queen named Guenloie, whereas he is elsewhere said to be the lover of Guinevere. Indeed, the same romance preserves clear traces of a tender relationship betwen Guinevere and Yder, even though he is actually represented as the lover of Queen Guenloie.[13] This confusion is due to the fact that the more mellifluous name Winlowen or Winlogee had been substituted by a few Breton *conteurs* for the Welsh Gwenhwyvar, although the great majority preserved the name as Guenievre. The author of *Yder* was attempting to reconcile two stories, one of which gave as the name of Yder's beloved Guenievre, and the other, Guenloie. But that these were one and the same person there can hardly be a doubt.

Now any Arthurian scholar, seeing Arthur's queen in a castle surrounded by great waters, approached by two entrances, would have at least a shrewd suspicion that this must be one of the versions of the abduction of Guinevere.[14] He would not, however, feel sure until he could detect among the extant literary versions some correspondences of detail with the Modena sculpture. One obvious feature of the Modena relief is the prominence of Galvaginus, who is, of course, Gawain. He alone bears an elaborately decorated shield and seems to be in combat with the more formidable of the queen's defenders. In the best-known forms of the abduction story, Crestien de Troyes's *Chevalier de la Charette* and the nineteenth book of Malory's *Morte d'Arthur*, Lancelot is the rescuer. But Miss Weston showed long ago that in Hartmann von Aue's *Iwein* it is distinctly implied that Gawain is the hero of the exploit. Let me quote: "A knight appears at Arthur's court and requires the king to grant him a boon — whatever he may ask. Arthur demurs, but finally yields to the knight's taunts and gives the required promise, when the knight demands the queen and carries her off. . . . The knights arm to pursue the ravisher; Kay is the first to overtake him, and is struck from his horse with such violence that his helmet catches in the bough of a tree, and he hangs suspended. . . . One after another all the knights are vanquished, and Guinevere is carried off. Gawain is not at

[12] Ed. J. D. Bruce, 85.
[13] *Yderroman*, ed. H. Gelzer, lvi.
[14] Bibl. of Guinevere abductions, G. Schoepperle, *Tristan and Isolt*, II, 528–40.

court; had he been there it would never have happened; he returns the next day, and rides at once in search of the queen. Later on we are told he has returned to court, and a few lines further on that in these same days the queen had returned from her captivity. Who freed her is not stated, but we are led to infer that it was Gawain. Lancelot is not once mentioned throughout the poem." [15]

Hartmann is not alone in representing Gawain as the rescuer of Guinevere. Heinrich von dem Türlin makes him the hero of her abduction by Gasozein,[16] and the *Livre d'Artus*, of her abduction by Urien.[17] Even though Crestien has made Gawain's failure a foil for the prowess of Lancelot, it was a deliberate perversion of a strong tradition which represented Gawain as the Queen's deliverer.

Four other features on the Modena archivolt are accounted for by the abduction story in *Durmart le Gallois*, a romance assigned to the second quarter of the thirteenth century: the castle of the abductor is surrounded by a wide marsh; [18] shields are hung on the sides of the keep; [19] the queen is found with her lover in the castle; [20] and Ydier, like Isdernus, wears no armor.[21] This last feature alone should convince us that we are on the right track. The subject of the sculpture must be the abduction of Guinevere.

How can we reconcile this conclusion with the manifest correspondence between the sculpture and the Carado of the Dolorous Tower episode, which Foerster detected? For the Dolorous Tower episode is an abduction not of Guinevere but of Gawain. Yet anyone examining carefully that episode will soon discover that it incorporates many incidents found in Crestien's account of the abduction of Guinevere,[22] and may properly suspect that the Dolorous Tower story is the result of a deliberate manipulation. By substituting Lancelot for Gawain as hero and Gawain for Guinevere as victim, the author of the *Lancelot* achieved the double result of avoiding a cumbersome repetition of the Guinevere abduction theme and of glorifying Lancelot at the expense of Gawain. Not only was such a procedure in accordance with the author's artistic purposes, but it

[15] J. L. Weston, *Legend of Gawain*, 69.
[16] *Krone*, ed. Scholl, 11608–12437. *Cf. Englische Studien*, XXXVI, 345.
[17] Sommer, *Vulgate Version*, VII, 65–7.
[18] *Durmart le Gallois*, ed. Stengel, ll. 4309–11.
[19] Ll. 4455 f.        [20] Ll. 4535–40.        [21] Ll. 4361 f.
[22] *RR*, XV, 266, n. 3.

may also have had the backing of precedent, for, as we shall discover later, [23] the tradition of Gawain's delivery from prison by Lancelot may represent almost as ancient tradition as Gawain's rescue of Guinevere. By reversing the author's process and making Gawain the hero of the Dolorous Tower episode and Guinevere the victim, we get most of the features we need to explain the Modena sculpture, and what the Dolorous Tower episode does not supply the *Durmart* version of the abduction of Guinevere does. With the aid of these survivals, one dating from the first quarter, the other from the second quarter of the thirteenth century, we can practically reconstruct the tale told by the Breton *conteur* at Bari during the winter of 1096–7.

Winlogèe, Artus' queen, escorted only by the unarmed knight Isdern, has gone out to a meadow. Suddenly there gallops out, from a wood near by, a giant knight, Carrado, who swings her from her palfrey to his horse. Her attendant seizes Carrado's rein in the attempt to stop him, but is beaten off. Carrado rides away with the Queen. Isdern goes back and gives the alarm. He himself takes spear and shield and starts in pursuit. There set out after him, fully armed, Galvariun, Galvagin, Artus, and Che. At length they arrive before a castle, surrounded by a marsh and approached by two opposite barbicans. Before one of them stands a huge ruffian, swinging a *baston cornu*, whose name is Burmalt. Apparently he withstands the assault of Artus, Isdern, and an unnamed knight. At the other entrance, Galvagin, Galvariun, and Che are met by the giant Carrado. Probably Che and Galvariun are overthrown. Galvagin, however, encounters Carrado and pursues him into the castle. When Galvagin breaks his sword, a damsel whom Carrado has abducted places Carrado's own sword, with which alone he could be killed, within Galvagin's reach, and with this Galvagin despatches him. The hero then proceeds, sees hanging upon the walls of the keep the shields of the knights whom Carrado has slain. He finds at last Winlogee with Mardoc, who has long loved her and to whom Carrado has delivered her. What is the fate of Mardoc is uncertain, but probably he throws himself on the Queen's mercy and is pardoned. Galvagin then brings her back to her husband.

It should further be noted that the *Vulgate Lancelot* ascribes

[23] Chap. XXXII.

to Carado, when he perceives that his mistress has betrayed him, this cry of reproach: "Alas, that which I loved best in the world has slain me, but now know I well that she loves another more than me." [24] The same romance says that his mistress was married to Melyans le Gai; [25] and the *Livre d'Artus* says that it was Gawain's amie Floree who was given in marriage to Melianz de Lis.[26] This correspondence raises a suspicion that the damsel who betrayed Carrado to Galvagin, in the story of the Modena archivolt, was Floree.

This sculpture, then, is a singularly well preserved example not only of Romanesque art in Lombardy at an early stage of its evolution, but also of Arthurian romance at a stage of which all other traces are lost. By comparison with later and more corrupt versions of the abduction motif, it is possible to read its riddle, to reconstruct the story told over the wine in that Apulian port eight hundred and thirty years ago.

But not far from Bari across the Straights of Messina lay "that fair field of Enna, where Proserpin, gathering flowers, herself the fairest flower, by gloomy Dis was gathered." And the story of Guinevere's abduction reminded Gaston Paris in 1883 of the abduction of the classic goddess of the fruits and flowers.[27] Does not Floree, the presumptive name of the lady carried off by Carrado, suggest that she is related to Proserpine? Does not Malory tell us that it was while the Queen was out a-Maying that Mellyagraunce seized her? [28] And is it not appropriate that her rescuer should be Gawain, who has been suspected of being a sun-hero? Still it must be confessed that these are confused hints, no more. But since it has been shown frequently that the exploits of Gawain correspond to those of the primitive Irish hero Cuchulinn,[29] let us follow the scent to Ireland. Perhaps there we shall find our abduction story in more archaic form. Perhaps we shall stumble on unmistakable myth.

[24] Sommer, *Vulgate Version*, IV, 136.
[25] *Ibid.*, 139.
[26] *Ibid.*, VII, 115.
[27] *Rom*, XII, 508. Paris is mistaken, I believe, in taking Gorre for the land of death, and Lot in interpreting Meleagant as Welsh Maelvas, Prince of Death. The analogue of Tigernmas has been destroyed by Meyer, *Sitzb. Preuss. Akad. Wiss.*, 1919, 545. Rhys's derivation from Mael-gwas, "Prince Youth," (*Arthurian Legend*, 51) seems more likely since the Welsh form is not Melvas but Melwas.
[28] Book XIX, ch. I.
[29] J. L. Weston, *Leg. of Gawain*, 17, 64.

# CHAPTER II

## THE RAPE OF THE FLOWER MAIDEN

In her study of the variant versions of the abduction of Guinevere and their Irish analogues Miss Schoepperle was the first to point out as a possible source the Irish legend of the abduction of Blathnat by Curoi and her rescue by Cuchulinn.[1] It was one of the three hundred and fifty "prime stories," to be related to kings and chiefs, which are mentioned in an incomplete list of the tenth century.[2] It was called the "Tragic Death of Curoi mac Daire." Several introductory or related stories are also found: "The Cattle-Raid of the Three Cows of Echaidh," "The Attack on the Men of Falga," and "The Elopement of Blathnait, daughter of Paill son of Fidaig, with Cuchulinn."[3] It may be remarked at once that the name Blathnat or Blathine means "Little Flower."[4]

The popularity of the tale is attested by the number of Irish versions, more or less condensed, which have survived,[5] and by the more numerous Arthurian abduction stories which it has influenced. The Irish versions have been published by the sound Celtic philologist, Thurneysen, but his accompanying study of the development of the legend has been shown to possess little scientific value.[5a] The most useful version for us is that found in the *Yellow Book of Lecan*, a fourteenth century manuscript.[6]

"Why did the men of Ulster slay Curoi son of Dare? . . . Because of Blathnait, daughter of Mend, who was carried off from the siege of the men of Falga, because of the three cows of Iuchna and the three men of Ochain, that is, the little birds that used to be on the ears of the cows, even Iuchna's cows, and a caldron was carried off with the cows. That was their calf. Thirty cows was the portion of the caldron. . . . Curoi son of Dare went with them to the siege, and they did not recognize

[1] G. Schoepperle, *Tristan and Isolt*, II, 427.
[2] E. O'Curry, *MS. Materials*, 584, 587.
[3] *Ibid.*, 585, 588, 590.
[4] R. Thurneysen, *Irische Helden- und Königsagen*, 432.
[5] *Ibid.*, 431–46.
[5a] *ZcP*, IX, 189; *Mitra*, I, 263.
[6] *Eriu*, II, 21 ff.

him, that is, they called him the man in the grey mantle. Every head that was brought out of the fort, 'Who slew that man?' said Conchobar. 'I and the man in the grey mantle,' each answered in turn.

"When, however, they were dividing the spoil, they did not give Curoi a share, for justice was not granted him. He ran in among the cows, and gathered them before him, collected the birds in his girdle, and thrust the woman under one of his armpits, and they went from them, he with his caldron on his back. And none among the men of Ulster was able to get speech with him save Cuchulainn alone. He [Curoi] turned upon the latter, and thrust him into the earth to his armpits, and cropped his hair on him with his sword, and rubbed cow-dung into his head and then came home.

"[After a year Cuchulainn found Curoi's stronghold.] He held converse with the woman, for he had loved her even before she was brought over sea; she was a daughter of Iuchna, king of the men of Falga. . . . He made a tryst with her again in the west on the night of Samain [Hallowe'en]. Moreover, a province of the Eraind set forth to go with Cuchulainn. It was on that day she gave counsel to Curoi, namely, that a splendid fortress should be built by him for his city, of every pillar-stone standing or lying in Ireland. It was the Clan Dedad who set out in one day for the building of the stronghold, so that he was alone in his fortress that day. This was the token that was between her and Cuchulainn, namely to pour the milk of Iuchna's cows adown the river in the direction of the Ulstermen so that the river might be white when she was washing him [Curoi]. So it was done. . . . She was then searching his head [for vermin] in front of the stronghold. 'Come into the stronghold,' said she, 'and get washed before the hosts come back with their burdens.' Just then he lifted up his head and saw the host of the Ulstermen coming towards him along the glen, both foot and horse. . . . Thereupon he goes inside, and the woman washes him, and she bound his hair to the bedposts and rails, and took the sword out of its scabbard, and threw open the stronghold. He heard naught, however, until the men had filled the house on him and had fallen on him. He rose up straightway against them and slew a hundred of them with kicks and blows of his fists. . . .

"Then it was the Clann Deda cast from them every pillar-stone which is standing and lying in Ireland, when they hear the

shouting, and came up to the slaughter around the fortress. . . .
When, however, they were slaying one another by the fortress,
Cuchulainn shore off the man's head. . . . Nevertheless the
slaughter increased on them every day from Hallowe'en till the
middle of spring."

Another version makes the following divergences from the
*Yellow Book* account: [7] Blathine is the daughter of Conchobar,
and is first carried off by Echde or Echaidh Echbel.  It is to
Echaidh that the marvelous speckled kine and the copper
caldron belong, which the Ulstermen in their turn carry off with
the maiden.  Curoi is said to be a young man.  He is promised
all the booty in return for slaying Echaidh, who pursues the
Ulstermen over the sea.  But for three years they put off the
complete fulfillment of the bargain and withhold Blathine, the
cows, and the caldron.  Finally Curoi carries her off, and
Blathine learns from him the secret of his life, which is an elaboration of the idea that he could be slain only with his own sword.
There was in a spring on the side of Sliab Mis a salmon which
appeared only at the end of seven years, and in the belly of the
salmon was a golden ball, and in the ball was Curoi's soul,
and only his own sword could cut the ball.  Cuchulinn carried
out the necessary measures, and Curoi died crying, "No secret to
women, no jewel to slaves!"

It is noteworthy that this variant has combined the tradition
that Curoi could be slain only with his own sword with a very
ancient and widespread theme — the treacherous wife who
betrays the seat of her husband's life in some "external soul."
Of this combination of treacherous wife and external soul the
legend of Samson and Delilah is doubtless the best known
version, and the narrative pattern we shall therefore call the
Samson and Delilah pattern.  As we shall see later, this feature
was highly elaborated in Welsh and modern Irish tales.

The versions given of this famous story by Keating and
O'Curry in more modern times agree on three noteworthy points. [8]
In both the caldron and the cows have been as completely
suppressed as they have been in the French versions of the ab-
duction of Guinevere.  Again both agree in making Curoi leave
Cuchulinn bound when the latter attempts to pursue him.
And again both are silent regarding Curoi's external soul, and

[7] *ZcP*, IX, 193–6.
[8] E. O'Curry, *Manners and Customs*, III, 79–82; *ITS*, VIII, 223–7.

afford only a bare suggestion that he was killed by his own sword.

But this point is emphasized in two old résumés of the story. "Cuchulinn reached him with his own sword, so that he left him behind on a litter on the noble shoulders of six men." [9] "Cuchulinn slew him [Curoi] with his own sword, after Blathnait had stolen it from him" [10] Moreover, the duration of the battle is again mentioned: "From November 1 till the middle of spring the battle of the Ulstermen continued." [11]

Now it is clear that this old Irish tale presents striking correspondences to the story of the Modena archivolt. The heroes correspond, for it has often been noted that Cuchulinn seems to be a prototype of Gawain. The name of the damsel who betrays Carrado seems to be Floree, whereas the name of Blathnat, who betrays Curoi, means "little flower." The general plot is the same: the abduction of a woman, the attack upon a castle to which she has been taken, the slaying of the abductor, and the rescue of the woman. In both stories the abductor is betrayed by his own mistress and killed by his own sword in the hands of the hero. Even the detail of the abductor's dying reproach to his mistress is common to both stories.

There are even further correspondences. The name of the abductor Carrado is close enough to that of the abductor Curoi mac Daire to make one suspect that it is a corruption of the Irish name — a suspicion which I shall prove elsewhere is fully justified. But it is even more startling to discover that in the churl Burmalt, who guards one of the gateways with his *baston cornu*, we have Curoi again. For in a famous scene in the Irish tale of *Bricriu's Feast* Curoi enters the hall of the Ulstermen disguised as a churl or herdsman, "great and hideous. An old hide next his skin, and a black tawny cloak about him. . . . In his right hand, an axe into which had gone thrice fifty measures of glowing metal." [12] In this disguise Curoi challenges the heroes to an exchange of blows with his ax. Now in the French romance of *Hunbaut* we find a churl who challenges Gawain to an exchange of blows, and this churl stands brandishing his ax before the gateway of an Otherworld castle; [13] in other words, he corresponds in station, appearance, and the weapon he uses to

[9] *ZcP*, IX, 205.      [10] *Ibid.*, 216.      [11] *Ibid.*, 212.
[12] G. L. Kittredge, *Study of G. G. K.*, 10 f.
[13] *Hunbaut*, ed. Stuerzinger, Breuer, ll. 1464–79.

the figure of Burmalt on the Modena sculpture. The Irish word for churl or herdsman which is regularly applied to the disguised Curoi is *bachlach*, and I have proved that this common noun was transformed into the proper name and appears in *Gawain and the Green Knight* as Bercilak.[14] It is hard to resist the conclusion that the same noun has been corrupted on its long journey from Ireland through Wales or Dumnonia and Brittany to Italy, and has turned up as the proper name Burmalt. We shall find our conclusion confirmed in Chapter XI.

The discovery that we have in Carrado and Burmalt Curoi himself in two forms provokes an examination of the third lord of the Otherworld castle, Mardoc. Now the two most famous abductors of Guinevere in Arthurian romance are Meleagant and Mordred, whose names in Welsh are Melwas and Medrot. Melwas could not possibly become Mardoc, but Medrot might very easily, through assimilation to the common Breton name Marcoc.[15] Medrot's abduction of Gwenhwyvar shows signs that, like Carrado's abduction of Winlogee, it goes back to Curoi's abduction of Blathnat, for in the *Didot Perceval* the scene of Arthur's battle with Modred is laid in Ireland,[16] and in the alliterative *Morte d'Arthur* Arthur is slain by his own sword Clarent, treacherously delivered to Mordred by Guinevere, who had it in her keeping.[17] We know so little of the uncontaminated Welsh forms of the Medrot abduction that it seems dangerous to go further.[18] But it is noteworthy that in Irish legend Mider's abduction of Etain forms a close parallel to Curoi's abduction of Blathnat,[19] and Rhys has already suggested that Mider is the original of Medrot.[20] The latter seems to have been a Brythonic name [21] substituted by the Welsh for Mider. But whether we trace Mardoc back to Mider or not, we can at least feel sure that as lover of Guinevere, and lord of the Other World, Mardoc goes back to the Welsh Medrot.

The story told by the *conteur* at Bari and carved over the doorway of Modena cathedral is rooted and grounded in the ancient legends of the Welsh and Irish. And since that story reveals that features found in thirteenth century romances like the

[14] *RR*, XV, 275 f.
[15] J. Loth, *Chrestomathie*, 150.
[16] Weston, *Leg. of Perceval*, II, 111.
[17] Ed. Björkman, 124.
[18] J. Loth, *Mab.*,[2] II, 247, 372.
[19] *RR*, XV, 278 f.
[20] *Arthurian Legend*, 35-9. *Cf.* Chap. XXXII. I do not accept the equation of Arthur with Airem.
[21] Loth, *op. cit.*, II, 236, n; *ZfSL*, XII,[1] 254 f.

*Vulgate Lancelot, Durmart, Yder,* and *Hunbaut* must repose on the same traditions as those found on the sculpture of 1099–1106, the scholars who maintain that Arthurian romance has little or no basis in Celtic tradition must be prepared to reconsider their judgment.

But is that Celtic tradition mythical? When faced with the fact that Cuchulinn is commonly regarded as a solar hero, that Blathnat means "little flower," that the battle for her possession lasted from the great Irish seasonal festival of November 1 to the middle of spring, can we resist the seasonal implications of the story? Here are the flower maiden, the abduction, the imprisonment of the maiden in the Other World during the winter. Let us go on to verify this interpretation.

Rhys and Gruffydd have studied the connections between the story of Blathnat and its Welsh analogue in the story of *Math Son of Mathonwy.*[22] The Welsh tale runs:[23]

Arianrod (Silver Circle) laid a destiny upon her son Llew (Lion) "that he shall never have a wife of the race that now inhabits this earth." Gwydion brought the youthful hero to Math. " 'Well,' said Math, 'we will seek, I and thou, by charms and illusion, to form a wife for him out of flowers. He has now come to man's stature, and he is the comeliest youth that was ever beheld.' So they took the blossoms of the oak, and the blossoms of the broom, and the blossoms of the meadow-sweet, and produced from them a maiden, the fairest and most graceful that man ever saw. And they baptized her, and gave her the name of Blodeuwedd (Flower Face)." One day while her husband Llew was absent, the huntsmen of Gronw or Goronwy Pebyr (the Strong) passed his palace, and after Gronw had killed the stag, he was invited in by Blodeuwedd. She at once fell in love with him, and they spent three nights together. Gronw on his departure urged her to find out by what means her husband Llew might come by his death. On Llew's return she learned through cajolery that he could be slain only by a spear which required a year to make, and only when he stood under a thatched roof with one foot on a bath-caldron and the other on a buck's back. Blodeuwedd at once informed Gronw, and at the end of a year he stood with the carefully wrought

[22] Rhys, *Hib. Lec.,* 239 f, 473 f; *Cymmrodorion Soc. Trans.,* 1912–3, 20–4. Baudis in attacking Gruffydd (*Folklore,* XXVII, 61) assumes, quite without warrant, that the external soul was essential to Curoi.

[23] Loth, *op. cit.,* I, 199 ff.

spear in ambush, while she persuaded Llew to take a bath.
After the bath he rose, setting one foot on the edge of the
caldron and the other on the back of a buck. Gronw then flung
the spear and pierced Llew in the side. Llew flew away in the
form of an eagle. Later, disenchanted, he avenged himself on
Gronw and Blodeuwedd.

This Welsh tale is another clear case of elaboration by blending. For its composer has seized on the Samson and Delilah
pattern (which seems to have been a comparatively late addition
to the Curoi story, being found in only one version) and has
proceeded to combine this version of the Curoi story with
another story containing the same Samson and Delilah pattern.
Miss Beckwith generously referred me to this analogue, already
studied in this connection by Baudis, the Egyptian tale of "The
Two Brothers," written down about 1300 B.C.[24] The part that
concerns us may be summarized as follows:

The younger of two brothers, Bata, kept his soul on the top of
an acacia tree. In pity for his loneliness the gods made him a
wife of marvelous beauty. A lock of her hair floated down to
Pharaoh, and his magicians told him it belonged to the daughter
of the Sun, "who had in her the essence of all the gods." Pharaoh sent and had her brought to him. She revealed where her
husband's soul was kept. Certain men went to the acacia tree,
cut it down, and at once Bata died. But he was later resusci-
tated by his brother.

Whatever the route by which this episode traveled to Wales,
there can be no doubt that in some way or other it has influenced
the story of Blodeuwedd, for here in addition to the Samson and
Delilah elements of the external soul and the treacherous wife, we
also have the wife created specially by the gods for a man
(or god). Still another folktale element — death dependent on a
certain grouping of circumstances — has been added.[25] But
for us the important point is the emphasis on the flower nature
of Blodeuwedd and her clearly marked descent from Blathnat.

Let us look at another derivative from the Blathnat abduction, first pointed out by Baudis,[26] the modern Irish folktale
of the Hung-up Naked Man. It is noteworthy that in one
variant of this tale Cuculin is the hero.[26a] I give a résumé of

[24] J. G. Frazer, *Balder the Beautiful*,[3] II, 135 f; *Folklore*, XXVII, 64 ff.
[25] *Mitra*, I, 161, 169. *Cf.* J. Curtin, *Hero Tales*, 304.
[26] *Eriu*, VII, 202.
[26a] J. Curtin, *Myths and Folklore*, 317.

the Donegal version, kindly translated for me by Mr. M. A. O'Byrne.[27]

The younger son of a widow, Eamonn, set out to seek his fortune. The first night he earned the gratitude of the Little Hound of the Rough Wood by giving her a bit of cake for her whelps, and she promised to be at his call. The next evening he came to a king's castle, and took service. He saw in the morning that the enclosure of the castle was full of spikes and that some of them bore human heads. His first task was to clean out a cow-house, on penalty of having his head placed on a spike if he failed. But the more he threw out, the more the muck increased. In despair he shouted for the Little Hound of the Rough Wood, and she produced a magic shovel, which quickly emptied the cow-house. She told him also to go down to the glen, where there were three giants who sought the hand of the king's daughter. He passed a naked man, hung up in a tree, who implored Eamonn to release him, but Eamonn went on. After a fierce contest with the giant, Eamonn leaped in the air, and struck off his head, and then leaped between the head and the body. "It was well for you," said the tongue in the head. "If I could get back on the head, you and all the men in the world could not cut it off again." As Eamonn returned, the Hung-up Naked Man again asked to be released but in vain. The second day Eamonn's task was to let a flock of ravens out of their house and bring them back in the evening. Again the Little Hound by providing a magic whistle enabled him to accomplish his task. His adventures in the glen with the Hung-up Naked Man and with a second giant practically repeat those of the previous day. The third day Eamonn was able to empty a lake with a tiny spoon provided by the Little Hound. The adventures in the glen were repeated. Eamonn killed the third giant, but on his return he consented to cut down the Hung-up Naked Man. The latter then declared that he would avenge the three giants, his brothers. He stripped Eamonn and tied him up in the tree where he had been. He then ran and carried off the

[27] Quiggin, *Dialect of Donegal*, 201. For analogues *cf.* J. G. Frazer, *op. cit.*, II, 126–33; Kittredge, *op. cit.*, 150 notes. Prof. Martha Beckwith has kindly added the following analogues: Somadeva, *Ocean of Story*, ed. N. M. Penzer, I, 124; M. Frere, *Old Deccan Days*, 1 ff; Stokes, *Indian Fairy Tales*, "Brave Hiralalbasa"; L. B. Day, *Folktales of Bengal*, Nos. 1, 4; Steele, *Tales of Punjaub*, "Prince Lionheart"; G. W. Dasent, *Popular Tales from the Norse*, "Giant Who Had No Heart in His Body." Penzer's note on the External Soul in Somadeva's *Ocean of Story*, I, 129 is most valuable.

king's daughter, no one knew whither. Eamonn was released
by a servant. The king was about to place his head on one of
the spikes, but Eamonn begged for a year and a day in which to
rescue the princess. The king agreed, and the youth set out.
He wandered fruitlessly for a long time. Finally he was entertained on three successive nights, first by an old man called the
Hawk of the Glen of Yellow Color, then by his brother called
the Brown Otter of the Lake of the Yew Tree, and on the third
night again by the Hawk of the Glen of Yellow Color. They
offered him their aid in time of peril, and tried to dissuade him
from his purpose. But the Hawk directed him finally to a little
boat, and a small boy rowed him to a far-off island. He entered a
large black castle, and the king's daughter welcomed him in the
Hung-up Naked Man's absence. She said that she had put a
spell on her abductor not to marry her for a year. Eamonn then
told her to pretend that she loved the Hung-up Naked Man
dearly, and grieved at the delay. Accordingly on the Hung-up's
return, he boastfully revealed the secret of his life. He could not
be killed till the briar tree down by the sea was cut; then a fox
would jump out, and none but the Little Hound of the Rough
Wood could kill him; then a duck would fly out of the fox, and
only the Hawk of the Glen of Yellow Color could kill him; the
duck on dying would lay an egg in the middle of the sea, and
only the Otter of the Lake of the Yew Tree could fetch it; and
only if that egg should strike the dark spot in the pit of his
stomach would the Hung-up Naked Man die. Of course, the
princess told the secret to Eamonn, and when the Hung-up
Naked Man had departed, the hero began to bring about his
death. All three of Eamonn's hosts appeared in the form of
animals and performed their respective parts. Finally the
Hung-up Naked Man approaches, growing weak and catching
his breath. Into his open mouth Eamonn hurls the egg, it
strikes the fatal spot, and the Hung-up Naked Man falls dead.
The lovers filled a ship full of treasure; a little metal boat with a
supernatural boatman, "fleeter than a March wind," took them
back to the house of the Hawk of the Glen of Yellow Color, who
again appeared as an old man. The lovers stayed on three
successive nights with the three old men, and brought them back
to the king's castle, arriving on the last day of the year granted
Eamonn by the king. Of course the lovers were married, and
they and their descendants are living in happiness and content.

One notices the intrusion of many folk-tale elements, particularly the development of the Samson and Delilah theme, as in the Blodeuwedd story. Extraordinary is the possible connection between the fact that the abductor in the Irish folktale hangs the hero up in a tree, and the fact that in Hartmann's *Iwein* the abductor hurls Kay out of his saddle so that he is suspended from the branch of a tree.[28] Even more extraordinary is the fact that the Hung-up Naked Man, who has taken the place of Curoi, the abductor, in the old Irish story, is a name applied to Jesus Christ on the cross. Let me quote Macalister: "The worshippers of the gods . . . retaliated by calling the Sacred Figure on the Crucifix *An Crochaire Tarrnoch-tuighthe*, a name still current in folk-tales told by good Christians, who are blissfully ignorant of its true meaning." [29] Why was the name for Christ substituted for Curoi's? Perhaps we shall find the answer as we pursue our mythological investigation.

Our next derivative from the Blathnat abduction sheds another light on Curoi's nature. The story forms the beginning of a French romance, *Li Atre Perillos* — written in the third quarter of the fourteenth century.[30]

A damsel rides up to Arthur's table at the Feast of Pentecost, asks a boon, and the king grants it. She is to have charge of the king's master cup, and is to serve him with it. Gawain is appointed her guardian, takes her to his hostel, and entrusts her to his sister. The next day the dinner is interrupted by a huge and beautiful knight, who rides up to the dais, places the damsel on his destrier, challenges the knights to overtake and fight him, and slowly departs. Gawain would have ridden after him at once had not courteous scruples prevented his leaving the table before the end of the dinner. Confident that his horse is swift enough to overtake the abductor in any case, he remains seated. Kay, however, after taunting Gawain, pursues the stranger knight, and is quickly humbled in the dust. Gawain finally starts, has some adventures of no significance to us, and on two successive nights, fails to overtake the damsel and rescue her from her abductor. He does contrive, however, to send messages which prevent their sleeping together. On the first night

---

[28] Ed. Benecke, Lachmann, ll. 4671–85.

[29] *PRIA*, XXXIV, 291. In Curtin's *Myths and Folklore of Ireland*, 275 ff Curucha na Gras (Hung on the Cross) plays a part like Gwrnach's in *Kilhwch*, and Gwrnach is certainly a Welsh descendant of Curoi. *Cf.* Chap. V.    [30] *Archiv*, XLII, 148–70.

he himself sleeps in a Perilous Cemetery, discovers there a most lovely damsel, fights a fiend, who keeps her in enchanted servitude, and by the power of the cross, slays him. This lady accompanies Gawain on his pursuit, and tells him that the abductor's name is Escanor, that his strength before noon is that of three men, but wanes with the declining of the sun, and that Gawain's mother feared for the outcome if her son should ever fight with Escanor. Gawain discovers lying by the road Escanor's shield, shining red in the sunlight. On the third day Gawain and his damsel overtake Escanor and his damsel in a forest. In the following combat Gawain catches up the spear which Escanor has dropped and with it slays his adversary's horse. At last he slays Escanor himself.

It is worth noting first of all that it is with Cuchulinn's own spear that Erc slays Cuchulinn's horse, the Gray of Macha, in the battle in which Cuchulinn himself fell.[31] Moreover the correspondence between this abduction story and that of Blathnat hardly needs to be pointed out. Blathnat, with her caldron, in Cuchulinn's possession, corresponds to the damsel, with her cup, under Gawain's protection. In the *Vulgate Lancelot* we actually find that a damsel who had come to Arthur's court and served him with her cup is called Lore,[32] a name Miss Weston recognized as a corrupt form of Floree,[33] so that the identity of the damsel with the cup and Blathnat, "Little Flower," is unmistakable. The abduction, the humiliation of a pursuer, and the death of the abductor produced by his own weapon, are features common to both stories. Significant is the fact that in the *Atre Perillos* the red shining shield [34] and the waxing and waning strength,[35] solar traits which one would expect to find attributed to Gawain, are attributed to the beautiful, gigantic knight, his adversary.[36]

[31] E. Hull, *Cuchulinn Saga*, 258 f.

[32] Sommer, *Vulgate Version*, III, 272.

[33] Weston, *Leg. of Gawain*, 46.

[34] *Archiv*, XLII, 163. *Cf.* Guillaume le Clerc, *Fergus*, ed. Martin, l. 537.

[35] *Archiv*, XLII, 163. *Cf.* Weston, *Leg. of Gawain*, 12; *Mort Artu*, ed. J. D. Bruce, 287 f.

[36] Another derivative from the Blathnat abduction is found in *De Ortu Walwanii*, ed. J. D. Bruce, 62–72. Milocrates, king of an island of dwarfs, has carried off the niece of the emperor. Coming as a spy to the palace, Gawain learns that the captured queen loves him and hopes by his means to obtain her freedom. He meets her and obtains from her Milocrates' sword and golden armor, concerning which it was fated that he who should first bear them should overthrow Milocrates. The next day when he cannot find

Our suspicions of a mythical background for the Blathnat abduction seem to be confirmed, for while the Welsh analogue stresses the flower nature of Blodeuwedd, both the modern Irish folktale and the fourteenth century French romance suggest that the abductor, who in one case is supplanted by a grotesque deformation of Christ and in the other is assimilated to the sun, is more than human.

---

them and sees them worn by Gawain, he knows he is doomed. Bravely he fights but is finally beheaded by his own sword. Another derivative is the Scotch tale of *Child Rowland*, which seems to go back through an English ballad to an Arthurian romance. (*Folklore*, II, 183 ff.) Burd Ellen is carried off by the King of Elfland. She is the daughter of King Arthur, and the two older of her three brothers seek her, but do not return. The youngest brother, Child Rowland, girt with his father's good claymore, goes to Merlin's cave, and is instructed to kill everyone he meets in Elfland, and to eat no food there. After a long journey, he slays in turn the King of Elfland's various herdsmen. He is directed finally by the henwife to a round green hill girdled with "rings," and after going round it thrice widdershins, he enters the hill. He finds it warm inside and lighted from the roof which was of transparent rock, incrusted with gems. Proceeding, he enters a lofty and splendid hall, with pillars of gold and silver, and clusters of diamonds in the arches; a great carbuncle hung from the roof, which turned round and shed a light like that of the setting sun. Seated here is Burd Ellen, who warns her brother of his fate, and under magic compulsion brings him a golden bowl of bread and milk. When Rowland refuses it, the King of Elfland enters with "Fi, fi, fo, and fum!" Rowland with his good claymore fells him in combat, but spares him on condition that his brothers are restored. With a small crystal of red liquor, the King brings them out of their magic sleep, and the four children of Arthur return in triumph.

# CHAPTER III

## CELTIC STORY-CHANNELS AND STORY-WAYS

Now that we find ourselves traversing the vast wilderness of Celtic romance, — like the knights of old who rode all day endlong and overthwart a great forest, — it may be best if we trace the paths we have followed, note a few landmarks, and get our bearings. In other words, dealing as we do with old and modern Irish tales, old Welsh and Breton legends, French, German, and English romances, we should know in what general relationship these various bodies of tradition stand to each other, what were the channels of transmission, and what the aims and habits of the story-tellers.

The most significant impulses and story-patterns arose in pre-Christian Ireland. There lies the chief fountainhead of all these streams.[1] There, of course, is the source of the modern Irish and Gaelic folktales, which until the present century were related by professional shanachies and the peasantry themselves. In ancient Irish tradition, too, is the source of the mythical tales which combined with the Romano-British tradition in Wales, Cornwall, and Devon to form the Arthurian legends. These legends passed from the Welsh and Dumnonian bards to the Breton *conteurs*, who could easily understand Welsh and at the same time speak French. Thus perfectly equipped to be the intermediaries between the Celtic-speaking and the French-speaking worlds, the Bretons adapted their stories to contemporary courtly taste, and soon won a public both in France and England. After that, the rest of Christendom succumbed to the charm of Arthurian legend as it reached them through the Breton and French *conteurs*. Even Wales felt the repercussion

---

[1] The soundest general work on the Celtic background of Arthurian romance is E. Windisch, *Das keltische Britannien bis zu Kaiser Arthur*, *Abh. d.k. Sächs. Ges. d. Wiss., ph.h.K.*, XXIX (1912), no. 6. The most serious defect is the failure to recognize that *Peredur*, *Owain*, and *Geraint* are mainly based on Breton-French sources. Competent accounts of Celtic mythology are Macculoch's *Religion of the Ancient Celts* and *Celtic Mythology*. Valuable also are Westropp's articles in the *PRIA*, XXXIII, XXXIV, J. MacNeill's *Celtic Ireland*, and Meyer's article on Donn in *Sitzb. Preuss. Akad. Wiss.*, 1919, 537.

and began to translate into Welsh the new Arthurian romances. By the year 1200 Merlin and Morgan le Fay had laid all Christian Europe under an enchantment. The conquests which Geoffrey of Monmouth attributed to a pseudo-historic Arthur were far surpassed by the conquests of the literary Arthur.

Let us follow the development of this great Celtic tradition in more detail, and turn back to Ireland. The great body of pagan Irish legends, to which the story of the abduction of Blathnat belongs, existed for a long period before the evangelization of Ireland in the fifth century, — how long, no one can say. The chariots in which the heroes of the sagas ride are reminiscences of a practise which probably died out in the first century A.D.[2] Nor can one say how far back in that past the Irish possessed in common with the Welsh such venerable deities as Govannon and Goibniu, Don and Dana, Manawyddan and Manannan. In the second century A.D. Tacitus witnessed to a general community of traditions between Britain and Ireland, between Brythons and Goidels.[3] Such a community of traditions is doubtless due in large measure to their common Celtic inheritance. But there is general agreement among scholars that at a later time the Welsh borrowed largely from the Irish. Probably the earliest datable borrowing can be set about 795 A.D., when the South-Welsh compiler of the *Historia Brittonum*, which goes under the name of Nennius, used three Irish documents.[4] But there must have been more fundamental borrowings from Irish oral tradition much earlier, at a time when Ireland was scarcely Christianized or was still quite pagan. This conclusion is confirmed over and over again by the discovery that French Arthurian romances, which are ultimately derived from Brythonic and Irish traditions, preserve with startling clarity of outline, as we shall see, the ritual and the myths of pre-Christian Ireland. An Arthurian romance of the thirteenth or fourteenth century will sometimes contain primitive pagan features which have disappeared from an Irish saga of the ninth century. I cannot resist the inference that a large body of Irish myth found its way into Welsh tradition by the sixth century at least.

But the process of borrowing did not stop. Miss O'Rahilly shows how during the tenth and eleventh centuries Irish letters revived from the staggering blow dealt them by the fierce Norse-

---

[2] *Proc. Brit. Acad.*, 1905–6, 135 ff.  [3] *Agricola*, sec. 24.

[4] C. O'Rahilly, *Ireland and Wales*. On relations between Ireland and Britain see also *RC*, XXXI, 421; *Cymmrodorion Soc. Trans.*, 1912–3, 18–26.

men, and how a large infiltration of Irish and Norse-Irish mer-
cenaries into Wales took place.[5] She concludes that to this
period we must assign the Irish influences patent in *Kilhwch* and
*Rhonabwy*. At any rate, it will appear from our study of the
different forms which the same Irish name took in Welsh that
the name must have been transmitted at quite different times
and through quite different channels.

Now it is well known that the people of Devon and Cornwall,
though cut off from the Welsh after the battle of Deerham
(A.D. 577), spoke the same language and maintained communi-
cation with their kinsfolk across the Bristol Channel. Gruffydd
has argued powerfully that "the superb mythology of Arthur"
developed in Dumnonia first, and spread later to Wales.[5a] At
any rate, we may be sure that the Irish myths mingled with
native Brythonic traditions, which were doubtless similar in
spirit and fundamental pattern. Curoi, Blathnat, Bran,
Manannan, and Findabair and the stories that clustered about
them became inextricably tangled with those that clustered
about Myrddin, Chei, Elen, Peredur, Avallach, Belli, and
Modron. This mingled strain produced after a considerable
period the *Four Branches of the Mabinogi, Kilhwch and Olwen*,
and the *Dream of Rhonabwy*, though both the latter show that the
Arthurian traditions of Brittany were filtering back into Wales.

Certainly as early as 1050 the insular Arthurian legend had
been taken up by the Bretons, who after five hundred years of
exile still looked back to Britain as their home and the scene of
their former greatness. Eastern Brittany through constant
contact with the French had become bilingual by the ninth
century.[6] The professional Breton *conteurs*, therefore, had only
to adapt this rich and colorful tradition which they took from
the Welsh to the taste of the more sophisticated and Christian
society of France and England in order to find a vast market for
their wares. And by the twelfth century they began to establish themselves as the most popular entertainers in Europe.
Not only the popularity of the Arthurian romances and Breton
lais themselves, but also the legends [7] of Brendan, Pope Gregory,

[5] O'Rahilly, *op. cit.*, 112–4.
[5a] *Cymmrodorion Soc. Trans.*, 1912–3, 30–4. *Cf.* W. J. Entwistle, *Arthurian Leg.*, 49, on Cornish singers in Spain ca. 1250. The form Modred is
Cornish. *ZfSL*, XII, 254.
[6] *Göttingische Gel. Anz.*, 1890, 789 ff.
[7] A. Nutt, *Voyage of Bran; ZrP*, XXX, 257; H. Sparnaay, *Verschmel-*

of Patrick's Purgatory, and the Celtic influence on the *Pèleri-nage Charlemagne*,[8] *Huon de Bordeaux*,[9] *Reinbrun, Hereward*,[10] *Amadas et Ydoine*,[11] *Ipomedon*,[11a] *Wolfdietrich*,[12] *Bataille Loqui-fer*,[13] and other non-Celtic stories demonstrate the amazing extent of their repertories and the vital art which alone can account for their stupendous success.

Scholars have debated at length whether the Anglo-Normans or the Bretons were the intermediaries between Wales and France.[14] After some investigation I have yet to find a single fact that shows that the Anglo-Normans played any consider-able part in the transmission of the Matter of Britain to the Continent. On the other hand, the evidence is overwhelmingly in favor of the hypothesis that the English and Anglo-Normans knew practically nothing of Arthur and his knights from Welsh sources. They, like the French, received the Celtic tradition only from professional Breton entertainers or from others who had imbibed the Breton tradition.

This sweeping generalization I make on the basis of two argu-ments. First, we have from the twelfth century many references to the *conteurs* as a class: not once are they called Welsh, but always when their nationality is specified they are called in Latin *Britones*, in French *Bretons*.[15] Now there were in both languages words which specifically applied to the Welsh, namely *Wallenses* and *Gallois*. If the Welsh played any considerable part in the propagation of the Arthurian legend among the French and English it seems incredible that these words are never used, but always the words which, even the advocates of Anglo-Norman transmission are compelled to admit,[16] referred,

---

*zung legendarischer und weltlicher Motive*, 25–56; P. de Félice, *L'autre monde;* G. P. Krapp, *Legend of St. Patrick's Purgatory.*

[8] *Englische Studien*, XXXVI, 340. *Cf*. Chap. XVII.

[9] C. Voretzsch, *Epische Studien*, 122; Engel, *Einflüsse der Arthurromane auf die Chansons de Geste.*

[10] Compare *Gesta Herwardi* with the Tristram legend.

[11] *RR*, XV, 215-65.          [11a] Weston *Three Days' Tournament.*

[12] H. Schneider, *Wolfdietrich*, 259 ff.

[13] L. A. Paton, *Fairy Mythology*, 49–51.

[14] Bédier, *Tristan de Thomas*, II, 122–4, 316; *ZfSL*, XIV[1], 161; *MLN*, XXVI, 65 ff. Bibl. in A. B. Hopkins, *Influence of Wace*, 114. The *Waldef* passage on which Gaston Paris laid such weight has been challenged by Brugger, Imelmann, and Miss Hibbard. *Cf*. *ZfSL*, XXXII[2], 138; *Bonner Studien zur Eng. Phil.*, IV, xxxiii; L. A. Hibbard, *Mediaeval Romance in England*, 102.

[15] *Moyen Age*, XXVIII, 234 ff.

[16] *Rom*, XXIV, 501.

when applied to contemporaries, to the Continental Celts, the Bretons.

The second argument is based on the name-forms found in English Arthurian materials. If the Anglo-Normans were intermediaries between Wales and the Continent, the name-forms in the romances and chronicles written in England ought to be closer to the Welsh forms than the names in French romances are. On the contrary, even Geoffrey of Monmouth, brought up in Wales, not only says that his professed source, the very ancient book in the "British" language came from Brittany, but also uses forms like Walgainus, Hiderus, Modredus, Caliburnus, which are far closer to the Galvain, Ider, Modred, Calibourne of the French romances than to Welsh Gwalchmai, Edern, Medrot, Caledvwlch.[17] Furthermore, in what is very probably the oldest piece of romantic Arthurian literature extant, excluding the Welsh, the *Lai du Cor*, an Anglo-Norman poem dated 1150–75, is preserved a local tradition about Cirencester, not fifty miles from the Welsh border. In this poem, if anywhere, we should find support for the theory of Welsh derivation. But the MS. furnishes the following names: Gauuein, Giflet, Iuuein, Mangounz de Moraine, Keerz, Gauwain, Kadoin, Iuwain, Arzur, Goher, Muz, Aguisiaus, Glouien, Kadoiners, Lot, Caratoun, Garadue, Galahal. In this earliest of poems about Arthur written in England there is not one name which suggests immediate borrowing from the Welsh. The name Garadue, on the other hand, points definitely to Brittany, where the name Caradoc sometimes assumes the form Caradec. And so far as I can detect there is in all the literature of this cycle written in England but one name which must have been taken from the Welsh, not the Bretons: Arthur. It is at least the only conspicuous example. This name demonstrates that Welsh tradition did have an infinitesimal direct influence in England, but it does not afford a pretext for supposing that the Anglo-Normans passed even that small contribution on to the French.

Another matter of the highest importance in tracing the development of the Arthurian legend and nomenclature is the fact that the Breton adaptations of Welsh myth had won such high prestige by the year 1100 that they returned to Wales as new and authentic stories of Arthur. Most scholars are aware of the obvious influence of Continental Arthurian traditions upon

[17] *ZfSL*, XII¹, 231 ff. *Cf*. Chap. XXXIV.

some of the Welsh triads and practically all admit that the
Welsh stories of *Peredur, Owain (The Lady of the Fountain)*, and
*Geraint*, found in late thirteenth century MSS., are adaptations of Continental romances.[17a] But it is not generally realized
that the process began much earlier.   Rhys ab Tewdwr on his
return from Brittany to take the crown of South Wales in 1077
brought with him the system of the Round Table, which at
home had been quite forgotten, and restored it as it was with
regard to poets and singers.[18]  M. Loth has pointed out French
influences in *Kilhwch and Olwen*, assigned to the early twelfth
century, and we shall presently see that the appearance of
Gwalchmai in that romance as a great hero shows the influence
of Breton stories about Galvain.

This demonstrated acquaintance of the Welsh with Breton
traditions at so early a date explains the curious fact that the
most influential of all the *conteurs*, the only transmitter of the
Matter of Britain to non-Celtic society whose name has been
preserved, is Bleheris, whose name is certainly Welsh Bleddri,
and who is definitely said to have been born and nurtured in
Wales.[19]  He seems between 1100 and 1137 to have established
at the court of Poitou a vogue for the Tristram and Gawain
romances, which later through the influence of Eleanor of
Poitou made itself felt throughout Europe.   Now it is highly
significant that though Bleheris was a Welshman, the romances
which claim to derive from him seem to belong as clearly as any
to the Bretonized tradition rather than the Welsh.   One may
look in vain for purely Welsh materials in the work of those
poets who cite Bleheris as their authority, Thomas and Wauchier
de Denain.   Brugger has rightly maintained that though Bleheris was an insular Celt, the legends which he vitalized and
propagated were those which had been acclimatized already for
some time on the Continent.[20]

To the Bretons, then, let us give the chief credit for remoulding
the fascinating but sometimes incomprehensible legends transmitted to them by their insular kinsmen.   As early as the sixth
century Venantius Fortunatus mentions the Breton *crotta*
(Welsh *crwth*) as an instrument that had made a reputation for
itself along with the Roman lyre and the Teutonic harp, and in

[17a] For the literature of the subject *cf.* J. D. Bruce, *Evolution*, II, 62 ff.
[18] T. Stephens, *Literature of the Kymry*, 422.
[19] *MLN*, XXXIX, 319; *Rom*, LI, 403 f.  Bibl. in *MP*, XXII, 123.
[20] *ZfSL*, XLVII, 169.

the eleventh century Dudo of St. Quentin calls upon the Breton harpers to aid the clerks of Normandy in spreading the fame of Duke Richard.[21]  Probably the lyric lais on themes which Marie de France and other poets have preserved in narrative form, were sung to the accompaniment of the *crotta*.  But these songs seem to have been little concerned with Arthur.  The Breton entertainers who spread his fame in the eleventh and twelfth centuries apparently did not rely on the charms of music or of verse.  Wauchier de Denain in the late twelfth century mentions minstrels who give the impression that they have related the whole story, when they have only "told a little of an adventure without rhyme." [22]  For at least a hundred years before Crestien composed what some scholars call the first Arthurian romance, about 1165, the Breton *conteurs* had been engaged in rationalizing, harmonizing, softening, and imbuing with courtly ideals this huge tangle of semi-barbaric fancies.  The only survivor of the purely Breton oral tradition is the sculptured story at Modena, the abduction of Winlogee by Carrado and her rescue by Galvagin.  But even so late an Arthurian romance as the *Atre Perillos* of about 1350 preserves in the story of the abduction of the damsel of the "master cup" and her rescue by Gawain what in my opinion is substantially a Breton *conte*.

The *conteurs* must have been not only adapters and composers, but also actors.  Peter of Blois in the second half of the twelfth century testifies: "The minstrels (*histriones*) tell certain tales about Arthur, Gaugan, and Tristan, the hearing of which moves the hearts of the listeners to compassion, and wounds them even to tears." [23]  The Bretons, too, possessed the use of a language which laid the world open to them, from Jerusalem to Dublin.[23a] It was the labor and the artistry of these wholly anonymous strolling entertainers of the twelfth century which first gave the Arthurian cycle its prestige and saved it from practical oblivion.

Let us turn now to consider the traditions, the conventions which so largely determined the development of the Matter of Britain not only in Brittany, but in its earlier stages in Wales and Ireland.  It will be far easier to understand what these composers and reciters made of their material if we understand first who they were and what they were trying to do.

---

[21] *Mon. Germ. Hist. Auct. Ant.*, IV, 163;  P. Paris, *Romans de la Table Ronde*, I, 7.

[22] E. Martin, *Zur Gralsage*, 28;  Wauchier, ed. Potvin, ll. 28373 ff.

[23] Migne, *Pat. Lat.*, CCVII, col. 1088.      [23a] T. Stephens, *op. cit.*, 421.

It is of the first importance to realize that these legends originated with men who inherited the traditions of the druids. I can do no better than quote excerpts from Hyde's *Literary History of Ireland:* [24] "That the Bardic schools, which we know flourished as public institutions with scarcely a break from the Synod of Drumceat in 590 . . . down to the seventeenth century, were really a continuation of the Druidic schools, and embodied much that is purely pagan in their curricula, is I think amply shown. . . . These instances that I have mentioned occurring in the books of the poets' instructions, are evidently remains of magic incantations and terrifying magic ceremonies, taken over from the schools and times of the druids and carried on into the Christian era. . . . After Christianity had succeeded in getting the upper hand over paganism, a kind of tacit compromise was arrived at, by means of which the bards or *files* and other representatives of the old pagan learning, were allowed to continue to propagate their stories, tales, poems and genealogies, at the price of incorporating with them a small share of Christian alloy. . . . But so badly has the dovetailing of the Christian and pagan parts been managed in most of the older romances, that the pieces come away quite separate in the hands of even the least skilled analyser, and the pagan substratum stands forth entirely distinct from the Christian accretion." It is scarcely necessary to add that everything points to an exactly analogous development in Wales. Neither professional storytellers nor their public were willing to give up their huge treasury of mythical narratives, the customary source of entertainment for generations untold. Thus, both in Ireland and in Wales these stories had been first the property of a pagan order which combined priestly functions with many others, and notably with that of reciting their pagan legends. Their priestly functions they had to relinquish to the servants of Christ, but they and their successors retained much of their sacred character and continued to make themselves agreeable by narrating under a thin disguise their wild and often most unedifying traditions of the gods. One should not forget that such stories as the abduction of Guinevere go back to stories learned and recited in the schools of the druids.

The narrative conventions of these Irish schools account for much in Arthurian romance. We have seen how the story

[24] Pp. 241, 243, 250.

carved over the Modena portal can only be explained as the in-
terweaving of variants of a famous theme; and we have noted
that the Carado of the Dolorous Tower episode in the *Vulgate
Lancelot* is the result of the ruthless blending of two quite different stories.   Was this the normal, the regular procedure in
Celtic composition?   The twelfth century *Book of Leinster*
states: "He is no poet (*fili*) who does not synchronize and harmonize all the stories." [25]   The Welsh copyists of mythical
materials did the same thing.   In the words of Gruffydd, "they
attempted to find some connection between tales or cycles of
tales which originally had no connection whatever, and were
therefore forced to invent new incidents or to introduce other
incidents from outside in order to establish this connection." [26]
The Bretons and French did likewise.   Crestien de Troyes,
Frenchman though he was, doubtless knew the aims and stand-
ards of his contemporaries, the Breton *conteurs*.   When, therefore, he speaks of his *Erec*, as a "mout bel conjointure" he seems
to recognize the composite nature of his material and to pride
himself on the skill with which the joining was done.[27]   Again
Thomas, another inheritor of Breton traditions (though it was
probably the Welshman Bleheris who wrought those traditions
into a work of art), states in an illuminating passage that he
knows many versions of the story of Tristram, and that it has
been his effort to harmonize them.[28]   He uses an expression "en
uni dire," which M. Bédier translates "donner au milieu de
variantes contradictoires de la légende, un récit logique et
cohérent." [29]

When hundreds of story-tellers wandered about, each elabo-
rating his own version of the exploits of Cuchulinn or Llew or
Gawain, hundreds of variants of the same incident arose.   To
reconcile the conflicting versions of every incident, to connect
incident logically and naturally with incident, such was the
*conteur's* aim.   The results were often absurd.   Timid souls
feared to tamper too much with traditions that had solidified.
Unskilful souls made feeble attempts to explain the inexplicable.
Too ingenious souls rashly endeavored to fit all the variants into
one great *tour de force*.   Of course the greater artists were comparatively ruthless.   The weeds must be sacrificed, however

[25] E. O'Curry, *MS. Materials*, 583.
[26] *Enc. Brit.*, ed. 11, V, 642.
[27] *Cf.* Nitze's discussion, *Rom*, XLIV, 16.
[28] Ed. Bédier, I, ll. 2107–56.          [29] *Ibid.*, II, 451.

brilliant their coloring, in order that the design of the formal garden might appear. But great artists are few in any period, and Arthurian romance was to suffer throughout its history from the fact that weeds and flowers, growing with riotous luxuriance were held in equal sacredness, with the result that one is dazzled with a profusion of color rather than charmed by any symmetry or sweep or harmony of pattern. Romances like *Tristan*, *Gawain and the Green Knight*, and *Gareth and Lynete* prove, however, that the French genius for clarity and coherence was not altogether lost upon this amorphous mass of story fragments.

Another convention of Celtic story-telling that the intelligent student of Irish and Welsh legend must take into account is a singular passion for finding a meaning in names. "To the *ollamh* [that is, the chief rank of professional story-tellers] belong the etymologies of names," declares the *Book of Lecan*.[30] And that they lived up to their responsibilities is demonstrated by the existence of treatises devoted to the explanation of place-names, the *Dindsenchas*, and of a treatise, the *Coir Anmann*, or "Fitness of Names," devoted to the elucidation of personal names. As one reads through the latter, he discovers that often several etymologies are given for the same name, and that it is distorted in the most obvious way in order to supply the requisite elements. For example: "Modgath Mor-olach 'greatly bibulous'. . . . Or Modgaeth Moroilech 'great cheeked,' for great were his *oile*, that is his two cheeks." [31] Or again take this erudite masterpiece: "Eogan was his name from parental origin, that is, *eo-genesis* i.e. good birth, for eo is εὐ-*bona*, but *genesis* is Eogan's *generatio*. . . . 'Tis from this that Eogan-acht is said of them (*scil*. his descendants), in virtue of the blessings which the men of Erin bestowed upon him for his hospitality and generosity towards them. . . . From this (comes) Eoganacht i.e. *bona actio*, i.e. a good act (it was) for him (Eogan) to save the men of Erin from starvation. [Or] Eogan-acht i.e. Eogan-icht, i.e. Eogan's protection to the men of Erin. Or Eogannecht that is Eogan's necht: *necht* 'children,' that is the seven Eoganachts are Eogan's children." [32] Now one hardly needs the authority of Whitley Stokes to assure one that "The etyma with which the *Coir Anmann*, like the *Dindsenchas*, abounds, are, as a rule, absurd." [33] Moreover, it is

---

[30] O'Curry, *op. cit.*, 240.
[31] *IT*, III, 289.
[32] *Ibid.*, 301.
[33] *Ibid.*, 285.

obvious that an *ollamh* in search of a picturesque or striking etymology was quite capable of changing the name to fit the requirements. It is not at all improbable, therefore, that the names of certain heroes, divine or semi-divine, as they have come down to us, are not the original forms. And we may properly be suspicious whenever we find a name explained by some striking anecdote. In such a case it is possible, even probable that the name has been modified in order that the story may be told to explain it.

Precisely the same phenomenon occurs in Welsh tradition. Gruffydd says: "The most important of these [changes in the *Mabinogion*] is the addition of what may be called the onomastic story of the well-known 'Ichabod' order. These were incidents woven, often most skilfully, into the fabric of the tale, to account for or to explain certain names, an exercise for which Welshmen and Jews have shown themselves fatally apt." [34]

The Bretons and French inherited this obsession for etymologizing along with the Welsh legends. No Arthurian student needs to be reminded of the attempt to explain the Isle of Avalon as the place where the sun *avaloit*, "went down"; [35] or of the deformations of the name Perceval in *Perlesvaus:* Par-lui-fet, Perd-les-vaus, which are supposed to mean "Self-created," and "Loses-the-valleys." In the *Estoire del Saint Graal* we find that the name Celidoine is said to mean "Given to Heaven," and Mordrain "Slow of Belief," [36] probably through an assumed connection with *Coeli-donum* and *Morans-credere*.[37] Perhaps the best-known piece of onomastic ingenuity is Helinandus' endeavor to find the origin of the word Gradale, a Latin form of our word Grail.[38] Unaware of its true derivation from Latin *cratalis* or *cratale*, a shallow dish,[39] he suggests first that the word *gradale* is connected with *gradatim*, because food was placed in the dish "in succession, one morsel after another." Then he says that the word is popularly pronounced *greal*, because it is "agreeable and acceptable to him who eats from it." A later attempt to read a meaning into the Saint Graal is found in Jacopo da Voragine, who towards the close of the thirteenth

---

[34] *Cymmrodorion Soc. Trans.* 1912–3, 59. *Cf.* D. E. Jenkins, *Bedd Gelert,* x–xiii.

[35] A. Nutt, *Studies on Leg. of Grail,* 78.

[36] Sommer, I, 75, 107.

[37] F. Lot, *Étude sur le Lancelot,* 211, n. 5.

[38] *MP*, XIII, 681.      [39] *Ibid.*

century says that "the English in their books call that vessel
Sanguinalia"! [40] And an even more ingenious corruption found
in England is the Sank Ryal or "Royal Blood." [41]

From all this may we learn to beware of the Celt when he
presents us with an etymology. Not always but often, the
derivation and even the form of the name which is offered as
proof of the derivation are both misleading. Not that the
Celt intended to deceive; more often than not he believed in his
own etymology. But we have a right to suspect his scientific
equipment if not his good faith. Nine times out of ten he puts
us on a false scent. And it is for us to look for the true origin
and form of the name elsewhere.

## A NOTE ON THE TRANSMISSION OF NAMES [42]

The discussion of names to follow may distress those who feel that
the development of Arthurian names should follow certain rigid phonetic laws. As a result of studying some of the generally admitted
derivations, I perceived that the names could not be phonetic equiv-
alents. The further I delved in the subject, the more it became patent.
What is phonetically impossible is factually probable.

Nor am I the first to reach this conviction. When Loth maintained
that the Welsh Tallwch could not be derived from Pictish Talorg because it conflicted with phonetic law, the eminent Celtist Smirnov replied: "M. Loth is a very trustworthy phonetician, but in a case like
this perhaps one ought not to lay too much weight on phonetics. One
is not concerned here with regular phonetic correspondences, but with
variant forms of a legendary proper name transmitted from one people
to another and exposed to many changes." [43] Likewise Bruce, referring
to another of Loth's applications of phonetic law, wrote: "It seems
mere pedantry to lay stress on the fact that French Iselt (Iseut) is not
quite exact in its phonetic correspondence to Welsh Essylt or Cornish
Eselt. Foreign names are seldom caught correctly, and the difference,
after all, is very slight." [44]

Because of their irrelevance the laws of phonetic development have
not come within the province of my studies. Most of them are con-

---

[40] *MLR*, XX, 443.

[41] *Seynt Graal*, ed. Furnivall, II, 337.

[42] I wish to express my gratitude to Prof. F. N. Robinson for suggesting
the insertion of this note, and for his criticism. His opinion of the main
contentions is as follows: "I find very little to criticize in your chapter. . . .
In general your explanation is clear, and it supplies the kind of defence that
I told you I thought the book would need in order to get a hearing from the
Celticists. I do not say that the work will convince them even with this
defence. For while your general contentions, as set forth in this apologia,
are by no means unreasonable, your special applications of the method will
appeal with different force to different men." Letter of Feb. 15, 1926.

[43] *Rom*, XLIII, 120.        [44] J. D. Bruce, *Evolution*, I, 183 f.

cerned with the sound changes which various languages go through in their development from a common root language. Of these Grimm's law is the most familiar example. As between Irish and Welsh a good instance is the fact that from a common original sound the Welsh developed the sound *g* or *gw*, where the Irish developed the sound *f*. For instance, *gwynn* corresponds to *finn*, *gwr*, to *fer*. But whereas this law certainly applies to sounds developed from a common root in an original Celtic language from which both the Brythonic and Goidelic languages derived, it does not apply at all to the direct transmission from the Goidelic to the Brythonic languages at a late date. For we find that in a text of the twelfth century, *Kilhwch and Olwen*, the Irish name Fergus appears in Welsh as Phercos:[45] the *f* has not become *g*. In fact, to expect that it would is about as sensible as to expect an Englishman to pronounce French *père* "fair," simply because according to Grimm's law Latin *p* and Germanic *f* are derived from the same root. Whenever we do find a phonetic correspondence of names, as for instance between the Irish Finn and the Welsh Gwynn or between the Irish Finndabair and the Welsh Gwennhwyvar, the explanation is not that the Welshman of the Dark Ages naturally reproduced these Irish sounds in this way, but either that the Welsh translated the Irish meaning of the name, — Finn and Gwynn both meaning "white," — or that these names go back to a common name in old Celtic. The laws of phonetic development in the two languages are really irrelevant when we are discussing cases, not of derivation from a common source, but of transmission from Irish to Welsh and from Welsh to Breton within the Christian era. Here we can be guided only by similarity of sound.

Furthermore, it should be noted, before one requires that names follow too rigid a formula, that both in Irish and Welsh there is an extraordinary looseness of forms, a looseness which would probably seem even greater if we had all the dialectal differences to be found in the various parts of Ireland and Wales. We may note that the foster mother of Lug is called both Tailtiu and Tallan, and his true mother, Etan, Ethne, Ethniu, Ethliu, Ceithliu. In Welsh likewise we have similar looseness. The name of the first British king converted to Christianity, whom Nennius calls Lucius, appears in Welsh both as Lles and Lleirwg.[46] Curoi mac Daire is rendered in Welsh MSS. both as Corroi map Dayry and Chubert map Daere.[47] Quite apart from the looseness created by the habit of etymologizing names, the Celts tended to give their proper names varying pronunciations of which the above are extreme examples.

Finally, if we are to impose rigid tests of phonetic equivalence we must give up even the few identifications of Arthurian and Celtic names already made. For it is notorious that Merlin is not an exact phonetic counterpart to Myrddin, Erec to Geraint, Gauvain to Gwalchmai, and Perceval to Peredur. Let me quote that conservative scholar, Bruce, on these names: "Geoffrey probably shrank from Latinizing the Welsh

[45] *RC*, XLI, 489.
[46] *Irish Nennius*, ed. J. H. Todd, Additional Notes, xiii f.
[47] *RC*, XLI, 489.

name [Myrddin] in the natural way as Merdinus, owing to the similarity to a French word of unpleasant associations which would have resulted, and so changed the *d* to an *l*."[48] "The Welsh, in adapting [French] romances, would cymricise names of all kinds more completely, substituting, for example, 'Geraint' for 'Erec,' with which they were not familiar."[49] "When Welshmen came to translate the Arthurian romances, they thought that in Perceval they recognized their native Peredur and they accordingly substituted the latter's name for Perceval; similarly they substituted Gwalchmei for Gawain."[50] In every case Bruce has been obliged to resort to some other explanation than direct and regular phonetic development. If anyone demands that every equation of names must conform to rigid and regular laws, he must start by denying that the names of Myrddin and Merlin, Geraint and Erec, Gwalchmai and Gawain, Peredur and Perceval have any connection whatsoever with each other. And in that case, he can indeed pride himself upon the scientific consistency of his position, but he will discover that he is the only scholar in the world equally consistent and equally courageous.

All who are not willing to adopt this extremist position regarding the transmission of proper names must be ready to agree that the most uncanny and unexpected changes *may* take place, and not much more than a rough similarity in sound *may* indicate the derivation of one name from another, or from a common source. But to assume identity of character on the basis of mere similarity in sound is, of course, sheer madness. The process must be safeguarded by certain tests: 1. Is there a demonstrated channel of transmission? 2. Is there a sustained or detailed similarity in nature or activities? 3. Is there a correspondence in relationships to identifiable characters? 4. Are intermediate forms between the two names discoverable? 5. Are any influences to be detected which would account for the abnormal features in the transmitted name? When, and only when, two or more of these conditions are met can one propose with some confidence an identification based on a rough similarity in the sound of the names.

The first condition scarcely need worry us in this connection, for the intercommunication between Ireland, Wales, and Brittany was not only natural enough for peoples speaking related tongues and possessing similar cultural heritages, but the direct testimony also is abundant. The existence of these channels of transmission has been amply demonstrated by Zimmer, Cross, and Miss O'Rahilly.

The fifth test deserves a little more treatment. In the passages from Bruce we have noted that several derived names are explained as substitutions. In other words, a story-teller does not render the name he hears as closely as he can: he merely uses a name to which his own tongue and the ears of his listeners are already accustomed, which resembles in sound the name he has heard but which existed already independent of it.[51] Another common and powerful force is that of assimilation. The story-teller does not substitute altogether another

---

[48] Bruce, *op. cit.*, I, 129.　　　[50] *Ibid.*, I, 192.
[49] *Ibid.*, II, 72.　　　[51] *ZfSL*, XXXI², 127 n. 5.

and independent name or word: he unconsciously, however, permits his attempt to reproduce the sound he hears to be attracted by a more familiar name or word.  The result is a cross between the sound suggested by the old name and the sound of the attracting word.  Another deflecting influence we have already given some attention to, and need not dwell on further: that is, etymologizing.  Etymologizing, assimilation, and substitution explain most of the strange developments of names in Arthurian romance; the differences in regional pronunciation of names and the striking looseness of sounds in the Celtic languages go far to explain the rest.  When one finds within the bounds of the same language that the place of Lludd Llurugawc in one version of a triad is taken by Llyr Lluyddawc in another,[52] one should not be surprised at finding substitutions and corruptions in names that have passed from one language to another.  Tests one must apply before one can pronounce that two personages of similar-sounding names are identical, but perhaps the least significant of the tests is complete conformity to phonetic laws.

[52] Loth, *Mab.*², II, 273.

# CHAPTER IV

## IRISH GODS OF SUN AND STORM

Now that we have taken our bearings and learned something of the trackways that lead through the dusky forests and wide launds of Celtic tradition, we may recommence our quest of the gods with better assurance of success. In particular, let us see if we may understand more clearly the nature of Cuchulinn and Curoi, and the part they play in the legend of the abduction of Blathnat.

There are doubtless those who shrug their shoulders at the mention of seasonal myth or of a solar interpretation. Ever since the too imaginative and sweeping theories of Max Müller and his school were exposed by Andrew Lang, and Mannhardt and Frazer made vegetation deities more fashionable than solar and culture heroes, it has been almost as much as one's reputation was worth to mention the sun in certain learned circles. It is hard for men of our day who live protected against heat and cold, and who are perfectly acquainted with the scientific causes for the stupendous pageantry of sunrise and sunset, the mysterious behavior of the moon and stars, the stunning flashes and detonations of the storm to take seriously this "highly poetical talk about the weather," as primitive myths have been ironically called. But for the savage it was different. Other men he found agreeable or disagreeable according to the case; yet being like himself, they were comprehensible and commonplace.

Not so the elements and their behavior. Five hundred years ago they were almost as complete mysteries as they were five hundred thousand years ago. They inspired the primitive man with awe, wonder, terror, and gratitude.

Miss Jane Harrison has put the situation admirably: [1] The savage "sees the black cloud rising, he feels a horrible oppression in the sultry air, he hears unearthly rumblings and watches flashes of lightning play across the sky. Finally he hears a noise over his head like a cartload of bricks; earth and sky, as Hesiod describes it, are jumbled together with an unspeakable din and he gives up all for lost. Presently it is all over, the sun is shining,

[1] J. Harrison, *Themis*, 89.

39

the trees glistening, the earth refreshed and glad.  If that were
all he might think there had been 'plenty devil about.'  . . .
But when he goes into the bush he finds a great tree split and
charred, or the body of his best friend lying on the road dead,
distorted.  Something has struck the tree and the man and
smashed them."

The play of these stupendous forces still inspires much of our
poetry; in the old days it inspired something which was both
poetry and science — myth.  The early gods were the mysterious
powers of nature in human form.  In spite of those who think
solar mythologies discredited, classical mythology alone numbers its sun-gods by the score.  Helios, Kronos, Zeus, Apollo,
Phaethon, Talus, Hercules, Phoebus, Admetus, Ixion, Aescula-
pius, Hyperion, Hades, Ares, Hippolytus, Janus, all had their
solar aspects.  Gilbert Murray has recently declared:[2]  "The
Young Sun returning after winter is himself a Kouros, and all
the Kouroi have some touch of the Sun in them."  It would
seem as if those who regard solar exegetics as a thing of the past
had not kept in touch with the brilliant work of the English
classicists, Gilbert Murray, A. B. Cook, and Miss Harrison.

Nor is the worship of the celestial powers restricted to Greece
and Rome.  Among the North American Indians of today,
among Egyptians of ten thousand years ago, among the Aztecs
and the Japanese, among the Norse and the Hindoos, at Tarshish, Carthage, Baalbek, Cuzco, Bath, Heliopolis the sun was
worshipped.  His names were many: Ra, Indra, Balder, Mith-
ras, Grannos, Tezcatlipoca.  It would be a work of supereroga-
tion to point out the wide diffusion of sun worship.

Its prevalence in Western Europe from the earliest times is
amply attested.  Déchelette in his *Manuel d'Archéologie Pré-
historique* declares:[3]  "It is in fact this cult of heliolatry which,
of all the beliefs of the Western barbarians in pre-Roman times,
has left in protohistoric art the clearest traces."  And he goes on
to devote fifty-six pages to the evidence.  Among the Gauls the
existence of solar deities is proved by the many inscriptions to
gods equated with Apollo, — Borvo, Grannos, Belinus, Maponos.[4]  The conception of the sun as a wheel was firmly rooted
both among Mediterranean and Germanic peoples, and Gaidoz

[2] G. Murray, *Five Stages of Greek Religion*, 46.
[3] II, 411.
[4] J. Rhys, *Hib. Lec.*, 21–8; A. Holder, *Altceltischer Sprachschatz, sub*
Belenos; *Bheft ZrP*, LX, 199.

has shown that the wheel appears frequently in Gallic sculpture, as an emblem carried by certain unnamed gods.[5]  Solar worship even survived for a while the introduction of Christianity.  The seventh century sermon of St. Eligius holds up to condemnation a long list of pagan usages and among them one finds this prohibition: [6]  "Let no one call the sun and the moon lords or swear by them, for they are but the creatures of God."  In Britain as late as the eleventh century the laws of King Canute prohibit completely "barbaric worship"; [7] more specifically the adoration of "the sun, the moon, fire, running water, springs, stones, trees of any kind, or blocks of wood."

In Ireland, too, it can be shown that heliolatry persisted from prehistoric times until long after the introduction of Christianity, and was even blended with Christianity.  In the British Museum *Guide to the Antiquities of the Bronze Age* we read: [8]  "At Trundholm in the north of Zealand an engraved bronze disk . . . has been found mounted on a miniature carriage drawn by a horse.  This was undoubtedly a ceremonial object, and connected with sun-worship, so that the discovery of more than one such disk in Ireland shows the extent of the cult before the first millennium B.C."

For the existence of heliolatry in the period that more nearly concerns us we have no less a witness than St. Patrick himself.  I do not believe that there is any scholar, however learned, who will claim to know more about Irish paganism of the fifth century than did St. Patrick.  In the *Confession*, universally admitted to be authentic, he says with obvious reference to the beliefs of his contemporaries: [9]  "That sun which we see, rises for us daily at God's command, but never will it reign nor will its splendor endure, but all who adore it will meet with the unhappy punishment of the wicked.  We, however, believe and worship the *true Sun Christ*, who will never perish; nor shall he perish who has done his will, but shall live eternally, even as Christ will live eternally."  In 697 the law of Adamnan was passed, for relieving women from service in battle, and was signed by a large

[5] H. Gaidoz, *Dieu gaulois du soleil*, 9; A. Bertrand, *Religion des gaulois*, 140 ff; J.-L. Courcelle-Seneuil, *Dieux gaulois d'après les monuments figurés*, 72 f.   *Cf.* on wheel J. Grimm, *Teut. Myth.*, tr. Stallybrass, II, 620.

[6] Migne, *Pat. Lat.*, LXXXVII, col. 523. *Cf. Rev. d. questions historiques*, LXV, 424–55.

[7] F. Liebermann, *Gesetze der Angelsachsen*, I, 313. *Cf.* Aelfric, *Homil.*, I, 366.

[8] P. 110.                    [9] *PRIA*, XXV, 252.

number of dignitaries of the realm, including bishops and abbots. But in spite of the entirely Christian auspices under which the ceremony was conducted, the "securities" invoked are, first, the sun, then the moon and all the other elements of God: and after these, the apostles and the saints.[10]   Eloquent testimony to the veneration which the sun still enjoyed in Christian Ireland! Cormac's *Glossary*, dated about 900, explains the word *indelba* as "the name of the altars of idols, because they were wont to carve on them the forms of the elements they adored there, *verbi gratia, figura solis.*" [11]   Could there be clearer, more striking witness than this of saints and bishops?

The memory of sun-worship on a magnificent scale persisted into the mid-eighteenth century, for Michael Comyn's tale, *The Adventure of the Sons of Thorolb*, relates: "It was a custom then to hold a meeting once in every third year on Buaile na Griene [Fold of the Sun] on the south side of Slieve Callan [near Ennis], to make sacrifice and adoration to the sun, upon an altar which was made of thin grey flags in that place.   And great numbers of bulls and rams used to be killed and roasted around those flags, and the blood and brains of those animals used to be spilled and rubbed upon that altar." [12]   Extraordinary though it may seem, as late as 1844 boys of the neighborhood on the first Sunday in August used to strew summer flowers on this altar and hold games in honor of a certain Crom Dubh, whom they called a god, and who was in all probability a name for the solar divinity.

Patrick's diplomatic designation of Christ as "Sol Verus" was not an isolated occurrence, but was common among missionaries to sun-worshippers.   Naturally it could be taken literally.   And in fact it was so taken: Gildas, writing in the century after Patrick and doubtless voicing prevailing conceptions among the Brythonic Celts, calls Christ "the true sun, showing to the whole world his splendor, not only from the temporal firmament, but also from the height of heaven, which surpasses everything temporal." [13]   Gildas could hardly say

[10] *Cain Adamnain*, ed. K. Meyer, 13.

[11] *Cormac's Glossary*, 94.   For other evidence on sun-worship in Ireland *cf. ITS*, IV, 223; M. O'Donnell, *Life of Columcille*, ed. O'Kelleher, Schoepperle, 357, 401; T. Moore, *Hist. of Ireland*, I, 57; Borlase, *Dolmens of Ireland*, III, 846–9; *Eriu*, VIII, 105.

[12] *PRIA*, Ser. 2, Polite Letters, I, 268–72; *PRIA*, XXXVI, C, 48 f, 56–59.

[13] Sec. 8.   For other examples of the identification *cf. RC*, II, 302;   F.

more explicitly that Christ shone in the sky. The same belief must have been current in Ireland, for not only has Hamilton discovered an Irish solar description applied to Christ, but also the indentification of Christ-worship with sun-worship can alone account for the curious statement in the life of St. Caillin: [14] "Sunwise Cathbad made every divination and prophecy because he believed in Christ." This remark makes rank nonsense, unless one takes Christ to be in a sense *Sol Verus*. But even more eloquent than any written record are those mute witnesses to the coalescence of heliolatry and Christianity, the weather-bitten but still majestic high crosses standing in their sequestered cemeteries at Clonmacnois and Kells. For each combines with the symbol of the Crucified the circle of the older divinity.[15]

Plummer has shown how profoundly solar conceptions have colored the lives of the Christian saints of Ireland. "It is in accordance with the pre-eminence of the Celtic Sun and Fire God that the solar should be the most prominent mythological influence in Celtic hagiology. . . . Aed is one of the names for fire; Buite means heat, Lassar (dim. Laisren) means flame, Samthann may have been etymologized as summer fire (Sam-thene)." [16] "Of miracles apparently solar in origin which recur with greater or less frequency we may enumerate the following: fiery manifestations at, or prior to birth or during childhood, heavenly light accompanying the saint, fantastic fire which does no hurt, luminous appearances at death or burial . . . while the stream in which he performs his ascetic devotions becomes hot." [17] If sun-worship has left the clearest traces on the lives of the Irish saints, it is incredible that it should leave no trace on the lives of the Irish pagan heroes.

In the face of this evidence it is hard to see how anyone can be supercilious about solar myths. Indeed, it would seem as if those who call themselves disciples of Frazer and Mannhardt, far outrun their masters in their skepticism. As Andrew Lang, one of the severest critics of the vagaries of mythologizers, himself says: [18] "Mannhardt was not the man to neglect or suppress solar myths when he found them, merely because he did

---

Cumont, *Textes et monuments*, I, 355; E. K.ʻ Chambers, *Medieval Stage*, I, 242. *Cf. Cambridge Medieval Hist.*, I, 9.

[14] C. Plummer, *Vitae Sanctorum Hiberniae*, I, cxxxv, n. 5.

[15] F. M. ffrench, *Prehistoric Faith*, 50, 64.

[16] C. Plummer, *op. cit.*, I, cxxxvi.

[17] *Ibid.*, cxxxvii ff.          [18] *Modern Mythology*, 55.

not believe that a great many other myths which had been claimed as celestial were solar. Like every sensible person, he knew that there are numerous real, obvious, confessed solar myths not derived from a disease of language. These arise from (1) the impulse to account for the doings of the Sun by telling a story about him as if he were a person; (2) from the natural poetry of the human mind." Lang, moreover, speaks with a drop of sarcasm of those who are afraid of solar myths. "'The scalded child dreads cold water,' and Müllenhoff apparently dreaded even real solar myths." Again Lang says: [19] "Mannhardt goes farther. He not only recognises, as everyone must do, the Sun, as explicitly named, when he plays his part in myth or popular tale. He thinks that even when the sun is not named, his presence, and reference to him, and derivation of the incidents in Märchen from solar myth, may sometimes be detected with great probability."

Given the unimpeachable testimony that the sun was worshipped in Ireland, I undertake without further apologies to re-open the question of solar elements in the Irish hero legends. Two facts must be kept in mind in this investigation. The first is the obvious pressure which lay upon every teller of heathen stories to suppress or disguise the mythological traits if he wished to avoid the powerful hostility of the most zealous clergy. MacNeill has acutely suggested that the reason why on one half of the ogham inscriptions of Kerry the name following *mucoi*, " of the clan," has been effaced, is the probability that the name was that of an eponymous ancestor, a pagan god.[20] In one story Lug, who of all the figures of Irish legend is most patently a god, asserts quite pointedly that he is of the race of Adam.[21] The story-teller clearly wished to avoid the charge that he was reviving the cult of the banished divinities. To be sure, certain figures appearing in story are explicitly said to be gods: Manannan, the Dagda, Ana, Dechtire, Conchobar, and the Tuatha De Danann.[22] Nevertheless we must not expect the signs of divinity

[19] *Ibid.*, 58.
[20] *Celtic Review*, X, 273.
[21] O'Curry, *MS. Materials*, 621.
[22] *Cormac's Glossary*, 4, 114; *IT*, III, 355; Rhys, *Hib. Lect.*, 144. It is, of course, possible that Conchobar, Dechtire, Conall Cernach and others whose stories interweave with those of plainly mythological personages and who themselves possess divine traits were both divine and human. As Cook puts it (*Folklore*, XVII, 35), "they were traditional or even historical kings, who, in accordance with the beliefs of their day, posed as embodiments of

to appear on the surface. To use Lang's word, they must be "detected."

Another all-important fact which neither the mythologizers in the Celtic field nor their opponents have grasped. Certain peoples considered the god of the sun and the god of the thunder and lightning to be one and the same. Jastrow says, "In many mythologies the sun and lightning are regarded as correlated forces." [23] Cook says, "These two conceptions of storm-god and sun-god, which to our way of thinking seem so diametrically opposed, are in point of fact by no means incompatible." [24] Cook figures an ancient vase in which the sun-god is shown in his chariot, with hand stretched out to grasp a winged thunderbolt, and he reminds us that two of the sun's steeds were named Bronte and Sterope, Thunder and Lightning.[25] Zeus himself was both the sun [26] and the cloud-gatherer, the lord of the thunderbolt. Déchelette, speaking of prehistoric symbolism, says: "Since primitive man attributed a common origin to the lightning and the rays of the sun, one may understand how the god of thunder is closely related to the divinities of the solar cycle, and one may easily explain the frequent association of solar symbols (horse, swan, wheel, swastika) with the ax." [27] Montelius, the great Swedish archaeologist, witnesses to the same dual conception in Teutonic mythology.[28] Windisch finds the same connection of sun-god and storm-god among the Gauls. "We know that the Celts conceived of the sun as a wheel. We have learned to recognize . . . a Gallic god with thunderbolt

---

the Irish sky-god. They would thus be brought into line with the early Greek kings, who claimed to be Zeus, and the early Italian kings, who were dubbed Jupiter." But it is for the historian to establish their historicity by scientific criteria. Gomme's argument (*Folklore as a Historical Science*, 101) that the Second Battle of Moytura must have taken place and that the Tuatha De Danann must have lived on this earth because the actual topography and the monuments of the plain of Moytura agree with the text is almost on a par with Caxton's argument that Arthur's knights must have existed because Gawain's skull was preserved at Dover, where the *Mort Artu* says that he died. After all, there is no denying that, whatever fragments of history may be embodied in the Irish sagas, there is an abundance of myth. And for the purposes of this book it makes no difference whether Conchobar or even Curoi is a deified hero or a euhemerized deity.

[23] M. Jastrow, *Religion of Babylonia*, 160.
[24] A. B. Cook, *Zeus*, I, 578.
[25] *Ibid.*, 337.
[26] *Ibid.*, 186.
[27] J. Déchelette, *Manuel d'arch. préhist.*, II, 482.
[28] *Folklore*, XXI, 60 ff.

and lightning, who carries at the same time a sun-wheel." [29]
An example of this very combination is found also among the
the Celts of Ireland.

Lug, probably the god whom Caesar refers to as the Mercury
of the Gauls, undoubtedly gave his name to some fourteen Gallic
towns named Lugudunum or Lugdunum, among which are to be
counted Lyons, Laon, Leyden.[30]  His importance in Ireland may
be judged by MacNeill's suggestion that "descent from Lugh
was the common claim of all the ancient Irish." [31]

Besides being the inventor of arts, he was, at least in Ireland,
a god of the sun.  Rhys was the first to point out the significant
passages in the *Fate of the Children of Turenn:* [32]  "The shining
of his face and of his brow was like the setting sun: it was impossible to look upon his visage, so great was its brilliance."
Again, "The aspect of his visage and of his brow was as bright
as the sun on a summer's day."  Finally when Bres utters his
astonishment that the sun should be rising in the west, the
direction from which Lug was approaching, the druids replied
that it was the splendor of the face of Lug Lamfada.  In the
*Second Battle of Moytura* the name of Lug is replaced by Samh-
ildanach, which means "Summer of Many Arts." [33]  But the
one point that shows that these are not mere rhetorical hyper-
boles employed to express Lug's magnificence is the singular and
hitherto uninterpreted detail, which is meaningless, even absurd
as a sign of beauty or greatness, but is appropriate enough in a
personification of the sun.  A gloss states that "a red color used
to be on him from sunset to morning." [34]  We know, of course,
the reason for the red glow with which the sun sinks below the
horizon and rises from it, but not so the Irishman or Anglo-
Saxon of a thousand years ago.  In a dialogue of Aelfric's we find
that two of the questions asked were: "Why is the sun red in the
evening?" and "Why shineth she so red in the morning?" [35]
This phenomenon which excited such curiosity naturally found
its way into the description of the sun-god.  It is highly unlikely
that the red color that was on Lug from sunset to morning has
any other explanation.

[29] E. Windisch, *op. cit.*, 200.
[30] *Rev. archéologique*, XXIV, 205.  *Cf. PRIA*, XXXIV, C, 141.
[31] J. MacNeill, *Celtic Ireland*, 57.
[32] Rhys, *Hib. Lec.*, 397; *Atlantis*, IV, 161, 163, 177.
[33] *Rev. arch.*, XXIV, 211.          [34] *RC*, XII, 127.
[35] J. Grimm, *Teut. Myth.*, tr. Stallybrass, II, 721.  *Cf.* Sébillot, *Folklore de France*, I, 36.

Lug also qualifies as god of lightning.  Of his spear it is said, "When battle was near it was drawn out; then it roared and struggled against its thongs; fire flashed from it; and, once slipped from its leash, it tore through and through the ranks of the enemy." [36]  His approach is thus described: "They saw a great mist all round, so that they knew not where they went because of the greatness of the darkness; and they heard the noise of a horseman approaching.  The horseman (Lug) let fly three throws of a spear at them." [37]  Furthermore his epithets *lamhfada loinnbheimionach*, "of the long arm and the mighty blows," are easily comprehensible.  In Ireland, therefore, we have the example of Lug to show that the forces of the sun and the thunder-cloud were combined in the same god.  Let us see whether this same mythological conception does not apply also to Cuchulinn and Curoi.

Cuchulinn was presumably a god, the son of a god and goddess; for Cormac about 900 attests that after his death people said, "A noble god was put to death;" and he was called the son of the goddess Dechtire, and was a rebirth of Lug.[38]

The signs of his solar nature have often been pointed out before, notably by Rhys and Miss Hull.  It was one of his taboos not to rise at Emain Macha later than the sun.[39]  On the Cattle-Raid of Cualgne the intense heat generated by his body melted the snow round him for thirty feet.[40]  His head is thus described: "Three crowns of hair he had: next his skin, brown; in the middle, crimson; that outside formed, as it were, a diadem of gold, for like the shining of yellow gold was each glittering, curling, beauty-colored thread as free and loose it fell down and hung between his shoulders." [41]  But most significant is the description of his contortions.[42]  "Then it was that he suffered his *riastradh* or paroxysm, whereby he became a fearsome and multiform and wondrous and hitherto unknown being. . . . Every limb and joint and point and articulation of him quivered as does a tree, yea a bulrush in midcurrent.  Within in his skin he put forth an unnatural effort of his body: his feet, his shins, and his knees shifted themselves and were behind him: his heels and calves and hams were displaced to the front of his leg-

[36] C. Squire, *Mythology of the British Islands*, 62.
[37] D'Arbois de Jubainville, *op. cit.*, 170.  *Cf.* Cook, *Zeus*, II, 704.
[38] *Cormac's Glossary*, 3.  E. Hull, *Cuchulinn Saga*, lvi.
[39] E. Hull, *op. cit.*, lxxvi.          [41] *Ibid.*, lxiii.
[40] *Ibid.*, lxv.                         [42] *Ibid.*, 174 f.

bones, in condition such that their knotted muscles stood up in
lumps large as the clenched fist of a fighting man." "Then his
face underwent an extraordinary transformation: one eye became engulfed in his head so far that 'tis a question whether a
wild heron could have got at it where it lay against his occiput,
to drag it out upon the surface of his cheek. . . . His lion's
gnashings caused flakes of fire, each one larger than fleece of
three-year-old wether, to stream from his throat into his mouth
(and so outwards). The sounding blows of the heart that panted
within him were as the howl of a ban-dog doing his office, or of a
lion in the act of charging bears. Among the aerial clouds over
his head were visible the virulent pouring showers and sparks
of ruddy fire which the seething of his savage wrath caused to
mount up above him. His hair became tangled about his head,
as it had been branches of a red thorn-bush stuffed into a
strongly fenced gap. . . . Taller, thicker, more rigid, longer
than mast of a great ship was the perpendicular jet of dusky
blood which out of his scalp's very central point shot upwards
and then was scattered to the four cardinal points; whereby
was formed a magic mist of gloom resembling the smoky pall
that drapes a regal dwelling, what time a king at night-fall of a
winter's day draws near to it. This distortion being now past
which had been operated in Cuchulinn, he leaped into the
scythed chariot. . . . Then he delivered a thunder-feat of a
hundred, one of two hundred, one of three hundred, one of four
hundred, and stood at a thunder-feat of five hundred." [42a]

It has been suggested that this extraordinary performance has,
as its foundation, the epileptic fits of a historical bravo.[43] Is it
not far more plausible to see in it the transformation of the sun-
god into the fire-shooting thunder cloud? The same hypothesis
explains the nature of the perplexing *gaebolga*. Meyer's interpretation of the word as really *gabul-gae*, a forked spear, which
has been accepted by MacNeill and Bergin, is a fitting description of the lightning.[44] At any rate, the museums show no
examples of forked spears, and it seems probable that the
*gaebolga* is a mythical weapon. In the *Sick-Bed of Cuchulinn*
the hero says: "I have hurled my spear, the mist has prevented

[42a] *Cf.* Cook, *Zeus*, II, 830.

[43] R. A. S. Macalister, *Ireland in Pre-Celtic Times*, 45.

[44] J. MacNeill, *Celtic Ireland*, 48 n. Poseidon's trident probably represented the lightning. *Cf.* Cook, *Zeus*, II, 805.

my seeing whether I have hit the mark; but if a man has been
hit, he is no longer living!" [45] This hurling of a spear from a
mist or cloud is a significant feaure, and as we shall see, it recurs
with another hero whose nature is demonstrably solar.

Let us now turn to Curoi mac Daire. He has been suspected of
being almost everything except a solar divinity: he has been
identified with the historic pirate Carausius, and called in turn
an actual chief of Munster, a genius of the sea, and a monster
with an external soul.[46] But let us note certain facts supplied by
*Bricriu's Feast*, a text of the ninth or even the eighth century.
We learn that when the rival heroes arrived by night at Curoi's
home, Curoi had gone on "an oriental expedition into Scythian
territory," and that "in whatsoever quarter of the globe Curoi
happened to be, every night over his fort he chanted a spell so
that it was as swift as a mill-stone." [47] When Curoi returned it
was in the morning.[48] When on another occasion, in the guise of
an uncouth giant, he enters the hall of the Ulstermen and takes
his stand by the fire, Dubthach Chafer-Tongue mocks him for
claiming the position of light-bearer to the house: "You are
more likely to burn the house down than to give light to the
household." [49] Thereupon Curoi replies: "Whatever my art
may be, surely it will be judged, however tall I may be, that the
whole household shall have light and yet the house shall not be
burned. Still that is not my only art; I have other arts besides.
However, the thing which I have come in quest of I have found
neither in Ireland nor in Scotland nor in Europe nor in Africa nor
in Asia as far as Greece and Scythia and the Orkney Islands and
the Pillars of Hercules and the Tower of Bregon and the Isles of
Gades."

An unexpected confirmation of Curoi's solar nature came to
me last summer. A graduate student of mine, Mr. Macleod, of
Highland Scotch ancestry and therefore heir to the traditional
lore of the Goidelic Celts, showed me a family ring, on which
were incised the device of a rayed sun and the motto "Luceo non
uro," — practically the Latin equivalent of Curoi's own words.

[45] D'Arbois de Jubainville, *Épopée celtique*, 207; literal translation A. H.
Leahy, *Heroic Romances of Ireland*, I, 182.

[46] *ITS*, II, 193, 197; *Eriu*, VII, 200; *ZcP*, IX, 189.

[47] *ITS*, II, 101, 103. I am greatly indebted to Prof. Ehrensperger for
verifying this translation.

[48] *Ibid.*, 113.

[49] Kittredge, *Study of G.G.K.*, 11.

Doubt there can be none that Curoi is a solar deity and that his home that revolves by night is the sky.[50]

The other side of Curoi's nature appears when in *Bricriu's Feast* he tests the three heroes on the plain.[51]  In each case "a dim, dark, heavy mist," "a hideous, black, dark cloud" comes up.  A giant, Curoi, appears and deals with his club a terrific blow "from top to toe" at the servant of the hero.  Again when Curoi enters the hall of the Ulstermen as a gigantic churl, he carries in his right hand "an ax into which had gone thrice fifty measures of glowing metal, and which would cut hairs against the wind for sharpness." [52]  When four nights later he deals a blow with this weapon, we read that "the creaking of the old hide that was about the fellow and the crashing of the ax — both his arms being raised aloft with all his might — were as the loud noise of a wood tempest-tossed in a night of storm." [53] Now this is an odd sound to accompany the stroke of an ax, but it has its explanation in the fact familiar to anthropologists that primitive peoples often conceived the thunder-weapon as an ax.[54] Déchelette declares that the double ax "was certainly related to the lightning or the thunder because it has given rise to anthropomorphic gods assimilated to Zeus (Zeus Labrandeus, Zeus Dolichenus), who bear at the same time the thunderbolt and the double ax." [55]  Curoi seems to belong in the same category. The most singular demonstration of Curoi's double nature lies in the fact that, whereas in the passages just quoted Curoi alone tests the courage of the heroes, another version of the Beheading Game furnishes in place of Curoi two testers.[56]  The three rivals for the Champion's Portion are sent first to Yellow Son of Fair to be judged, and he sends them on to Terror Son of Great Fear. To anyone aware of Curoi's dual nature these enigmatic names would be quite comprehensible.  Yellow Son of Fair would be Curoi the Sun, Terror Son of Great Fear would be Curoi the lightning.  This interpretation will find ample support in Chapter VI.

[50] On revolving castles *cf.* Sypherd, *Studies in Chaucer's Hous of Fame,* 144 ff, 173 ff.

[51] *ITS*, II, 43–51.

[52] Kittredge, *op. cit.*, 11.

[53] *ITS*, II, 127.

[54] C. Blinkenberg, *Thunderweapon in Religion*, 1 ff, 88 ff; A. B. Cook, *Zeus*, II, 505 ff.

[55] *Cf.* note 27.

[56] *ITS*, II, 97–101.

Cuchulinn and Curoi, then, are both sun-gods. The story of the abduction and rescue of Blathnat is the story of the passing of the flower-maiden from the possession of one sun-god to another's. The substitution of the "Hung-up Naked Man" and "Hung-up on the Cross" for Curoi may be explained by the tendency to identify Christ with the sun. At least, the same phenomenon may be observed in Breton folktales, of which Luzel writes:[57] "The Breton *conteurs* quite often confuse the Sun with the Eternal Father. Thus, in a tale where the hero should go to find the Sun in his palace in order to ask him various questions, the Eternal Father has taken the place of the orb of day."

The statement that a year elapsed between the abduction of Curoi and the discovery of Blathnat by Cuchulinn, as well as the statement that the struggle for her possession lasted from the first of November, the great seasonal festival of the Gaels, to the middle of spring, is a part of the myth. The story of Guinevere's abduction was also originally a seasonal myth, in which Arthur, Gawain, or Lancelot, on the one side, and Modred, Mardoc, Carrado, or Meleagant on the other, took the parts of the rival gods.

Let us now see if we can divine more exactly the relationship between Curoi and Cuchulinn.

[57] *RC*, II, 302. For survivals of sun-worship in Brittany *cf.* Sébillot, *Folklore de France*, 36 f, 60 f.

# BOOK TWO
## THE YOUNG GOD AND THE OLD

# CHAPTER V

## CUROI, GWRI, AND GAWAIN

Curoi and Cuchulinn, as we have seen, both betray the dual nature of sun and lightning god. There are other marked resemblances, even proofs of identity. Henderson suggested in his edition of *Bricriu's Feast* that "for some (non-Celtic?) tribe of Erin, Curoi may have filled the position of Cuchulinn." [1] This we shall find is not precisely right, but that some close relationship existed is borne out by the evidence. In the first place, both seem identified with Lug. We have the explicit statement that Cuchulinn was a rebirth of his father Lug.[2] Likewise Curoi is generally called the son of Daire, who in ancient tradition was equated with Lugaid,[3] and in a certain story the sons of Daire are all named Lugaid,[4] a name which MacNeill declares to be practically a variant of Lug.[5] It would seem, therefore, as if one had a right to call Curoi, Lug son of Lug, just as Cuchulinn is also Lug son of Lug. Furthermore, we learn that Lugaidh mac-na-tri-Con, the slayer of Cuchulinn, was so called because he was said to be the son of three Cu's: Curoi, Cuchulinn, and Conall Cearnach,[6] — another hint that as the father of the same man, Curoi and Cuchulinn were identical. Again, both Curoi and Cuchulinn are said to be so precocious that they took arms at the age of seven.[7] Finally, we have seen that in the various versions of the Blathnat abduction, when Cuchulinn and the men of Ulster went to attack the fortress of her father, the principal part was played by Curoi, who appeared as a young man disguised in a gray mantle. It was he who in one version performed prodigies of slaughter in the fortress, and who in another version, when overtaken at sea by the avenging Echde, slew him single-handed.[8] But in what may be an older

---

[1] *ITS*, II, 196.
[2] E. Hull, *Cuchulinn Saga*, lvi, lix.
[3] *Miscellany of Celtic Society*, ed. J. O'Donovan, 9.
[4] *Ir. Texte*, III, 319.
[5] J. MacNeill, *Celtic Ireland*, 49 f. On Daire *cf. PRIA*, XXXIV, C, 162; *ZcP*, XII, 327.
[6] E. O'Curry, *MS. Materials*, 479.
[7] *ITS*, II, 101.
[8] *Eriu*, II, 21; *ZcP*, IX, 194.

version of the story, that in *Cuchulinn's Phantom Chariot*, Cuchulinn takes the place of Curoi, both in playing the chief part in the attack and in rescuing the Ulstermen when overtaken by a storm on their return.[9] May it not be that the version of *Cuchulinn's Phantom Chariot* is the earlier, and that the other versions represent an effort to combine the form which makes Cuchulinn the hero with an even earlier, lost form which makes Curoi the hero of the same exploit?

But even more striking than the resemblances between Curoi and Cuchulinn are the differences. It is astonishing that Cuchulinn, the Irish Achilles, is almost always represented as very small, a boy in size. His first name was Setanta Bec, "the little," and he is called "little Cu," *mac bec*, "the little boy."[10] On the Cattle Raid of Cualgne he is said to be only seventeen years old.[11] His beardlessness was a subject of jest.[12] Cuchulinn is distinctly a boy hero.

Now whereas Curoi is also described as a youth when he aids the Ulstermen on their expedition to carry off Blathnat, the three cows, and the caldron, yet, as we have seen, he appears in the disguise of a *bachlach* or herdsman of enormous size.[13] In *Bricriu's Feast* we are told that as the heroes of Ulster were sitting in their hall at the close of day, "they saw a herdsman, great and very hideous, coming toward them into the house. It seemed to them that there was not among the Ulstermen a hero who would reach half his size. . . . An old hide next his skin, and a black, tawny cloak about him, and upon him the bushiness of a great tree, the size of a winter-fold in which thirty yearlings could find shelter. Fierce yellow eyes he had in his head, each of those two eyes standing out of his head as big as a cauldron that would hold a large ox. As thick as the wrist of any other man each one of his fingers. In his left hand, a block in which was a load for twenty yoke of oxen. In his right hand, an ax into which had gone thrice fifty measures of glowing metal; the handle was so heavy that it would take the strength of six oxen to move it; it would cut hairs against the wind for sharpness." I believe, therefore, we can detect a tendency to differentiate Curoi from Cuchulinn by emphasizing the difference in

---

[9] E. Hull, *op. cit.*, 282–5. Significant is Thurneysen's remark (*ZcP*, IX, 198) "Für Curoi ist im *Siaborcharpat* kein Platz."

[10] *Mesca Ulad*, ed. W. M. Hennessy, xiv.

[11] O'Curry, *MS. Materials*, 509.

[12] Rhys, *Hib. Lec.*, 436.    [13] G. L. Kittredge, *Study of G. G. K.*, 10 f.

size, though, to be sure that differentiation was never made consistent or uniform in all the texts.

This conception of Cuchulinn as identical with Curoi, except in so far as he is inferior in stature and age, suggests a re-interpretation of the name Cuchulinn. Our knowledge of the etymologizing habits of the Irish story-tellers should put us particularly on our guard whenever we meet a story that is introduced to explain a name. In the case of Cuchulinn there is the well-known incident of the struggle of the boy hero with the "Hound of Culann," a giant smith.[14] Both Baudis and Nutt have independently surmised that this tale was probably invented to explain the name.[15] If it was, we have the analogy of numerous other examples to warn us that the name Cu-Chulainn may itself be a corrupt form, intentionally distorted in the first place to supply an excuse for the story, and then established by the popularity of the story as the one and only form. Perhaps we may infer the true derivation of the name from the fact that not only is Cuchulinn a Curoi in miniature, but he also is referred to in the *Cattle Raid of Cualgne* frequently by diminutives like Cucan and Cucucan, which would mean "little Hound" or "Little Cu." [16] Now the latter might refer to Curoi, since he is mentioned along with Cuchulinn and Conall as one of the "three Cu's" from whom Lugaidh mac-na-tri-Con derived his name,[17] and since the Irish built up their pet names by adding diminutive endings to shortened forms of proper names.[18] Therefore, there is a possibility that Cucan and Cucucan as applied to Cuchulinn may mean "Little Curoi." May I suggest that the original form of the name Cuchulinn, before it was modified as an excuse for the Hound of Culann tale, was a hypocoristic development from Curoi?

When we observe that in the seasonal myth of the abduction of Blathnat, which we have already studied, the boy Cuchulinn takes over the weapon, the flower bride, and presumably the caldron and cows of the slain Curoi, may we not tentatively conjecture that Cuchulinn is a diminutive Curoi, the little Curoi, the young sun-god, who like Zeus kills the old sun and lightning god and takes over the symbols of his power?

[14] E. Hull, *op. cit.*, 140 f.
[15] *Eriu*, VII, 208; *Folklore Record*, IV, 26.
[16] *Mitt. Anthrop. Ges. in Wien*, XXXIX, 110.
[17] See note 6.
[18] Pokorny, *Historical Reader of Old Irish*, 23.

We shall find this conjecture corroborated if we study the other account of a contest between Curoi and Cuchulinn, the Beheading Game episode,[19] which, as we have seen, occurs in two versions in the *Feast of Bricriu*, and the ramifications of that story in Arthurian romance, which Kittredge has studied with such clarity, completeness, and scholarly caution.[20]  I have already quoted the passage in which the heroes of Ulster see Curoi approaching in the disguise of the *bachlach* or herdsman, and also the passage in which Curoi when mocked at as claiming the position of light-bearer for the house replies that the whole household shall have light and yet the house shall not be burned, and adds that this is not his only art, and that in his journeyings in the East, including Asia, Greece, the Pillars of Hercules, and the Isles of Gades, he has not found any man who would fulfil the rules of fair play for him.  He then announces what the bargain is to be: "Whoever it is of you that is able except these two (Conchobar and Fergus), let him come that I may strike off his head tonight and he may strike off my head tomorrow night." Munremar then undertakes the perilous task, but fails to appear when it is his own turn to suffer decapitation.  Loegaire behaves in the same way.  On the fourth night the *bachlach* returns in great wrath, reproaches the Ulstermen for their cowardice, and even taunts Cuchulinn.  "Thereupon Cuchulinn leaped toward him.  He dealt him a blow with the ax so that he sent his head to the top rafter of the Red Branch, so that the whole house shook.  Cuchulinn caught up his head again and gave it a blow with the ax so that he made fragments of it.  The *bachlach* rose up after that.  On the morrow the Ulstermen were watching Cuchulinn to see whether he would avoid the *bachlach*, as the other heroes had done. . . .   As they were there, then, at the close of day, they saw the *bachlach* approaching them. . . . Then Cuchulinn went to him and stretched his neck across the block.  'Stretch out your neck, wretch!' said the *bachlach*. . . .   Then Cuchulinn stretched out his neck so that a grown man's foot would have fitted between each two of his ribs, and he stretched his neck until it reached the block on the other side. The *bachlach* raised his ax so that it reached the roof-tree of the house.  The creaking of the old hide that was about the fellow and the crashing of the ax— both his arms being raised aloft with all his might — were as the loud noise of a wood tempest-tossed

[19] *ITS*, II, 117–29.        [20] *A Study of Gawain and the Green Knight*.

in a night of storm. Down it came then . . . on his neck, its blunt side below, — all the nobles of Ulster gazing upon them. 'O Cuchulinn, arise! . . . Of the warriors of Ulster or of Ireland, none is found to be compared with you in valor or in prowess or in truth.'"

There are seven versions of this story in Arthurian romance: two versions of *Gawain and the Green Knight,* the *Livre de Caradoc* inserted in the first continuation of Crestien de Troyes's *Conte del Graal, Hunbaut,* the *Mule sanz Frain, Diu Krone* and *Perlesvaus.* Kittredge has declared that at least four of these are independent of each other,[21] and I go so far as to believe that all seven are independent of each other. The minute traits of the Irish story which crop up four or five centuries later in these romances show that the currents of tradition which carried them down must have been extraordinarily uncontaminated. For example, just as the dying reproach of Curoi to Blathnat turns up in the similar speech of Carado of the Dolorous Tower in the *Vulgate Lancelot,* so also certain speeches of Curoi, the *bachlach,* are reproduced in substance in *Gawain and the Green Knight.*[22] Details, such as the stretching of the neck, crop up in other romances.[23] I believe that there is far more original tradition in the whole group of versions than has been detected so far. In *Bricriu's Feast* Curoi wears a black tawny cloak,[24] and, as we have seen, in the abduction story he is called "the man in the gray mantle." Yet both in *Gawain and the Green Knight* and the prose *Perceval* version of the Caradoc, the challenger is dressed in green.[25] This transformation is entirely explicable by the fact that one of the Irish words for gray, *glas,* also may mean green.[26] We know that Curoi disguised is regularly called a *bachlach,* that is, a herdsman or churl.[27] This word is pronounced today as if it were trisyllabic, — bachelach. Now in *Gawain and the Green Knight,* the latter is called, as Hulbert has shown,[28] Sir Bercilak. Hulbert has also shown that a corresponding figure of a huge old knight in the False Guinevere story is called Barzelack in Fueterer's *Lancelot,* Bertelak in the English prose *Merlin,* and Bercelai and Bertolais in the French *Vulgate Lancelot.* If we bear in mind that, as Lot has observed, the insertion of *r* is met with more than once in Welsh,[29] and that a *c* is

[21] *Ibid.,* 25.
[22] *Ibid.,* 16.
[23] *Ibid.,* 45.
[24] *Ibid.,* 11.
[25] *Ibid.,* 31.
[26] *Ibid.,* 197.
[27] *ITS,* II, 116 ff.
[28] [J. M.] *Manly Anniversary Papers,* 12.
[29] *Rom.,* XXV, 2.

constantly mistaken for a *t* in manuscript transmission, I think
there can hardly be any question that all these names, including
Sir Bercilak, are derived from the Irish *bachlach*. Furthermore,
Hulbert pointed out that a love affair between Cuchulinn and
Curoi's wife was one of the most famous of Irish stories,[30]
and even the account of a three days' visit of Cuchulinn's to
Curoi's castle is to be found in *Bricriu's Feast*. And although we
do not find these traditions combined in the Irish, yet there is
nothing more certain than that the Celtic story-tellers regarded
it as the essence of their art to combine into harmony the various
stories about a given figure. It is entirely possible, therefore,
as Hulbert has maintained, that *Gawain and the Green Knight*
may represent with some fidelity a combination already made
in Ireland. When we note that not one of the Arthurian
versions of the Beheading Game reproduces the feature common
to both the Irish versions — the three rivals for the Champion's
Portion, — we are even led to ask whether both these extant
Irish versions have not been forced into a pattern peculiar to
*Bricriu's Feast*. In that case the Arthurian versions in restrict-
ing the adventure with the headcutting stranger to one champion
are more original than the extant Irish versions.

Now one notable difference between the story of *Gawain and
the Green Knight* and the Irish stories is the fact that Bercilak
appears on New Year's day to have his head cut off and that it
is exactly a year later that Gawain meets Bercilak to have his
own head cut off; whereas in the Irish stories no date is mentioned and the return blow is set for the next day. It is easy to
see why if the original story had set a year's interval between the
two blows, the author of *Bricriu's Feast* should have suppressed
this fact in order that the pattern of the three rivals should not
force him to postpone the dénouement of the episode till the
end of three years. It is also easy to see that if the year's
interval goes back to an authentic Irish original, how clearly it
fits into a mythic interpretation of the story, and how completely
it corroborates our hypothesis that Cuchulinn is a diminutive
Curoi. The Beheading Game would then be simply the tale of
the encounter of the old and the young sun-god, when the
old god is beheaded on condition that the young god shall himself lose his head a year later.

It is obvious that this myth, if such it be, is not perfectly

[30] *MP*, XIII, 439.

logical. It should not be the old god who at the year's end tests the young god, but the young god should now himself be decapitated, not merely tested, by a third god, and so on *ad infinitum*. This is precisely what we do find in the *Perlesvaus* version of the Beheading Game, a succession of golden coronaled youths who have been annually slain; an indication that the logic of the myth was understood by the inventor of that version. But myths cannot be completely logical, especially if they are forced into entertaining story-patterns. The game of alternating blows or pluck-buffet provided a story-pattern which was inconsistent, to be sure, with the myth, but effective as entertainment. And the Irish *fili* who concocted the story doubtless cared more about pleasing his patrons than about the hopeless task of making myths logical. So he merely remarked: "So much the worse for the myth!" and gave us this charming story.

But it is when we trace the figures of Curoi and Cuchulinn down through the Welsh into Arthurian romance that we find conclusive evidence that Cuchulinn is simply little Curoi. In the first place as Henderson says: "The name Cu Roi is often written Curui. . . . The Egerton variant for sec. 80 once has Curi. . . . Nor must we forget a phonetic fact which may easily be illustrated in Ireland as well as in the Highlands, viz., *ui* being sounded as an *i*, somewhat like *ee* in English seed." [31] The name, then, may well have passed into Welsh pronounced Cooree. In Wales there were opportunities for the initial letter to remain as it was or to become voiced. No traces of a form Cwri survive in Welsh, though there is quite a little evidence in Arthurian nomenclature to prove its existence. Various forces might change the initial *c* to a *g*. Old Welsh *cant* became Middle Welsh *can* or *gan*. We find that Cascordmawr, the original epithet of Eleuther, became Gosgorddvawr.[32] The Welsh laws of lenation would have operated to produce G at the beginning of the name Cwri in most of its occurrences,[33] and the attractive force of the word *gwr*, "man," would have tended to fix the form Gwri. So far as the names are concerned there is far less difficulty in explaining how Curoi became Gwri than in explaining how it became Chubert, an acknowledged derivation as we saw in Chapter III.

Now Rhys long since pointed out that the mythical Welsh

[31] *ITS*, II, 194. For names derived from Curoi, consult Chart A, p. 356.
[32] *Annales de Bretagne*, XV, 530.
[33] J. Strachan, *Introd. to Early Welsh*, 8 ff.

figure Gwri corresponds in a way to Cuchulinn.[34]  They were
both precocious in their growth, Gwri at the age of four striving
with his father's servants to take the horses to water.  Moreover,
to quote Rhys, "the allusion to the colt born at the time of
Gwri's own birth deserves special notice, as it has its counterpart in the story of one of the obscure incarnations of Lug
before he was born . . . Cuchulainn."  Two colts were born
at the same time as the divine child, and though the story relates
that this particular rebirth of Lug died in infancy, the divine
father directed that the two colts be kept for his other rebirth,
Cuchulinn.  Baudis came to the conclusion that this strange
tale represented a fusion of two similar stories.  "According to
one story Cuchulainn had a horse, or two horses, which were of
the same origin as himself."[35]  In that case, there would be a
striking parallel between the birth of Cuchulinn and that of
Gwri, and there is a possibility that Gwri is the youthful Curoi
or Cuchulinn.

Furthermore, Welsh myth knows both a little Gwri and a big
Gwri, Gwr-van and Gwr-nach.  Gwrnach is called a giant;
his castle is the largest in the world.[36]  Just as in *Bricriu's
Feast* the three Irish heroes enter Curoi's castle at the day's
end, so the three Welsh heroes enter Gwrnach's castle at the
day's end.  And Gwrnach is slain with his own sword by Kei
as Curoi is slain with his own sword by Cuchulinn.[37]  Gwrvan or
little Gwri only appears in a catalogue of the names of Arthur's
knights,[38] but his epithet Gwallt Avwyn, which seems to mean
"hair like reins," that is, long, streaming hair, is the solution of
a most perplexing problem.

For it has generally been assumed that the name of Gawain,
who, as we have seen, plays the rôle of Cuchulinn both in the
rescue of the flower maiden and in the Beheading Game was
derived from the Welsh Gwalchmai.  To be sure, there were
difficulties.  No influences could be detected that would produce
the *n* in Galvain; Rhys himself had to admit that he could not
tell why a solar deity should be called "hawk of May," presumably the meaning of Gwalchmai;[39] and finally there seemed
no connection between Gwalchmai and Cuchulinn.  The

---

[34] *Hib. Lec.*, 501.  *Cf. Folklore Record*, IV, 23, 26.

[35] *Folklore*, XXVII, 49.  *Cf. PRIA*, XXXIV, C, 330; *Intern. Cong. Rel.*,
III, vol. 2, 240.

[36] Loth, *Mab.* [2], I, 318.                [38] *Ibid.*, 277.

[37] *Ibid.*, 321.                              [39] *Arthurian Legend*, 13.

phonetic difficulty is aggravated when one realizes that the earliest form of Gawain is that on the Modena portal — Galvagin, which is even further away from Gwalchmai than Galvain. But everything becomes perfectly clear if one sees in Galvagin the Welsh epithet of Gwrvan, Gwallt Avwyn. For Gwrvan is no other than little Gwri and is therefore identical with Cuchulinn.

Confirmation of this theory is abundant. Beside Galvagin on the Modena sculpture is Galvariun, whose name seems almost as clearly derived from the epithet of Gwri, Gwallt Euryn, meaning Golden Hair. Galvariun in turn can correspond to only one figure in the Dolorous Tower story, namely Galeschin, and it is easy to see how a French scribe might misread the unfamiliar name and assimilate it to the familiar adjective *galesche* (Welsh). This Galeschin is called Duc de Clarence. Now, according to Lot, in the thirteenth century there was no place of this name in England and no title, but on the contrary, it was the popularity of the *Lancelot* which caused this name to be given to the castle of Clare in Suffolk.[40] Since Clarence is not a place name, it can hardly have any other than its proper meaning of "light." And what more appropriate epithet for the youthful Gwri than "Golden-Hair, Lord of Light"?

Again, Lot identified long ago Gwrvan with a certain Gorvain who appears in Raoul de Houdenc's *Meraugis de Portlesguez*.[41] "Note particularly," says Bruce, "the manner in which Gorvain, so prominent in the beginning, drops out of the action entirely for almost the whole of the remainder of the story." [42] He might have added: "Note particularly how Gawain becomes prominent in the action when Gorvain drops out." There is every indication that the author was following a source in which a character Gorvain Galvain was called by one name for a stretch and then by another, and very naturally he took the two names for two separate characters. And who can Gorvain Galvain be but Gwrvan Gwallt-Avwyn?

The solar nature of Gawain has often been pointed out. Again and again in the romances it is said that his strength increases until noon and then decreases.[43] And in Crestien de Troyes's *Ivain* it is explicitly said Gawain is the sun.[44] Crestien

[40] *Étude sur le Lancelot*, 143, n. 12.
[41] *Rom.*, XXIV, 326.  [43] *Mort Artu*, ed. J. D. Bruce, 287 f.
[42] *Evolution*, II, 208.  [44] Ll. 2398–2403.

goes on to give it a metaphorical turn, but I shall revert to the
passage in a later chapter and show that, whatever Crestien
thought of the statement, his source knew perfectly well what
he was talking about, and intended it to be taken mythologically.

What about Gwalchmai, who manifestly corresponds to
Gawain in certain Welsh romances? The name occurs in five of
the *Mabinogion*. In the two which embody native Welsh
tradition it is a significant fact that Gwalchmai is hardly more
than a name in a catalog.[45] Loth has pointed out that the
transcribers of *Kilhwch* and *Rhonabwy* belong to a period when
French and Breton influences were beginning to be felt as is
shown by the mention of that very Alan Fergant Duke of
Brittany (1088–1109), whom we have already met at Bari and
by the use of the French word for spear.[46] It is entirely possible
therefore that the slight acquaintance which these transcribers
show with Gwalchmai is derived from Brittany. To be sure, in
three other Welsh stories, *Peredur*, *Owain*, and *Geraint*, Gwalchmai plays a considerable part; but these are precisely the
stories which are regarded by practically all scholars as adaptations of Continental romances. All the facts agree with the
supposition that the name Gwalchmai is a Welsh substitution
for Breton or French Galvain, and not vice versa.

Though the processes I have traced offer the only explanation so far put forward for the organic connections between
Arthurian and Irish tradition, the processes themselves may
seem too strange, the conceptions too fantastic for acceptance.
Is not the notion of two gods, so different in nature and so
removed in size, yet both essentially the same, a figment of a
disordered brain? Is it not ridiculous to suppose that the divine
epithets flew off and became deities on their own account?
Yet both these absurdities are well-recognized phenomena in
classical mythology. Cook, in his exhaustive study of Zeus,
declares: "Not once, nor twice, but many times in our survey
of the Mediterranean lands — in the Archipelago, at Kyrene, in
Magna Graecia, in Crete, at Baalbek, and elsewhere — we have
had occasion to notice the younger god side by side with the
older god, of whom he was in a sense the younger self." [47] And
in Gaul, too, we find sculptured a mature god with caduceus
and winged cap, and beside him a boy god.[48] The first is doubt-

45 Loth, *Mab.* ², I, 282, 288, 373.     47 A. B. Cook, *Zeus*, I, 780.
46 *Contributions à l'étude*, 45.          48 *RC*, XXVII, 319.

less the Mercury, who according to Caesar was the chief of the Gallic pantheon and who is perhaps identical with the Lug after whom so many Gallic towns were named. The sculpture at any rate proves the existence among the Celts of this dual concept. The second phenomenon of divine epithets which start independent careers of their own is attested by Farnell: "The bright personal deities of Greek polytheism throw off their epithets as suns throw off satellites, the epithets then becoming the descriptive names of subordinate divinities or heroines." [49]

The conceptions, the phenomena which we have been obliged to assume in order to connect Gawain with Cuchulinn are neither irregular nor unique: they are the commonplaces of classical mythology. And when we recapitulate the evidence, we must see that the whole structure fits together. True, much of the evidence on the intermediate stages is not direct and obvious; if it had been, we should not have had to wait all these years for a solution of this central problem. Accordingly, if the organic connection between Irish and Arthurian legend, which has been maintained by such admirable scholars as Kittredge, Nutt, Brown, Cross, and Miss Schoepperle, exists at all, we must be prepared to find the evidence often indirect and confused. The solution proposed in this chapter, based on the theory that Cuchulinn originated as a diminutive Curoi, though superficially it may seem improbable, finds abundant confirmation under close scrutiny. 1. The postulate that Cuchulinn was a diminutive Curoi and that Curoi corresponds to Welsh Gwri alone offers an explanation for the correspondence between the birth-stories and *enfances* of Cuchulinn and Gwri. 2. It alone explains the contrasted forms in *Kilhwch and Olwen:* Gwrnach, which means big Gwr, and Gwrvan, which means little Gwr. 3. It alone explains the marked correspondence in nature and story between Curoi and Gwrnach (big Gwr). 4. It alone explains the fact, so often observed by scholars, that Gawain seems to be a representative of Cuchulinn, for Gwrvan's (Little Gwr's) epithet Gwallt Avwyn offers the only plausible source of the form Galvagin on the Modena sculpture (1099–1106), the earliest form of the name Gawain. 5. It alone explains the fact that in spite of the acknowledged influence of Irish legend on the Welsh, Cuchulinn, the supreme hero of by

---

[49] Farnell, *Greek Hero Cults*, 86. Loth (*Mab.*[2], I, 79 f) says: "The epithet is often more significant and tenacious than the name."

far the largest group of ancient Irish sagas, is named in Welsh
only in a twelfth century poem, for it would appear that those
Irish from whom the Welsh derived so much of the materials of
the Arthurian legend did not use the name Cuchulinn as commonly as Little Curoi.   6.  It alone explains why Guiglain,
whose name is so close in sound to Cuchulainn, appears in
Arthurian romance as Gawain's son, for Gawain represents both
the older and the younger Curoi.   Now when a key which at
first sight may seem rather queer and complicated actually fits
into such a complex structure of facts, and throws the bolt, then
it should not be discarded until another key, as good or better,
can be produced.

Before we pass on, let us note the significance of the fact that
the original form Curoi seems to have affected Welsh far more
than the derivative Cuchulinn, which occurs only once and then
in a late poem.[50]   Likewise the names in Arthurian romance
which we shall find based upon Curoi and his epithets are of
far more importance than the name of Gawain's son, Guiglain,[51]
which is certainly based on Cuchulainn.   What does this extraordinary reversal of the importance of these two heroes mean?
We know that Cuchulinn was the chief star of the Ulster galaxy;
whereas Curoi is represented as a king of Munster and his
traditional fortress stands today on Slieve Mish in County
Kerry.[52]   Quiggin in the *Encyclopædia Britannica* states as a
certainty that Curoi mac Daire was the central figure of a
Munster cycle of legends, now lost.[53]   He probably had in mind
the *Exploits of Curoi* mentioned in the tenth century list of the
*Book of Leinster*.[54]   Was this body of Munster myth the main
source of the Welsh Gwri legend?   Certainly it is significant
that the story of the abduction of Blathnat, which not only has
left its imprint on Welsh myth, but has also stamped itself
deeply upon Arthurian romance, shows a marked sympathy
and admiration for Curoi, the Munsterman, while Cuchulinn
and Blathnat are cheapened by contrast.[55]

The disappearance of the Munster mythological cycle may

---

[50] Skene, *Four Ancient Books*, I, 255.

[51] This in the opinion of Zimmer and Schofield is the original French
form.   *Cf. SNPL*, IV, 138;   *ZfSL*, XIII, 17.

[52] *Ulster Journ. of Arch.*, 1860, 111;   *Roy. Soc. Ant. Irel. Journ.*, XXIX, 5;
XL, 288;   XLI, 46.

[53] *Enc. Brit.*, ed. 11, V, 627.

[54] O'Curry, *MS. Materials*, 589.

[55] *Cf.* A. Nutt, *Cuchulinn, the Irish Achilles*, 24.

perhaps explain why the essential relationship between Irish and Arthurian legend has been so long concealed. If we take it that the name Cuchulinn represents a hypocoristic, etymologized development of Curoi, converted into a separate individual and popularized mainly in Ulster, we can understand why it should have made so insignificant an impression on Welsh literature and so weak an impression on Arthurian nomenclature. For it would seem that the Ulster cycle of which Cuchulinn is the hero had little effect, until late, upon Brythonic tradition. Whereas it would seem as if a Munster cycle in which the same figure played a large part mainly under the name of Curoi or Little Curoi must have been the source of the Brythonic traditions regarding Gwri and Gwrvan and ultimately of Arthurian romance. Other figures, Lug, Manannan, Bran, Mider, we shall see, must have been prominent in the Irish legends which passed into Welsh and French. But Curoi and Cuchulinn are the key figures. To understand their nature and relationship is to open suddenly the mountainsides into the glittering palaces of the *Sidhe*.

# CHAPTER VI

## YELLOW SON OF FAIR

In discussing the Beheading Game in *Bricriu's Feast*, we noted that there is another version of the same episode in this text. Here Curoi's place is taken by two enigmatic persons called Yellow Son of Fair, who is proposed as an umpire to judge between the three rivals, and Terror Son of Great Fear, who actually carries out the test. We should by examining this story and its analogues in Arthurian romance be able to determine whether the interpretation of Yellow Son of Fair and Terror Son of Great Fear as representatives of the solar and stormy aspects of the same deity is correct.

There is the usual dispute as to which of the three heroes, Loegaire, Conall, or Cuchulinn, shall have the Champion's Portion at the feast.[1] "'Hold!' quoth Sencha, 'do as I bid.' 'We will,' they said. 'Go forth to the ford of Yellow, son of Fair. He will adjudge you.' Accordingly the three heroes went to the abode of Yellow. They told their wants and the rivalries which brought them. 'Was not judgment given you in Cruachan by Ailill and Meve?' said Yellow. 'In sooth there was,' quoth Cuchulinn, 'but those fellows don't stand by it.' . . . 'It is not easy for another to adjudge you then,' quoth Yellow, 'seeing ye did not abide by Meve and Ailill's arrangement. I know,' he continued, 'one who will venture it, viz., Terror, son of Great Fear, at yonder loch. Off then in quest of him; he will adjudge you.' . . . To Terror at his loch they accordingly went. Yellow had given them a guide." Then follows the story of the Beheading Game, but both Conall and Loigaire refused even to accept the bargain; the scribe, however, adds that "other books say that they made that bargain with him, — namely, Loegaire to cut off his head the first day, — and that he (Loegaire) avoided him, and that Conall avoided him in the same way." But Cuchulinn accepted, and carried through the adventure much as in the other Irish account.

Kittredge has declared that this version "had no effect on French literature, and is of interest only for the earlier history

[1] *ITS*, II, 97–101.

of the tale." [2] He, however, did not possess the clue which we have already discovered to the meaning of this variant. With that clue we shall find that this form of the story had a profound influence on the source of *Gawain and the Green Knight*, and on other stories as well. If we are right, the story should mean: The hero first goes to Curoi in his solar aspect. He is then sent by Curoi to be tested by himself in his thunderous aspect. The hero is accompanied by a guide. Precisely these three points are incorporated in the story of *Gawain and the Green Knight*.

For the Green Knight in his capacity of host to Gawain betrays that he is the old sun god: we learn that he is "a huge warrior," "of great age," that "broad and bright was his beard and all beaver-hued," "with a face as fierce as fire." [3] This last phrase, as Tolkien and Gordon point out, is applied in the *Wars of Alexander* to the sun-god.[4] Furthermore at Gawain's request the Green Knight assigns him a servant to guide him to the Green Chapel.[5] Finally at the end of the poem the Green Knight reveals his identity with the host with face as fierce as fire.[6] Both in nature and in function, then, Sir Bercilak the host corresponds to Yellow Son of Fair.

Even more strikingly does the Yellow Son of Fair story seem to have affected the sources of the Welsh romance of the *Lady of the Fountain* or, as Brown calls it, *Owain*, an adaptation of a Breton *conte*.[7] At Arthur's court the minor hero Kynon relates the following tale: [8]

He set out to test whether he was superior to all other knights, and at night-fall came to a large and lustrous castle. On approaching he saw two youths with yellow curling hair, each with a frontlet of gold upon his head, and clad in a garment of yellow satin. Each was shooting daggers with blades of gold. Near them was a man in the prime of life, clad in a robe and a mantle of yellow satin; round the top of his mantle was a band of gold lace. On his feet were shoes of variegated leather, fastened by two bosses of gold. He took Kynon to his castle, and twenty-

---

[2] Kittredge, *Study of G. G. K.*, 74.

[3] Ll. 844–6. *Cf.* Plummer, *Vit. Sanct. Hib.*, I, cxl note.

[4] *Sir Gawain and the Green Knight* (Oxford, 1925), 96.

[5] Ll. 1077, 2074, 2089 ff.

[6] Ll. 2358 ff.

[7] The completest study of this romance and its French counterpart is R. Zenker's *Ivainstudien*, *Bhft. ZrP*, LXX.

[8] Loth, *Mab.²*, II, 5–27.

four damsels more lovely than Gwenhwyvar, when she appeared
at the offering on the feast of the Nativity or of Easter ministered
to his wants.    When dinner was half over, the host asked the
purpose of his journey, and on being told, directed him to an adventure that would test his superiority.   He is to follow a certain
path till he comes to a giant herdsman, who will in turn direct
him to the adventure of which he is in quest.   Kynon meets the
giant herdsman, (of whom we shall have more to say in chap.
XIII,) and is told to ascend a wooded steep, on the summit of
which he will find a tall tree.   He is to pour water from a fountain on a marble slab near by.   There will follow a mighty peal
of thunder, then a shower of hail, carrying away every leaf of the
tree.    After the storm a flight of birds will come, alight on the
tree, and sing most sweetly.   But he will be interrupted by a
knight on a coal-black horse, clothed in black velvet, and with a
pennon of black linen upon his lance, with whom he must encounter.   Kynon followed these instructions, and everything
happened as foretold by the giant herdsman.   Kynon, however,
was worsted in the conflict with the black knight, and returned
to Arthur's court.   Owain, on hearing the story, set out the
next day to see if he might fare better in the adventure.   "When
he approached the castle he saw the youths shooting their
daggers in the place where Kynon had seen them, and the
yellow man, to whom the castle belonged, standing hard by.
And no sooner had Owain saluted the yellow man than he was
saluted by him in return.   About the middle of the repast, the
yellow man asked Owain the object of his journey," and told
him how to reach the green tree and the fountain.   Owain met
the herdsman, and having done as Kynon did at the fountain,
was attacked by the black knight.   Owain, however, dealt him a
mortal wound, so that he fled, with Owain in pursuit, back to his
vast and resplendent castle, and there later died.   Owain
eventually married his widow.

Crestien de Troyes's *Ivain*, which is based, perhaps at several
removes, on the same Breton *conte* as *Owain*, preserves fewer
original traits than the Welsh, omitting altogether references to
the yellow garb of the host, but it retains one feature which
reveals its relationship to *Gawain and the Green Knight*.[9]   For
instead of the twenty-four damsels, there is but one lady, and
she very fair.   She is left alone with Calogrenant (who corre-

[9] *Yvain*, ed. Foerster, 1906, ll. 226–55.

sponds to Kynon), and takes him into a little pleasaunce encircled by a wall, where she entertains him so gaily that he is most annoyed when night comes and his host seeks him out for supper. But since the damsel, his host's daughter, sits opposite him he is content. One detects here in simple form the tradition of the loving hospitality which Blathnat extends to Cuchulinn, and Bercilak's wife to Gawain.

It seems impossible not to detect in the Welsh *Owain* and the French *Ivain* precisely the same fundamental myth that we have discovered in the story of Yellow Son of Fair and Terror Son of Great Fear, and in *Gawain and the Green Knight*. For it is clear that the yellow man who plays the part of host to the hero and sends him on his way is, like Yellow Son of Fair and like Sir Bercilak, the old sun god; that the adventure consists in a combat with the storm god. Only the god has the right to bring on the storm, and when the youthful god attempts to do so he must try conclusions with the old god whose right has been invaded. When he has destroyed the old god, then he must in turn act as defender of the storm-making spring.

The old tradition of the love affair between young Curoi or Cuchulinn and old Curoi's wife, which has been so distorted in *Gawain and the Green Knight* as to give us simply the temptation motif, still survives in *Owain* and *Ivain*. For not only does the young sun god, Owain or Ivain, slay the storm god and take his place, but he also marries his wife, just as Cuchulinn slew Curoi and took Blathnat.

It is perhaps worth noting that though the defender of the fountain is described as being clad all in black and riding a black steed as became a thunder god,[10] nevertheless his name is Esclados the Red, suggesting a dual nature.[11] Furthermore, though Owain as his successor in the defense of the fountain also rides in black armor, yet when he appears as his successor to the hand of his wife, he wears a coat and mantle of yellow satin with a broad band of gold lace like his host, who represents the sun.[12]

The Breton *conte*, then, from which both Crestien's *Ivain* and the Welsh *Owain* are ultimately derived, is based in the first half on the same fundamental myths as *Gawain and the Green Knight*: the struggle between the young sun-god and the old storm-god, and the young god's succession to the old god's privileges and

[10] Loth, *op. cit.*, II, 14     [11] L. 1970.     [12] Loth, *op. cit.*, II, 26.

powers. In this interpretation of *Ivain* and *Owain* I have been anticipated by Nitze,[13] who saw in Esclados a figure like the Priest of Nemi, the King of the Wood, defender of sacred waters, wedded to the goddess Diana, who becomes the consort of his slayer. Nitze, however, derived the story from a survival of the Diana cult in France, to the existence of which we have considerable testimony.[14] But the connection with the story of Yellow Son of Fair is too vital to permit of any other than Irish origin. Furthermore, the correspondence which Brown has shown between the scenarios of *Ivain* and of the Irish *Sick-bed of Cuchulinn* [15] confirms beyond a shadow of doubt the fundamental indebtedness of *Ivain* and *Owain* to the stories of Cuchulinn. But the name, Owain son of Urien, is drawn from history.

We have another survival of Yellow Son of Fair in the *Joie de la Cour* episode in Crestien's *Erec*. The hospitable host who entertains the hero before his combat with the host's nephew, and who himself acts as guide to the adventure bears the name Eurain. Philipot suggested that this name might be derived from the Welsh adjective *euryn*, meaning "golden." [16] This derivation fits in so well with the yellow or fiery coloring ascribed in *Owain* and *Gawain and the Green Knight* to the hospitable host that it may be accepted. But through some confusion Erec's adversary instead of being, according to formula, a god of storm possesses the traits which Malory in Book VII ascribes to the Red Knight of the Red Launds. For he dwells beside a sycamore tree, is summoned by a horn, is of gigantic stature, wears vermeil arms, and it can hardly be accidental that right after we are told that the hour of noon is past he becomes so exhausted that his breath fails him and he confesses himself beaten.[17] Clearly this is a vestige of the solar trait, familiar in Arthurian romance, viz. strength which gradually fails as the sun goes down. Moreover, his name, Mabonagrain, must derive in part, as Lot showed, from Welsh Mabon,[18] which in turn goes back to the Apollo Maponos of Gallic and Romano-British inscriptions.[19] Since in chapter IX we shall see

---

[13] *MP*, III, 267, VII, 145.

[14] See Zenker, *op. cit.*, 101 n. 5.

[15] *SNPL*, VIII, 34–45.

[16] *Rom.*, XXV, 258.

[17] *Erec*, ll. 5547–6007.

[18] *Rom.*, XXIV, 321 f; XXV, 284. *Cf. RC*, XXXIII, 452 ff; *SNPL*, IV, 125 f.

[19] E. W. Hübner, *Inscriptiones Britanniae Latinae*, 58, 80, 309; Rhys, *Hib. Lec.*, 27 f.

that Erec also is a sun-god, the combat, though in many ways sophisticated and confused, is essentially a myth.

There remains another version of the mythological pattern of solar host and storm giant in *Perlesvaus*, a French prose romance written between 1191 and 1212.[20] Luckily we possess the same episode in a simpler form in *Kilhwch and Olwen*.[21] A comparison of the two versions supplies a complete check on the results of the last two chapters, — a check on the derivation of Arthurian names from Welsh Gwri and Gwallt Avwyn, on the identification of Gwrnach with big Curoi, on the splitting of Curoi into solar host and storm giant. Both stories are concerned with the quest of the hero for a marvelous sword. Kilhwch may not win the hand of Olwen until he secures among other talismans the sword of Gwrnach the Giant. Likewise Gawain may not enter the Grail Castle till he conquers a sword in the possession of Gurgalain.[22] Of Gwrnach's castle we read that no guest ever returned thence alive; of Gurgalain's, that many knights have gone thither for the sword but never thence have they returned. Nevertheless, Gwrnach the Giant's head is cut off and his sword brought back to Arthur's court, and in the French romance a giant's head (not Gurgalain's) is cut off, and the sword brought back to the Grail Castle.[23] These correspondences, added to the suggestion of affinity in the names, justify the conclusion that the two tales are related.

Differences there are, to be sure, yet the most marked difference turns out on examination to be the most striking proof of kinship. In the Welsh tale the hero has to contend with but one person, a giant who resembles Curoi in the fact that his castle is visited by the hero in company with two other warriors at nightfall, that he can be slain only with his own sword, and that his head is cut off. In the French romance the hero has to do with two persons; he is entertained by a solar host who sends him off to battle against a giant with an ax. In other words, just as Curoi split into Yellow Son of Fair and Terror Son of Great Fear, Gwrnach has split into Gurgalain and the giant with an ax. Gurgalain's solar nature betrays itself in his very name, which naturally resolves itself into Gwr Gwallt Avwyn, "with Hair like Reins." Another connection with the sun is suggested by the

---

[20] *MP*, XVII, 165, 611.

[21] Loth, *op. cit.*, I, 318–20.

[22] Potvin, I, 64 f. Alternative forms Gorgalan, 73 f; Gorgaran, 74; Gurgalan, 65.　　　　　　　　　　　　　　　　　[23] *Ibid.*, 76 ff.

fact that his sword turns bloody at noon.[24]  He welcomes Gawain just as does the solar host, Sir Bercilak.  He sends the hero on to fight against a giant with an ax, just as Yellow Son of Fair and Sir Bercilak send the hero on to be tested by a giant with an ax. Gawain strikes off the head of the giant with the ax, just as Cuchulinn strikes off the head of Terror Son of Great Fear. The setting for the encounter both in *Perlesvaus* and *Gawain and the Green Knight* is desolate and mountainous.

The episode of Gurgalain in *Perlesvaus* is of the highest significance.  It is inconceivable that any Frenchman could have through sheer chance or the exercise of his imagination invented a name which so completely fits in with all we have discovered about the descent of Irish and Welsh divine names and solar epithets into Arthurian nomenclature; could have constructed a narrative which on the one hand echoes the Welsh tale of the quest for Gwrnach's sword, and on the other evinces a knowledge of the fact that Gwrnach was Curoi, and that Curoi could always be split up into a solar host and a storm giant.  Even the most skeptical must realize that only the complicated derivations and the mythological principles we have outlined in these two chapters can explain the episode of Gurgalain's sword.

Can one conceive that mere chance has led us from Gawain to Gwrvan, and from Gurgalain to Gwrnach; and that mere chance has represented in this story Gwrvan in the rôle of Cuchulinn and Gwrnach in the rôle of Curoi as Yellow Son of Fair? More clearly than ever we see that the figure of Cuchulinn, whatever be the origin of his name, was regarded by the Welsh, who received these tales straight from the Irish, as a younger Curoi.

[24] *Ibid.*, 74.

# CHAPTER VII

## MOULDS FOR MYTHS

THE cautious critic who has been willing to go with us so far as to concede that both Cuchulinn and Curoi are divine embodiments of the sun and storm, and that their struggle for the possession of Blathnat is a seasonal myth, may yet stickle at placing the same interpretation on *Gawain and the Green Knight*. What if Gawain be the younger god, what if the meeting take place near the time of the winter solstice, what if there be a year's interval? The two latter features are not present in the extant Irish versions, and the story does not relate the successive death and displacement of a series of gods. Furthermore, the plot both in the Irish and Middle English versions is simply that of a test — a test of the hero's courage and good faith. Why look for more than a plain folklore motif?

Now there are two replies. One must be reserved till Chapter IX, where we can detect mythical meanings cropping up again in connection with the Beheading Test, — mythical meanings which could not have been extracted from *Gawain and the Green Knight* or its source. The other is a demonstration that myth was habitually run into the moulds of folklore. And the fact that a given story exhibits a pattern which often has no mythical significance by no means proves that this story cannot have such a meaning.

For example, we have already seen that the story of Blathnat follows the Samson and Delilah pattern.[1] Does that prove it destitute of seasonal significance? We have seen, too, that one version of the story supplies Curoi with an external soul. Baudis, having observed this folklore motif in one ancient version and several of its modern Irish descendants, rashly concluded that Curoi was nothing more than a giant with an external soul. But we know that this folklore motif is far less essential than Curoi's solar nature. When this ancient myth reappears as the folktale of the Hung-up Naked Man it has absorbed, besides the external soul, other familiar formulae: the impossible tasks, the helpful animals, the circumstantial death. But because this

[1] *Cf.* J. G. Frazer, *Folklore in the Old Testament*, II, 480 ff.

tale can be expounded correctly as a patchwork of folklore commonplaces, we are not forced to deny that it goes back to a seasonal myth. In fact, in the Welsh tale of Blodeuwedd, her mythical nature is clearly preserved, though the death of her husband is elaborated according to folklore formula. Myth and folktale are not, therefore, mutually exclusive terms, nor should the recognition of narrative patterns originating in the human sphere blind us to the existence of cosmic meanings beneath those patterns. Too long has Arthurian romance been regarded as a vast storehouse of curiously shaped but empty boxes.

It does not therefore destroy but rather fortifies our position if we proceed to study the folklore moulds into which the conflict between big and little Curoi has at various times been cast. If, as seems certain, that conflict once meant the overthrow of the enfeebled sun-god by his more vigorous successor, we should expect to find the same meaning poured into more than one mould.

Most obvious of these narrative patterns is the game of pluck-buffet. Kittredge has dealt so fully with the motif that I need hardly say more than that the game is found as far afield as Australia and the Philippines, either as story or practise, and is common in medieval literature.[2] The conception is too simple to force us to believe in any common source in the Stone Age; and many of the forms may well have sprung up independently. It is certainly a bit of folklore which had originally no seasonal significance and required no deities for actors. But some Irishman has seen how effective the story might become if instead of two brawny bravos with their spears or clubs the two participants were the old storm god and the young sun god, with the lightning itself for an ax.

Another common pattern is the Father and Son Combat, of which *Sohrab and Rustum* is the classic example. There is no hint in the Irish versions of the Beheading Test of any paternal relation between Curoi and Cuchulinn, but Nutt, Miss Weston, and Henderson seem to have had an intuitive feeling that the situation called for such a motif to give it poignancy.[3] And it is easy to see that if Cuchulinn had his origin in a diminutive Curoi, it would be natural to make him Curoi's son. Now Celtic legend was familiar with the theme of a combat between father and son, who do not recognize each other at first. Cuchulinn

<hr />

[2] *Study of G. G. K.*, 21 f, 218 ff.
[3] *ITS*, II, xlv: Weston, *Leg. of Gawain*, 95–8.

thus kills his son Conlaoch: in the Irish story of Elotha and Bres, and in the Breton lais of *Doon* and *Milun* the combat ends in mutual recognition.[4] This very formula of a combat ending happily in recognition appears in Arthurian romance, which relates an encounter between Guiglain and his father Gawain,[5] between Galaad and his father (Lancelot)[6] whose baptismal name was Galahot,[7] and between Degare or Degore and his father.[8] The names here are significant, for Guiglain = Cuchulinn, Gawain = Curoi, Galaad and Galahot are probably, as I shall show in Chapter XVI, developments like Gawain from a solar epithet beginning with Gwallt, and Degore, in spite of its implied derivation from French *esgaré*, quite likely is a corruption of Gwri. There can be little doubt that in the Welsh stage at any rate, traditions of a combat between a father and son, identical in origin with big and little Curoi, had developed. Whether we can go so far as to say that the testing of little Curoi by big Curoi in *Bricriu's Feast* was, as Nutt, Henderson, and Miss Weston surmised, a disguised form of this ancient motif is doubtful. But it is certain that not only have modern scholars but also one ancient romancer has felt the closeness of the situation in the Champion's Bargain to the familiar theme of the filial encounter, and has made the testing enchanter the father of the hero. This is the version of the Beheading Game related in the *Livre de Caradoc*, an insertion in the first continuation of the *Conte del Graal*.[9] The Father and Son Combat is a narrative pattern which if not actually present in *Bricriu's Feast* and *Gawain and the Green Knight* is not far removed. It was only a question of time before the myth of Curoi's testing of Cuchulinn would be run into that mould.

The Father and Son Combat is itself a theme that suggests comparison with, and assimilation to other themes. Speaking of the fight between Cuchulinn and his son Conlaoch, Miss Weston, with one of her characteristic flashes of insight, remarks:[10] "As I interpret it, the father and son combat in heroic

---

[4] M. A. Potter, *Sohrab and Rustum*, 22, 46 f, 101. Lugaid mac-na-tri-Con, who killed Cuchulinn, was said to be his son as well as Curoi's.

[5] Potvin, l. 20671.

[6] Sommer, *Vulgate Version*, VI, 40.

[7] *Ibid.*, III 3.

[8] Ed. Laing. *Cf.* L. Hibbard, *Mediaeval Romance in England*, 301–5.

[9] Potvin, III, 125–33.

[10] *Leg. of Lancelot*, 109.

tradition really represents the 'slayer who shall himself be slain,'
the prehistoric combat of the Golden Bough, . . . influenced
by the doctrine of rebirth, as set forth by Mr. Nutt in vol. II
of the *Voyage of Bran;* i.e. it is a conflict of the god with his reborn and rejuvenated self, and as such has a very real place in
Celtic tradition." Her reference, of course, is to Frazer's
famous study of the King of the Wood, the Priest of Nemi, who
has already been put forward by Cook as a prototype of the
Green Knight.[11]   Let me quote part of Frazer's memorable
chapter.[12]

"In the sacred grove [beside the volcanic lake of Nemi] there
grew a certain tree round which at any time of day, and probably
far into the night a grim figure might be seen to prowl.   In his
hand he carried a drawn sword, and he kept peering warily
about him as if at every instant he expected to be set upon by an
enemy.   He was a priest and a murderer; the man for whom he
looked was sooner or later to murder him and hold the priesthood
in his stead.   Such was the rule of the sanctuary. . . .   To
gentle pilgrims at the shrine the sight of him might well seem to
darken the fair landscape, as when a cloud suddenly blots the
sun on a bright day.   The dreamy blue of Italian skies, the dap-
pled shade of summer woods, and the sparkle of waves in the
sun, can have accorded but ill with that stern and sinister figure.
Rather we picture to ourselves the scene as it may have been
witnessed by a belated wayfarer on one of those wild autumn
nights when the dead leaves are falling thick and the winds seem
to sing the dirge of the dying year.   It is a sombre picture set to
melancholy music — the background of forest showing black and
jagged against a lowering and stormy sky, the sighing of the
wind in the branches, the rustle of the withered leaves under foot,
the lapping of the cold water on the shore, and in the foreground,
pacing to and fro, now in twilight, now in gloom, a dark figure
with a glitter of steel at the shoulder whenever the pale moon,
riding clear of the cloud-rack, peers down at him through the
matted boughs. . . .

"In his character of the founder of the sacred grove and first
king of Nemi, Virbius [a god of vegetation] is clearly the mythical predecessor and archetype of the line of priests who served

---

[11] *Folklore,* XVII, 333–41. I do not accept Cook's connection of **Daire**
with the oak, or of the Green Knight with Virbius.
[12] *Golden Bough,* ch. I.

Diana under the title of Kings of the Wood, and who came like him, one after another, to a violent end. It is natural therefore to conjecture that they stood to the goddess of the grove in the same relation in which Virbius stood to her; in short that the mortal King of the Wood had for his queen the woodland Diana herself."

As is well-known, Frazer interpreted this savage custom as a survival of a belief in the annual sacrifice of kings who represented the god of vegetation; and probably Virbius was such a god. Macalister has shown that there are traces of a similar practise among the early Irish.[13] "Omitting the kings of the Fir Bolg and of the Tuatha De Danann, I find 110 kings enumerated in *Flaithiusa hErenn* as having reigned from Eremon down to Conn Cet-chathach, the grandfather of Cormac mac Airt. Of these 80 are said to have been killed by their successors. As we have already seen, the 'official historians' explained this as a blood-feud, going back to the time when Eremon, the first king, killed his brother Eber at the battle of Geashill. . . . But in the light of the wealth of illustrative examples which Sir James Frazer has collected from all over the world, we must see in this organized slaying of the king by his successor something other than a blood-feud extending through a large number of generations, and involving relationships spread over impossible lapses of time. Doubtless the 'official historians' were puzzled by the regularity with which each king met his death at the hands of his successor, and felt obliged to explain it. Not knowing the system of the Arician priesthood, they had to cast about elsewhere; and they found a blood-feud as the easiest way of accounting for the perplexing fact. The genealogies were manipulated accordingly, the slayer of a slayer being assumed to be a relative of the first victim; but the result only makes obvious the impossibilities of the 'blood-feud' theory." Thus we have evidence that in Ireland the royal representative of the god was a "slayer who shall himself be slain." When we remember that Baudis has indicated that these royal representatives shared in the solar nature of divinity,[14] we have a situation very close in its significance to that in *Gawain and the Green Knight* as we have interpreted it. The kings of Ireland were, like Cuchulinn, solar beings who slew and then after a period were themselves slain.

---

[13] *PRIA*, XXXIV, C, 326 f.     [14] *Eriu*, VIII, 105.

The struggles and deaths of sun-gods naturally came to be associated with the periodic changes of the solar year. Grimm and Frazer have shown how under the form of a ritual combat, annually recurring, our forefathers were wont to celebrate the passing of the old year and the triumph of the new.[15] In Uker-mark on Christmas day a fight took place between persons representing Summer and Winter.[16] A similar ritual was held on Mayday on the Isle of Man and in South Wales.[17] An aged Welshman thus described the battle: "When I was a boy, two companies of men and youths were formed. One had for its captain a man dressed in a long coat much trimmed with fur, and on his head a rough fur cap. He carried a stout stick of blackthorn and a kind of shield, on which were studded tufts of wool to represent snow. His companions wore caps and waist-coats of fur decorated with balls of white wool. These men were very bold, and in songs and verse proclaimed the virtues of Winter, who was their captain. The other company had for its leader a captain representing Summer. This man was dressed in a kind of white smock decorated with garlands of flowers and gay ribbons. On his head he wore a broad-brimmed hat trimmed with flowers and ribbons. In his hand he carried a willow-wand wreathed with spring flowers and tied with ribbons. All these men marched in procession, with their captain on horse-back heading them, to an appropriate place. This would be some stretch of common or waste land. There a mock encounter took place, the Winter company flinging straw and dry under-wood at their opponents, who used as their weapons birch branches, willow-wands, and young ferns. A good deal of horse-play went on, but finally Summer gained the mastery over Winter. Then the victorious captain representing Summer selected a May King and the people nominated a May Queen, who were crowned and conducted into the village." This ritual combat had its mythical counterpart. The god Gwynn and Gwythyr fight for the maiden Kreiddylat and will fight for her every first of May till the Judgment Day.[18] Geoffrey of Mon-mouth makes Kreiddylat or Cordeilla daughter of Leir, the

[15] J. G. Frazer, *Golden Bough*,[3] IV, 254 ff; Grimm, *Teut. Myth.*, tr. Stallybrass, II, 764 ff.

[16] Thorpe, *Northern Mythology*, III, 147.

[17] A. W. Moore, *Folklore of the Isle of Man*, 112 f; M. Trevelyan, *Folklore and Folkstories of Wales*, 25.

[18] Loth, *Mab.*[2], I, 284 f.

Welsh god Llyr. May 1 was a great seasonal festival of the
Celts. The implications of such a combat clearly correspond to
those of the struggle between Curoi and Cuchulinn for Blathnat.
In Welsh folk ritual and myth, therefore, we discover the seasonal
combat, and in Irish pseudo-history traces of a belief that the
divine king gave way to his slayer. We have but to combine
these two elements, and we have the annually recurring encounter between the old god and the young, in which the latter
triumphs, only to succumb a year later himself. The placing of
the event on January 1, as in *Gawain and the Green Knight*, is
probably due to the attraction of the Christian festival. Chambers has shown that similarly the St. George plays, containing
the old ritual elements of combat, death, and resurrection of the
god, have been transferred to Christmas from Mayday and
Easter.[19] And that the original tradition concerning the Beheading Game placed it, along with the Welsh seasonal combats,
in the month of May, seems strongly suggested by the Caradoc
version, for here the challenging magician appears at Arthur's
court at the Feast of Pentecost.

Further evidence that the Priest of Nemi concept was in the
air, so to speak, and was utilized by Celtic story-tellers in
the patterning of their myths is abundant. Nitze, as we saw in
the last chapter, detected in it *Ivain* and *Owain*. Lot recognized
it in the Tertre Devée episode in the *Vulgate Lancelot*,[20] and it is
found in *Meraugis de Portlesguez* [21] and the Balaain story.[22] In
these last three versions, where Boors, Gawain, and Balaan are
the incumbents of the office after slaying their predecessors, the
names take us back, as later chapters will show, to Curoi. It
seems plain that at an early stage in the development of the
legends of Curoi's combats with his younger self, some were
cast in the mould of that primitive system best illustrated by·
the Priesthood of Nemi.

The narrative pattern which has most deeply affected the
story of *Gawain and the Green Knight* is the test pattern. In its
first form, we may believe, the encounter between Cuchulinn
and Curoi was represented as a true quarrel, a genuine life-and-
death struggle; and the loving passages between Cuchulinn and
Blathnat in the ultimate source of *Gawain and the Green Knight*

[19] E. K. Chambers, *Med. Stage*, I, 226.
[20] F. Lot, *Étude sur le Lancelot*, 447.
[21] Ed. Friedwagner, ll. 3132 ff. *Cf.* L. A. Paton, *Fairy Mythology*, 275.
[22] *Huth Merlin*, ed. G. Paris, Ulrich, II, 54 f.

by no means consisted of a calculated temptation on her side and a virtuous rebuff on his, but were lusty and passionate enough. Thus they are represented in the abduction and rescue story we have studied. The complete overturning of these established relationships is due to the thorough-going application of the concept of the old god as a tester of the younger.

This concept is perhaps implicit in the custom of the Priest of Nemi; it is clearly dominant in the story of Jason's struggles to win Medea, the grand-daughter of the Sun, from her father. And I believe that the root idea in *Bricriu's Feast* is the testing of three competitors for supremacy among the gods by several of the old gods. What had originally been isolated tales of combat were now recast in order to fit into this new narrative machinery. Perhaps the conception of Curoi as Cuchulinn's father, which appears to have been prevalent at one time, prompted a softening of their traditional antagonism. At all events, there arose the radically new conception of Curoi as a benevolent tester of Cuchulinn. The next step was naturally to fit Blathnat into the same scheme. The result is apparent in *Gawain and the Green Knight*, where the lady's function is to test the hero's loyalty, as it is her husband's to test his courage. Never would one suspect from this poem or *Bricriu's Feast* that Cuchulinn and Blathnat were celebrated lovers, and Curoi and Cuchulinn notorious enemies.

Since we shall hereafter concentrate our attention on the mythical significance of Arthurian romance rather than on the narrative formulae derived from folklore and folk-custom, let me emphasize the fundamental importance of the test pattern for this whole mass of Celtic legend. It was doubtless a series of tests which Eamonn had to carry out to win the king's daughter when he was set to cleaning the cow-house, collecting the ravens, and emptying the lake with a spoon.[23] Old Irish literature contains stories of strange perils and difficult tasks which the heroes had to adventure in order to win the "sovereignty," a euhemerist substitution for the godhead. The same theme recurs countless times in Arthurian romance. Every young knight when he appears on the scene must demonstrate his supremacy as a drawer of swords, an embracer of hideous hags, a crosser of perilous bridges, a sleeper in haunted cemeteries. The Grail legend itself is, to all intents and purposes, the

[23] Confirmed *RR*, X, 86.

account of the success or failure of various knights in meeting a series of tests. The supreme test is the one which curiously enough seems easiest — the mere requirement that the hero ask the purpose of the mysterious lance and vessel.

The fact that tests of one kind or another are of frequent occurrence both in human life and in the tales of the folk does not compel us to believe that the ordeals and perils of Arthurian romance possess no meaning save such human meaning as appears on the surface. If we can identify the actors with gods, if we can discover that their acts have results that resemble the operations of Nature, then we can be sure that, no matter how clear the folklore patterns, they are but the moulds for myths.

# CHAPTER VIII

## GARETH AND LYNETE

THE tale of Gareth and Lynete, made famous by Tennyson, not only is one of the best stories in Malory's *Morte d'Arthur*, but also affords a clearly recognizable re-combination of many of the motifs found in *Gawain and the Green Knight* and other stories we have examined. Since the romance is well known, it seems unnecessary to retell it.

Now who was Gareth? He was the younger brother of Gawain, and his name has been long recognized by scholars as a variant of Gaeres, Gaheries, Guahries or Gwarehes.[1] In Malory's story we find beside Gareth his brother Gaheryes, and it is surely no accident that the two brothers should marry sisters of such similar names as Lynet and Lyones.[2] It is furthermore significant that in Crestien's *Ivain* there is forced upon our notice a traditional love affair between Gawain and Lunete.[3] A little research will show that *Kilhwch and Olwen* supplies a variant form of Gwri Gwallt Euryn, namely Gware Gwallt Euryn. Gware with the addition of the French nominative *s* would naturally appear as Guares or Gares, and from this might easily be formed by mistake an oblique case Garet, just as Bohort is an oblique case wrongly constructed from Bohors. And Garet, of course, is Gareth. Since Gareth and Gawain are both derived from a hypothetical Gware Gwallt Avwyn, and both are represented as lovers of Lunete, there must have been a strong Breton tradition concerning the loves of Gaere Galvain and this damsel, which accounts for Crestien's strangely parenthetical treatment of the affair, as if he realized it did not belong in his story, but knew that his audience would be surprised if the two lovers were brought together without a hint of their relationship.

Like Eamonn in the folk-tale of the Hung-up Naked Man and many other Irish heroes including Finn, and like the Arthurian Perceval, Lancelot, and Carduino, Gareth is the son of

---

[1] These forms are found in W. Foerster, *Wörterbuch*, 11; J. L. Weston, *Leg. of Perceval*, I, 248 n; *Joseph of Arimathie*, ed. Skeat, 71.

[2] Book VII, ch. 35.

[3] L. 2398.

a widow.[4] Like Finn and Guiglain, Gareth is not known when he appears at court under the name given him at birth. Finn's original name was Demne or Glaisdic, but he was called Finn, "the Fair" on account of his shapeliness. Guiglain on arriving at Arthur's court cannot tell his real name, but says that his mother calls him Beaufis, "Fair Son," and Arthur thereupon declares that he shall be called Libeaus Desconus, "the Fair Unknown." Similarly, Gareth cannot tell Arthur his name, and Kay dubs him Beaumains, "Fair Hands." Gareth, then, as widow's son and as the bearer of a nickname containing the element "Fair," seems to be directly in the line of Celtic heroes.

The opening adventure in Gareth's story parallels closely that of Guiglain.[5] We have seen how both heroes are welcomed at Arthur's court, and given new names. The first adventure takes place when a damsel rides up asking succor for her mistress, and Arthur, bound by his promise to the hero, assigns him to the task. The damsel is indignant at Arthur's treatment of her request and pours scorn on the youth. He, however, accompanies her in her own despite, and eventually wins her reluctant admiration by his prowess. The parallel between Gareth, Guiglain, and Gawain is accentuated by the fact that in Crestien's *Conte del Graal* a proud damsel, l'Orgueilleuse de Logres, mocks at Gawain, though apparently she needs him as her champion, and he follows her in spite of her scorn.[6] The episode, however, is far more confused than in the Gareth and Guiglain stories.

Gareth's exploits consist of successive combats with four brothers, clad respectively in black, green, red, and dark blue (Inde) arms.[7] The reasons for these colors we have already learned. Red, like yellow, is the color of the sun. Black and dark blue suggest the thunder cloud, and green also, being a mistranslation of the Irish word which means also gray, has the same origin. It should not escape us that the Green Knight's name, Partolype or Pertylope,[8] is more than faintly reminiscent of Bercilak, Bertolais, and other corruptions of the Irish *bachlach*, Curoi disguised as the churl in the dark dun mantle. The names

[4] References for this paragraph may be found in *MP*, XVIII, 213 f; *SNPL*, IV, 4–6; L. A. Paton, *Fairy Mythology*, 176–85.

[5] *SNPL*, IV, 7–14.

[6] *Contes del Graal*, ed. Baist, ll. 6441–6865.   *Cf.* Chap. XXVII.

[7] Ch. 7, 8, 10, 11.

[8] Malory, ed. Sommer, I, 250, 259.

of his brothers, Percard, Persant, and Perrymones, are possibly intentional variants of his own name. And just as Sir Bercilak entertains Gawain at his castle and sends a servant as guide, so Sir Pertylope, the Green Knight, entertains Gareth at his castle and conveys him on his way.[9] Besides the Red Knight, Sir Perrymones, Gareth overcomes the Red Knight of the Red Launds, Sir Ironside.[10] The latter possesses traits proving that his color is not the only indication of his kinship with the sun. His strength like that of Gawain himself increases till noon. A hint of the tradition that he could be slain only by his own sword survives in the account of his fight with Gareth. "At sometime they were so amazed that either took other's sword instead of his own." Now in all these three respects the Red Knight of the Red Launds corresponds to Escanor.[11] For Escanor's shield shone red in the sunlight; his strength increased till noon, equaling that of three men; and in the confusion of the combat Gawain takes Escanor's spear and with it brings down his horse. Even more complete perhaps is the parallel which the Red Knight of the Red Launds, Sir Ironside, presents to a character in the Middle English romance of *Eger, ˙Grime, and Graysteel*. For there seems to be a connection between the names Ironside and Graysteel. Both, moreover, were clad in red arms,[12] both grew stronger with the rising of the sun in the heavens,[13] both besieged a lady and had slain many of her presumptive rescuers until the hero overcame him. A peculiar sign of the Celtic origin of the Middle English romance has been pointed out by Miss Hibbard, who noted that the Lady Loospaine, whom Graysteel besieges, had between her eyes a spot which made Grime forget all else, like the love spot which made the Irish hero Diarmaid irresistible to women.[14] Celtic mythology is certainly the common birthplace of Sir Graysteel and Sir Ironside.

In connection with the colors of the various opponents of Gareth it is noteworthy that Gareth himself, by the aid of a magic ring, shifts the colors of his panoply in the midst of a tournament, but the color which he retains longest and which the author most dwells on is yellow. The herald cries: "This is

[9] Ch. 8, 9.
[10] Ch. 15–17.
[11] See ch. II.
[12] Ed. D. Laing, ll. 137, 1499.
[13] *Percy Folio MS.*, ed. Furnivall, Hales, I, ll. 891–4.
[14] L. Hibbard, *Mediaeval Romance in England*, 316.

Sir Gareth of Orkney in the yellow arms!" [15] The color we may assume has the same solar connotation which we have found elsewhere. And when it is said that Arthur was able to detect Gareth's identity throughout his various chameleon-like metamorphoses by his hair,[16] we hardly need to be reminded that Gware's epithet was Gwallt Euryn, "Golden Hair," another solar feature.

A significant point, — though its full significance will not become apparent till we attack the problem of the Grail, — is the healing power attributed to Lynete and her double Lyones. Just before his conflict with Sir Ironside, Gareth receives from Lyones through her dwarf food and wine to make him strong, and a cup of gold " that is rich and precious." [17] Evidently the precious cup played a part in strengthening the hero. After the desperate combat between Gareth and Gawain, Lynete not only stops the combat but also staunches their wounds on the spot and later heals them.[18] Even more uncanny is the way in which Lynete picks up the head of the knight with the ax who by her means has attacked Gareth during his rendezvous with her sister.[19] She "took up the head in the sight of them all, and anointed it with an ointment thereas it was smitten off; and in the same wise she did to the other part thereas the head stuck, and then she set it together and it stuck as fast as ever it did." A second time, when Gareth had cut the head into a hundred pieces and thrown them out of a window, Lynete brings them together again, anoints them, and puts the head back. It was doubtless the same powerful salve which she applied to Gareth himself, which within fifteen days made him "never so fresh nor so lusty." [20] Quite certainly Lynete-Lyones was the possessor of a precious cup and a marvelous healing power.

The adventure of the knight with the ax to which I have just alluded has already been cited in connection with the Beheading Game by Kittredge.[21] Perhaps a brief outline may be useful.[22]

Gareth, having vanquished all the enemies of the Lady Lyones, is accepted finally as her betrothed. Before their marriage they arrange an assignation in the hall where Gareth has his couch. Lynete decides to prevent its consummation, and by her subtle crafts a knight with many lights about him comes upon the

---

[15] Ch. 30.

[16] Ch. 29.

[17] Ch. 14.

[18] Ch. 33.

[19] Ch. 22, 23.

[20] Ch. 26.

[21] *Study of G. G. K.*, 265.

[22] Ch. 22, 23.

lovers with a long gisarm in his hand. As we have seen, Gareth cuts off his head and Lynete replaces it. Ten nights later much the same happens. We are told mysteriously that during this second combat between Gareth and the knight with the ax there was great light, as it had been the number of twenty torches, both before and behind. Again the stranger loses his head and Lynete replaces it.

Though we do not have here the Beheading Game or bargain as it is found in *Bricriu's Feast* and in *Gawain and the Green Knight*, yet surely certain traditional features of both these stories are present in the scenes from Gareth and Lynete. Is the strange light that accompanies the knight with the ax unrelated to the taunt hurled at Curoi with his ax that he seems to claim the position of light-bearer for the house, and to Berci-lak's face that was as fierce as fire? Are not both Gareth and Gawain involved in a situation which combines both the tempta-tion motif and the beheading test motif? And since Lyones, the temptress, and Lynete, the accomplice in the beheading test, are identical, do we not here have essentially the same general situ-ation that we have in *Gawain and the Green Knight* — a woman and an enchanter with an ax conniving together to test the hero? That it is really the same woman who tempts the hero and tests his courage is confirmed by the curious adventure of Lancelot in Crestien's *Charette*,[23] also adduced by Kittredge,[24] in which a damsel harbors Lancelot on condition that he lie with her. As he enters her chamber to keep his promise, he finds her at-tacked by a knight, and the door guarded by two knights and four men with axes. Lancelot lays about him so vigorously that the damsel is soon out of danger, but then she dismisses "the men of her household," and they depart obediently. Lancelot then lies beside the damsel, but his love for Queen Guinevere enables him to withstand this test of his chastity. That the damsel's rôle is that of somewhat dispassionate instrument is revealed by the coolness with which she takes his neglect. In short, in the *Charette* as in Gareth and Lynete, and *Gawain and the Green Knight*, we have three variations on the same basic theme: the testing of the hero by an enchantress and by one or more ax-bearing men who act in collusion with her.

The romance of Gareth and Lynete, then, though it appears only in that compilation from French sources which was finished

[23] Ll. 941 ff.                    [24] *Op. cit.*, 263.

by Malory in 1469, yet bears abundant marks of its authenticity as a true scion of the Celtic stem. Probably its immediate source, as Miss Scudder has suggested,[25] was a twelfth century French romance, — doubtless, like Gareth himself, one of the freshest and lustiest of the products of that spring-time of Arthurian romance.

[25] V. Scudder, *Morte d'Arthur*, 222.

# CHAPTER IX

## LUG, LANCELOT, AND LOT

LET us return to the subject of the Beheading Game. One of the seven Arthurian versions occurs in *Perlesvaus*, which we have already had occasion to note contains authentic Celtic mythology. The hero of the episode is Lancelot, and the story may be summarized as follows:[1]

Lancelot comes to a Waste Land, "wherein wonned neither beast nor bird, for the land was so poor and parched that no victual was to be found therein." He enters a city of which the walls and churches were ruinous. There is no sign of any inhabitants, until before a great palace he hears lamentation for a young knight who is about to go to his death. Presently the fated knight comes forth in a red jerkin, with a girdle and chaplet of gold. He charges Lancelot on pain of death to cut off his head with the ax he is carrying. But Lancelot must promise first to return a year hence at noon and submit his own head to the ax. Reluctantly Lancelot agrees, cuts off the young knight's head, and departs. As he looks back, he sees no trace of body or head, but hears far off mourning and cries for vengeance. A year later,[2] true to his promise, Lancelot returns at the hour of noon to the Waste City and finds it empty as before. The brother of the slain knight meets him, whetting the ax, and fiercely announces that his time has come. Lancelot cries out on Guinevere, takes three blades of grass, and stretches his neck on the block. The knight strikes a blow with the ax but misses. Happily at this instant two fair damsels appear, and one, who is the lover of the knight with the ax, cries to him to spare Lancelot. Then the hero learns that though a score of knights have visited the Waste City and beheaded one of the kinsmen, none before Lancelot has returned to keep his covenant. But Lancelot by his loyalty has preserved the land in the possession of the damsels. There is now great rejoicing, the city is again peopled with the fairest folk in the world, and the streets are thronged.

[1] Potvin, I, 102–4; S. Evans, *High History*, Everyman ed., 104–6.
[2] Potvin, 231–4; *High History*, 245–8.

The implication is, though there is no direct statement, that neither the city nor the land are longer waste, but are again re-edified and fertile. Lancelot is greatly honored.

We can readily perceive that this version of the Beheading Game preserves the mythological meaning more clearly than *Gawain and the Green Knight* in two respects. First, the fertility of the land and the prosperity of the people are restored by the successful termination of the adventure. Secondly, the pluck-buffet pattern is so far discarded as to supply instead of one victim who loses his head, a succession of kinsmen with golden chaplets who are beheaded in turn, probably at yearly intervals at the hour of noon. In these features we may properly detect traces of a myth in which year after year a golden chapleted god is slain, and thereby his successor renews the fertility of the land and the welfare of the folk.

Since this story seems to preserve such archaic features, let us see whether Lancelot may not be as ancient a figure as Cuchulinn. Of the former name M. Lot has said: [3] "This name is not certainly Celtic. It recalls Lancelin, a Germanic diminutive or hypocoristic form of Lantbert, Lantfrid, etc. There is no doubt that Lancelin has influenced and deformed a Celtic name which no one has succeeded so far in reconstituting." He has recently proposed [4] that the Celtic original of Lancelot was a certain Llenlleawc the Irishman, who in *Kilhwch and Olwen* [5] performs an exploit similar to Cuchulinn's expedition to the Other World to carry off the three cows, the caldron, and the maiden Blathnat. Arthur went in his ship Prydwen to Ireland with his men to secure a caldron from Diwrnach. After being entertained, Arthur demanded the caldron and was refused. Bedwyr then seized it and gave it to a servant. "And Llenlleawc the Irishman seized Caledvwlch [Excalibur] and brandished it, and slew Diwrnach the Irishman and his company." Then Arthur's men returned with the caldron, full of money, to Wales.

Another expedition of Arthur and his men in the ship Prydwen is related in the very archaic Welsh poem called the *Harryings of Annwn*. The following translation is based on those of Rhys, Stephens, and Squire.[6]

[3] *Rom*, XXV, 12.
[4] *Rom*, LI, 423. On this whole group of names consult Chart B.
[5] Loth, *Mab.*², I, 334.
[6] Malory, Everyman ed., I, xxiii; C. Squire, *Mythology of the British Islands*, 319; Stephens, *Literature of the Kymry*, I, 184.

The Head of Annwn's caldron — what is it like?
A rim of pearls, it has around its edge;
It boils not the food of a coward or perjurer(?).
The bright sword of Llwch was lifted to it,
And in the hand of Lleminawc it was left.
And before the door of Hell's gate lamps were burning,
And when we accompanied Arthur, a brilliant effort,
Seven alone did we return from the fortress of the Perfect
    Ones.

It is surely not rash to recognize here a variant of the other expedition of Arthur's men, in which the mythological element has been more clearly preserved. We may then equate the sword-brandisher Llenlleawc with Lleminawc. Since the *Harryings of Annwn* seems to give a more primitive account, we may tentatively assume that the form Lleminawc is closer to the original than Llenlleawc. It is doubtful whether the two names mentioned in two succeeding lines, Llwch and Lleminawc, refer to the same person. But since we find several times in old Welsh literature a figure called Llwch Llawwynawc,[7] one of Arthur's knights, we may regard Llwch Lleminawc and Llwch Llawwynawc as variants of the same name. The question remains which is the original form.

Loth has construed Llawwynnyawc to mean "of the white hand." It is possible, however, that Llawwynnyawc was an attempt at etymologizing some unfamiliar word. We have already seen that Llenlleawc was an Irishman, and it seems reasonable to look in that quarter for a possible prototype. And indeed we discover no other than Lug himself, Lugh Loinnbheimionach, "Lug of the mighty blows," god, as we have seen, of the sun and lightning, who is at once the father of Cuchulinn and identical with him.[8] Lugh Loinnbheimionach, then, is at the head of the line, and very naturally is followed in Welsh by Llwch Lleminawc and its variants. It was probably the Bretons who, knowing that Llwch in Welsh place-names means "lake" came to the conclusion that Llwch Lleminawc or Llawwynawc must mean Llawwynawc of the Lake. This name in turn felt the attraction of the French name Lancelin, which occurs early in Brittany,[9] and became Lanceloc of the

---

[7] Malory, *op. cit.*, xix; Skene, *Four Ancient Books*, I, 262; Loth, *op. cit.*, I, 264, 276; *RC*, XVI, 84.

[8] E. Hull, *Cuchulinn Saga*, lvi f. *Cf.* Lonn-bem-nech, *RC*, XII, 127.

[9] *ZfSL*, XIII¹, 47 f; XIV¹, 180.

Lake. When written down in manuscript, the final c was read as t, and so at last appeared Lancelot du Lac. It was probably this development of his name which suggested the story that the Lady of the Lake was his foster-mother, though Lug's palace was placed under Lloch Corrib.[10]

The probability that Lancelot is no other than Lug of the mighty blows, the great sun and storm god of the Gauls and Irish, makes it quite natural that he like his *alter ego*, Cuchulinn-Gawain, should be the hero of the Beheading Test. The version in the *Perlesvaus* may not go back to an Irish myth about Lug, but certainly its source was a tale in which the mythical nature of the adventure and of the hero was well understood, although the exigencies of the plot had already confused them. Perhaps in its primitive form the story ran thus: Lug comes into a Waste Land, barren and desolate, where no birds sing. He enters a ruinous and deserted city. A young chief with a golden coronal meets him and offers him the kingship on condition that he exchange blows with the ax. The chief is one of a long series of brothers who have thus yearly been slain. Lug smites off the chief's head, whereat the land becomes fertile and the city is filled with folk, who hail Lug as king. But at the year's end the woods and fields once more wither and decay, and the brother of Lug's predecessor appears and claims the fulfillment of the bargain. Lug loyally submits his head to the ax. Whereupon the brother proclaims that by his courage and good faith Lug has won the perpetual sovereignty of the land, which henceforth shall enjoy an eternal spring.

This derivation of Lancelot from Lug is corroborated in many ways. It explains the fact that Gawain and Lancelot play such similar rôles, for of course Cuchulinn was Lug's *alter ego*. It explains the fact that in *Diu Krone* Lancelot possesses a solar attribute in the distorted form of strength which increases from noon till night.[11] It is supported in the most remarkable way by the fact that Lug's name with his other epithet Lamfada, "of the long arm" has come down as Laquins de Lampadaiz or Lampades or Lambeguez.[12] Laquins seems to be the French word Lac, translated from Welsh Llwch, plus the diminutive *in*. Such diminutive forms are not unusual in Arthurian

[10] J. MacNeill, *Celtic Ireland*, 51. *Cf.* also Paton, *Fairy Mythology*, 175 n.
[11] Ed. Scholl, ll. 2089–92.
[12] Raoul de Houdenc, *Meraugis*, ed. Friedwagner, ll. 4578, 2080, 2014.

romance; for example, Banin from Ban, Galehodin from Gale-hot. And we shall see that besides the notion of a big and little Curoi, the notion of a young god corresponding to an old one of the same name runs through the whole of Arthurian romance. It is interesting also to note that just as Galvain split off from Gorvain, Lancelot from Lac, so here we have the familiar corruption Lambegues, usually encountered alone, still attached to Laquin: a conclusive proof that the process we have discovered in the case of Lancelot and Gawain was not unique.

We possess further corroboration of the fact that Lac as a part of a name in the French romances is a translation of the Welsh Llwch, which in turn is derived from the Irish Lug. For we know that Lug is not only the *alter ego* of little Curoi, he is also the father. In Crestien's *Erec* Lac is the father of one whose name has developed through natural processes from that of Curoi. For Curoi as we have seen became Gwri, and Loth has pointed out that the original form of the name of Lac's son was Guerec.[13]  Guerec was a historic figure famous in Brittany, and the eternal urge to lend familiarity to the strange Welsh names which we have discerned in the case of Winlogee, Mardoc and Lancelot very naturally led the Bretons to substitute the familiar name Guerec for the unfamiliar Gwri. Guerec in French degenerated into Erec, the name under which Crestien introduces us to Lac's son. Guerec also found its way back to Welsh ears, and not being recognized as a corruption of Gwri, suggested in turn the name of a Welsh hero, Geraint, familiar as the son of Erbin. Thus Geraint the son of Erbin and Erec the son of Lac are both derived from Gwri the son of Llwch.

But the objection may properly be raised: Gwri is not represented in the *Mabinogion* as the son of Llwch, but as the son of Pwyll. Very true. But Welsh scholars have already suggested that other traditions probably made Gwri the actual son of Manawyddan or Teyrnon, his step-father and foster-father.[14] And in consideration of the fact that the paternal relationships of Celtic heroes and heroines are often very muddled — Blathnat, for example, has five fathers, Perceval six [15] — it is far from im-

---

[13] *Rom.*, XXV, 588.  It is interesting to see how the divine Gwri and Guerec, Count of Nantes, have both contributed to the narrative of Erec's coronation. To the former are due the dazzling crowns and the robe displaying the sea, earth, heavens, stars, moon, and sun; to the latter the localization at Nantes.

[14] *Folklore*, XXVII, 50; *RC*, XXXIII, 455.

[15] *RR*, XV, 277; *MP*, XVI, 342 n.

probable that Gwri was according to one tradition the son of Llwch.

This supposition is supported not only by the strong Irish tradition which makes Cuchulinn (little Curoi) the son of Lug, and by the Breton tradition which makes a presumptive Guerec son of Lac, but also by another tradition which makes Guerhes, Gaeres and Gauvain all sons of Loth. The names of the sons must be derived from Gwri, Gware and Gwallt Avwyn and the father's name has been shown by Loth to be derived from Llwch or Lloch.[16] Thus we are forced to believe that there was traditional justification for assuming that Gwri, Gware, or Gwrvan was the son of Llwch; especially when we note that the name of Loth's fourth son, Agravain, is easily formed from Gware-van, Little Gware, the intermediate form Garravain being found in Crestien's *Erec*, though merely as a name.[17] *Kilhwch and Olwen*, which supplies the forms Gwrvan Gwallt Avwyn and Gware Gwallt Euryn also mentions in the same list three Gwairs, two of whom are apparently "sons of Llwch Llawwynnyawg from beyond the raging sea." [18] Gruffydd has already argued that the name Gwair, is a variant of Gwri.[19] Here, then, is Welsh evidence for Gwri or Gwair as the son of Llwch.

A few more facts point to the identity of Lac, Loth, and Lancelot. Both Lac and Loth are Kings of Orcanie.[20] In the *Estoire del Saint Graal* there is a King Orcan, of whom the following significant points may be made: [21] 1. His baptismal name was Lamer. 2. He is in very close and confused relationship with a King Luces. 3. In his island he challenges and fights adventurous knights beneath a pine in a way which closely parallels the behavior of Lancelot in the Isle de Joie.[21a] 4. He is an ancestor of Gawain. Is not the inference natural that here we have a confused survival of Llwch King of Orkney, father of Gwri Gwallt Avwyn, and that the name Lamer (like Lambegues) is a corruption of Lamfada? At any rate the doubter may turn on to Chapter XXXIV, where he will find some confirmatory material.

So, bewildering though the prospect may seem, we must face the fact that Lug gives us in Welsh Llwch Lleminawc, Llwch

---

[16] *RC*, XVI, 84 ff.
[17] L. 170.
[18] Loth, *op. cit.*, I, 276; *Mabinogion*, ed. Nutt, 111.
[19] *RC*, XXXIII, 461.
[20] Sommer, VII, 15, 37, 146; I, 280.
[21] *Ibid.*, I, 272–80.      [21a] *Ibid.*, V, 403.

Llawwynnawc and Llenlleawc; in Arthurian romance Loth, Lac, Lancelot, and ˙ Lambegues. While Curoi gives us in Welsh Gwri, Gware, Gware-van, Gwair, and (through the repercussion of Breton Guerec) Geraint; and in French romance Guerhes, Gaeres, Agravain, Gauvain, and Erec. Such a confusion, of course, is the inevitable result of a wide-spread oral transmission by many generations of individual *conteurs*. Each marked difference in pronunciation, each original interpretation led to the making of a new character. If we are embarrassed by such a number of sun-gods when there is only one sun, so was Cicero, long since, puzzled at a similar *embarras de richesse*.[22] Celtic myth has just as much right to numerous solar divinities as classical mythology.

Moreover the conversion of the names of one god into the names of other gods, who develop various ties of kinship to the god with whom they were originally identical, is a phenomenon well recognized by classical mythologists. Let me quote Miss Macurdy:[23] "Like many of the Sun and Moon epithets, this one [Hyperion] becomes a relative of the divinity in question, in this case the father of the Sun. . . . Again Titan, at Titane, is called the brother of the Sun. . . . Perhaps the most famous son of the Sun who was developed from an epithet is Phaethon, whose story all the world knows. The epithet appears once in the *Iliad* and once in the *Odyssey* to mark the sun in his brightness, and in the twenty-third book of the *Odyssey* it has become a name for a steed of Dawn. . . . The subject is inexhaustible." This last statement is equally true of Arthurian nomenclature, where we have to deal not only with the splitting off of epithets, but also with the multiplication of names passing from one speech to another and being copied by careless or too ingenious scribes.

The matter is further complicated in the case of Curoi by the fact that he is a notorious shape-shifter. Like Conchobar,[24] like Manannan and Mongan,[25] he was a Proteus. Of Manannan we read that he "was worshipped by the peoples as a god because he transformed himself into many shapes." [26] This passage clearly

[22] *De Natura Deorum*, III, 21.
[23] Article to be published: "Hippolytus and Sun Epithets." See Saintyves, *Saints Successeurs des Dieux*, 288 ff.
[24] *Archaeological Review*, I, 150, 231.
[25] *SNPL*, VIII, 42 n.
[26] *RC*, XXIV, 276.

implies that shape-shifting was a sign of divinity. We have already detected Curoi as the youth in the gray mantle, the gigantic churl with the ax, Yellow Son of Fair, and Terror Son of Great Fear. Of the last it is said that "he used to form himself into whatever shape he pleased," and "he was called the Wizard from the extent of his forming himself into many shapes." [27] We have had fair warning, therefore, and we must not be surprised if when we pull off the disguises of a number of traditional figures in Welsh myth and Arthurian romance, we discover more than once Curoi himself at his old tricks.

[27] Kittredge, *Study of G. G. K.*, 17.

# CHAPTER X

## DISENCHANTMENT BY DECAPITATION

THE singular penchant which Curoi displays in so many stories for losing his head seems to have suggested to certain story-tellers that his purposes were not wholly disinterested. Perhaps there was "something in it for him." This suggestion naturally combined with the sudden transformations of which Curoi was capable, from the huge and ugly Terror Son of Great Fear into Yellow Son of Fair. And so we discover in two Middle English romances, doubtless modeled upon French sources, the motif of disenchantment by decapitation. We have seen in the Irish stories that Curoi plays two rôles: that of helpful companion on Cuchulinn's expedition to the Other World, and that of the tester of Cuchulinn. Both the English romances combine these traditional motifs, and both conclude with the disenchantment of the figure corresponding to Curoi by the severing of his head.

The first romance (preserved in two versions) is the *Carl of Carlisle*.[1] Like the preceding myths we have studied, it falls into a regular folklore pattern, known as the Giant's Daughter, which Kittredge thus summarizes:[2] "A hero makes his way to the Other World and desires to marry the daughter of its ruler. The god is angry or reluctant, and wishes to destroy or eject the intruder. At best, he is under the necessity of testing the suitor's worthiness to become an immortal. In any case, he either tries to kill the aspirant (sometimes in single combat, often by trickery) or sets him dangerous or apparently impossible tasks. . . . In the end, the bride is won, for the god is either baffled and subdued or else he is satisfied to accept the hero as son-in-law. . . . Many tales of this type are frankly mythological." Elsewhere he remarks that "the general type is well enough represented by Jason and Medea."[3] We shall see how through the pattern the traces of mythological significance still appear.

While Arthur is sojourning at Cardiff he goes hunting with his knights. Gawain, Kay, and Bishop Baldwin take refuge for the night in the castle of the Carl of Carlisle. (Carl is the equiva-

[1] Kittredge, *Study of G. G. K.*, 301, 85–9, 257–73.
[2] *Ibid.*, 232 f.
[3] *Ibid.*, 262.

lent of churl.) He is described as a giant dreadful to see with gray beard and long locks. Four beasts are lying by the fire — a bull, a boar, a lion, and a bear. They threaten the guests, but when the Carl tells them to lie down, they dread him so sorely that they creep under the table. He bids bring in wine, but is dissatisfied when it is brought in four-gallon cups. Then the butler brings a gold cup holding nine gallons. After an adventure in which Gawain shows his superior courtesy, they sit down to supper with the Carl's wife, a most beautiful lady. The Carl tells Gawain to hurl a spear at him from the buttery door and hit him in the face. Gawain obeys, but the Carl lowers his head and the spear breaks on the wall. The Carl after dinner bids him go to bed with his wife and kiss her, but when he goes further the Carl shouts, "Whoa there! That game I forbade thee." But he rewards Gawain's obedience by giving him his daughter instead. Next morning the Carl shows Gawain ten cartloads of bones of men slain by his beasts for their disobedience. After dinner (according to the Percy MS.) the Carl gives Gawain a sword and commands him to strike off his head, and when he refuses threatens to cut off Gawain's head. Finally Gawain performs the deed, and the Carl rises, a man of Gawain's own size. He thanks the knight for freeing him from the spell which had forced him for forty years to slay all who would not obey him. He will now found a chantry for souls. The three knights depart, Gawain taking the daughter, to whom the Bishop marries him. The next day Arthur dines with the transformed Carl, and makes him one of the Round Table.

This story harmonizes with the Irish legends of Curoi in the following particulars: Both Curoi and the Carl are huge and ugly churls. Of Curoi it is said that "As thick as the wrist of any other man each one of his fingers," [4] and of the Carl that "His fingeris also, I wys," were as great "as any lege that we bere." [5] Both have wives of supreme beauty, with whom the hero falls in love. The castles of both are visited at nightfall by three heroes. Both apply tests to the heroes. Both are shape-shifters and at times assume a handsome aspect. Furthermore, the equation of Curoi with Lug explains the nine-gallon bowl of wine, for a description of Lug's palace mentions a silver kieve with hoops of gold, full of red ale.[6]

[4] *ITS*, II, 117.  [5] *Sir Gawayne*, ed. F. Madden, ll. 266 f.
[6] D'Arbois de Jubainville, *Irish Mythological Cycle*, tr. Best, 170.

A Welsh version of the Giant's Daughter theme accounts for other features in the *Carl of Carlisle*.[7] In *Kilhwch and Olwen* we may recognize the old sun and storm god not only in Gwrnach, but also in Yspaddaden, the Chief Giant. His brother Custennin acts as Hospitable Host to the heroes. He himself is by no means as friendly to them as is the Carl of Carlisle, but like the Carl his function is to put them through numerous tests. Each time they come into his presence he flings a poisoned spear at them, and each time one of the heroes catches it, and returning it wounds the giant. And singularly enough it is his daughter Olwen whom Kilhwch weds, just as it is the Carl's daughter whom Gawain weds. Furthermore just as the Carl has slain all previous visitors, so none who had sought Yspaddaden's daughter had returned alive.

The *Carl of Carlisle* also contains features corresponding to certain Arthurian traditions about old Curoi. Like the Green Knight, the Carl tests the young hero by means of his wife, though the circumstances are quite different; like the Green Knight and the churls of *Hunbaut* and the Mule without a Bridle,[8] he submits to decapitation by the hero.

We have seen that the Carl is disenchanted and regains his youthful shape and normal size when Gawain decapitates him. Hitherto the mythical idea behind these stories of the meeting between the young and the old sun-god is apparently that the old god tests the young god to determine whether he is fit to supplant him. In some cases the old god is actually destroyed by the young god. But as we see here and as we shall see in many cases[9] to follow, another mythical conception existed besides, almost antithetic to this: namely, that the young god, having survived the tests of the old god, restored his vigor, brought back his youth. This same conception of the disenchantment of the old god by decapitation is found also in another Middle English poem, *The Turk and Gawain*.[10] Here is the story:

Into Arthur's court there comes a man, not tall but broad, shaped like a Turk. He challenges to an exchange of buffets. Gawain gives him a heavy blow, but the return blow is to be

[7] Loth, *Mab²*, I, 296–9, 346, 291.

[8] *Hunbaut*, ed. Stuerzinger, Breuer, pp. 61 ff.

[9] See ch. XVIII, XXVI.

[10] *Percy Folio MS.*, ed. Furnivall, Hales, I, 90–102. *Cf.* Kittredge, *op. cit.*, 118–25, 274–81.

given elsewhere.  Gawain rides northward with him for two days.  When Gawain complains of hunger, the Turk leads him right into the side of a hill, which closes over them.  "The murk was come and the light is gone; thunder, lightning, snow, and rain, — thereof enough they had."  They reach a castle where the board is spread with meats and drinks, but no person is visible.  At first the Turk forbids Gawain to eat but relents and serves him plentifully.  They leave the castle, sail over the sea to the home of the King of Man.  The Turk warns Gawain of the giants whom they will encounter, but promises to help him.  On their arrival the King of Man inveighs against Arthur's men and particularly the clergy.  He bids bring in a tennis ball of brass, and nine giants, half as tall again as Gawain enter, hoping to beat out Gawain's brains in the game.  Here a gap in the text leaves us merely to infer that the Turk successfully copes with the giants and the ball of brass and also throws an axle tree.  A giant then lifts a huge brazier.  Gawain in terror bids his "boy" perform the feat, and the Turk swings it so that the coals fly about.  The King of Man then threatens Gawain with death and leads him to a caldron of boiling lead by which stands a giant with an iron fork.  The Turk, who was clad in invisible gray (?), threw the giant first into the caldron, and then the King of Man.  Another gap allows us to suppose that the Turk deals Gawain a return blow.  Then he gives him a sword and bids him strike off his head and let the blood flow in a golden basin.  Gawain reluctantly does so and the Turk rises up a stalwart knight, named Sir Gromer.  They release the prisoners, and return to court.  Arthur makes Gromer the King of Man.

Now this expedition to the Isle of Man recalls Keating's version of the opening of the story of the *Death of Curoi:* [11]

"The champions of the Red Branch went to pillage an island in the ocean near Alba called Manainn . . . And when Curaoi heard that the champions were setting out on that expedition, he put on a disguise by magic, and went with the party; and when they were about to plunder the island in the guise of jugglers, they apprehended great difficulty in seizing on the dun, . . . both on account of its strength and of the great skill in magic of those who were defending it.  Then Curaoi, who was disguised as a man with a *grey cloak*, said that if he got his choice

[11] *ITS*, VIII, 223.

of the valuables in the dun, he would capture it for them. Cuchulainn promised him this; and thereupon they attacked the dun with the man in the grey cloak at their head. He stopped the magic wheel that was in motion at the door of the fortress,[12] and enabled all to enter; and they plundered the dun, and took from it Blanaid and all the precious valuables it contained."

Another version runs: "Finally Cuchulinn went. As he stepped into the boat, a young man overtook him, of rude appearance: a grey tunic, a grey mantle, a copper fibula in his mantle." [13]  The earliest account of the *Attack on the Men of Falga* equates the Men of Falga with the Men of the Isle of Man.[14] It relates that Cuchulinn alone overcame them, and finally by means of the *gaebolga* and *cleittine* vanquished the King of Man himself.  In the *Destruction of Da Derga's Hostel* three of the nine Men of Falga are described as grayish giants, clad only in their shaggy hair, carrying iron flails with chains and knobs attached to them.[15]  In *Bricriu's Feast* these giants are apparently transferred to another Otherworld realm, for Cuchulinn successfully encounters three groups of nine monsters.[16]  Finally, as we have seen, the raid of Cuchulinn upon the castle of Blathnat's father always specified among the booty a caldron, sometimes filled with milk and sometimes with treasure.[17]

Thus we see that the traditions concerning the Attack upon the Men of Falga furnish us with most of the essential features of the central part of *The Turk and Gawain*.  First, there is Cuchulinn, the original of Gawain.  Then there is the young or small man in gray who accompanies and helps the hero.  There is the sea voyage and the location in the Isle of Man.  There is the encounter with giants who wield heavy shafts.  There is a caldron, though the uses are different in the two stories.  There is the final struggle with the King of Man himself.  Can one escape the conclusion that *The Turk and Gawain* is based on *The Attack on the Men of Falga?*

Another striking Irish parallel which shows Curoi at his old tricks of metamorphosis is found in *Cormac's Glossary*.  I quote Kittredge's account: [18]  "Senchan with his retinue of poets and

---

[12] *Cf. Chevalier du Papegau*, ed. Heuckenkamp, 72.
[13] *ZcP*, IX, 194.
[14] R. Thurneysen, *Irische Helden- und Königsage*, 430.
[15] *RC*, XXII, 303, 305.          [17] Rhys, *Hib. Lec.*, 261.
[16] *ITS*, II, 107.          [18] *Op. cit.*, 276.

students visits the Isle of Man — the scene of the Turk's exploits. A frightfully ugly youth asks permission to accompany them and climbs into the boat. He is described in great detail: 'Rounder than a blackbird's egg were his two eyes; . . . black as death his face; . . . yellower than gold the points of his teeth; greener than holly their butt; . . . his belly like a sack; . . . his neck like a crane's neck.' . . . On their arrival, they find an old woman on the strand. Learning that the leader of the party is 'Senchan, Poet of Ireland,' she asks an answer to a problem, and it is unwarily promised. She then speaks two verses of poetry and calls for the other half of the quatrain. All the poets are nonplussed. The ugly lad springs forward and supplies the missing lines. The same test is repeated. Senchan recognizes her as a lost poetess, for whom there has been much searching. 'Then she is taken by Senchan, and noble raiment is put upon her,' and she accompanies the bards to Ireland. 'When they came to Ireland they saw the aforesaid youth before them; and he was a young hero, kingly, radiant; a long eye in his head: his hair golden yellow: fairer than the men of the world was he, both in form and dress. Then he goes sunwise round Senchan and his people, *et nusquam apparuit ex illo tempore.*'"

It is natural to suspect that this helpful youth, who goes to the Isle of Man, who is transformed into a radiant youth with golden hair, "more fair than the men of the world," and who goes sunwise round the poet is again Curoi. And when we note that Lug, to whom he is constantly assimilated, boasts among his many "arts" that of a poet,[19] it is fair to suppose that like Apollo the Irish sun gods were also gods of poetry. This conclusion is borne out by the statement that the Welsh Gwair, who is, as we know, Gwri, "sang grievously at the harryings of Annwn, and will remain a bard till doom." [20]

Since in this story Curoi is transformed at the end of his helpful expedition to the Isle of Man, we may plausibly reason that the transformation of the helpful companion in *The Turk and Gawain* is also based on tradition. The fact that this metamorphosis is accomplished by means of decapitation seems simply an attempt to combine the motif of Curoi's shape-shifting with the familiar motif of being slain by the young sun god and the

---

[19] D'Arbois de Jubainville, *op. cit.*, 99.
[20] Malory, Everyman ed., I, xxiii.

equally familiar motif of being healed or restored by the young sun god.  All three combine in the stories of Curoi's disenchantment by decapitation as found in *The Carl of Carlisle* and *The Turk and Gawain*.

# CHAPTER XI

## THE PORTER OF THE OTHER WORLD

THE Beheading Test is also found in the romance of *Hunbaut*, written in the first half of the thirteenth century.[1] Here the part of Curoi is taken by a churl huge and black, ugly and hideous, who grasping his ax with both hands plants himself before the gate of the castle of the King of the Isles. When he has proposed his bargain, Gawain strikes off his head with the ax and by preventing him from seizing his severed head causes his body to fall lifeless on the spot.[2] We can hardly avoid comparing this *grant vilain* before the gate of the Otherworld castle with the big churl Burmaltus before the gate of the Otherworld castle, as depicted over the portal at Modena. The only difference is that one wields an ax, the other a *baston cornu*. And this resemblance takes on greater significance when we note that in the story of Carado of the Dolorous Tower, which is so closely related to the Modena sculpture, a *grant vilain* appears before one of the two entrances of the Dolorous Tower, discreetly retiring, however, to a position above the gate on Ivain's approach; and that in the *Mule Sanz Frain* Gawain on his departure from the Otherworld castle sees the *vilain*, with whom he has played the head-cutting game, stationed likewise over the gateway.[3] Clearly we have to deal with a well-marked tradition that the churl, whom we have come to recognize as Curoi in disguise, played the part of Porter of the Other World. There is no trace in Irish that Curoi performed that function, but in the Welsh he is clearly to be detected in Glewlwyd Gavaelvawr.

Glewlwyd Gavaelvawr means "brave gray one of the mighty grasp" or "dusky hero of the mighty grasp,"[4] an apt description of Curoi as the man in gray. Glewlwyd in four Welsh texts fills the rôle of porter. In *Owain* he welcomes strangers and guests to Arthur's court.[5] In an ancient poem we find Arthur and his knights, Llwch Llawynnawc, Bedwyr, Kei,

---

[1] Ed. Stuerzinger, Breuer, ll. 1464 ff.
[2] *Cf. supra* p. 19 and Kittredge, *Study*, 149 f.
[3] Ed. R. T. Hill, ll. 1012 f.
[4] Rhys, *Hib. Lec.*, 372.
[5] Loth, *Mab.*², II, 3.

Mabon, Manawyd and others attacking an Otherworld castle.[6]
The poem begins: "Who is the porter?" "Glewlwyd Gavaelvawr." In *Geraint* Glewlwyd is the chief porter of Arthur's
castle, performing the office, however, only on the three high
festivals of the year.[7] In *Kilhwch* Glewlwyd plays an important
rôle as porter of Arthur's castle, and it is here that he betrays his
identity with Curoi.[8] When the young hero, Kilhwch, asks,
"Is there a porter?" Glewlwyd replies: "I am Arthur's porter
every first day of January." He refuses to admit Kilhwch until
he has consulted Arthur. He goes in and addresses the king as he
sits at the board with his knights in words that echo the speech
of Curoi, the *bachlach*, as he addresses Conchobar and the heroes
of Ulster. Curoi, it will be remembered, declares: "The thing
which I have come in quest of I have found neither in Ireland
nor in Scotland nor in Europe nor in Africa nor in Asia as far as
Greece and Scythia and the Orkney Islands and the Pillars of
Hercules and the Tower of Bregon and the Isles of Gades."
Glewlwyd entering the hall of Arthur declares: "I was heretofore in Kaer Se and Asse, in Sach and Salach, in Lotor and
Fotor; and I have been heretofore in India the Great and India
the Lesser; and I was in the battle of the two Ynyr, when the
twelve hostages were brought from Llychllyn. And I have also
been in Europe, and in Africa, and in the islands of Corsica, and
in Caer Brythwch and Brythach, and Nerthach; and I was
present when formerly thou didst slay Mil Du the son of Ducum,
and when thou didst conquer Greece in the East. And I have
been in Caer Oeth and Annoeth, and in Caer Nevenhyr; nine
supreme sovereigns, handsome men saw we there, but never
did I behold a man of equal dignity with him who is now at the
door of the portal."

Glewlwyd and Curoi, therefore, present the following points of
similarity: both are gray men; both use the same formula in
speaking of their achievements; both Glewlwyd and the French
development of Curoi as the churl who challenges to a beheading
game are found in the rôle of porters or gate-keepers of the
Otherworld castle. Furthermore Glewlwyd betrays Irish connections, not only by his use of Curoi's formula, but also by
announcing that only the craftsman bringing his craft may
be admitted, like the porter in the Irish *Second Battle of*

---

[6] Malory, Everyman ed., xviii ff.

[7] Loth, *op. cit.*, II, 122.          [8] *Ibid.*, I, 254 ff.

*Moytura.*[9]   At a later point in *Kilhwch,* also, Glewlwyd betrays Irish affinities by the juxtaposition of his name to that of Lloch Llawwynnyawc, whom we have identified with Lug.   Do we need further proof that Glewlwyd is but another development of Curoi?

If we turn to the pages of French romance we shall discover that many guardians of gateways begin to have a familiar look. Singularly enough, whenever they are named, the names seem to be deformations of those attached to the three lords of the Otherworld castle in the Modena sculpture.   Although Carado of the Dolorous Tower, according to the text of the *Vulgate Lancelot* printed by Sommer, carried no ax in his struggle with Lancelot inside his castle, yet the illumination of the scene in the MS. formerly in the Yates Thompson collection shows Carado wielding an ax.[10]   This is possibly coincidence, but earlier in the same romance appears a King Claudas, nine feet tall, bushy-browed, snub-nosed, red-bearded, thick-necked, with a wide mouth and notched teeth.   From his shoulders down, however, he is as finely made as one could imagine.[11]   He defends the gate of his castle alone against Lambegues, with a huge and heavy ax, for "he was the man in the world who most loved an ax in a great mêlée." [12]   Knowing that Lambegues goes back to the same original as Lancelot, it is hard to resist the impression that Lambegues' opponent, Claudas, with his ax is identical with Lancelot's opponent, Carado(s), with his ax, and that both go back to Curoi with his ax.

Burmalt as Porter of the Other World also has his descendant in the knight whom Boors meets at the gateway before the bridge of Corbenic.[13]   The *Vulgate Lancelot* gives his name as Brunout or Brumaut, and Malory as Bromel.[14]   He is said to love the lady Elaine, who dwells within the castle, and hopes to bar the entrance to her lover Lancelot, and avenge himself on his rival.

The third lord of the Other World sculptured at Modena, Mardoc, also seems to have taken his turn as porter, for it has been suggested that Mador de la Porte derives his epithet from

[9]  *RC*, XII, 77–9.
[10]  H. Yates Thompson, *One Hundred MSS,* ser. VI, pl. 37.
[11]  Sommer, III, 26.
[12]  *Ibid.,* 61 f.
[13]  *Ibid.,* V, 294 f;  327 n.
[14]  Bk. XI, ch. 3, 4.

his service in that capacity, and his name is often and more authentically written Madoc, and once as Madoc li Noirs de la Porte.[15] This Madoc or Maduc le Noir does not appear precisely in the rôle of keeper of a gate, but in the *Livre d'Artus* he employs the gruesome custom of allowing stranger knights to enter his hostel, attacking them while they are eating, unprepared and unhelmed, and then affixing their heads to stakes.[16] The last-mentioned practise is attributed in both the romances of the Fair Unknown to a knight called Malgiers le Gris or Maugis, described in the English poem as "black as any pitch." [17]  He defends the bridge before the Isle d'Or in precisely the same way as Brumaut the bridge before Corbenic, and is, like Brumaut, an unsuccessful lover of the lady within.  Nor is it hard to see how the name Malgiers or Maugis might be derived from Mardoc, for we have nearly all the necessary intermediate forms in names which certainly belong to a lord of the Other World not unlike Mardoc.  The development would be: Mardoc, Malduc, Malduz, Mauduiz, Maugis.[18]  It seems to me highly probable that Malgiers le Gris, the pitch-black Maugis, and Madoc le Noir de la Porte are all derived from Mardoc functioning, like Carrado and Burmalt, as Porter of the Other World.

The *Vulgate Lancelot* provides two more instances of gatekeepers armed with axes.  In the Valley of the False Lovers the hero comes to a stair, and overcomes in succession three knights thus equipped.[19]  Again, Lancelot, in order to end the enchantments of the Douloureuse Garde, is obliged to procure certain keys from a cave.[20]  He passes one peril after another and finally meets a black-headed man, with eyes and teeth like live coals and a flaming mouth.  The monster brandishes an ax in both hands, but Lancelot after withdrawing rushes suddenly upon him, sweeps him off his feet, and finally strangles him.  In Crestien's *Charette* also Lancelot comes to a wooden tower held by a knight and two ax-men, who vainly try to prevent his passage.[21]

[15] Sommer, VII, 242 n. 2.
[16] *Ibid.*, 143.
[17] *SNPL*, IV, 37.
[18] Weston, *Leg. of Lancelot*, 15 and n.  The form Maugis is probably a substitution of the name of the famous enchanter of the Carolingian cycle.
[19] Sommer, IV, 121.
[20] *Ibid.*, III, 190 ff.
[21] *Charette*, ll. 2212–50.

I might go on listing indefinitely from the pages of Arthurian romance Porters of the Other World, who are more or less reminiscent of Curoi. But surely we have seen enough to convince us of the existence of a vigorous tradition concerning the activities of Curoi as guardian of the gateway to the land of which he was also lord.

A curious development in this traditional porter of the Other World is the fact that in some romances, instead of being a huge black giant or churl, he is a dwarf. The porter who appears before the entrance of the Dolorous Tower in the *Vulgate Lancelot* is according to Sommer's text "un grant vilain greignor de lui (Yvain) asses." But in the text summarized by Paulin Paris we find instead a "petit vilain." [22] In the romance of *Fergus* by Guillaume le Clerc the hero meets before a tent a porter, whose skin is black, whose hair is bushy, who carries a *baston*, and is exceedingly ugly of countenance.[23] In brief, he corresponds exactly to the descriptions of Curoi as the churl, except that he is only three feet tall. That he is, however, in spite of his stature but another of the forms of Curoi, is strengthened by the fact that the gray Turk, who is Gawain's helpful companion on his expedition to the Isle of Man and who is certainly Curoi, is described as a dwarf. This theory also explains the cryptic remark which Lancelot makes to a dwarf who, according to the *Vulgate Lancelot*,[24] beats him with a stick: "I am honored to be touched by so high a person as you are." Accordingly I believe we shall not be far wrong if we regard the many dwarfs who mysteriously appear and disappear in Otherworld castles, — for instance in those of Brun de Morois, and Pelles, — as manifestations of the ubiquitous god.

[22] P. Paris, *Romans de la Table Ronde*, IV, 310.
[23] Ed. Martin, ll. 2819 ff.
[24] Sommer, V, 237. On dwarfs *cf.* Chap. XX and L. A. Paton, *Fairy Mythology*, 124.

# CHAPTER XII

## THE MULE WITHOUT A BRIDLE

WE HAVE seen the primitive mythological conception of the struggle between the old god and the young, elaborated according to several patterns furnished by folklore: the Samson and Delilah pattern, the pluck-buffet pattern, the giant's daughter pattern. We have seen in Gareth and Lynete a story where various versions of the contest have been worked into a series of contests, so that the hero meets and vanquishes the old god in many forms. In the Mule without a Bridle we possess what seems a quite conscious use of this last principle: the introduction of the old god in various disguises as tester of the hero.

The Mule without a Bridle story is extant in two forms. One is the French poem, *La Mule sanz Frain,* by the Champagne poet Paien de Maisieres,[1] dated early in the thirteenth century. The other forms a part of the huge compilation *Diu Krone,* made by the Austrian poet, Heinrich von dem Türlin, about 1220.[2] It has been generally held that Heinrich followed Paien's poem, for no better reason, as far as I can see, than the closeness of the two versions and a reluctance to add to the list of lost sources. But with Orlowski,[3] I hold that Heinrich supplies too many features which clearly have their source in tradition and not in his own brain to be regarded as a *remanieur* of Paien. He must have drawn on a fuller version of the story. In my summary, therefore, I follow Heinrich, inserting details here and there from Paien's poem.

But first let us run over the various disguises in which we have detected Curoi the shapeshifter: the churl with his ax, the knight whose strength wanes after noon, the hospitable host, the helpful companion, the enchanter contriver of a revolving castle, the keeper of wild beasts, the creature with an external soul, the handsome knight (Bercilak) who is transformed into the shape of a churl, the dwarf porter. And then let us note that it is a recognized principle of Celtic narrative

[1] Ed. B. Orlowski as *La Damoisele à la Mule.* Ed. R. T. Hill.
[2] Ed. G. H. F. Scholl, *Bibl. Litt. Ver. Stuttgart,* XXVII.
[3] Pp. 62 f.

110

that the same supernatural figure should appear in various forms without revealing his identity at all or until the end. Let me quote from Hyde's introduction to *The Lad of the Ferule:*[4] "The reader familiar with Irish story-telling will understand that all this machinery of the hounds, the hunting, and the ferule was put in motion by a mysterious being, a god in fact (a similar being appears in some stories as Lugh, and in others as Manannan), to the end that he might save Tir na n-Og [the land of Youth]. It is he who appears as the messenger with the two hounds, and an untrue tale about the Queen of Pride. It is he again who, having by means of his hounds placed Murrough in a dilemma, takes service with him as his gillie; and it is he who finally entices him down into Tir na n-Og and makes use of him to set free the country. I feel quite certain that this is the way the story would be understood, and was meant to be understood, by all native Irish readers." In the Highland-Scotch *Lay of the Great Fool*,[5] which Nutt brought forward as corresponding in certain details to the Perceval story, we discover another example of this procedure: While the hero is left on guard over the treasure and the wife of his absent host, a young wizard enters and snatches a kiss from the woman. The Great Fool will not let him escape, until at last the intruder reveals that he is not only his host in a new shape, but also a sorcerer whom the hero had encountered earlier, and indeed is his own bespelled brother into the bargain. In the Welsh *Peredur*,[6] an adaptation from a Breton romance, there appears at the end a yellow-haired youth, who declares to the hero: "It was I that came in the form of the black maiden to Arthur's court, and when thou didst throw down the chessboard, and when thou didst slay the black man of Ysbidinongyl, and when thou didst slay the stag, and when thou didst go to fight the black man of the cromlech. And I came with the bloody head in the salver, and with the lance that streamed with blood. . . . And I am thy cousin." If we keep in mind this frequently tacit procedure on the part of Celtic story-tellers, and the way in which apparent hostility is often, as we have seen, a camouflage for real goodwill on the part of supernatural beings, we shall discover that the Mule without a Bridle is not such a hopeless hodgepodge as has been supposed.

[4] *Lad of the Ferule, ITS*, ed. D. Hyde, viii–x.
[5] A. Nutt, *Studies in Legend*, 160 f.      [6] Loth, *Mab.*[2], II, 118.

The story of the Mule appears in Heinrich's poem [7] attached
to the story of the Rival Sisters, which is found separately in
*Ivain*.[8] The King of Serre, dying leaves his kingdom to his two
daughters and with it a bridle which has the talismanic virtue
of preserving the kingdom for its possessor. The elder daughter,
Amurfina, seized both bridle and kingdom, and in order to
forestall the younger, who might appeal for aid at Arthur's
court, she lures Gawain to her castle and makes him her lover.
But Gawain (like other heroes of romance, notably Ivain and
Perceval) feels the call of duty or adventure, and finds his way
back to Arthur's court (ll. 7647–9128). Meanwhile the younger
sister Sgoidamur, dispossessed of her inheritance, arrives at the
same destination, riding a mule without a bridle. Her appeal for
aid is first answered by Kay. He sets off on the mule, traverses a
dark forest full of leopards and lions, who fall on their knees before the mule. After a deep, dark valley infested by reptiles, he
comes to a sunny plain, and rests beside a fountain. But when
he arrives before a black river, wide and deep, and the mule
tries to jump upon a steel bridge over it, no wider than a hands-
breadth, Kay in terror returns to the court.

Gawain then sets out in his place, passes the Perilous Bridge,
and comes to a castle, with heads mounted on stakes, whose
walls are high and glass-like and revolve like a mill-stone.
When the gate comes round, he spurs the mule through, but
with the loss of its tail. The streets are deserted, but presently
a dwarf appears. Then a handsome man in splendid apparel
is seen, only to turn into an ugly shape. (In Paien we hear
nothing of the handsome man, but a huge black churl, with
bushy hair, emerges from a cave.) This is a learned clerk,
Gansguoter, uncle of the sisters, builder of the turning castle,
and slayer of many adventurous knights. He bears a broad ax,
and announces that before Gawain may receive the bridle he
must engage in several contests. Gansguoter takes him to a fair
chamber, gives him food, and proposes the first test, the Beheading Game. Gawain accepts and decapitates the magician, who,
however, turns up the next morning, sound in wind and limb,
to carry out the rest of the bargain. Gawain has to stretch his
neck on the block as if it were gutta percha. Gansguoter spares
him. The wizard then provides armor for the second test, a
combat with two lions, and leads them out of a vault. Gawain

---

[7] Ll. 7647–9128, 12584–13901.     [8] Ed. Orlowski, 48–50.

is victorious. The third test is a conflict with a knight who has placed the heads of those whom he has vanquished on the stakes outside. Gawain finds him lying wounded on a couch, but at the hero's approach he is cured, and fights with him till noon. Then Gawain deals him a fatal stroke, and Gansguoter sets his head on the remaining stake. The wizard provides new arms for the fourth test, brings in two dragons, and Gawain slays them. At this cries of joy are heard from the maidens delivered from terror of the beasts. The knight goes to his love Amurfina, and is welcomed. Next day they start back taking mule and bridle. (Paien tells how the churl causes the castle to cease revolving, and stands over the gate as Gawain departs; also how the beasts of the perilous forest now kneel down in homage to Gawain as well as to the mule.) Sgoidamur rejoices when she sees the hero returning with the bridle, and offers him her love, but Gawain, already pledged to her sister, arranges that Sgoidamur marry Gasozein. And the weddings of the two sisters are celebrated together (ll. 12584–13901).

Now when we examine this tale, the Rival Sisters motif is clearly extraneous, and is accountable for most of the apparent madness of the poem, such as Gawain's total ignorance of the castle, its customs, and its inhabitants, when he is supposed to have dwelt there already as the lover of its mistress. But the genuine traditional elements in the story are apparent: Gawain's journey to the turning castle is paralleled by Cuchulinn's journey to the land of Scathach, as Brown pointed out,[9] for both ride a guiding animal, both pass through a perilous glen filled with monsters, and both cross a very narrow bridge.[10] The correspondences between the Mule without a Bridle and *Bricriu's Feast* are almost uncanny. Kittredge has shown [11] that Paien's version of the Beheading Test is closer to the Irish than any other romance in three respects: the churl is bushy-haired, the interval is only one day, and the hero stretches his neck at the demand of the tester. Just as the Mule without a Bridle describes a wizard contriver of a castle which "revolves as strongly as a mill-stone moves," [12] so *Bricriu's Feast* tells how Curoi chanted a spell over his fort every night, "till the fort revolved as swiftly as a mill-stone." [13] Other features which

---

[9] *PMLA*, XX, 688–94.　　[11] Kittredge, *Study of G. G. K.*, 44 f.
[10] Rhys, *Hib. Lec.*, 450.　　[12] Ll. 440 f. *Cf. Krone*, ll. 12960 f.
[13] *ITS*, II, 103. *Cf. Arthur of Little Britain*, ed. Utterson, 222 f; *Durmart*, ed. Stengel, ll. 10900 ff; *SNPL*, VIII, 80 f.

this castle shares with the Irish Otherworld fortress are the heads on stakes [14] and the glass wall.[15] A common tradition, also, must account for the fact that in Paien's poem the churl with his ax emerges from a cave and that in *Gawain and the Green Knight* Sir Bercilak in the form of a churl comes out of a hole in the earth,[16] and that while Paien's churl is black as a Moor, Bercilak's coloring is a mistranslation of the ambiguous Irish word for gray.

But perhaps most impressive of all the evidences of the genuine tradition which produced the Mule without a Bridle is the apparent awareness of its originator of the identity of Curoi behind all his transformations, and his apparent intention to train the vine of his narrative on the traditional framework of the successive appearances of the shapeshifter. Quite explicitly Heinrich tells us that the churl who puts the hero through the Beheading Test is the contriver and lord of a revolving castle and he permits us to catch a glimpse of him as a handsome man, splendidly appareled, before he is metamorphosed into the churl. We who are aware of some of Curoi's other shapes, can detect him in the dwarf, in the hospitable and helpful activities of the churl, in the keeper of wild beasts, and in the knight who fights the hero till noon is past and then succumbs. This same knight's sudden recovery from his wound on the arrival of the hero is doubtless due to the primitive conception mentioned in the last chapter — that the young god restores the old god's vigor, — and thus may appropriately be attributed to the old god. Clearly the originator of the story must have been conscious of the fact that all the male figures whom Gawain encounters in the castle and their performances are the traditional forms and performances of old Curoi.

This conviction becomes even stronger when we scrutinize the Mule himself. That he is no ordinary beast is clear from the way all the animals of the forest kneel before him. Brown pointed out [17] that in the *Chevalier du Papegau*, a fifteenth century romance based on a twelfth century original,[18] Arthur follows for two days a strange beast with two snow-white horns and a bright red coat.[19] At the end of the second day when Arthur

---

[14] *RR*, IX, 21.

[15] Rhys, *op. cit.*, 155 f, 263 f.

[16] Ed. Tolkien, Gordon, l. 2221.

[17] *PMLA*, XX, 697.

[18] *Beiträge zur Geschichte der deutschen Sprache*, XXI, 413–7.

[19] Ed. Heuckenkamp, 64 f. *Cf.* A. Gregory, *Gods and Fighting Men*, 294–8.

dismounts under a tree bearing the most fragrant blossoms in the world, he sees coming toward him a venerable man in white, who on being questioned announces that he is the beast who has led Arthur there, and that he is the ghost of King Belnain of the Realm of Damsels.   Now Gansguoter is himself just such a shapeshifting lord of a realm of damsels.   In the story we have just been studying, Heinrich mentions no male figure in the castle except the various shapes which Gansguoter himself assumes.   When Gawain has finally slain the dragons, it is a cry of maidens which he hears.   Another castle of Gansguoter's, described by Heinrich, the Schastel Mervillos, though various males inhabit it, is nevertheless a hardly disguised Castle of Ladies.[20]   Gansguoter is, therefore, like Belnain, lord of a Kingdom of Damsels.   And so since Belnain expressly says that he has played the part of the guiding beast, I have no doubt that the Mule without a Bridle was another of Gansguoter's or Curoi's manifold forms.   Quite clearly throughout this romance, just as in the Champion's Bargain, the *Carl of Carlisle, Gawain and the Green Knight,* and elsewhere, the old god takes the part of a benevolent tester of the young god, sometimes helping him in the performance of his tasks, always ready to acclaim his success.   It is a natural development from such a conception that the old god should bring the young god to the scene of his trial, and that is just what the marvelous mule does.

But what of the bridle?   What is its meaning?   Kittredge says without hesitation on the analogy of a certain folktale that "It is by virtue of the bridle that the mule can resume his human shape.   Its loss condemns the bespelled man to retain the form of an animal until it is recovered."[22]   But if we recognize in the mule the magician who changes his shape so many times before Gawain places the bridle on the animal's head, we cannot admit that the bridle, whatever its significance in other stories, could have meant for the originator of this plot a talisman essential for the return of the bespelled animal to its normal shape.

[20] See particularly ll. 20399, 20457, 20745.   *Cf.* Weston, *Leg. of Gawain,* 33 f.   Probably Belnain is a corruption of Belian, name of a king of a realm of damsels in *Wolfdietrich.*

[21] The conception of a god in the form of a mule was familiar at least to the Continental Celts, since we find in Gaul inscriptions to Mars Mullo, — a deification of the pack animal as an essential auxiliary of the god of war. *Cf. Corpus Inscriptionum Latinarum,* XIII, 3071;   Holder, *Altceltischer Sprachschatz, sub* Mullo.

[22] Kittredge, *op. cit.,* 250.

Hartland suggests that in the very analogue which Kittredge adduces — the Magician and his Pupil — the halter has a slightly different function. "The halter is probably the external soul. So long as it is free, its owner cannot be held within the purchaser's power." [23] To secure the halter, in other words, is to obtain perpetual and absolute control of the magic mule. And is it not, then, precisely such a talismanic symbol of sovereignty as Heinrich asserts the bridle to be? Is this not practically the implication of Paien when he makes the younger sister say: "When the bridle is given back to me, then the castle will be yours and my kisses and the other favor"? [24] How can the castle be given to anyone who had not mastered the lord of the castle, who, as we know, is the mule himself? A similar meaning appears in the fact that it is to the mule alone that the animals kneel before the talisman has been won, but afterwards, according to Paien, they kneel before Gawain as well as the mule. In Wauchier de Denain's continuation of the *Conte del Graal* [25] a damsel gives Perceval a white mule and a ring, explicitly said to give the possessor power over the beast. Ring and bridle have apparently the same magic virtue.

As we have seen in the *Ivain* story and shall see in others to come, the tests are the condition on which the young god takes over the powers of the old god. In the Mule without a Bridle, then, if we eliminate the Rival Sisters theme, we have a fairly coherent, logical tale. The Old God, like Curoi, plays throughout the part of a benevolent tester of the Young God. He comes and carries him to the scene of the tests. He then puts him through one ordeal after another. He finally leads him to the two symbols of his victory: the bridle which confers sovereignty, and the bride who, like other well-known ladies in Celtic romance, is the Sovereignty.

We have seen in the Gareth story that the damsel messenger Lynete is unquestionably identical with the damsel of the castle, Lyones. The splitting of the one person into two was probably due to the fact that in the earlier forms of these tales the maiden-messenger, after summoning the hero, disappears and then reappears in the land to which she has summoned him. It was inevitable that the two appearances of the same maiden should be misinterpreted as two maidens, two sisters. The same

[23] S. Hartland, *Legend of Perseus*, II, 56.
[24] Ll. 105–7.                    [25] Nutt, *Studies*, 17

phenomenon seems to have produced the two sisters Amurfina and Sgoidamur. It is, therefore, the old god's beautiful wife who appears with him to summon the young god to win the symbol of his divinity; and it is she who awaits him in the Other-world kingdom as the prize of his victory.

# CHAPTER XIII

## THE GIANT HERDSMAN

KITTREDGE suggested in connection with the Mule without a
Bridle that the churl who is in charge of the lions and dragons is
identical with the Giant Herdsman whom we have encountered
in *Owain* and *Ivain*.[1] Likewise Brown surmised that the Hospitable Host in the same stories is identical with the Giant Herdsman.[2] Miss Paton, in turn, was sure that Esclados the Red, the
defender of the fountain, was but a form of the Giant Herdsman.[3]
Cook showed the keenest penetration, asserting that the Hospitable Host, the defender of the fountain, and the Giant Herdsman, all in a sense represented the Otherworld King.[4] Our
previous study has shown that all but the Giant Herdsman are
shapes of old Curoi. We shall now see that the intuitions of
these eminent scholars are justified, and shall discover in the
Giant Herdsman also the protean god.

In the first place, let us note that the word *bachlach*, which is
applied to the disguised Curoi, has not only the general meaning
of churl but also the special sense of a staff-man (*cf.* Latin
*baculum*) or herdsman. And surely he is gigantic enough. He
curiously corresponds to a figure in the *Destruction of Da Derga's
Hostel*, who appears on the road to King Conaire: a huge, black-
haired *bachlach* or herdsman, with a forked iron pole, who when
asked who he is, replies in the cryptic words: "Fer Caille (the
Man of the Wood)."[5] This Fer Caille suggests identification
with the *bachlach* Curoi because when he is inside Da Derga's
Hostel, he takes his stand in front of the fire,[6] just as Curoi does
in the hall of Conchobar. This same figure, moreover, can be
definitely identified with two of the Giant Herdsmen of
Welsh romance.

He is accompanied by a monstrous spouse, huge, hideous, big-
mouthed. In *Kilhwch and Olwen* there is a Giant Herdsman,
whose wife is likewise a powerful hag.[7] The hero and his com-

---

[1] *Study of G. G. K.*, 256.  [4] *Folklore*, XVIII, 47.
[2] *SNPL*, VIII, 114.  [5] *RC*, XXII, 41–3.
[3] *PMLA*, XXII, 269.  [6] *Ibid.*, 309.
[7] Loth, *Mab.²*, I, 289; Guest, *Mab.*, ed. Nutt, 116.

panions, on approaching the castle of Yspaddaden Penkawr, "the fairest of the castles of the world," "beheld a vast flock of sheep, which was boundless and without an end. And upon the top of the mound there was a herdsman, keeping the sheep. And a rug made of skins was upon him; and by his side was a shaggy mastiff, larger than a steed nine winters old. Never had he lost even a lamb from his flock, much less a large sheep. He let no company pass without doing some hurt or harm. All the dead trees and bushes in the plain he burnt with his breath down to the very ground." When the heroes drew near to the mound they asked, "Truly art thou the Head?" The herdsman replied, "There is no hurt to injure me but my own." When asked his name, he said, "I am called Custennin the son of Dyfnedig (*dyfn* = deep), and my brother Yspaddaden Penkawr oppressed me because of my possessions." When Custennin's wife ran to welcome Arthur and his men, Kai prudently allowed her to embrace a billet of wood rather than himself, and she squeezed it so that it became a twisted coil. Evidently she was a powerful monster.

All this is significant, for Custennin corresponds directly to Curoi in his disguise as a herdsman clad in a hide; his monstrous spouse relates him to the Fer Caille. His admission that he is the Head,[8] doubtless the Head of Annwn, saying that there is no hurt to injure him but his own, affords firm ground for the supposition that he is a god. His relationship to Yspaddaden, who has already been shown to be one of the prototypes of the Carl of Carlisle, again proves him akin to Curoi.

Custennin has a son, whom we should naturally expect to betray signs of the younger god. He has yellow curling hair. He rises up out of a stone chest, where he has been secreted for fear of his uncle, and thereby shows kinship with the young Llew Llaw Gyffes,[9] whom Rhys and others equate with Lug.[10] The part Custennin's son plays in *Kilhwch and Olwen* is almost as important as that of the hero himself.[11] When Kai and Bedwyr had entered the castle of Gwrnach the Giant, a young

---

[8] Cf. *Branwen the Daughter of Llyr*, where the phrase "the Entertainment of Bran" seems synonymous with "the entertaining of the Noble Head." The story as I show in Chap. XV has been distorted because the latter phrase was taken in a physical sense.

[9] Loth, I, 192.

[10] Rhys, *Hibbert Lectures*, 237; C. Squire, *Mythology of the British Islands*, 262. For proofs see Chap. XXXIV.

[11] Loth, *Mab.*[2], I, 319 ff; Guest, *Mab.*, ed. Nutt, 132.

man, "the only son of Custennin the herdsman, got in also. And he caused all his companions to keep close to him as he passed the three wards, and until he came into the midst of the castle. And his companions said unto the son of Custennin, 'Thou hast done this! Thou art the best (*goreu*) of all men.' And thenceforth he was called Goreu." We have seen reason to suspect that when such an anecdote is told to explain a name, an originally meaningless name has been distorted to furnish a plausible etymology. Can Goreu be Gwri, who was also the son of a Head of Annwn? In the Gwrnach episode, where Gwrnach himself is old Curoi, we should expect one of the three champions who bring about his death to represent little Curoi, and though Kai is the chief hero of this exploit, Goreu alone could be conceived of as little Gwri. And in the final episode of the book, the beheading of Yspaddaden Penkawr, who is but another name for the old god, it is Goreu himself who seizes the giant by the hair of his head, drags him to the keep, cuts off his head, and places it on a stake on the citadel.[12] The suspicion that his real name is Gwri is strong. And his relationship to the Giant Herdsman is then easily understood.

The Fer Caille has but one eye and one foot,[13] and thereby identifies himself with another of the Giant Herdsmen of Welsh romance. In *Owain*, an adaptation from a Breton source, Kynon is told: [14] "A little way within the wood, thou wilt meet with a road branching off to the right, by which thou must proceed, until thou comest to a large sheltered glade with a mound in the centre. And thou wilt see a black man of great stature on the top of the mound. He is not smaller in size than two of the men of this world. He has but one foot; and one eye in the middle of his forehead. And he has a club of iron, and it is certain that there are no two men in the world who would not find their burden in that club. And he is not a wicked man, but he is exceedingly ill-favored; and he is the woodward of that wood." Kynon finds the black man as he has been told. " 'Then,' he says, 'I asked him what power he held over these animals.' 'I will show thee, little man,' said he. And he took his club in his hand, and with it he struck a stag so that he brayed ve-

[12] Loth, I, 345 ff; Nutt, 147.
[13] *RC*, XXII, 41.
[14] Loth, II, 9 f; Nutt, 170 f. The herdsman god, as well as the sun-god, seems to have supplied attributes to the Irish saints. *Cf.* C. Plummer, *Vitae Sanctorum Hiberniae*, I, cxlvi.

hemently, and at his braying the animals came together, as numerous as the stars in the sky, so that it was difficult for me to find room in the glade to stand among them. There were serpents and dragons and divers sorts of animals. And he looked at them, and bade them go feed; and they bowed their heads, and did him homage as vassals to their lord."

In size and ugliness this herdsman corresponds to the herdsman Curoi; in his preternatural control over the animals he reminds us of the Mule without a Bridle, to whom the animals bowed, of Gansguoter, and of the Carl of Carlisle — all hypostases of Curoi. His one eye, one foot, and iron club relate him to the other *bachlach*, the Fer Caille, who seems to be Curoi under an alias. And curiously enough, we read of Lug himself (who seems to be essentially the same sort of being as Curoi) that he "sang this chant below, as he went round the men of Erin, on one foot and with one eye." [15] Now these apparently grotesque features may have had some meaning. Cook maintains, after adducing certain arguments, that there is a presumption in favor of identifying the one round eye of the Cyclops with the shining orb of the sun.[16] In *Kilhwch* one of the companions of Arthur, named Sol, had this peculiarity that he could stand all day upon one foot.[17] The author of *Kilhwch* seems to use this form Sol instead of the usual *sul*, meaning sun.[18] When, therefore, Sol, the Fer Caille, and Lug, all of whom have clear solar affinities, are described as standing on one foot, we cannot doubt that this was a wide-spread Celtic conception of the anthropomorphized sun.

Crestien's *Ivain*, derived ultimately from the same Breton source as *Owain*, depicts a similar Giant Herdsman.[19] Calogrenant, narrating his adventures, says: "I found in a glade wild bulls at large, all of which were fighting among themselves. . . . A churl, who looked like a Moor, tall and hideous beyond measure (so passing ugly a creature no mouth could describe) I saw sitting on a stump, a great club in his hand. . . . His hair was in tufts. . . . He was clad in a garment so strange, for he had neither linen nor wool, but had fastened to his neck two hides newly flayed from two bulls or beeves. . . . He was

[15] *RC*, XII, 99.

[16] A. B. Cook, *Zeus*, I, 313.   *Cf.* Settegast, *Polyphemmärchen*, 23, 32.

[17] *Mab.*, ed. Nutt, 112.

[18] Dinsul, the usual Cornish form for Mount of the Sun, appears *Ibid.*, 104 as Dinsol.          [19] Ll. 279–355.

seventeen feet in height." He declared that he was master of the beasts and that when he wrenched the horns of one of the bulls, the others trembled for fear of him, and gathered about him to ask mercy.

The appearance of this herdsman, ugly, clad in hides, bushy-haired, corresponds closely to that of Curoi the herdsman, more than twice the size of any Ulsterman, hideous, clad in an old hide, and "upon him the bushiness of a great tree." The circle is complete. The Fer Caille, Custennin, and the herdsmen in *Owain* and *Ivain*, all reveal their identity with each other and with Curoi, the Giant Herdsman.

It is possible that Curoi was not alone in possessing this particular disguise. Cuchulinn in one of the riddling replies which he returns to Emer when he comes to her as a suitor, says:[20] "I am the nephew of the man that disappears in another in the wood of Badb." Later he explains that the reference is to Conchobar, brother of Cuchulinn's mother Dechtire.[21] Besides shapeshifting, Conchobar presents another analogy to Curoi, in that, though he does not seem to have been supplanted by "the Hung-up Naked Man," much is made of the fact that he was born at precisely the same hour as Christ.[21a] The similarity of his nature to Curoi's may extend to the trait that the shape he adopted in the wood of Badb was that of a Giant Herdsman. But of that we have no assurance.

The Fer Caille and the Giant Herdsman in *Owain* possessed, as we remember, but one foot and one eye. Brown has pointed out that such a one-eyed, one-legged, and often one-handed monster survives in modern Irish and Gaelic folktales, under the name of the Fachan.[22] And it is possible that Curoi appears in the Finn cycle and elsewhere under the name of Goll or "The One-Eyed." In the twelfth century text, *The Youthful Exploits of Finn*, the son of Daire the Red was called Aed, meaning "Fire," but having lost one eye he was thereafter called Goll, that is, the One-Eyed.[23] Now MacNeill has shown that the

---

[20] *Archaeological Review*, I, 150.

[21] *Ibid.*, 231.      [21a] K. Meyer, *Death Tales*, 9, 17.

[22] *PMLA*, XX, 682 f. For bibl. of Polyphemus legends see A. B. Cook, *Zeus*, II, 988. *Cf.* F. Settegast, *Polyphemmärchen in altfranzösischen Gedichten.* A probably mythical MacCuill, called a Cyclops, appears in a very early legend of St. Patrick as frequenting a mountainous region and slaying in a cruel fashion strangers who passed by. Cf. J. D. Bury, *Life of St. Patrick*, 267; N. J. D. White, *St. Patrick, His Writings and Life*, 92–4.

[23] *MP*, XVIII, 213.

Eochus, Nuadas, Aillils and Daires of myth, though they possess distinguishing epithets, nevertheless are either identical or else have so borrowed each others' qualities and histories as to be essentially composite figures that can be treated as one.[24]  Brown goes far toward admitting that Aed, son of Daire the Red, is a fire deity.[25]  And in that case, Curoi mac Daire may be identical with "Fire," son of Daire.   There is nothing fantastic in this conclusion to anyone who has probed about in Celtic mythology. It suffered, as Westropp, remarks, from a plague of alias-names which obscure the identity of the various gods.[26]  "The Dagda" seems to be but the title of Eochaid Ollathair, "the All-Father," who had various other appellations.[27]  The *Fitness of Names* itself asserts that "Oengus was the original name for Cairbre Musc, Eochu for Cairbre Rigfota, Aillil for Cairbre Baschain." [28] Examples might be multiplied.   It is possible, therefore, that Curoi enjoyed not only the aliases of "Yellow Son of Fair" and "Terror Son of Great Fear," but also of "Fire," "The One-Eyed," and "The Man of the Wood."

[24]  J. MacNeill, *Celtic Ireland*, 61.
[25]  *MP*, XVIII, 213 n.
[26]  *PRIA*, XXXIV, C, 54.
[27]  *Kittredge Anniversary Papers*, 239 n. 1;  *ITS*, XV, 283;  *Eriu*, VIII, 17;  *RC*, XII, 125.
[28]  *IT*, III, 317.

# CHAPTER XIV

## MERLIN THE SHAPESHIFTER

THE metamorphoses of Curoi are matched in Arthurian romance by the well-known transformations of Merlin.[1] Curoi vaunts his arts, and Merlin his "crafts." Curoi, under the name of Terror Son of Great Fear, used to form himself into whatever shape he pleased,[2] and the same was true of Merlin. Among the shapes which we have seen Curoi assume are those of a Giant Herdsman and of a Man of the Wood; the earliest accounts of Merlin show him in the same guises. However, an influential group of scholars have asserted that there was practically no independent Celtic tradition about the name of Merlin, and that it was merely the caprice of Geoffrey of Monmouth in foisting upon this insignificant figure certain Oriental tales of remarkable prophecies which had already been fastened by the Welsh to the name of a certain Lailoken, that started Merlin upon his career.

Now Gaster has shown conclusively that as Merlin is first clearly represented under his own name in Geoffrey of Monmouth's *History*, his story is based upon Talmudic legends regarding Solomon and Asmodeus, which are already attached in Nennius to a marvelous youth called Ambrosius. Gaster concludes:[3] "Given the practice of assimilating old legends to new surroundings and spelling the past in the letters and ideas of the present, of substituting better known names for less known ones and making a romance out of the ancient tales of Greece and Palestine, then this legend can only be the reflex of the oriental tales and motives, not even skilfully worked up. One can easily detect the seams in the coat. The latter part of the Merlin legend entirely belies the first. There is absolutely no connection between the later adventures of Merlin at the courts of Vortigern, Uter, and his son, and the incidents at the beginning of the tale." Let us grant everything Gaster has

---

[1] For Merlin bibliography see Bruce, *Evolution*, I, 129–51. Add *Philological Quarterly*, IV, 193; *Univ. of Illinois Studies in Lang. and Lit.*, X, no. 3; *Kittredge Anniversary Papers*, 191.

[2] *ITS*, II, 97.

[3] *Folklore*, XVI, 425.

claimed; but let us also note the admissions he has incidentally made. First, that before Geoffrey adopted him, Merlin's name was already well known, and therefore the centre of a tradition. Second, that even in Geoffrey's *History* Merlin's career is a composite. Thirdly, that Talmudic and apocryphal legends explain only a part of that composite. As Miss Weston at once showed,[4] Layamon gives a more primitive account of Merlin's birth. "The story discussed by Dr. Gaster only touches a very small part of the Merlin legend and offers no parallel to the shape-shifting which was so marked a feature of his career, nor to his 'wood-abiding' madness and his prophecies." Parry has pointed out a remarkable parallel to the *Vita Merlini* in the Irish *Frenzy of Suibhne*,[5] and Sullivan long since pointed out an Irish parallel to the story of Vortigern's tower.[6]

We may agree, then, that there was a Merlin and that he was famous before Geoffrey exploited him. Who or what he was originally I do not pretend to know. The Welsh poems in which he figures are to me too obscure to shed any light, and since their date is most uncertain there is little profit in discussing them. They prove, however, that there was a Welsh tradition independent of Geoffrey of Monmouth.[7] It is possible that he was a historic bard of the sixth century who, like Arthur, took on supernatural traits. It is also possible that the process was reversed and that we have in Myrddin a degraded god whose special domain was poetry and prophecy. But from the first when he appears in the full blaze of Geoffrey's *History* he is far more than human.

As has been long recognized, Geoffrey took the story of Merlin's birth from Nennius' account of the birth of one who is never called Merlin. In the well-known story,[8] Vortigern, being told by his magi that a certain tower may never be built unless he sprinkle the earth with the blood of a fatherless child, has brought before him a boy whose mother swore that he had no father, for she had never had intercourse with any man. The boy reveals supernatural knowledge, and the king asks his name. He replies, "I am called Ambrosius," that is, the Immortal. So far the story is quite consistent. But a new and really in-

---

[4] *Ibid.*, 427.
[5] *Philological Quarterly*, IV, 193.
[6] O'Curry, *Manners and Customs*, I, cccxxxiii.
[7] *Phil. Quar.* IV, 203–5.
[8] Nennius, *Mon. Ger. Hist., Auct. Antiq.*, XIII, 181–6.

congruous element enters at this point, for the boy's declaration that he is Ambrosius is followed by the gloss: "That is, he meant that he was Embreis the Chief or Emperor." And presently the story is utterly confused by the boy's assertion that his father is a Roman consul. This narrative Liebermann characterizes as "a nauseous farrago attached, not without self-contradiction and impossible miracles" to the historical leader of the Britons, Ambrosius Aurelianus, celebrated by Gildas.[9] Liebermann adds, "I venture to charge Nennius with blending the half-druidical boy of miraculous origin with the historical prince." But is this blending without meaning or motive? Does it not seem probable that some stupid person has taken the ambiguous remark, "I am called Ambrosius," without a glimmer of its double meaning and quite prosaically proceeded to equate the wonder child with the historic hero of Gildas, Ambrosius Aurelianus, the general of Roman descent who successfully fought the Saxons? Hence the absurdity, and hence the curious combination of sage and ruler which both Ambrosius and Geoffrey's Merlin, who was modeled on Ambrosius, present.

But it may well be asked, what right, besides that of making sense of the story, has one to interpret the name Ambrosius as the Immortal One? First, there is the almost universal habit of supernatural beings to give cryptic answers regarding their identity.[9a] We have noted it particularly in the case of Custennin in *Kilhwch* and of the Fer Caille in *Da Derga's Hostel*, both shapes which we shall presently see Merlin assuming. Secondly, the story of the wonder child's birth as it developed in the case of Merlin presents clearer and clearer affinities to the stories of divine birth. In Geoffrey's *History* Merlin's mother declares:[10] "One appeared unto me in the shape of a right comely youth and embracing me full straitly in his arms did kiss me, and after that he had abided with me some little time did as suddenly evanish away so that nought more did I see of him. Natheless, many a time and oft did he speak unto me when that I was sitting alone, albeit that never once did I catch sight of him. But after that he had thus haunted me of a long time I did conceive and bear a child." Geoffrey offers the explanation that the supernatural visitor was an incubus. But Layamon,

<hr />

[9] *Essays in Medieval History presented to T. F. Tout*, 40. See *SNPL*, X, 18.

[9a] *Poetic Edda*, tr. H. A. Bellows, 197.     [10] Book VI, ch. 18.

who was using a version of Wace expanded from Breton tradition, makes the divine paternity even clearer. The child's mother relates:[11] "When I was in bed in slumber, with my soft sleep, then came before me the fairest thing that ever was born, as if it were a tall knight, arrayed all of gold. This I saw in dream each night in sleep. This thing glided before me, and glistened of gold: oft it kissed me and oft it embraced me; oft it approached me and oft it came to me very nigh." Now whether this had any relation to the original birth story of Myrddin or whether the wonder-child of Nennius was Myrddin, no one can tell. But at any rate the story of Ambrosius' birth was recognized as that of a divine child and was developed accordingly. That cannot be gainsaid, even though the more orthodox clerics who got hold of the story had to interpret the divine father as an incubus or a devil.

Even more striking is the fact that Merlin, the inheritor of Ambrosius' story is without exception the most clearly deathless figure in Arthurian romance. Native Welsh legends say that he departed with nine bards into the sea in a Glass House, and that nothing was heard of him since; or that he dwells in a Glass House in the Isle of Bardsey.[12] In 1810 a Breton tradition is recorded, which said that Merlin was inclosed by his mistress in a tree on the Ile de Sein.[13] In the French romances we have the practically uniform story of the beguiling of Merlin by his love and his eternal imprisonment.[14] In the *Vulgate Merlin* Niniane confines him in the Forest of Broceliande in walls of air, which to others present only a thick mist but to him is the fairest tower in the world.[15] In the *Vulgate Lancelot* she seals him asleep in a cave.[16] In the *Prophecies* the Lady of the Lake imprisons him in a tomb where his body wastes away but his soul lives on for all who come.[17] In Malory we learn that the Damsel of the Lake, Nyneue, made Merlin go under a stone and wrought so that he came never out for all the craft he could do.[18] The *Didot Perceval* closes with stating that Merlin retired to an *esplumeor* or cabin, and that no one had seen him since.[19] Only

---

[11] Ed. Madden, II, ll. 15706-14.
[12] Rhys, *Hib. Lec.*, 155.
[13] A. Plumptre, *Narrative of Three Years' Residence in France*, III, 187.
[14] L. Paton, *Fairy Mythology*, 204-27.
[15] Sommer, II, 452.
[16] *Ibid.*, III, 21.
[17] Pp. xliv, lxiv–lxviii.
[18] Bk. III, ch. 5, 6; Bk. IV, ch. 1.
[19] Weston, *Leg. of Perceval*, II, 112.

the *Huth Merlin* makes his imprisonment in the tomb by Niniane end in death.[20]  But in so doing it violates what is practically a uniform tradition of Merlin's immortality.  I do not believe, therefore, that Geoffrey's identification of Merlin with Ambrosius was wholly arbitrary.  Whoever the wonder-child was who called himself Ambrosius, he shared with Merlin the trait of immortality.  There is every reason, then, to believe that the ambiguity of the statement, "Ambrosius vocor," led to the confusion of the Immortal One with Ambrosius Aurelianus.

Merlin reappears in Geoffrey's *Vita Merlini*, but the figure is so different from that in the *History* that it can hardly be the fabrication of Geoffrey, who would certainly have attempted some sort of harmony between the accounts.  As a matter of fact we hear nothing of the marvelous birth, of Vortigern and Uter, and very little of Arthur.  The only feature which the Merlin of the *Vita* has in common with the Merlin of the *History of the Kings of Britain* is the prophetic power.  I think the conclusion is hardly avoidable that Geoffrey is following two separate traditions.  This difference is responsible for Giraldus Cambrensis' conclusion that there were two Merlins: Merlin Ambrosius and Merlin Silvester (of the wood) or Celidonius.[21]

In the really charming *Vita*, Merlin, overcome with sorrow at the death of his three brothers in battle, flees to the forest, where he appears in the rôles already shown to be characteristic of Curoi — wild man of the woods and ruler of wild animals. Let me translate: "He enters the forest and delights in hiding beneath the mountain ash-trees.  He gazes on the wild beasts feeding in the glade.  He eats the fruit of herbs, he eats herbs, he eats the fruit of trees and the berries of the bramble-bush. He becomes a man of the woods (*silvester homo*) as if he had been born among them." [22]  "There was a spring on the topmost peak of the mountain, surrounded on all sides by hazel trees and dense thickets.  There Merlin took his seat; from it he gazed on all the woods, the courses and games of the wild beasts.  The messenger [of his sister Ganieda] ascends to this point, and with soft step he goes up the hill seeking the man.  Finally he espies the spring and Merlin seated behind it on the grass." [23]

[20]  Ed. G. Paris, J. Ulrich, I, 264, II, 198.
[21]  *Itinerarium Cambriae*, Bk. II, ch. 8.  *Cf. Annales de Bretagne*, XV, 334.
[22]  Ed. J. J. Parry, ll. 75–80.
[23]  Ll. 138–44.

Merlin is enticed by the messenger back to the court of his brother-in-law Rodarchus. But arrived there, he declares that "To these things he prefers the forest and the spreading oaks of Calidon, the high mountains and the green meadows below." [24] The king has him chained, but Merlin after startling him with his soothsaying, returns to the forest, and there for years he spends his life with the wild herds and from a mountain top watches the courses of the stars. One night he discovers in the heavens signs that his wife Guendoloena is unfaithful. "He passes through all the woods and glades, collecting all the herds of stags into a host, together with fallow deer and roe-deer. He sat on a stag, and driving the host before him he hastens at dawn to the place where Guendoloena is being wed." [25] He calls Guendoloena to look out at the gifts he has brought her, and she wonders at the sight of him riding the stag, at the animal's tameness, and at the multitude he alone is driving before him "as a herdsman is wont to lead his sheep to pasture." [26] Guendoloena's new spouse laughs at him, and Merlin in anger tears the antlers from the stag, hurls them, and kills him.

As "wood man" and as "herdsman" Merlin corresponds to Curoi as the Fer Caille and *bachlach.* Further evidence that the tradition of the *Vita* has ultimate connections with the Irish is the fact that at one point Merlin instructs his sister to make a secluded house in the forest with seventy doors and seventy windows, in order that he might observe the stars.[27] In the *Imram Snedgusa* of the 9th or 10th century, one of the Otherworld islands contains a royal dwelling with a hundred doors.[28] And as already stated, Parry has shown the remarkable parallel to the whole *Vita* supplied by the *Frenzy of Suibhne.*[29]

It is, of course, true that the stories of Curoi and Geoffrey's stories of Merlin show so far no correspondences in detail. Only the divine birth and the rôle of man of the forest and giant herdsman suggest an equation. But it must be remembered that Geoffrey by explaining Merlin's mysterious father as an incubus, by reducing his prophetic powers to that of a merely human astrologer, and by his use of stories culled from Eastern legends shows that the version he followed was by no means the pure Celtic tradition. The question of Merlin's true

[24] Ll. 241 f.          [26] L. 463.          [28] *RC*, IX, 14.
[25] Ll. 451–5.          [27] L. 555.          [29] *Phil. Quar.*, IV, 199 ff.

nature and of his connection with Curoi can be solved by observing whether in the later Arthurian romances he possesses the distinctive traits assigned him by Geoffrey or those which are associated with the mythical figure of the Giant Herdsman. That the Merlin of Geoffrey's *History* has greatly influenced later romances is clear, but the real issue is round the Merlin of the *Vita*. Do we detect Merlin in the French romances as an astrologer, as a madman, as related to Rodarchus, Ganieda, and Guendoloena? If not, if we find instead that his identity with the mythical Giant Herdsman and his shape-shifting are developed, then it is clear that the *Vita* did not initiate the conception of Merlin Silvester or Celidonius, but rather that the mythical conception is independent and naturally earlier. It is Arthurian romance which has preserved the tales of the Bretons more clearly than Geoffrey or any other source. And there Merlin seems quite clearly to have inherited the nature of the old sun-god.

In the *Vulgate Merlin* he comes to the messengers of Uther Pendragon "like a wood-cutter, a big ax at his neck, wearing big shoes, a short coat all torn. His hair was bristly, his beard large, and he looked much like a wild man of the woods." He bids the messengers tell Uther to come to the forest of Northumberland the next day, and there he will meet Merlin. Sure enough one of the king's followers discovers "a great multitude of beasts and a very ugly man in disguise who was tending these beasts." After appearing successively as a comely man, well arrayed, and as a beautiful boy, Merlin finally visits the king in his own semblance and admits that it was he who was transformed into the man of the woods and the herdsman.[30]

Again Merlin approaches the lodges of Arthur by the river in the guise of a carl shooting wild fowl. "He wore great cow-hide boots, a coat and surcoat of coarse wool and a hood, and was girded with a knotted thong of sheep-skin. He was big and tall and black and bristly, and seemed right cruel and fierce." [31]

Again Merlin "took on an aged aspect, and was again in an old coat of coarse wool all torn and rent, and though he had before been tall and stout, now he was short and hump-backed and old, and his head was a composite, and his beard was long. He held a club beside his neck and drove a very great multitude of beasts before him." [32]

---

[30] Sommer, II, 36–8.    [31] *Ibid.*, 122.    [32] *Ibid.*, 180.

But Merlin's power of metamorphosis and his predilection for the shape of a wild man or churl comes out more clearly in the Grisandole story in the same *Vulgate Merlin.*[33] Miss Paton has studied this story and concluded that it is based not on Geoffrey but on an independent Celtic tradition.[34] Instead of riding on a stag as in the *Vita,* Merlin actually assumes the form of a huge stag of five branches, with a white fore-foot.[35] Again he comes on the scene as a black man, shaggy, barefoot, wearing a torn coat, and allows himself to be captured.[36] Before leaving the emperor's court, he writes on the wall in Hebrew letters that the wild man and the stag were Merlin.[37] All through the *Vulgate Merlin,* then, we have evidence of a powerful tradition which made far more of Merlin's penchant for shape-shifting than Geoffrey does, and also stresses his peculiar fondness for the rôle of the Giant Herdsman or churl. It is in the *Livre d'Artus,* however, that he is most clearly presented in this character. Let me translate the passage in full.[38]

"It came to his (Merlin's) mind to go and divert himself in the forest of Broceliande and to do something for which he should be spoken of forever. So on the day when the three messengers departed from Calogrenant, he transformed himself into such a shape as no man ever saw or heard of before. He became a herdsman, a great club in his hand, clad in a great hide, the fur of which was longer than the breadth of the largest hand known, and it was neither black nor white but smoked and browned and seemed to be a wolf-skin. He took his place in a great clearing on the border of a ditch, right over the bank, leaning on an old mossy oak, and held his club down to the bottom of the ditch and bent over it. He was large, bent, black, lean, hairy, old with a great age, shod without in marvelous leggings that reached his girdle. He was transformed so that his ears hung down to his waist, wide as a winnowing fan. He had eyes in his head as large and black as a —, and a head as big as a buffalo's, and hair so long that it brushed his girdle, all bristly, stiff, and black as ink. His mouth was as large and wide as a dragon's, and gaped up to the ears; his teeth were white; and his thick lips were always open so that the teeth showed all

[33] *Ibid.,* 281 ff.
[34] *PMLA,* XXII, 234 ff.
[35] Sommer, II, 283. Cf. *Folklore,* XVII, 435 n. 6; E. K. Chambers, *Mediaeval Stage,* I, 258 f.          [37] *Ibid.,* 291.
[36] Sommer, *op. cit.,* II, 284.          [38] *Ibid.,* VII, 124–6.

around. He had a hump behind on his spine, as big as a mortar. His two feet were where the heels ought to be in an earthly man, and the palms of the hands where the backs should be. He was so hideous and ugly to see that no man living would not be seized with great dread, unless he were brave and valiant. He was so tall when he stood up that a rod of eighteen feet would not reach him, and in proportion to his height he had the breadth of a thin man. His voice was so loud when he spoke that it seemed like a trumpet when he spoke a little loud. When Merlin had turned himself into this shape and placed himself on the road by which Calogrenant was traveling, he caused by his art stags, hinds, bucks, and all manner of wild beasts to come and graze around him; and there were such a multitude that no one could tell the number. He ruled them so that when he scolded one roughly, it did not dare to eat or drink till he commanded."

When Calogrenant saw the "hom sauvage" he set himself in a posture for defense, but turned toward him to ask the way. To his question, what man he was, the herdsman replied: "Vassal, what would you do? I am such as you see, for I am never anyone else, and I watch over the beasts of these woods and the forest, of which I am wholly lord. For there is no beast so bold that when I have chidden or rebuked it will dare to eat or drink until I bid. They go to drink in a fountain of mine near by, which a friend of mine guards." Then follows a description of the storm-making fountain and its defender, Brun sans Pitié. "Now tell me," said Calogrenant, "on what you live. Have you a manor in the neighborhood where you sleep or a retreat where you take your meat and whatsoever you need to live?" He answered that he ate nothing but herbs and roots of the wood just like these other beasts; "for I do not care for other food, and these are all my arts, and I have no desire to have an abode but only a rough oak where I may rest at night, and when it is cold and stormy, to be clad as you see. If it is cold and I need to warm myself, I have a fire as long as I like; and if I wish to eat meat I always have as much as I want." "Truly," said Calogrenant, "you are a lord when you thus have your desires." The "hom sauvage" then directs Calogrenant to a hermitage, where he is well entertained before going on to the fountain.

Now anyone familiar with Calogrenant's meeting with the

Giant Herdsman as he relates it in Crestien's *Ivain* [39] will detect at once a close resemblance to the account we have just quoted from the *Livre d'Artus*. Besides the name of the hero and the location in the forest of Broceliande and the general similarity in the situations, there are the following correspondences in detail: the clearing, the stump, the club, the herdsman's blackness, huge head, large hanging ears, wide mouth, hump back, hide covering, and his height of seventeen or eighteen feet. In *Ivain* the dialog at times is almost identical with that in the *Livre d'Artus*. In the former Calogrenant asks: "What man art thou?" "Such as thou seest. I am never anyone else." "What dost thou do here?" "I was watching over these beasts throughout this wood." And after describing the method by which he tamed their fierceness, the Herdsman says, "Thus I am lord of my beasts." It seems therefore highly probable that the author of the *Livre d'Artus* used *Ivain* or, since we know that Crestien stuck close to his source, the source of *Ivain*. But Miss Paton, Freymond, Zenker have contended that the *Livre d'Artus* embodies in its picture of the Giant Herdsman certain authentic features from tradition not supplied by Crestien.[40] The bulls that constitute in *Ivain* the forest herd [41] are replaced in the *Livre d'Artus* by stags, hinds, and bucks. Now in *Owain* the Giant Herdsman summons the animals by striking a stag; in the *Vita* Merlin rides upon a stag, and in the *Frenzy of Suibhne* the mad prophet sings, "Thou stag, . . . pleasant is the place for seats on the top of thy antler points." Again *Ivain* does not mention the Herdsman's diet of roots and herbs; but the *Vita* expressly says that Merlin eats the fruit of herbs, herbs, the fruit of trees, and the berries of the bramble-bush. Since, however, the *Livre d'Artus* shows no other signs of connection with the *Vita*, I believe it must have derived these two traits from the Merlin tradition, not from that book. It is furthermore worthy of note that whereas the normal development in Arthurian romance is continually to minimize the supernatural element, the Merlin of the *Livre d'Artus*, unlike the Merlin of the *Vita*,[42] has no fear of the elements, but boasts his supernatural powers as coolly as in *Ivain* or *Owain*.

[39] Ll. 279–355.
[40] *PMLA*, XXII, 269 f; *ZfSL*, XVII ¹, 56 n. 1; *Bhft ZrP*, LXX, 245.
[41] Certain MSS. mention lions, leopards, bears. *PMLA*, XX, 686 n. 1.
[42] L. 84.

The conclusion of it all is that Merlin the Shapeshifter manifests a predilection for precisely the same forms as Curoi, — the churl, the Giant Herdsman, the Man of the Woods, — and that this predilection was not an arbitrary invention of Geoffrey's, but was an established tradition into which Geoffrey or his source introduced some Oriental stories of prophetic power.[43] And accordingly it seems that when the legends of Curoi swept over Wales and certain story-tellers were passing them on as stories of Gwri, Gwrnach, Gwrvan, Gware, and so forth, other story-tellers, recognizing the similarity of Curoi to their own Myrddin, attached some of these stories to him. It is exactly the same process as occurred when the Romans attached the Greek legends of Aphrodite to Venus, of Hera to Minerva, of Hermes to Mercury, of Kronos to Saturn. In much the same sense, then, as we say that Vulcan is Hephaistos or Diana is Artemis, we may say that Merlin is Curoi.

Other clues lead us to the same destination. We have already noted that Merlin on one occasion transformed himself into a stag with a white fore-foot. In the lai of *Tyolet* [44] and in the Dutch *Lancelot* [45] we find a story in which the stag and his white foot seem to play a part analogous to that of the mule and his bridle, which we have already studied. A damsel appears at Arthur's court and promises either her own hand or that of her queen to the knight who shall bring her the stag's foot. Kay sets out but turns back in fright. The hero, however, successfully encounters seven lions which guard the stag, cuts off the white foot, whereupon a knight immediately appears, who deals him a treacherous blow. Here the False Claimant motif is interwoven, but in the *Tyolet* version the story ends properly with the marriage of the hero to the damsel for whom he had procured the stag's white foot. Miss Weston perceived that the stag was "the enchanted relative of the princess who sought the hero's aid," and I have little doubt that, like the mule, he is the old god transformed, and that his white foot is his external soul, or at least the seat of his power. Irish gods who took on the stag's shape were Donn and Mongan.[46] And in view of

---

[43] Cuchulinn possesses prophetic powers. *Archaeological Rev.*, I, 70.

[44] *Rom*, VIII, 45–50.

[45] Weston, *Leg. of Lancelot*, 30–32.

[46] *PRIA*, XXXIV, C, 160; K. Meyer, A. Nutt, *Voyage of Bran*, I, 26; II, 78 f.

the recognized phenomenon that Irish saints absorbed characteristics of pagan deities, it is not without significance that Patrick transformed himself into a stag.[47] Miss Weston also notes the fact that Merlin transforms himself into a stag with a white forefoot, and that in the *Queste del Saint Graal* a stag guarded by four lions actually turns into Christ with the four Evangelists.[48] In identifying the stag, certainly a metamorphosed god, with Christ, the author of the *Queste* has done exactly what we saw had taken place in the modern Irish folktale, where the part of Curoi is played by the Hung-up Naked Man. The author makes a like substitution when he implies that the mysterious voice which is constantly heard threatening or commanding, is that of God, while a similar voice in the *Didot Perceval* is said to be that of Merlin.[49]

Another of Merlin's protean changes brings us to the same conclusion. In the well-known story of the begetting of Arthur as we have it in Geoffrey of Monmouth Merlin transforms himself and Uter in order to gain access to Igerna. Miss Schoepperle demonstrated that the part of Uter is due to a misinterpretation of the phrase applied to Arthur, *mab uter*, meaning either "terrible (or wonderful) youth," or "son of Uter." [50] Gruffydd has advanced the theory that according to one tradition at least the father of Arthur was really Merlin.[51] This view gains support from a statement in the *Livre d'Artus* that Merlin carried Arthur's mother away to the Chastel de la Merveille.[52] Now oddly enough, in *Diu Krone* the enchanter who carries Arthur's mother to the same castle is Gansguoter,[53] and Gansguoter, we have seen, is manifestly Curoi. So once more we are forced to recognize a tradition which equated Merlin with Curoi.

Merlin's extraordinary interest in the fortunes of Arthur thus becomes clearly motivated. To be sure, in the *Didot Perceval* he displays equal solicitude for the hero, who is son of Alain le Gros,[54] and in the *Huth Merlin* he watches over Balaain, the son

[47] C. Plummer, *Vit. Sanct. Hib.*, I, cxxxii, cxxxvi; *Tripartite Life*, ed. W. Stokes, I, 47.
[48] Ed. Pauphilet, 234 f.
[49] Weston, *Leg. of Perceval*, II, 21, 56.
[50] *Vassar Mediaeval Studies*, 4 f.
[51] *Cymmrodorion Soc. Trans.*, 1912–13, 79.
[52] Sommer, *op. cit.*, VII, 244.
[53] Ed. Scholl, ll. 20380 ff.
[54] *Cf.* Weston, *Leg. of Perceval*, II, 230.

of the King of Northumberland. One must grant that in these heroes Merlin's interest is not paternal. Nevertheless in all three cases Merlin, the old god, seems to act as a sort of omniscient and omnipotent arranger of tests and master of ceremonies, with all good will conducting the heroes through the trials and struggles which fall to their lot.

It is fitting then, that we should close this part of the book with Merlin for he exemplifies in his attitude toward Arthur, Perceval, and Balaain that curious mingling of the kindly helper and contriver of perilous tests for the young god which we have found so characteristic a tradition of Celtic and Arthurian romance. It is also fortunate that in Merlin at last we have a god who can produce explicit evidence of his divinity. Doubtless some readers have thought that while the various figures considered did possess supernatural traits, it was rash to call them divine. But of Merlin — and as we shall see later — of Morgan le Fay, the Grail Bearer, and the original of the Fisher King, the word god or goddess is actually used. Not only does a Welsh triad call Britain Merlin's Close,[55] not only does *Claris and Laris* refer to Merlin as he "who knows all, does all, and sees all." [56] But also the *Vulgate Lancelot* states that he "knew all the wisdom that can descend from the devils, and therefore he was so feared of the Britons and so honored that all called him the holy prophet and all the lesser folk their god." [57]

[55] Rhys, *Hib. Lec.*, 168.
[56] *Claris and Laris*, ed. J. Alton, l. 22236.
[57] Sommer, III, 19. *Cf. Rom*, XXII, 515.

# BOOK THREE
THE CULT OF THE GRAIL

# CHAPTER XV

## THE ANCESTORS OF GALAAD

THE legends of the Grail are perhaps the most tantalizing in all Arthurian romance. That "saintisme vaiselle" is of all enigmas the most enigmatic. The very meaning of the word Grail has from the earliest times been so obscure as to prompt various ingenious interpretations,[1] though now the best scholarly judgment accepts the derivation from Latin *cratalis**, meaning a bowl.[2] But what the vessel itself signified, what the quest, what the strange consequences of asking a simple question, and what the multitudinous phantasmagoric adventures that led to and away from it — what all these might mean has allured the minds of multitudes to the study of these ancient romances. Scholars, poets, mystics have followed in the track of Perceval, Lancelot, Boors, and Galaad, and hoped to find somewhere along their mazy wanderings some hermit to expound the mystery, to meet some errant damsel riding a white mule, who would answer their questions, or to hear a celestial voice revealing from the clouds the meaning of these high adventures and these solemn symbols.

There is no questioning the fact that the scholars who have offered the three chief solutions for the problem of the Grail have been able to make out an excellent case.[3] The Grail as Celtic talisman, as fertility symbol, as Christian relic, — each conception is supported by masses of detailed evidence. The judicious scholar is driven to admit that the Grail has signified many things to many men at many times. Each interpretation is partially true for us just as it was true for the redactor who placed that particular interpretation on it. There is, of course, no doubt that from about 1190, when Robert de Boron wrote his *Joseph*, to our own day the predominant interpretation of the Grail has been Christian: the statement that the Grail was the cup of the Last Supper and the cup in which Joseph of Arimathea caught the blood of the Crucified are explicit. Though Wolfram von Eschenbach and Heinrich von dem Türlin conceive the Grail itself differently, yet both regard it as Chris-

[1] *Cf.* Chap. III.    [2] *MP*, XIII, 684.    [3] Bruce, *Evolution*, I, 219–89.

tian. Scholars like Pauphilet, Miss Peebles, and Miss Fisher,[4] who have interpreted for us the Christian ideology of the Grail romances, are performing a great service in illuminating the later stages of the tradition.

Yet the Christian aspect of the legend is but one aspect, — the least baffling, the least mysterious. Before Boron there was Crestien's *Conte del Graal*, written between 1174 and 1177, the earliest datable Grail story extant. In his account of the strange scene in the castle of the Maimed King there is not a trace of Christian symbolism or association. The glittering vessel borne by a maiden is called "*a* graal," not "the Graal," as if it were not the one and only cup of the Last Supper, but simply a bowl. Later in the poem, to be sure, the published text does mention the host or sacred wafer of the mass as kept in this "graal," but Brown has shown good reason to suspect that this is a scribal interpolation.[5] The exiguousness of the Christian connections of the Grail in Crestien is significant. Throughout the romances of this cycle, moreover, glimmerings of seasonal myth, of phallic ritual, of Celtic vessels of plenty, of divine weapons, can be spied here and there. To study the Grail Legend is to dig down through the ruins of buried cities, to uncover layer after layer of extinct civilizations and forgotten religions. The problem is not simple, nor is the answer. It will be our task in the following chapters to distinguish as clearly as possible the various non-Christian strata which underlie the Temple of the Grail.

Prosaic and plodding though the prospect may seem, let us begin by studying the names of the ancestors of the Grail hero Galaad. We have found that many a mystery yields its secret to this method of investigation. We shall, I believe, discover the same clear indication of Celtic origin that we have found elsewhere.

The most extended account of the early history of the Grail, its origin as a relic which had touched the lips and held the blood of the Savior of the World, its acquisition by Joseph of Arimathea, its transportation to Britain, and the many marvels and miracles which attended those who cared for it until the time of Arthur, is in the first part of the Vulgate cycle, called the

---

[4] A. Pauphilet, *Études sur la Queste del S. Graal; Bryn Mawr Monographs*, IX; L. A. Fisher, *Mystic Vision in the Grail Legend*.

[5] *MLN*, XLI, 226.

*Estoire del Saint Graal.*[6] It contains the names and the stories of the ancestors of the Grail hero, who in this cycle is Galaad. Among the ancestors is a Celidoine. He is distinguished by his precocious youth, his gift of prophecy, his knowledge of the stars, his occasional solitary sojourns in the forest. Now Merlin in his function of the Man of the Wood had a special epithet Merlin Silvester or Celidonius. Giraldus Cambrensis, indeed, on the basis of the diverse activities of Merlin and the length of time over which his activities extended, concluded that there were two Merlins, Merlin Ambrosius and Merlin Silvester or Celidonius.[7] But Lot has shown that they were indeed one.[8] The latter appellation means "of Scotland." As Giraldus puts it, he was called Celidonius "from the Caledonian Forest in which he prophesied." Certain essential features of the story of Merlin are his precocious youth, his gift of prophecy, his knowledge of the stars, his life in the forest. Is it possible that Celidoine is Merlin Celidonius?

In spite of the fact that Celidoine is exactly the form which Celidonius would take when Gallicized (Antonius > Antoine), yet this identification must seem highly improbable at first glance to those who know the story of Celidoine. For the *Estoire del Saint Graal* is an edifying story of missionary enterprise, of the discomfiture and conversion of heathen kings, of the miraculous escapes of the propagators of Christianity, of voyages in self-propelled ships, and so forth. It is perfectly clear that the author has drawn on all manner of Oriental and Western pious legends, on the Bible, on Robert de Boron's *Joseph*, and so forth.[9] As Lot has said, the author was a learned clerk, one who worked with conscious purpose.[10] Does either of these facts eliminate the possibility that one of his sources was Celtic tradition, and that Celidoine is Celidonius? Are there other traces of the legendary lore of Wales and Ireland?

At the very beginning of the *Estoire* we find, as Nutt pointed out,[11] an introduction which seems closely related to Celtic hagiological tradition. The author relates that as he lay in his

---

[6] Sommer, I.

[7] *Itinerarium Cambriae*, Bk. II, ch. 8.

[8] *Annales de Bretagne*, XV, 333.

[9] Bruce, *op. cit.*, I, 386–91. Even Bruce, however, admits the influence of the Celtic *Voyage of St. Brendan* (p. 391, note 36).

[10] F. Lot, *Étude sur le Lancelot*, 212.

[11] *Studies on the Legend*, 264.

hut in one of the wildest parts of Britain, 717 years after the
Passion of Christ, Christ appeared to him and gave him a book
which would silence his doubts regarding the Trinity. The
next day, Good Friday, he is lifted up to Heaven, and sees the
Trinity itself. But on Easter the precious book has disappeared
and a voice tells him that he must go to Norway under the
guidance of a snow-white beast, with the head and neck of a
sheep, legs of a dog, body of a wolf, and tail of a lion. He
follows the guiding beast, which reminds us in more ways than
one of the beast in the *Chevalier du Papegau;* [12] passes an Adventurous Pine; spends a night in the castle of a hospitable
knight; celebrates mass in a nunnery; and on the third day
finds the book in a beautiful chapel. He returns with it and at
God's command begins copying it with divinely provided pen,
ink, parchment, and knife. In two versions of the Brendan
legend, the Celtic origin of which is unquestioned, we learn that
the saint burns a book which contains too many marvels for
his belief. In one version the voice of God rebukes him and
tells him that he must wander on the ocean for nine years till
he has verified what he has read. In the other version he must
wander till he find again the book he has destroyed, which
would be resting upon the tongue of an ox with burning eyes.
The parallel is clear. It is conceded on all sides that the Brendan
legend is an ecclesiasticized form of the pagan legend of the
*Voyage of Bran.* And it would seem as if the *Estoire,* which in
the first few pages introduces us to a guiding beast and a hospitable host, bade fair to contain other elements from Celtic
paganism.

In the *Estoire* there is among the ancestors of Galaad, as we
have noted, a Celidoine. Let us compare him more closely with
a possible Celtic prototype, the Welsh god, Merlin Celidonius.[12a]
To be sure, the story of Celidoine reads for the most part like
one of these apocryphal stories of evangelism. It may even be
that chance accounts for the fact that he was born at midday
the first of June, and that the sun appeared as at rising and the
stars came out at the moment of his birth [13] — signs of a solar
nature in the child.[14] It may also be chance that as the child

[12] *Cf.* Chap. XII.
[12a] Heinzel suggested the connection, *Denkschriften K. Akad., Wien, p. h.
Cl.,* XL, 144.
[13] Sommer, I, 108.
[14] Hermes was born at sunrise. Pauly-Wissowa, VIII, 779.

Merlin was to be slain to provide the foundations of a tower,[15] so Celidoine was to be slain by hurling down from a tower.[16] But it cannot be coincidence that both Merlin and Celidoine are distinguished for their life in the woods, their preternatural knowledge, and their study of the stars. Merlin's life in the forest is stressed both in Geoffrey's *Vita* and in the story of Grisandole.[17] Celidoine twice in the course of the *Estoire* is represented as living in the forest. It is said that when he was borne away miraculously from the tower, he was put down on an island. "When he saw himself in such a strange place, closed on one side by a savage forest and on the other by mountains and great, marvelous cliffs, which he was not accustomed to see, then he was not at ease but sore afraid, and began to complain to himself." [18] Again in the middle of the *Estoire* when Joseph of Arimathea and his company come to Galafort in Britain they find that Celidoine has already arrived there before them, and that he has been spending the four months since his arrival in a forest nearby.[19]

Of all the characters in the *Estoire* Celidoine is most distinguished for his preternatural knowledge. It is said of him that at the age of ten he knew more than any other child of his age.[20] Compare the statement in Geoffrey's *History* concerning the boy Merlin: "All they that stood by were no less astonished at such wisdom being found in him." [21] It is Celidoine who discomfits the philosophers of King Ganor, as Merlin discomfits the wizards of King Vortigern. Perhaps the most striking coincidence lies in the fact that Celidoine prophesies the death of King Label, who had caused him to be brought as a prisoner from the forest, and whose daughter he later marries,[22] and that Merlin prophesies the death of King Rodarchus, who on a previous occasion had caused him to be brought as a prisoner from the forest, and who had previously married Merlin's sister.[23]

---

[15] Geoffrey of Monmouth, *Historia*, Bk. VI, ch. 17.

[16] Sommer, I, 110.

[17] Geoffrey of Monmouth, *Vita*, ll. 74 ff; 416 ff; 533 ff. Sommer, II, 88, 284–91.

[18] Sommer, I, 142.

[19] *Ibid.*, 219.

[20] *Ibid.*, 143.

[21] Geoffrey, *History*, Bk. VI, ch. 19.

[22] Sommer, I, 143, 147, 243.

[23] Geoffrey, *Vita*, ll. 121 ff, 478 ff.

Again our suspicions of identity are reinforced when we read that, like Merlin, Celidoine "knew all the course of the stars so that it was a marvel, and thereby he was able to know concerning things to come." [24] Celidoine prophesies the invasion of the Saxons just as Merlin did. [25] The *Queste del Saint Graal* echoes this astronomical knowledge of Celidoine's: "He knew the course of the stars and the planets and the behavior of the firmament as well or better than the philosophers knew it." [26] And most significantly it adds: "He was the first Christian king who ruled the realm of Scotland." We know from Giraldus that Merlin derived his title Celidonius from his association with Scotland. Though successfully disguised in saintly wrappings, Celidoine is the old Welsh prophet and god, Merlin.

This identification suggests that other ancestors of Galaad might be masquerading divinities. There can be no doubt that the author of the *Estoire* was deliberately connecting stories that he knew about the cup of the Last Supper with the Celtic traditions about Arthur. Since his theme is the transference of the Grail to Britain and its preservation there under the care of a series of guardians, we may expect to find among these guardians, ancestors of the Grail hero, some whose names are distinctively Hebraic, and some whose names are Celtic. Here is a list of Galaad's maternal ancestors: Bron (brother-in-law of Joseph of Arimathea according to Robert de Boron) heads the line, and is followed in succession by Alain le Gros, Josue, Aminadap, Catheloys (or Cartelois), Manaal, Lambar, Pellean, Pelles. [27] Parallel with this line, all of whom but Bron are Keepers of the Grail, is a line of kings closely associated with the Grail. The two lines meet when King Pelles' daughter conceives a child by Lancelot. Lancelot's family tree starts with a heathen king Evalach, and his brother-in-law, Seraphe. On their conversion to Christianity they take the names of Mordrain and Nasciens. [28] From Nasciens there descended seven kings and two knights, as follows: Celidoine, Marpus, Nasciens II, Alain le Gros, Ysaies or Helyas, Jonas, Lancelot I, Ban, Lancelot II (the hero of the Lancelot cycle), and Galaad. [29]

[24] Sommer, I, 291.
[25] *Ibid.*, 292. Geoffrey, *Vita*, ll. 948.
[26] Sommer, VI, 97.
[27] *Ibid.*, I, 286–90.
[28] *Ibid.*, 74 f.
[29] *Ibid.*, 293; *cf.* VI, 97.

Clearly these lists of the ancestors of Galaad contain a number of Biblical names: Josue, Aminadap, Jonas, Ysaies. There are four, moreover, whose derivation seems uncertain: Seraphe, Helyas,[30] Marpus and Catheloys. The remainder, including Celidoine, we may properly suspect of Celtic origin: the two Alains, Pelles, Pellean, Lambar, Manaal, Bron, the two Nasciens, the two Lancelots, Ban, Evalach, Mordrain. Alain is the Breton Alan, which might easily have been substituted for Welsh Arawn, Prince of Annwn (the Other World),[31] just as Winlowen was substituted for Gwenhwyvar. Pelles or Pelle[32] suggests Belli, and Pellean the variant Belin or Bellinus. There seem to to have been various human Belis in Welsh history,[33] and the name may be connected with Irish Bile.[34] But we shall accumulate abundant proofs before we get through that Beli came to be used almost interchangeably with Belin, and that the latter was a divine name, probably going back to the Apollo Bellinus or Belinos of the inscriptions.[35] The name Pellinor which has worried scholars by its perverse occurrence, time and again, in places where one expected Pelles or Pellean,[36] is very simply explained as Beli Mawr, "Beli the Great," a common appellation. In fact, Bellinor occurs in the *Prose Tristan* as a form of Pellinor.[37] Lambar recalls the epithet of Lug, Lamfada, which we know must have been represented in Welsh or Cornish because of its survivals in Lampadaiz or Lambegues.[38] Manaal suggests a corruption of Manawyddan, or Manawyd, the name of the Welsh sea-god. Bron has been proved by Nitze to be derived from the Irish and Welsh god Bran.[39] Ban also is found in the form Brauz,[40] hardly to be explained unless the common original were Bran plus the French nominative ending in *s* or *z*.

[30] *Cf.* Chap. XXXI.

[31] Mabinogi of *Pwyll Prince of Dyved*. On Annwvn *cf. Folklore*, XVIII, 121; *ZcP*, I, 29.

[32] F. Lot, *op. cit.*, 243.

[33] J. Rhys, J. B. Jones, *Welsh People*, 41–3; *Bhft ZrP*, LX, 199 f.

[34] *Ibid.*

[35] Holder, *Altceltischer Sprachschatz, sub* Belenos.

[36] *MP*, XVI, 122, 347.

[37] E. Löseth, *Tristan en Prose*, 498. At an uncertain date the laws of lenation caused Beli Mawr to be pronounced Beli Vawr; but this pronunciation could also produce French Belinor, for Belivor would be written Beliour, which might easily be misread Belinor.

[38] *Cf.* Chap. IX.

[39] *Medieval Studies in Memory of Gertrude Schoepperle Loomis.*

[40] Crestien de Troyes, *Erec*, ed. Foerster, variant reading, l. 1975.

Ban is usually called Ban de Benoic, easily accounted for as a misunderstanding of Bran le Benoit, an exact translation of the Welsh Bendigeid Bran, or "Bran the Blessed." Evalach occurs in the *Queste* as Anelac,[41] a form which points to a common original Aualach, the Welsh god Avallach, put forward by Rhys as the original of Evalach.[42] Lancelot du Lac we have already traced back through Welsh Llenlleawc or Lleminawc, epithet of Llwch, to the Irish god Lugh Loinnbheimionach.

There remain Nasciens and Mordrain. Both these names are under suspicion of being corrupted. The spelling of Nasciens seems due, as Moland ingeniously suggested,[43] to an attempt to connect it with *nascor*, for the name seems to mean "first-born in the truth." Likewise Mordrain is said to mean "slow of belief," [44] and Moland proposed that the romancer connected the name with Latin *moror* and *credere*.[45] The conjecture that Mordrain is a substitution for some form like Morcred is strengthened by the occurrence, in Gerbert de Montreuil's form of the conversion legend, of the variant Mordrach.[46] At any rate, both Mordrach and hypothetical Morcred clearly suggest the name of Arthur's nephew (or son) Mordrec,[47] which undoubtedly derives from the Welsh Medrot or Medrod. In a certain Welsh triad we find mentioned together, as "men of such gentle, kindly, and fair words that anyone would be sorry to refuse them anything," Nasiens, King of Denmark, and Medrod.[48] The correspondence of these names to the Nasciens and Mordrain or Mordrach of Grail tradition can hardly be accounted for by chance. The connection of Nasiens with Denmark need not baffle us, since Zimmer has demonstrated that Geoffrey's Gormundus, King of the Africans, is really the Viking Godrum, leader of the "black heathen." [49] For the Irish and Welsh used thus to refer to the Danes. The *Annales Cambriae*, for instance,

[41] Nutt, *Studies*, 268.

[42] J. Rhys, *Arthurian Legend*, 324, 337. *Cf*. Chap. XIX.

[43] L. Moland, *Origines littéraires de la France*, 38.

[44] Sommer, I, 75.

[45] See note 43.

[46] Nutt, *Studies*, 24. Probably the name Maurdrannus cited by Bruce, *MLN*, XXXIV, 385 ff, had some influence.

[47] *Huth Merlin*, ed. Paris, Ulrich, I, 204 ff.

[48] Foerster, *Myvyrian Archaiology*,[2] 393a.

[49] *Gött. gel. Anz.*, 1890, 823. *Cf*. Loth, *Mab.*[2], I, 362, where Edern son of Nudd, the Arthurian hero Ider, is prince of the men of Denmark, who were clothed in jet-black with white borders, and were referred to as the jet-black troop.

calls them *gentiles nigri*. The Gormundus parallel shows that it was quite easy for Nasiens King of Denmark to become Nasciens King of the Saracens, who were of course more familiar to Bretons of the twelfth century as "black heathen" than the Danes. Nor need the fact that Medrot developed into Mordred, the villain of Geoffrey of Monmouth and later Arthurian tradition, prevent our identifying Medrot with Mordrach or Mordrain, for the triad quoted shows that the Welsh sometimes at least conceived him in a favorable light.[50] We may feel satisfied, then, that this triad preserves for us the originals of Nasciens and Mordrach.

Of those names in the lists of the ancestors of Galaad which are not obviously Biblical an extraordinary proportion seem to be either corruptions of the names of Welsh gods or else deliberate modifications of such names for the purpose of etymologizing. This hypothesis is confirmed when we find two of them, Bron and Manaal, closely corresponding in name to two possessors of magic caldrons which may be equated with the Grail. Manawyd, who corresponds to Manaal, is said to be Perpetual Keeper of the Caldron of Britain.[51] In later chapters we shall see how strong was the connection of Manawyd or Manawyddan with the Grail cycle. Bron's counterpart, Bran, as Nutt showed,[52] possesses a caldron, the property of which was that if a man were slain and were cast therein, tomorrow he would be as well as ever he was at the best, except that he would not regain his speech. Nutt, moreover, pointed out that the Irish Bran, the great voyager, and his Welsh namesake, possessor of a reviving caldron and according to a triad promulgator of Christianity in Britain, would naturally be selected for the rôle to which he is assigned by Robert de Boron: that of Grail Keeper, voyager, and Christianizer of Britain. Nitze has published in *Medieval Studies in Memory of Gertrude Schoepperle Loomis* a powerful case for the identity of Bron and Bran.

One more point must be noted here. The Welsh word *Pen*, meaning the Head or Chief, was a common title for the Old God. We remember how Kilhwch asks Custennin, "Art thou the Head?" and receives the apt reply, "There is no hurt to in-

[50] *Cf.* Chap. XXXIII.
[51] *Irish Nennius*, ed. J. H. Todd, lviii.
[52] Nutt, *Studies*, 219 f.

jure me but my own." [53]   Pwyll and Arawn are called **Pen Annwn** or Chief of the Other World.[54]   If we realize that **Pen** also means head in the physical sense and that the Old God had a notorious fondness for decapitation, it becomes easy to understand the strange tale in the Mabinogi, *Branwen*, of the Entertainment of the Noble Head.[55]   We learn that after his wounding at the battle in Ireland, Bran instructed his men to cut off his head, and carry it to London to be buried.  He said, "A long time will you be upon the road," and mentioned particularly Harlech and the island of Grassholm off Pembrokeshire as places where they would sojourn long.  Of the Entertainment of the Head we read that they stopped at Harlech and "they provided meat and liquor, and sat down to eat and drink."  In the island of Grassholm they found "a fair and regal spot overlooking the ocean; and a spacious hall was therein. . . . And that night they regaled themselves and were joyful.  And of all they had seen of food laid before them, and of all they had heard of they remembered nothing; neither of that nor of any sorrow whatsoever. And there they remained four-score years, unconscious of having ever spent a time more joyous and mirthful. . . . And it was not more irksome to them . . . than if the Blessed Bran had been with them himself.  And because of these four-score years it was called the Entertaining of the Noble Head."  Most significantly we find in the colophon references to the "Entertainment of Bran" and the "Sojourning of the Head." [56]   It seems highly likely that the whole story is invented to explain the phrase, "the Entertaining of the Noble Head," which doubtless referred to the ambrosial feasts of the god Bran, localized at Harlech, where he was said to have held his court, and also on the island of Grassholm.  Bran *is* the Noble Head.

This supposition finds strange confirmation in the story of Bron in Robert de Boron's *Joseph*.[57]   Here the company of the faithful starts out on long wanderings in far-off lands.  They become hungry and complain to Bron (not, significantly, to Joseph, their leader).  Bron is to catch a fish (a story invented to explain his sobriquet, the Rich Fisher) — and it is to be

---

[53] *White Book Mabinogion*, ed. J. G. Evans, 237.  *Mabinogion*, ed. Nutt, 117.  *Cf.* Chap. XIII.

[54] *Mabinogion*, ed. Nutt, 4, 9.

[55] *Ibid.*, 39–43.

[56] *Ibid.*, 42 f.

[57] Robert de Boron, *Joseph*, ed. F. X. Michel.

placed on the table with the Holy Vessel. Joseph is to sit where Christ sat at the Last Supper with Bron on his right and an empty place for Bron's son, the Siege Perilous. The Grail then serves as a tester of the righteous, who alone are filled with the sweetness and desire of their hearts. Joseph is instructed by an angel to consign the Grail to Bron, the Rich Fisher, who is to be commander, lord, and master of the Grail.[58] Not a word of the severing of Bron's head, but a very distinct implication that Bron himself, like Bran, is a Noble Head. Another bit of evidence lies in the *Didot Perceval*,[59] where we read that the Fisher King, Bron, dwelt in "the isles of Ireland, in one of the fairest places of the world. And know that he was in the greatest misease that ever man was and had fallen into a great malady." When we realize that Bran had been wounded in the foot before the Noble Head sojourned in the Isle of Grassholm in the midst of the Irish sea, and his followers reveled in "a fair and regal spot overlooking the ocean," the parallel is too clear to miss. But again there is no severed head. That feature is due to a misunderstanding.

Of the twenty three names assigned by the *Estoire del Saint Graal* to the ancestors of Galaad six, then, are definitely identifiable with those of Welsh gods for reasons given above. Here are the corresponding names in parallel columns.

| | |
|---|---|
| Lancelot I | Llenlleawc |
| Lancelot II | Llenlleawc |
| Celidoine | Celidonius |
| Bron | Bran |
| Ban de Benoic | Bendigeid Bran (*le Benoit*) |
| Manaal | Manawyd |

And if we compare eight others with the names of eight other Welsh deities we can hardly attribute the correspondence to chance.

| | |
|---|---|
| Pelle | Belli |
| Pellean | Belin |
| Evalach | Avallach |
| Mordrain | Medrod |
| Nasciens I | Nasiens |
| Nasciens II | Nasiens |
| Alain | Arawn |
| Alain | Arawn |

---

[58] Ll. 3341, 3349.     [59] Weston, *Leg. of Perceval*, II, 12 f.

I venture to state that if anyone were to compûte mathe-
matically the probability that a limited set of names in one
language would correspond so closely to a limited set of names
in another language through mere accident, the odds against it
would be thousands to one.   It would be virtually an impossibility.

Probably the man who first transformed Welsh gods into ancestors of the Grail hero believed, like Wace, that the fables
about Arthur and the Matter of Britain in general were not all
false and not all true; but that the embellishments of the
story-tellers had overlaid a real basis in fact.  He probably
found an account in which the Welsh gods had already been
euhemerized, some of them into kings, some into Keepers of the
Holy Vessel.  This he blended as best he could with the Joseph
conversion legend as he found it in Robert de Boron.   And
with great learning he filled in from all the apocryphal conversion
literature he knew the deficiencies in his Welsh outline of a
dynasty of euhemerized gods.   But like a true medievalist,
while he combined sources with reckless abandon, he did not
throw his sources over altogether.  He was not an original writer
in any modern sense, and it seems clear that his source told more
about Bron, Nasciens, Celidoine and Mordrach than about the
other kings, and that we are able to detect clear signs of that
source only in the case of Celidoine because we know far more
of the Welsh tradition of Merlin Celidonius than of the three
others.

# CHAPTER XVI

## THE GRAIL HEROES

THE names of the Grail Kings as they are given in the *Estoire* show almost exactly what we should expect in a work which was attempting to trace back a Celtic legend to a Christian source: a group of names of which a fair proportion are plainly Biblical, and a larger proportion are more or less clearly corruptions of Celtic names. We have seen that the Celtic names for the most part are those of the more venerable Welsh gods, Bran, Manawyddan, Merlin Celidonius, Arawn, Beli. Let us now look at the names of the heroes who are prominent in the Grail quest.

Here they are: Gawain, Lancelot, Perceval, Boors, Galaad. We already know that Gawain is derived from the Welsh epithet Gwallt Avwyn, applied to Gwrvan, or the little Gwri, who in turn represents little Curoi or Cuchulinn. We have also seen that Lancelot du Lac goes back through the Welsh Llwch Lleminawc to the Irish god Lugh Loinnbheimionach. Boors is also easily disposed of, for the name is usually found in French in the form Bohors. Now Lot has noted that the substitution of *b* for *g* is not a rare occurrence in the romance MSS.[1] Do we find the name Gohors? In what is perhaps our earliest Arthurian poem in French, the *Lai du Cor* (1150–75), there is mentioned a King Gohors.[2] He apparently corresponds to King Bohors, the father of the young Grail Quester. On the first page of the *Vulgate Lancelot* we read:[3] "On the marches of Gaul and Little Britain there were in old times two kings who were brothers. . . . One of the two kings was named King Ban of Benoich, and the other king was named King Bohours of Gannes." Ban we identified in the last chapter with Bran, and the land of Bran was a name applied to north-eastern Wales.[4] Adjoining it was the Wirral peninsula, known as the Retreat of Gwri.[5] The lands of Bran and Gwri would therefore lie together on the borders of Britain and Wales. Can one doubt

---

[1] *Étude sur le Lancelot*, 148 note 8. *Cf. MP*, XVI, 348.
[2] Ed. H. Dörner, l. 421.
[3] Sommer, III, 1.
[4] *Internatl. Cong. for Hist. of Religions*, III, vol 2, 236 f.
[5] *Ibid.*

what has happened? The French author has substituted for Galles Gaule, and has therefore been compelled to substitute the Continental or Little Britain for the insular. Bran le Benoit, we know, has become Ban de Benoich. Gohors of Galles has become Bohours of Gannes. Gohors, of course, can be no other than Bran's neighbor, Gwri, his name developing in much the same way that Gaheres developed from Gware. When we note that there is an older and a younger Boors, we can hardly avoid equating them with Big Gwr and Little Gwr, or Gwrnach and Gwrvan Gwallt Avwyn. The names Boors and Gawain, then, are simply derived from the two parts of the name Gwr(i) Gwallt Avwyn. And everything works out as it should, for we shall see in the next chapter that both Boors and Gawain are credited with the same adventures in Castle Corbenic, — adventures which go back to an ancient Irish tradition concerning adventures of Cuchulinn in Curoi's castle. Boors, the Grail Quester, is then clearly descended from little Gwri and Cuchulinn.

Now Gwri, according to the *Mabinogi* of *Pwyll Prince of Dyved*, was given a second name by which he was known afterwards, namely Pryderi, meaning "anxiety." A story is told to account for this curious name. His mother Rhiannon had given birth to Gwri, but while she and her attendants slept, the child disappeared, and the attendants in order to avoid blame asserted that Rhiannon had devoured him. She was accordingly condemned to sit outside the gate of the palace, tell her story to all strangers, and offer to carry them to the palace. Meanwhile Teirnyon on the night of the first of May discovered a young child left by a monster arm, which had been carrying off his newly born colts. The child grew with astonishing precocity, and revealed a marked resemblance to his father Pwyll. On this discovery Teirnyon journeyed to Pwyll's palace bringing the boy. They sat down to meat with Pwyll and Rhiannon, and the story of the boy's birth was disclosed. Then Rhiannon exclaimed, "I declare to Heaven that if this be true, there is indeed an end to my trouble." "Lady," said Pendaran Dyved, "well hast thou named thy son Pryderi. . . . It were more proper that the boy should take his name from the word his mother spoke when she received the joyful tidings of him." Gruffydd properly remarks: "The explanation of Pryderi is a very poor one, and carries with it its own refutation." [6]

[6] *Cymmrodorion Soc. Trans.*, 1912–3, 59 note.

Now we have learned to suspect that when such a forced anecdote is told to explain a name, it is only a cover for etymologizing some similar name. Now the word for "trouble" or "anxiety" exists in two forms, Pryderi and Pryder.[7] And if we search for a Welsh name for which Pryder might well have been substituted we do not have to search far.

For Peredur is a fairly common name in Celtic literature.[8] An old Welsh poem attributed to Aneurin records that at the battle of Cattraeth, fought at the beginning of the sixth century, Peredur of the steel arms, along with all the rest of the host of Mynyddawc, was slain.[9] In the *Annales Cambriae* we are told under the date 580 that "Guurci et Peretur moritur." [10] A genealogy of the tenth century tells us that these two heroes were the sons of Eleuther Cascordmaur, and Geoffrey of Monmouth mentions in his *History* a King Peredur brother of Elidur and another Peredur son of Eridur, one of Arthur's knights.[11] Since both Eridur and Elidur are admittedly corrupt forms of Eleuther, both these Peredurs are identical with the Peredur of the *Annales*. Another old Welsh poem speaks of the valor of the sons of Eliffer at the battle of Arderydd, dated about 575,[12] and Geoffrey in his *Vita Merlini*, introduces a Peredurus, king of the North Welsh, who fought in that battle, but was not slain.[13] Finally there is in the *Dream of Rhonabwy* a knight of Arthur's, Peredur of the Long Lance,[14] and the same Peredur, son of Evrawc, is doubtless the titular hero of another Welsh tale.[15]

Whether there were one or more historical Peredurs, who were slain or not slain at the battle of Cattraeth or that of Arderydd, I do not know. It is quite possible. All I am concerned to show here is, that the Peredur, son of Eleuther, and brother of Gwrgi, who was said to have fallen in battle, betrays signs of identity with Pryderi, and that under the latter name he is a mythological figure. I shall leave till later chapters the complete demonstration that Pryderi, like Peredur, corresponds to

---

[7] Guest, *Mabinogion*, ed. Nutt, 24 note.
[8] On Peredur see Lot in *Annales de Bretagne*, XV, 530. I am not convinced, however, that Peredur was a hero of Cumbria. Loth, *Mab.*[2], II, 47.
[9] W. F. Skene, *Four Ancient Books*, I, 386.
[10] Loth, *Mab.*[2], II, 373.
[11] Book III, ch. 18: Book IX, ch. 12.
[12] *Univ. Illinois Studies in Lang. and Lit.*, X, No. 3, 128, 18.
[13] *Ibid.*, 30, 32.
[14] Guest, *Mabinogion*, ed. Nutt, 162.
[15] *Ibid.*, 244.

Perceval. But one suggestion of the identity of Pryderi and Peredur I may cite here. As I have said, the *Annales Cambriae* record the death of Peredur and Gwrgi in the same year, 580. Of this tradition the Mabinogi of *Math* seems to afford a vague reminiscence.[16] For it relates that Gwydion,[17] ruler of North Wales, overcame in battle Pryderi, ruler of South Wales,[18] and forced him to flee with great slaughter. "And that he might have peace, Pryderi gave hostages; Gwrgi Gwastra gave he and three and twenty others, sons of nobles." The slaughter however, continued, and Pryderi was slain in single combat with Gwydion. It is related that the hostages were released from prison. "So that youth [apparently Gwrgi] and the other hostages that were with him were set free to follow the men of the South." That is the last we hear of Gwrgi. Whether he was slain later as well as Pryderi we shall probably never know, but it cannot be without significance that a Gwrgi should be closely associated with the deaths of both Peredur and Pryderi.

We have therefore some reason to believe that Pryderi is a name substituted by the South Welsh for the more wide-spread original form Peredur. And the assumption explains a number of facts, for both Peredur and Pryderi seem to be counterparts of Perceval. Peredur son of Eridur is included in Geoffrey's list of Arthur's knights, and Peredur the son of Evrawc is the titular hero of a Welsh romance which contains many adventures corresponding to those of Perceval in Crestien's *Conte del Graal*. In fact, no one will deny that Peredur is the Welsh counterpart of Perceval. Pryderi, under his first name of Gwri, was the original of Gawain,[19] whose career at many points parallels that of Perceval. And in chapters XVIII, XX, and XXII, we shall see how neatly the rôle of Pryderi himself in Welsh tradition corresponds to that of Perceval in the *Conte del Graal*, *Perlesvaus*, and *Didot Perceval*. Thus Peredur and Pryderi are both equated with Perceval and therefore with each other. If Peredur was a historic king, he like Arthur must have been apotheosized. Nothing else can explain his identification with Gwri. Nothing else can explain the fact, pointed out by Lot, that the familiar trait of increasing in strength till noon is attributed to him.[20]

---

[16] *Ibid.*, 62–4.

[17] On the derivation of Gwydion from the Celtic deity Vitionos *cf. International Congress for the History of Religions, Transactions*, III, vol. 2, 241.

[18] *Cf. ZcP*, I, 291.

[19] *Cf.* Chap. VI.      [20] *Rom*, XXIV, 323.

Nothing else can explain why his descendant, Perceval, in the *Perlesvaus* is distinguished by shields bearing the sun, the stag, and the cross: [21] the first two being forms of the pagan deity, and the third the symbol of the Christ, with whom the pagan deity was equated.

Finally, there is Galaad. Now the name in this form, as Heinzel showed,[22] is certainly the Biblical Gilead, which the Latin Vulgate renders Galaad. Moreover, the author of the *Queste*, as Pauphilet showed,[23] was aware that Galaad, which means "Mount of Testimony," had been interpreted by the Cistercian abbot Gillebert in his *Sermon on the Canticles* as Christ, "upon whom are heaped all the testimonies of the prophets, of John, of the Father, and of his own works." But to end our inquiry here would be as incautious as to conclude that because the author of *Perlesvaus* interpreted the name as "loses the valleys" that was the true origin of the name. There can be no doubt whatsoever that the form Perlesvaus is a substitution for Perceval, which in turn is a substitution for Peredur. Now when we find mentioned in the *Lai du Cor*, a poem fifty years or so older than the *Queste*, a King Galahal,[24] and when other derivatives from Welsh solar epithets containing the element Gwallt are scattered about in Arthurian texts, we should at least look for any indication that Galaad is an ingenious substititute for a name derived from the Welsh.

As in the case of Pryderi, we must leave the conclusive demonstration for later chapters, namely XXV, and XXXII. Here I can only put forward some hints. In the first place, if Lancelot has been proven the counterpart of the Welsh Llwch Llawwynnyawc and of King Loth,[25] he should have a son to correspond to Gwair and Gawain. Now practically all we know of Gwair is that he was imprisoned in an island of the sea.[26] In this respect Galaad, who was imprisoned in the isle of Sarras,[27] may be equated with Gwair. His name, moreover, is by no means remote from the earlier form of Gawain, Galvain. And in Galaad's devotion to the service of Perceval's sister we may have a rarefied form of the loves of Gawain and Floree. In the *Queste* we are told that Perceval's sister took from Galaad

[21] Potvin, I, 26, 39, 62.

[22] Heinzel *Über die französischen Gralromane*, 134 f.

[23] *Études sur la Queste*, 137.

[24] Ed. Dörner, l. 500.              [26] Rhys, *Celtic Folklore*, II, 679.

[25] *Cf*. Chap. IX.                   [27] Sommer, VI, 196.

the sword which he wore and girded him with the Sword with the Strange Hangings.[28] "And when she had hung it at his side, she said to him: 'Certes, sire, now reck I not though I die; for now I hold me the most blessed maiden of the world, which hath made the worthiest man of the world knight. For wit ye well ye were not in right case when ye were not dight with the sword which for you was brought upon this earth.' 'Damozel,' said Galaad, 'ye have done so much that I shall be your knight all the days of my life.'" Now in *Perlesvaus* and *Didot Perceval* the father of Perceval is Alain le Gros,[29] and in the *Livre d'Artus* Alain has a daughter Floree, beloved of Gawain.[30] The suggestion is that in the dark backward and abysm of time Perceval's sister was Floree, whose name occurs more frequently than any other as that of Gawain's *amie*.[31] It seems likely, therefore, that just as the Biblical Galaad supplanted the pagan epithet as the name of the Grail hero, so his spiritual devotion to Perceval's sister is the sublimation of a frankly mundane love. If it be objected that the equating of Galaad with Gawain demands a greater degree of correspondence in their adventures than this faintly recognizable identity of their ladies, let the reader suspend judgment till he has at least read Chapter XXV.

The Grail heroes, Gawain, Lancelot, Boors, Perceval, and Galaad, all may claim to be young sun-gods who have descended into Arthurian romance from the realms of Celtic mythology. In fact, it would be logical and natural if other descendants of youthful gods should find a place in the Grail Quest. And so they do. In the solemn scene in the castle of Corbenic [32] when Josephe appears in the vestments of a bishop and performs the miracle of the Eucharist, there strangely are added to the three heroes, Galaad, Perceval, and Boors, nine other knights from Gaul (probably a substitution for *Galles*, Wales), Ireland, and Denmark. Christ himself rises from the Grail, and feeds the twelve kneeling companions with the bread of His body. He tells them that they are twelve because He first administered the sacrament to the twelve apostles. But when we

---

[28] *Ibid.*, 163.

[29] Potvin, I, 332. Many corruptions appear in *MS*.

[30] Sommer, VII, 85.

[31] O. Piper, *Höfisches Epik*, II, 211 f; Heinrich von dem Türlin, *Krone*, l. 1294; *Merveilles de Rigomer*, ed. Foerster, Breuer, ll. 10627 f; Potvin, III, 46; etc. *Cf.* Chap. II.

[32] Sommer, VI, 188–91.

find in *Perlesvaus, Sone de Nansai,* and the *Vulgate Lancelot* [33] feasts of twelve which have no eucharistic associations, and that in the first two romances the feast takes place within the precincts of the Grail, we may well doubt whether the number twelve was not a pagan, perhaps solar, feature. At any rate it is remarkable that the one knight named by the author of the *Queste* as sharing with Galaad, Perceval, and Boors the supreme reward of their holy and ascetic strife is Claudin the son of Claudas,[34] who has not even been mentioned in the *Queste* before. It is still more remarkable when we note that Claudin is the son of that Claudas, whom we beheld not many pages back brandishing his ax before the city gate, and who seemed to be modeled on old Curoi. Claudin himself then would be a young Curoi, and would correspond to Gawain, Galaad, and Bors. The pseudo-Robert de Boron *Queste* furnishes the names of the other eight knights,[35] and they are interesting even though their traditional value may be doubted. One, Persides li Gallois, is clearly a corrupt form of Perceval li Gallois. Another is Lambegues, whom we have identified with Lancelot.[36] There is also Boors' son, Helianz le Blanc, whose name, as we shall see in Chapter XXXI, probably had solar significance. Another of the nine names is Melians de Danemarche, which like its cognate Meleagant is derived from Welsh Melwas, a divine title probably meaning the Prince Youth.[37] It would be foolish to lay too much stress upon the significance of these latter names, but the fact that Claudin, the son of a figure derived from the giant Curoi with his ax, should join at the feast of the Grail Galaad, Perceval, and Boors, who in a sense are no other than Cuchulinn, seems to say the least a strange coincidence. For it points to the conclusion that as the old gods are represented in the Grail Cycle as guardians of the sacred cup, so the younger gods appear as seekers of the vessel. Their names give them away.

[33] Potvin, I, 87; *Sone de Nansai,* ed. M. Goldschmidt, ll. 4829–40; Sommer, *op. cit.,* IV, 264. Laura Hibbard Loomis is preparing an article on the solar twelve in the romances.

[34] Sommer, VI, 192.

[35] *Rom,* XXXVI, 574.

[36] *Cf.* Chap. IX.

[37] Rhys, *Arthurian Legend,* 51.

# CHAPTER XVII

## THE GRAIL CASTLE

Having seen that both Grail Heroes and Grail Kings show traces of descent from Welsh and Irish gods, we may well turn our attention to other features of the Grail tradition. Let us see how far the Grail Castle conforms to Celtic traditions concerning Otherworld dwellings.

Highly significant is Nitze's careful study [1] of the parallels between the Grail Castle as described by Crestien in the *Conte del Graal* and the houses of Irish saga. Perceval entering finds the Fisher King lying on a couch in the midst of the hall. Before him is a fire on a hearth. According to the corresponding passage in Wolfram, Parzival sees besides the couch of the Fisher King a hundred others, and there are three fires in all. Now Nitze has shown that the numerous couches, the central fireplace, with the couch of the chief before it, are regular features in the arrangements of the Irish palace hall, but totally unlike those of a twelfth century French castle. Wolfram's detail of the three fires is matched by the three fire-places in the Mead Hall of Tara. Bruce's attempt [2] to explain these details by assuming that Crestien "purposely made his description archaic," is worthless since he did not show any other source than the *contes bretons* from which Crestien could have derived these not only archaic but also Celtic details.

Besides these general resemblances in architectural features, the Grail Castle shows other resemblances to Celtic fortresses or palaces, especially to the Otherworld fortress of Curoi. We saw in Chapter XI that a certain Brumaut [3] or Bromel, [4] who defended the bridge of the Castle of the Grail, was derived from Curoi in the guise of a churl, famous as a porter of the Other World. The castle of the Grail, then, is an Irish Otherworld fortress, and in a sense, Curoi's fortress.

Again we have seen that Curoi's fortress which revolved every night was really the sky; and though it may seem haz-

[1] *Studies in Honor of A. Marshall Elliott*, I, 19.
[2] Bruce, *Evolution*, I, 275.
[3] Sommer, V, 294 f; 327 note.          [4] Malory, Bk. XI, ch. 3, 4.

ardous to suggest it, the *Jüngere Titurel* of Albrecht von Scharfenberg contains an elaborate description of the Grail Temple which seems to reflect that ancient image.[5] Of course, most of the details in the German poem are comparatively late inventions, but a few seem to point to the original conception. Zarncke, indeed, suspected that "various hands at various times" had contributed to the description.[6] The Grail Temple was round. The dome was covered with blue sapphire, strewn with carbuncles which shone like the sun, whether the night was light, dim, or dark. The golden sun and silver moon were also set in the dome, and were moved by a hidden mechanism through their courses. The rest of the Temple seems as clearly to be a miniature replica of the earth, the whole forming a sort of microcosm. The walls were green with emerald. The arches were like green bows of gold, filled with birds. Vines intertwined through the arches and hung down over the stalls. Below sprouted all manner of flowers, white and red roses on green stems, and all manner of herbs, both stalk and foliage of gold colored with green.

The parallel between the Grail Castle and Curoi's fortress is even more strongly revealed in the account of the perils endured by Boors, Gawain, and Galaphes in the Palace Adventurous of the Grail Castle and in the perils of Curoi's castle as described in *Bricriu's Feast*. Let me begin with the account of Gawain's adventures at Corbenic, the Grail Castle, related in the *Vulgate Lancelot*.[7] I quote freely from Miss Weston's fine translation.[8]

Gawain comes towards evening to a castle surrounded by water, where he desires to lie for the night. On his arriving and announcing his name, the knights made the greatest joy in the world. "There came forth from a chamber, a knight, who led with him many other knights; and he was the fairest man that Sir Gawain had beheld since he left his own land." The King welcomed the stranger, and while they were speaking a dove entered with a censer. "There came forth from the chamber wherein the dove had entered a damsel, the fairest he had beheld any day of his life. . . . She came forth from the chamber bearing in her hands the richest vessel that might be beheld by the eye of mortal man. 'Twas made in the semblance of a

[5] O. Piper, *Höfisches Epik*, II, 465 ff.
[6] *Sächsische Gesellschaft d. Wiss., Abh.*, Phil. Hist. Kl., VII, 391.
[7] Sommer, IV, 343–7.     [8] J. L. Weston, *Gawain at the Grail Castle*, 54 ff.

chalice, and she held it on high above her head. . . . The King
and his knights, as the damsel passed them by, all kneeled low
before the holy vessel; and forthwith were all the tables re-
plenished with the choicest meats in the world. . . . Sir
Gawain followed her with his eyes as long as he might, and when
he saw her no more he looked on the table before him, and saw
naught that he might eat, for 'twas void and bare. . . . And
when he saw this he was sore abashed, and knew not what he
might say or do, since he deemed well that he had in some point
transgressed. . . . So he withheld him from asking till that they
were risen from the table, but then all gat them forth from the
palace . . . and when he himself would have gone forth into
the courtyard below he might no longer do so, for all the doors
were fast shut."

Presently a dwarf appeared and was about to strike Gawain
with a staff, but Gawain wrested it from him, and the dwarf
departed. "Sir Gawain looked toward the head of the hall and
saw there one of the richest couches in the world, and he made
haste towards it for there would he lie. But even as he set
him down he heard a maiden cry upon him, 'Ha! Sir knight,
thou diest an thou liest there unarmed, for 'tis the Couch
Adventurous, but look ye, yonder lie arms, take them and lie ye
down an ye will.'" Gawain armed himself. "But scarce had
he set him down when he heard a cry, the most fell he had ever
heard, and he thought him well 'twas the voice of the foul fiend.
With that there came forth swiftly from a chamber a lance
whereof the blade was all afire, and it smote Sir Gawain so
hardly that despite shield and hauberk it pierced his shoulder
through and through. And he fell swooning, but anon he felt
how one drew out the lance. . . . Long time did Sir Gawain
abide there, and when night fell — so that he saw but ill save
for the light of the moon, which shone through more than forty
windows, which were all open — then he looked towards the
chamber which was nighest him and beheld a dragon, the
greatest he had ever seen. . . . Its eyes were red and swollen,
and its mouth huge and gaping." The dragon played about,
turned on its back, cast forth from its mouth five hundred young
dragons. Then a leopard entered and fought with the dragon.
Then followed a combat between the old and the young dragons,
till both old and young died. "Then the windows of the hall
clap to, the one after the other, with so great a noise it seemed

the palace must fall; and there came therein a wind, so great and so strong that it swept clear the rushes from the floor."

Then after a while twelve damsels entered weeping, and said, "Dear Lord God, when shall we be delivered from this pain?" They kneeled to pray at the door where the dove had entered, and then after a great while departed. "Sir Gawain saw come forth from a chamber a great knight, all armed, shield at neck, and sword in hand;" and after bidding the hero depart, he fought with him till both were exhausted. "And so spent and so weary were they that they might not lift their heads, but lay on the ground even as they had swooned. Great while they lay thus, . . . then the palace began to shake, and the windows to clap together, and it began to thunder and lighten, as 'twas the worst weather in the world, save that it rained not." There followed the sound of sweet chanting, "Glory and praise and honor be unto the King of Heaven!" but Gawain could see nothing and "deemed not they were of earth, but rather things spiritual." "Then he saw come forth from a chamber the damsel who the even before had borne the holy vessel before the table. And before her came two tapers and two censers. And when she came even to the middle of the palace she set the Holy Grail afore her on a table of silver. . . . And all said with one voice, 'Blessed be the Father of Heaven.' When the song had endured long time the damsel took the vessel and bare it into the chamber whence she came, and then were the voices silent as they had departed thence, and all the windows of the palace opened and closed them again, and the hall grew dark so that Sir Gawain saw naught, but of this was he well aware that he felt hale and whole as naught had ailed him, nor might he feel aught of the wound in his shoulder, for 'twas right well healed. Then he arose joyous and glad at heart, and went seeking the knight who had fought with him, but he found him not. Then he heard as it were a great folk that drew nigh to him, and he felt how they laid hold on him by the arms and the shoulders, and the feet and the head, and bare him forth from the hall, and bound him fast to a cart that was in the midst of the court, and forthwith he fell asleep.

"In the morning when the sun was risen Sir Gawain awoke, and lo! he was in the vilest cart in the world, and he saw that his shield was bound on the shaft afore him, and his steed was made fast behind. But in the shafts was a horse so thin and so

meagre to look at that it seemed scarce worth twopence."
A damsel with a scourge appeared and drove the shameful cart
through the streets of the town, and the people threw mud, dirt,
and rags at Gawain. Beyond the bridge, the damsel unbound
him and said that the castle was named Corbenic. He departed
on his own horse lamenting bitterly. He came to the Secret
Hermit, who on learning of his adventures exclaims, "Ha, Sir,
God help ye, for truly 'twas great mischance when ye saw, and
yet wist not what ye saw! . . . 'Twas the Holy Grail, in which
the blood of Our Lord was received and held." The Hermit
furthermore explained the combat between the dragon and the
leopard, and between the old dragon and its young as an allegory
of the wars between Arthur and Lancelot, and between Arthur
and Mordred.

Now such an allegorizing of an episode in the night of perils
surely indicates that the episode has been tampered with. When
we turn to the Mule without a Bridle we find what seems to be
the uncorrupted form of this episode, namely successive combats
between certain monstrous animals and the hero himself.[9]

Also significant is the form which Gawain's humiliation takes.
For in *Bricriu's Feast* we find Cuchulinn applying almost the
same form of humiliation to a vanquished champion. "Cuchulinn took Ercol (Hercules) himself bound behind his chariot
along with him to Emain." [10] This parallel seems to point to an
Irish origin for the whole episode.

There are in the Vulgate Cycle two other accounts of the perils
of the Palace Adventurous. According to the *Estoire del Saint
Graal* the first to endure them was a certain heathen king, a
leper, by name, Galaphes.[11] Being cured by the sight of the
Grail, brought by Alain, he was baptized, changed his name to
Alfasein, and built the castle of Corbenic to preserve the "most
holy vessel." This Galaphes [12] "lay one night in his chief
palace, and his bed was made in the middle of the palace, right
fair and rich. In the evening when he had slept he awoke and
saw before him the holy vessel covered with red samite, and
before it a man whom he did not know in the semblance of a
priest at the sacring of the mass. Around him he heard more
than a thousand voices which gave thanks to Our Lord, and he
seemed to hear around him the sound of wings and a flutter (?)

---

[9] *Cf.* Chap. XII.
[10] *ITS*, II, 89.

[11] Sommer, I, 286–8.
[12] *Ibid.*, 288 f.

as great as if all the birds of the world were there. When this laudation was ceased and the holy vessel had been borne back whence it came, a man came before him all in flames and said: 'King Alfasein, in this palace neither thou nor any other should sleep. For hardly ought a mortal man to dwell in the place where the holy vessel is so honored as thou hast seen.' . . . Then he let fly a spear which he held and smote him through both the thighs so that it appeared on the other side, and then said to the king: 'Now let others beware of remaining in the Palace Adventurous, for let them know that verily he who henceforth shall lie there shall not escape death or departing in shame, if he be not utterly a good knight.' Then he departed and withdrew his spear."

A far longer account is that of the adventures of Boors in the *Lancelot*.[13] It is essentially the same as that of Gawain's adventures, with some changes and additions. Boors, after his encounter with Brumaut at the gate of Corbenic, enters and is welcomed by King Pelles and his daughter (Malory calls her Elaine), who had formerly been the Grail Bearer, but because of her intrigue with Lancelot had been supplanted by another. There is quite a domestic scene in which Boors gives news of Lancelot, and Galaad, aged two years, is presented to his father's cousin. Then we have the dove with the censer, and the damsel of the Grail, which provides food for all present. After the meal Boors announces his determination to test the adventures as Gawain had done. The dwarf is not mentioned nor the warning voice. As soon as Boors sat on the Perilous Bed, "there began so great a crashing that no one in the world would not be frightened. For at once arose a wind so great that it caused all the windows, of which there were more than a hundred, to bang together. When this had ceased there issued from a chamber a great, long lance of which the head seemed like a burning candle, and it came towards Boors as hard as lightning," and wounded him in the shoulder. He could not see who had thrown it but felt it being withdrawn, and the lance returned to the chamber. The combat with the huge knight is introduced at this point instead of after the weeping damsels as in the Gawain version, and is elaborated by the fact that the knight regains his strength in the middle of the struggle by entering the Grail chamber. Boors forces him at last to go to

[13] *Ibid.*, V, 295–303.

Arthur's court and surrender. When Boors returns to the bed, there comes through the windows a flight of arrows and bolts and wounds him sorely. The windows shut and the missiles cease. Boors then engages with a lion and cuts off his head. There follows the same spectacle which Gawain had seen, of the dragon, the leopard, and the young dragons. Then a pale, thin man with two serpents coiled about his neck enters,[14] and plays on the harp a lai concerning a debate between Joseph of Arimathea and Orfeus the Enchanter. He then tells Boors that he will not be delivered from his pain until the good knight come. On his departure, an aged man habited like a priest, preceded by censers and four children bearing candles, bears into the hall a lance from whose point issued drops of blood, and tells Boors that it is the "Lance Vengeresse," but he will not know what that means until the Perilous Seat shall have found its master. Then we have the twelve weeping damsels who pray at the door of the Grail chamber. A little before midnight Boors sees a growing light in front of the chief chamber as if the sun had his habitation there. When he attempts to enter he is stopped by a sword. Nevertheless he sees within a table of silver with a bishop kneeling before it. When the bishop rises and lifts the samite cover from the Grail on the altar, Boors is blinded with its brilliance. Being warned by a voice, not to look longer he returns to seek the bed, but not finding it, spends the night on the pavement of the hall. Boors' adventures conclude quite differently from those of Gawain, for he is not humiliated at all, but Pelles entering the next morning rejoices that he has passed the night safely.

Now it must be something more than coincidence that these three versions of the perils of the Palace Adventurous are attached to Gawain, Galaphes, and Boors, — names of which two, as we have seen, are simply developments from the one name Gwri Gwallt Avwyn, and the third seems to rest under the same suspicion as Galahal and Galaad, namely, that it is a corruption of the same or a similar Welsh epithet, being related to Welsh Gwalhavet [15] as Galvain is to Welsh Gwalchmai. We have reason to suspect a strong traditional basis for this series of nocturnal adventures in the hall of the Grail Castle.

[14] It is worth noting that Welsh tradition knows a Gwgon who was a year with a snake around his neck. Rhys, *Celtic Folklore*, II, 690.

[15] Loth, *Mab.*², I, 282.

Proof of the existence of such a tradition is also found in the
nocturnal adventures experienced by Gawain in the Chateau
Merveil. Three versions exist: in Crestien de Troyes's *Conte del
Graal*,[16] in Wolfram von Eschenbach's *Parzival*,[17] and in Heinrich
von dem Türlin's *Krone*.[18] The similarity of these adventures in
Chateau Merveil to those in the Palace Adventurous of Corbenic
seems due to the identity of the two castles, for in the Welsh
*Peredur* the castle where the Grail procession appears is called
the Castle of Wonders.[19] Crestien's account of Gawain's adventures in this castle of wonders, except for a few additions from
Wolfram and Heinrich, will form the basis of the following
summary. Gawain comes to a deep and wide river, and des-
cries on the other side, built on a cliff, the richest fortress
ever seen. A mysterious boatman ferries him across, and most
hospitably entertains him at his house, which is so comfortable
and fine that a count might well tarry there. The next morning
early Gawain looks out at the great castle (which Wolfram and
Heinrich call the Chateau Merveil), and on asking his host to
whom it belongs, receives the strange reply that he does not
know. Gawain is naturally amazed that the boatman, who is in
the service of the castle, should not know who his lord is, but is
still met with the declaration of complete ignorance. The host is
ready enough, however, to say that the castle is defended
by enchanted bows and arbalests. A clerk wise in astronomy
has so devised that none may live in the hall an hour who is a
coward, traitor, or liar.

Let us pause to dwell on the fairly obvious fact that the
hospitable boatman corresponds to the Hospitable Host in
*Gawain and the Green Knight*, in *Ivain*, and *Owain*.[20] In Wolfram von Eschenbach's version of this episode the parallel is
carried so far that Gawain wakes in the morning to find his host's
daughter seated beside his bed,[21] just as in *Gawain and the Green
Knight* the hero wakes to find his host's wife about to sit on his
bed.[22] In Heinrich von dem Türlin's version the host is called
Karadas,[23] a name which appears on the Modena sculpture as
Carrado, and there applies to the traditional figure descended
from Curoi the abductor, just as clearly as the name Karadas

---

[16] Ed. Baist, ll. 7190–886.
[17] Bks. X, XI.
[18] Ed. Scholl, ll. 20100–20962.
[19] Loth, *Mab.*², II, 114, 120.

[20] *Cf.* Chap. VII.
[21] Book XI.
[22] Ll. 1182 ff.
[23] L. 20270.

is applied by Heinrich to the traditional figure descended from Curoi, the hospitable host. The host's professed ignorance of the name of his lord, the sire of Chateau Merveil, is best explained by the supposition that it was in a sense himself. '

Let us return to Crestien's story.[24] Gawain and his host approach the castle and pass a lame man, with a silver leg (*eschace*), who keeps a mysterious silence, and is said to be very rich in rents. Gawain and his guide then enter the palace, with its five hundred windows, its doors of ivory and ebony, and its pavement of many colors. In the midst of the floor was a bed of gold with a coverlet of samite and bedposts containing shining carbuncles, mounted on wheels. (In *Diu Krone*[25] a pure and beautiful maiden meets them, and with four squires serves Gawain, when evening comes, with an excellent repast.) Then his host of the night before departs, and Gawain takes his seat on the Perilous Bed, armed. (Wolfram says that Gawain had to leap on the bed, which was rolling around the floor.) At once the bed-cords cry out, bells hanging beneath the bed ring, the windows fly open, and with a crashing sound arrows and bolts shoot in at Gawain, from whom or what he cannot see. Presently the windows closed and Gawain drew out the bolts from his shield and flesh. Then a churl in a hide (in *Diu Krone*[26] the man with the silver leg) opened a door, and a lion sprang out and brought Gawain to his knees. But he rose and smote off the lion's head and paws so that the latter hung by the claws to his shield. As soon as he had slain the lion (in *Diu Krone*[27] the next morning), the host returned with glad countenance, announced the end of the enchantments, and praised God therefor. Then youths entered, welcoming Gawain as the awaited hero. When he had been disarmed, a maiden with a golden circlet entered, followed by other maidens. (In *Diu Krone*[28] she, like Amurfina in the Mule without a Bridle story, is to be Gawain's bride, the reward of his valor.)

In this narrative there are several traces of Celtic origin. The bed with its shining carbuncles is apparently derived, as Nitze noted,[29] from a couch like that of Conchobar, which is de-

[24] L. 7612.
[25] Ll. 20594 ff.
[26] Ll. 20890 ff.
[27] Ll. 20833 ff.
[28] Ll. 21031 ff.
[29] *Studies in Honor of A. M. Elliott*, I, 34; *ITS*, II, 3.

scribed in *Bricriu's Feast* as "set with carbuncles and other precious stones, which shone with a lustre, . . . making night like unto day."

Another Celtic feature is the mysterious man met at the entrance of the palace, who is called the *eschacier*, has a silver *eschace* or artificial leg, and is busy carving with a knife a stick of ashwood. In one manuscript the reading, however, is *eskiekier* or money-changer: and some such form is doubtless responsible for Wolfram's description of the man as a wealthy merchant. Crestien says that the *eschacier* is rich with great rents: Wolfram says that the merchant's booth contains great treasure, and that both merchant and treasure will belong to Gawain if he is victorious. Later he says in Book XIII that Klinschor, the builder and lord of Chateau Merveil, will give castle and kingdom to Gawain. The equation of merchant and lord of the castle is strongly suggested. All this is explained if we turn our attention to a Welsh lord of the Other World, Eudaf,[30] who according to the *Dream of Maxen Wledig* [31] sits in an ivory chair in the magnificent hall of an Otherworld castle, carving chessmen (French *eschac*) with a file, and who is lord of the castle. Everything clears up if we only realize that the original story told of a lord of a castle, who like Eudaf sat before his hall carving *eschacs* (chessmen) for his rich *eschaquier* (chessboard). This figure then is Celtic.

Furthermore, it requires no great perspicacity to see that while Gawain goes back to Cuchulinn, his host who entertains him lavishly, guides him to his great adventure, is no other than Curoi; and we may properly have our suspicions that as in the Mule without a Bridle it is Curoi who appears as a churl in a hide and lets a lion loose at the hero to test him. Our suspicions are completely confirmed when we find in the Irish a story in which Curoi leaves his castle, Cuchulinn arrives, is entertained by the beautiful Blathnat, sits in a perilous watching seat, endures an attack by various monsters, and a fight with a giant, and finally receives the congratulations of Curoi on his exploit. Here is the account from *Bricriu's Feast:* [32] of course, as usual one must allow for the scheme of the three competing heroes

---

[30] Two Welsh genealogies go back to Eudaf Hen (The Old), perhaps the divine ancestor, as Beli is in others. *Cymmrodor*, VIII, 85 f.

[31] Guest, *Mabinogion*, ed. Nutt, 84 f.

[32] *ITS*, II, 101–13.

on which that book is composed. The original tale, doubtless, related the testing of one hero only.

"On the morning of the morrow the three heroes, Cuchulinn, Conall and Loigaire, then set off to Fort Curoi. . . . That night on their arrival Curoi was not at home. But knowing they would come, he counselled his wife regarding the heroes. . . . His wife acted according to his wish in the matter of bathing and of washing, providing them with refreshing drinks and beds most excellent. . . . When bedtime was come, she told them that each was to take his night, watching the fort until Curoi should return. . . . The first night Loigaire the Triumphant took the sentry. . . . As he kept watch into the later part of the night, he saw a giant approaching him far as his eyes could see from the sea westwards. Exceeding huge and ugly and horrible he thought him, for in height, it seemed to him, he reached unto the sky, and the broad expanse of the sea was visible between his legs. Thus did he come, his hands full of stripped oaks, each of which would form a burden for a wagon-team of six. . . . One of the stakes he cast at Loigaire, who let it pass him. Twice or thrice he repeated it, but the stake reached neither the skin nor the shield of Loigaire. Then Loigaire hurled a spear at him and it hit him not." The giant then seized Loigaire and tossed him out of the fort. The same fate befell Conall on the second night. "The third night Cuchulinn went into the seat of watch." He first killed twenty-seven spectres. "While he was there far on into the night, tired and sad and weary, he heard the rising of the loch on high, as it were the booming of a very heavy sea. How deep soever his dejection, his spirit could not brook his not going to see what caused the great noise he heard. He then perceived the up-heaving monster, and it seemed to him to be thirty cubits in curvature above the loch. It raised itself on high into the air, sprang towards the fort, opened its mouth so that one of the palaces could go into its gullet. Then he called to mind his swooping feat, sprang on high, and was as swift as a winnowing riddle right round the monster. He entwined his two arms about its neck, stretched his hand till it reached into its gullet, tore out the monster's heart, and cast it from him to the ground. . . . Cuchulinn then plied it with his sword, hacked it to atoms, and took the head with him into the sentry-seat along with the other heap of skulls. While there, depressed and miserable in

the morning dawn, he saw the giant approaching him westwards
from the sea. . . . Then the giant cast one of the branches at
Cuchulinn, who let it pass him. He repeated it two or three
times, but it reached neither the skin nor the shield of Cuchulinn.
Cuchulinn then hurled his spear at the giant, but it reached
him not. Whereupon the giant stretched his hand towards
Cuchulinn to grip him as he did the others. Cuchulinn leapt the
hero's salmon-leap, and called to mind his swooping-feat, with
his drawn sword over the monster's head. As swift as a hare he
was, and in mid-air circling round the monster till he made a
water-wheel of it. 'Life for life, O Cuchulinn,' quoth he.
'Give me my triad of wishes,' quoth Cuchulinn. 'At a breath
they are thine,' he said. 'The Sovranty of Erin's Heroes be
henceforth mine, the Champion's Portion without dispute, the
precedence to my wife over the ladies of Ulster forever.' 'It
shall be thine,' quoth he at once. Then he who had been con-
versing with him vanished he knew not whither." Cuchulinn
then displayed his exuberance in a series of marvelous leaps.
"He thereupon entered the house and heaved a sigh. Then
Mind's [or Midir's] [32a] daughter, Blathnat, wife of Curoi, made
speech: 'Truly, not the sigh of one dishonored, but a victor's
sigh of triumph.' The daughter of the king of the Isle of the
Men of Falga knew full well of Cuchulinn's evil plight that
night. They were not long there when they beheld Curoi coming towards them, carrying into the house with him the stand-
ard of the "three nines" slain by Chuchulinn, along with
their heads and that of the monster. He put the heads from
off his breast on to the floor of the stead, and spoke: 'The gillie
whose one night's trophies are these is a fit lad to watch a king's
keep for aye. The Champion's Portion, over which you have
fallen out with the gallant youths of Erin, truly belongs to
Cuchulinn.'"

Now Brown pointed out long since that the giant is Curoi.[33]
"I do not see how there can be any reasonable doubt that the
giant whom Cuchulinn overcomes at Curoi's fort and compels to
promise him the sovereignty, is Curoi in one of his magic shapes.
Curoi has purposely absented himself just before the arrival of
the heroes, and he returns directly after the sudden vanishing
of the giant. What more natural than that he should himself
test the heroes, just as we are expressly told that he did in the

[32a] *Ibid.*, 137.                    [33] *SNPL*, VIII, 55 note.

beheading game? Furthermore if the giant is not Curoi, how can he promise the sovereignty, inasmuch as Cuchulinn is sworn to abide by the decision of Curoi?"

Now knowing, as we do, something of Curoi's nature, we may properly conclude that the stripped oaks or stakes which the gigantic shadow cast at Loigaire, and the branches which the same giant threw at Cuchulinn are probably corrupt developments from some symbol of the lightning. This conception would account for the wind, the thunder, and lightning in the account of Gawain's visit to Corbenic; the man in flames who cast his spear at King Galaphes; the wind that slammed the windows, and the shower of arrows and bolts in the account of Boors' second visit to Corbenic; and the shower of bolts in Crestien's story of Gawain's visit to Chateau Merveil.

But we have already seen that Curoi and Lug are very similar figures and we saw in Chapter IV a description of Lug's spear which almost exactly fits the description of the flaming spear which wounds Gawain and Boors in the hall of Corbenic. Lug's spear "roared and struggled against its thongs; fire flashed from it." [34] Compare this with the account of Gawain's night in the Palace Adventurous: [35] "He heard a cry, the most fell he had ever heard, and he thought him well 'twas the voice of the foul fiend. With that there came forth swiftly from a chamber a lance whereof the blade was all afire." And with the account of Boors' experience in the same place: [36] "There began so great a crashing that no one in the world would not be frightened. For at once arose a wind so great that it caused all the windows of which there were more than a hundred to clap together. When this had ceased there issued from a chamber a great, long lance of which the head seemed like a burning candle, and it came towards Boors as hard as lightning."

The Grail Damsel who bears her sacred vessel through the hall of Corbenic supplying miraculously the choicest meats in the world, and that pure and beautiful maiden who in *Diu Krone* feeds Gawain "as a dear guest," [37] have they not their counterpart in the beautiful damsel Blathnat, who hospitably entertains the heroes and provides them with refreshing drinks? Without going into detail, let me point out that in Wolfram's *Parzival* one of the Grail maidens is called Florie von Lunel;

[34] C. Squire, *Mythology of the British Islands*, 63.    [36] *Ibid.*, V, 298.
[35] Sommer, IV, 344.    [37] L. 20624.

and we have seen in Chapter II that the maiden cup-bearer in Arthur's court is the heroine of an abduction story parallel to that of Blathnat, and that her name, Lore, is a recognizable corruption of Floree, and is therefore a translation of Blathnat, which means "little Flower." It is noteworthy, too, that *Diu Krone* stresses the anxiety of the maiden over Gawain's fate, and her joy when in the morning she discovers him unharmed.[38] Are these not elaborations of the hints in *Bricriu's Feast:*[39] Blathnat "knew full well of Cuchulinn's evil plight that night;" and in the morning she exclaimed on hearing Cuchulinn's sigh: "'Truly not the sigh of one dishonored, but a victor's sigh of triumph.'"

In passing, too, let us observe that the test is not merely a test of the hero's prowess on a particular occasion. Like many other tests which we shall encounter in dealing with the Grail cycle, it requires of the hero that he be without taint of cowardice or deceit from birth. Crestien, as we have seen,[40] informs us through the mouth of the host, that no man who is a coward, a traitor, or a liar can remain alive in the hall one hour, and Heinrich himself declares[41] that he who could endure the perils of the enchanted bed must have been without evil from childhood up. Since, therefore, in the account of Gawain's unsuccessful trial in the Palace Adventurous at Corbenic, it is clear that the Grail does not serve him because of his unworthiness, we may fairly suppose that the Grail itself refuses food to the coward and the deceitful. This function of the Grail as a tester of bravery and good faith we shall see is of fundamental importance in ascertaining its origin.

Let us now look back and see how far the story of the visit of the three Irish heroes to Curoi's fortress will account for features in the narratives which the romances give us of the nocturnal perils of Corbenic and Chateau Merveil. I shall refer to the stories as Gawain-Corbenic, Boors, Galaphes, and Gawain-Merveil.

1. Arrival at nightfall. Gaw. Corb.; Boors.
2. Lord of castle supposedly absent. Gaw. Merv.
3. Castle has magic properties. Gaw. Merv.
4. Entertainment by beautiful lady on arrival. Boors; Gaw. Merv. (*Krone*).

[38] Ll. 20743 ff: ll. 20799 ff.
[39] *ITS*, II, 113.
[40] Ed. Baist, ll. 7517 ff.
[41] Ll. 20601 ff.

5. Hero, armed, takes seat to watch the night through. Gaw. Corb.; Boors; Gaw. Merv.; Galaphes.
6. Attack by storm god:
     a. Gigantic figure. Gaw. Corb.; Boors.
     b. Shower of missiles. Gaw. Corb.; Boors; Gaw. Merv.
     c. Single lance. Boors; Galaphes.
     d. Forces giant to surrender. Boors.
7. Attack by monster. Boors; Gaw. Merv.
8. Ignominious outcome (Loigaire, Conall). Gaw. Corb.
9. Lord of castle returns in morning, congratulates hero. Gaw. Merv. (Krone).

One of the most extraordinary instances of the survival of genuine Celtic tradition in unexpected places is found in the romance of *Arthur of Little Britain*, translated by Lord Berners from an unpublished French text of the fourteenth century. No Arthurian studies, so far as I know, even mention this realistic and interesting romance, which deals with the adventures of a mere knight of Brittany, ostensibly distinct from the great British king. But when we note that Layamon implies that King Arthur was fostered in Brittany,[42] and that his sword Clarent [43] seems to be no other than the sword Clarence [44] which Arthur of Little Britain wins, we may presume that the distinction between the two heroes is comparatively late. Now in this neglected romance Arthur accomplishes a series of adventures in the Otherworld castle which bears many marks of authentic tradition and strangely fits into the contentions of this chapter. Significantly enough, he is accompanied by a certain Baldwin, in whose name after allowing for the common confusion of *b* and *g*, we may recognize a corruption of Galvain. Baldwin, therefore, goes back ultimately to Cuchulinn, and was doubtless the original hero of the adventure.

Arthur of Little Britain, accompanied by Baldwin, sets out to end the enchantments of Porte Noire, a marvelous castle, given by the Queen of Faery, Proserpine, to her godchild and replica Florens, and watched over by an enchanter, Master Steven, the beloved servant of Florens.[45] Arthur, after being entertained and directed to his destination by a hospitable squire, crosses a

---

[42] L. 19834. *Cf. SNPL*, X, 163.
[43] Alliterative *Morte Arthur*, ed. Björkman, 124.
[44] Berners, *Arthur of Little Britain*, ed. Utterson, 157.
[45] *Ibid.*, 43–9. On Proserpine and Florens *cf.* Chap. XXX.

ARTHUR OF LITTLE BRITAIN AT PORTE NOIRE

Note Steven (thrice repeated), images with flails, giant bearing ax, and lions.

narrow bridge over a river.[46]    Steven, aware of his approach,
mounts (like Gansguoter) on the walls of Porte Noire.    On the
far side of the river Arthur encounters twelve knights on foot
"with hatches and maces of steel."    Among them was a gigantic
churl, under whom Arthur fell, but luckily the churl's head was
cut off accidentally by one of his fellows.[47]    Arthur, victorious,
passed into a hall, and then into a chamber, where "was por-
trayed how God did create sun and the moon, and in the roof
were all the seven planets wrought with fine gold and silver, and
all the situations of the heavens, wherein were pight many
carbuncles and other precious stones."[48]    Here were divers beds,
and the richest was in the midst of the chamber.    Four images
of gold in the corners blow their horns in succession.    At the
first blast, the doors and windows open and shut; there is a roar
of water and a great wind.    At the second and third blasts a
lion attacks Arthur, but he overcomes both.    At the fourth a
great giant enters, biting his teeth as if "they had been hammers
striking on a stithy."    He was clad in a serpent skin, and bore
an ax that would cut asunder everything it touched.[49]    Arthur
slays him, and proceeds to lie down on the fairest bed.    An
image at the head shoots a silver arrow.[50]    One window flies
wide; the wind bursts the glass in others.    It thundered terribly,
and a burning spear would have consumed Arthur had he not
dodged.    As it was, it burned up a knight on another bed,
descended through the chamber, and sank in the earth.    Then
suddenly the palace began to revolve like a wheel, so that
Arthur had to embrace the image which alone stood fixed.    A
great voice cried: "It is ended, it is ended!"

When the castle became still, Baldwin sought out his master
and washed his wounds.    After Arthur had released two prisoners, dined, and shaved, he destroyed another enchantment,
two copper images with flails.[51]    Then he was brought before the
enchanter Steven, who knew all that Arthur had done.[52]
"Sir, we have long trusted for the wealth and honor that is now
come to you; therefore now ye be welcome as the chief sovereign

---

[46] *Ibid.*, 128–35.

[47] *Ibid.*, 138.

[48] *Ibid.*, 139.

[49] *Cf.* Kittredge, *Study of G. G. K.*, 11, where we read that Curoi's ax
would cut hairs against the wind for sharpness.

[50] *Cf.* on similar automata *MP*, X, 516.

[51] *Ibid.*, 523.                          [52] Berners, *op. cit.*, 148.

knight of all the wide world." Later they supped in the chamber of the Marvelous Bed, and Steven's servants brought vessels of gold and silver. "They were as richly served," we read, "as though they had been in the house of Florens: but though she were not there, yet she paid for all their expenses." [53]

It is hard not to recognize Blathnat here. Her name, her close connection with the enchanter, her entertainment of the hero, distorted though they have been, are still distinguishable. Steven's subordination to Florens and his mounting on the walls correspond to the Gansguoter traditions in the Mule without a Bridle.[54] The narrow bridge, the fight with the gigantic, ax-bearing churl at the gate, the marvelous bed, the slamming doors and windows, the combat with two lions, the flaming spear, the whirling castle: these are all, we know, authentic survivals of Celtic myth. To be sure, they are so common in Arthurian romance, that one might suspect the whole adventure of being a late composite from French materials. However, not only does the rôle of Florens tell against the suspicion, but also the clear recognition that the flaming spear is the lightning, and the resemblance between the congratulatory speeches of Steven and Curoi. Manifestly, too, this romance offers the clue to perplexing features of the marvelous bed in Wolfram and Crestien. For in *Arthur of Little Britain*, when the bed revolves, we are not surprised since it is carried round by the whirling castle, which is so familiar to us in the traditions of Curoi. But Wolfram's version says nothing of the revolving castle, and the bed alone rolls about on wheels. Crestien has almost but not quite suppressed this mythical element: the bed, though stationary, is provided with wheels. His version, though earliest in date, is the least primitive.

The two images with flails in *Arthur of Little Britain* [55] also seem to have originated in the Irish Other World. For in the *Destruction of Da Derga's Hostel* we encounter three men in rough coats of hair, carrying iron flails,[56] who are said to be the Men of Falga whom Cuchulinn spared when he slew the other six on the Isle of Man, as we saw in Chapter X. Gigantic figures with flails were certainly among the foes which the hero had to overcome in the Irish Other World. Perhaps most curious of all is the apparent survival here as in *Titurel* of the

[53] *Ibid.*, 150.
[54] *Cf.* Chap. XII.
[55] *Cf.* L. A. Paton, *Fairy Mythology*, 131.
[56] *RC*, XXII, 303, 305.

conception that the Other World is the sky. At any rate it is this conception which seems to lie behind the celestial orbs which deck the roofs of the Grail Temple and of the Porte Noire, and also behind the nocturnal revolutions of Curoi's castle.

These conclusions fit in perfectly with what we have learned regarding Corbenic and Chateau Merveil. The whole episode in the Palace Adventurous is based upon the scene in Curoi's castle. The figure of Brumaut, who defends the gate of Corbenic, is again Curoi. And the Chateau Merveil, where to be sure the Grail does not appear but in which events so similar to those in the Grail Castle occur, connects us again with Curoi. For the account in *Diu Krone* gives us the Hospitable Host, Karadas, who guides the hero to the adventure, who leaves him at nightfall, who tests him with a rain of missiles and by loosing a lion upon him, who returns to congratulate him in the morning and to announce the reward of his prowess, — all familiar activities of Curoi, the old god. And Gansguoter, the builder of the castle and contriver of its enchantments, is we know a development of Curoi.

But the Grail Castle is not merely the fortress of Curoi. As we proceed we shall see that it is also identifiable with the abode of other Welsh gods, Manawyddan, Bran, and Beli, who were imagined as dwelling especially in Happy Isles beyond the sunset. The Castle of the Grail is a composite of Celtic conceptions of the dwelling of the gods.

# CHAPTER XVIII

## FISHER KING AND MAIMED KING

In the last chapter we had presented to us an account of Gawain's visit to the Chateau Merveil which through certain features betrayed its descent from Irish stories about Cuchulinn's visits to Curoi. There is the host who entertains the hero before sending him on to his other self to be tested: there is the beautiful damsel who entertains the hero; there is the watch through the night in the hall of the castle, from which the lord is supposedly absent; there are the churl in his hide, the shower of missiles, the fight with a monster, the congratulations of the host. But there are other features which are not explained by anything we know about the visits to Curoi's castle, but seem to find their explanation in another Irish legend.

The narrative framework into which Crestien sets the adventures of Gawain at the Chateau Merveil is as follows, though complicated by many minor adventures: [1] The knight discovers in a castle garth under a tree a most beautiful damsel with a narrow circlet of orfreys upon her head. Though from the first she mocks him, as Lynete mocks Gareth, it is quite clear that the damsel is really like Lynete a fairy guide. At any rate, they ride off together, meeting many adventures. Finally they come in sight of the Chateau Merveil, the richest fortress ever seen. The palace contains six hundred windows, at which stand damsels, clad in samite and cloth of gold, gazing out at the meadows and adorning their shining hair. The damsel messenger enters a boat, and invites Gawain to join her, but he first engages in combat with a knight. When he returns victorious, to the damsel, "he could not find her at all, neither the boat nor herself, and it displeased him sore that he had lost her so that he did not know what had become of her. While he thought about the damsel, he saw approaching a boat, which a boatman guided, coming from the castle." [2] He announces that he has been sent by the damsels of the castle, and Gawain after delivering to him the vanquished knight as toll, is ferried across. Then follow the various adventures at the boatman's house and

---

[1] Ed. Baist, ll. 6440–7435.     [2] *Ibid.*, ll. 7330–8.

at the Chateau Merveil. The morning after the testing,[3] the beauteous damsel with the circlet welcomes him with her maidens, and says: "My lady the queen sends you, fair sir, dear greetings and commands us all to hold you for our rightful lord." After offering him homage and presenting him with furred robes they depart. Gawain ascends a tower with his boatman host, and expresses a desire to hunt in the surrounding forests. But the host replies that those whom God so loves that those of the castle hail him as lord and master must never issue forth. Later he is received by the queen herself and one hundred and fifty damsels, and a magnificent banquet follows, lasting as long as a winter day and consisting of all he desired. The next day Gawain asks the queen's permission to speak with the damsel who has guided him thither and whom he sees with a knight in a meadow outside the castle. The queen at first refuses, but Gawain replies that he would hold himself evil apaid if he could not issue forth from the castle, and prays God that he may not remain there long a prisoner. At the boatman's intercession the queen consents on condition that Gawain return that night. Gawain promises and departs.

Now here we have five striking features: a guiding damsel who suddenly vanishes, having accomplished her mission; a meeting with a mysterious being in a boat on the water; a castle of damsels who welcome the hero as their lord and master; a feast of every desirable food; a strict prohibition from departure, finally relaxed by the queen of the maidens on condition that the hero return.

Miss Weston has already pointed out that some of these features seem to be derived from an Irish visit to the Other World,[4] but she failed to note that all five are to be found. In the *Voyage of Bran*,[5] a woman in strange raiment appeared in the royal house, and sang a song describing the happy isles. When she had finished, she "went from them, while they knew not whither she went." The next morning Bran and his company set sail, and after two days and nights saw a man in a chariot approaching over the sea, who said that he was Manannan the son of Ler. He sang a song saying that what to Bran in his coracle looked like the clear sea, was for him in his chariot a

[3] *Ibid.*, ll. 7862–8330.
[4] Weston, *Leg. of Gawain*, 36 ff.
[5] K. Meyer, A. Nutt, *Voyage of Bran*, I, 4, 16, 28, 30–34.

flowery plain. After rhapsodizing on the joys of the Other World and telling his own errand to Ireland, he concluded: "Steadily then let Bran row, Not far to the Land of Women." Indeed Bran and his men soon arrived, and saw the leader of the women at the port. She invited him ashore; Bran did not venture, but she drew him in by a magic thread. "Thereupon they went into a large house, in which there was a bed for every couple. The food that was put on every dish vanished not from them. . . . No savor was wanting to them." After a long time homesickness seized one of the men. Bran proposed to return to Ireland. The woman at first forbade but finally allowed them to go on condition that they did not step on shore. They sailed back, only to tell of their wanderings. Bran "wrote these quatrains in Ogam, and then bade them farewell, and from that hour his wanderings are not known." The implication, of course, is that he returned to the Land of Women.

Here we have precisely the features which are necessary to round out the story of Gawain at the Chateau Merveil: the maiden messenger who vanishes, the god met upon the water, the Land of Maidens, the long and miraculous feast, and the prohibition against departure. The fact that Bran meets Manannan riding in a chariot, not in a boat, does not prevent our identifying the boatman of Chateau Merveil with the sea-god, for Manannan possessed a magic coracle, the Wave-Sweeper.[6] Crestien in representing the boatman as Hospitable Host was making a composite figure of Curoi and Manannan. Indeed the whole adventure of Chateau Merveil is a composite of visits to the homes of Curoi and Manannan.

Another story of a visit to the home of Manannan, which Nutt and Brown have already connected with the Grail legend,[7] is found in the *Adventures of Cormac.*[8] One dawn in May Cormac is standing alone at Tara, when he is approached by a gray-haired warrior, in purple mantle, gold-threaded shirt, and shoes of white bronze, who says he is from a land where there is no age, decay, sadness, or hatred. He consents to give Cormac a magic branch,[9] if he will grant three wishes. In fulfilment of the bargain the warrior later appears three times and carries away

[6] *Atlantis,* IV, 193. On magic boats see L. A. Paton, *Fairy Mythology,* 16 note.

[7] Nutt, *Studies in Legend,* 193 f: *PMLA,* XXV, 40 f.

[8] *IT,* III, 211–6.

[9] *Cf.* on magic boughs *Folklore,* XII, 431.

Cormac's daughter, son, and wife. Cormac pursues, is over-taken by a mist, and finds himself in a great plain. He enters a palace with beams of bronze, and wattled with silver. In the garth is a fountain. There sits a splendid warrior and a yellow-haired maid with a gold helmet, loveliest of women. Cormac is bathed by invisible means, and an abundance of food and ale is provided. His host displays a gold cup of strange work-manship and many designs, which breaks in pieces when three lies are told in its presence, and is restored whole when three truths are uttered. He gives it to Cormac, and reveals himself as Manannan son of Ler, King of the Land of Promise. On the morrow Cormac wakes to find himself and his family on the green of Tara. The cup which he had received from Manannan was used to distinguish between truth and falsehood with the Gael. But it did not remain after his death, and we may infer that it returned to the abode of Manannan.

Now if we eliminate from this story the three wishes and the abduction of Cormac's wife, which seem to be extraneous fea-tures, we have left a visit to an Otherworld castle, which sud-denly becomes visible, a venerable god of the sea, a beautiful damsel, a feast, a cup which was used to distinguish between truth and falsehood. These same elements, though with many changes and additions, may be distinguished in Crestien's narrative of Perceval's visit to the Grail castle.[10] The knight comes upon an old man fishing from a boat on a river, who in-vites him to his castle. When Perceval tries to find the castle, he seeks in vain until it suddenly appears ahead of him. In the hall he discovers the fisherman, wearing a purple robe, arrived before him. A youth bears in a bleeding lance. A damsel of great beauty follows with a *graal*, or shallow dish, glittering with gems. Perceval fails to ask whom it serves. There ensues a great feast. But the next morning Perceval wakes to find the castle deserted, rides out alone, and the drawbridge rises suddenly behind him. He learns that his host was the Fisher King, who was wounded in both thighs in battle but would have regained health and lands if Perceval had asked the question. In the *Didot Perceval*, which contains nearly the same series of in-cidents,[11] Perceval later returns to the Fisher King's castle, succeeds in the test, heals thereby the King, and on his death three days later becomes his successor as Guardian of the Grail.

[10] Ed. Baist, ll. 2956–3552.   [11] Weston, *Leg. of Perceval*, II, 58–60, 82–4.

Now the resemblance between this adventure and that of Cormac lies not in the details but in that general significance and sequence of events which we have detected in other parallels between Irish and Arthurian legend. It should be said further that the difference between the two traditions is lessened if we note that the manner in which Manannan's cup tests falsehood seems remodeled on the basis of another legendary crystal vessel, used for purposes of ordeal,[12] and it may originally have "distinguished between truth and falsehood with the Gael" by refusing food to the unworthy in a manner more like the feeding vessel of Corbenic. Moreover, though Perceval's unsuccessful visit to the Grail castle terminates in his departure from the empty edifice, Gawain's unsuccessful visit as recounted by Wauchier de Denain ends in his waking on a lofty cliff beside the sea.[13] "Strangely did he marvel in that he found himself there, and saw neither house nor castle, neither hall nor keep." This termination, needless to say, corresponds to the end of Cormac's visit to the palace of Manannan. All these facts, therefore, lead us to the conclusion already reached by Nitze, that "Manannan and the Fisher King are to all intents and purposes (originally) the same person." [14] Nevertheless it must be admitted that in three important points the Irish and Arthurian traditions differ: Manannan is not discovered fishing; he is not maimed or infirm; there is no procession of Grail or spear.

Accordingly let us look for any other links which might serve to connect Manannan with the Fisher King. Both, as has been pointed out before, are explicitly said to be addicted to shape-shifting.[15] Manannan [16] is one of the Tuatha De Danann, a divine race, and is closely connected with the gods Lug and Cuchulinn, who we know have their many representatives in Arthurian romance. In the *Cattle-Raid of Cualnge* Cuchulinn wears a mantle of invisibility given him by Manannan.[17] In the *Fate of the Children of Turenn* Lug is equipped with Manannan's coat of mail, breastplate, and sword, and rides his steed.[18] It has even been suggested that Lug is in a sense

[12] The vessel of Badurn. *IT*, III, 209.
[13] Weston, *Gawain at Grail Castle*, 27 f.
[14] *Studies in Honor of A. M. Elliott*, I, 44.
[15] *PMLA*, XXV, 37; *RC*, XXIV, 276; Potvin, II, l. 222.
[16] On Manannan *cf. PRIA*, XXXIV, C, 149; *Folklore*, XVII, 141.
[17] Thurneysen, *Irische Helden- und Königsage*, 180.
[18] Joyce, *Old Celtic Romances*, 37 ff.

Manannan.[19]  At any rate we have found among the ancestors of
Galaad not only Lambar and Lancelot, who derive their names
from Lug's epithets Lamfada and Loinnbheimionach, but also
Manaal, whose name seems related to Manannan's or rather its
Welsh counterpart Manawyd or Manawyddan.

Of Manawyd we know that he was Perpetual Guardian of the
Caldron of Britain; [20] that he dwelt in a certain Otherworld
castle called Kaer Sidi, — "Neither age nor plague harms him
who dwells therein;" [21] that in Kaer Sidi is kept a pearl-rimmed
caldron of the Head of Annwn,[22] doubtless identical with the
Caldron of Britain; that this caldron would not boil the food of
a coward or perjurer, — a fact which betrays kinship with
Manannan's cup of truth.   Manawyd was closely associated
with his step-son Pryderi,[23] who is also represented as a dweller
in Kaer Sidi.[24]  Now Pryderi we have had reason to suspect is
Perceval, and Rhys equated the pearl-rimmed caldron of Kaer
Sidi with the Grail.[25]  When we recall Crestien's account of
Perceval's visit to the Grail Castle, it is hard to escape the conviction that the young hero, who in spite of his first failure,
later succeeds to the kingship of the Grail and Castle, is Pryderi,
the Fisher King is Manawyddan, and the jeweled dish is the
jeweled caldron of Kaer Sidi.

Certain difficulties remain, however.   The *Didot Perceval* calls
the Fisher King Bron, and makes him grandfather of Perceval.
But we have already noticed that the Grail Kings are practically
interchangeable, and there is a special reason for equating Bran
and Manawyddan,[26] for they are brothers, sons of Llyr, the Sea.
We may almost suspect that when the Irish Bran son of Febal
crosses the sea to the Isle of Women he is really taking Manannan's place while Manannan is in Ireland, just as Pwyll takes
the place of Arawn in the Welsh story.   If the Fisher King were
to bear any name in the Grail romances other than some form of
Manawyddan, it would be some form of Bran.   We have seen,

[19] *Folklore,* XVII, 141; Nutt, *Voyage of Bran,* I, 292 f.
[20] *Irish Nennius,* ed. J. H. Todd, lviii.
[21] Rhys, *Arthurian Legend,* 301; *Celtic Folklore,* II, 678.
[22] Malory, *Morte d'Arthur,* Everyman ed., I, xxiii.   There is every reason, as we shall see in the next chapter, to identify Caer Pedryvan and Caer
Sidi.
[23] *Cf.* Mabinogi of *Manawyddan.*
[24] *Cf.* note 21.
[25] Rhys, *Arthurian Legend,* 300, 305, 310.
[26] *Cf.* Nutt, *op. cit.,* 219.

too, that Bran was the possessor of a magic caldron, which restores the dead to life, and that he lent himself early to a Christian development of the Grail tradition, since he is said to be the first to bring the faith of Christ to the nation of the Cymry.[27] He is therefore as fully qualified as Manawyddan to play the rôle of Fisher King and Grail King. The difficulty in the relationship between Manawyddan and Pryderi is really no difficulty because Nutt has pointed out that probably one tradition made Pryderi true son of Manawyddan, instead of step-son,[28] and in Robert de Boron's *Joseph* the Grail hero is variously said to be son or grandson of Bron, the Grail Keeper.[29] Consistency in relationships is almost the last thing to demand from the Arthurian romances.

All this goes to show that the two sons of Llyr, Bran and Manawyd, were virtually identical, that both of them reappear in the mysteriously rich and powerful host whom the young knight, Gawain or Perceval, before his testing, encounters sitting in a boat. This habitual appearance of the host upon the water was due to the fact that Manawyd and Bran were preëminently sea-gods. But the *conteurs*, puzzled to account for this habit, invented the explanation that because of his infirmity, the lord of the castle spent his time in the sedentary occupation of fishing, and called him the Fisher King.[30] This title in turn provoked the curiosity of Robert de Boron, and he concocted the fable that Bron caught a fish at the direction of a heavenly voice, whence he obtained the name of the Rich Fisher.[31]

Crestien describes the Fisher King as wounded; the *Didot Perceval* as aged and sick. And though other versions tend to distinguish between Fisher King and Maimed King, yet almost all the Guardians of the Grail show a tendency to suffer from mysterious ailments, particularly wounds in the thigh or leg. Lot has pointed out the repetition of this theme as one of the artistic defects of the Vulgate cycle, remarking: "What a multitude of the maimed! Josephe smitten in the thigh; his father, Joseph of Arimathea, in the leg; Caleb Alphassam [the converted Galaphes] pierced by a spear through the thighs; likewise Pellehan, father of King Pelles; Nascien, blinded for an

---

[27] See Nitze's article in *Medieval Studies in Memory of Gertrude Schoep-perle Loomis.*

[28] Nutt, *Voyage of Bran*, II, 17.   [30] Ed. Baist, ll. 3470–82.

[29] Nutt, *Studies*, 81.   [31] Nutt, *Studies*, 208.

instant; Mordrain blinded and paralysed for several centuries. The divine vengeance has displayed scant variety in its manifestations." [32]  And again in speaking of the Maimed King he says: [33]  "At the end of the *Estoire* he is called Pellehan.  In the *Lancelot*, where he does not appear till very late, as has been said, he has not yet a name.  In the *Queste*, where he is mentioned many times, he is named only once and the form of his name differs from that in the *Estoire:* it is Pellinor in the passage where the sister of Perceval relates to Galaad the circumstances of her punishment. . . .  (Here) certain manuscripts read Pelles, which is an obvious absurdity."

If one concedes that all these names except Joseph and Josephe are really those of Welsh gods, and that the names of these gods are interchangeable, the tangle of absurdities begins to unravel. In the Grail stories, when the young god comes to be tested, the result of his success is at first to heal the old god, but the old god conveniently dies shortly after to make way for his youthful successor.  Miss Weston showed further that the success of the young god in the test seems, moreover, to bring about the general renewal of life and fertility in the land.

But, it may be asked, what reason have we to believe that any such conceptions prevailed among the Irish?  Let me quote at length from Macalister's illuminating study of Tara: [34] "The king of Temair [Tara] was a god incarnate.  This is the all-important fact which results from the study of the traditions of the early kingship that have come down to us. . . .  When a good king was on the throne the gods condescended to take up their abode within him; when the king was illegitimate, they withdrew themselves. . . .  Contrast these characterizations from the *Lebor Gabala:* 'Good was that king Eochu mac Eirc; there was no rain in his time, but only dew; there was no year without its harvest; falsehood was expelled from Ireland in his time.'  'In evil case was Ireland in the time of Coirpre, for the earth did not yield her fruit, because there was but one grain in the ear, one acorn on the oak, one nut in the hazel; the creeks were unproductive, the cattle were dry, so that there was an intolerable famine throughout Ireland for five years in which Coirpre was king.'  We have seen in the last section that Eochu mac Eirc was the impersonation of the Divine Wisdom, at the

---

[32] Lot, *Étude sur le Lancelot*, 269.
[33] *Ibid.*, 241.                                  [34] *PRIA*, XXXIV, C, 324.

head of the 'epic' pantheon: and though the historians have made him into a king, he retains sufficient godhead to secure the blessings named for his people. . . . As Dr. Baudis points out, this idea is also at the basis of the prohibition of the rule of a blemished king." The euhemerized god Nuada, after losing his arm at the First Battle of Moytura, was forced to retire from the kingship. His successor Bres was satirized for his churlishness so that great red blotches broke out over his face, disqualifying him in turn.[35] By this time Nuada had acquired his famous silver arm, and was able to resume his throne. There can be no doubt, therefore, that the Irish believed that the health or sickness of the god and his earthly representative, the king, reflected themselves in the abundance of the crops and the yield of the cattle.[36] Nevertheless, it is significant that only the Welsh Bran affords a clear prototype of the Maimed King, and the names of most of the Maimed Kings of romance are of Welsh derivation.

Miss Weston has brought to bear on this point one of the most significant of Grail texts, the late thirteenth century romance of *Sone de Nansai*.[37] In a passage concerned with the wounding of Joseph of Arimathea, Guardian of the Grail, we read: "Neither peas nor wheat were sown, no child was born to man, nor maiden had husband, nor tree bore leaf, nor meadow turned green; neither bird nor beast had young, so sore was the king maimed." All these functions were clearly thought of as bound up with the vigor of the divine king. And his malady, to the precise nature of which we shall devote some attention in a later chapter, brought about the Enchantment of Lorgres or England, of which the Welsh name was Lloegyr.

Since in this passage and others the enchantment of Britain seems to have stretched over a period of years, we might interpret the phenomenon as a prolonged famine and pestilence. But in the next chapter we shall discover evidence that the wounds of the Otherworld King were conceived as breaking out anew annually. In that case we may properly believe that the catastrophe which accompanied the wounding of the king was

[35] *Folklore*, XVII, 29.

[36] On connections of kings and fertility *cf. Kittredge Anniversary Papers*, 191, note 4; *MP*, XXII, 85; *Eriu*, II, 86, VIII, 101 ff; *Destruction of Da Derga's Hostel*, ed. W. Stokes, 20, 56; *Tripartite Life*, Rolls ed., 507; *Cymmrodor*, X, 217.

[37] *Rom.*, XLIII, 403 ff.

rather the desolation of winter; and his infirmity signifies the low vitality of natural forces, particularly the feeble winter sun.

At any rate, whatever the malady of the king may have meant, two conceptions clashed in the accounts of its termination: one, the restoration of the old god's powers; the other, his supersession by the young god. So we have in the healing of the Maimed King and his prompt demise thereafter an attempt to reconcile these two natural conceptions. The result in the Mule without a Bridle is even more ironic, for Gawain has hardly brought healing to the wounded knight by his advent, when he gives him a fatal wound. But after all it makes little difference for we know him to be the Immortal One.

Miss Weston's interpretation of the Maimed King and the task of the hero I accept, though stressing rather the solar than the vegetation aspect of the characters. Manawyddan and Bran were, like Manannan, more than sea-gods, and so came to play a part in the drama of terrestrial fertility. Manannan boasts: [38] "When we desired to plow that field outside, then it was found plowed, harrowed and sown with wheat. When we desired to reap it, then the crop was found stacked in the field. When we desired to draw it into that side out there, it was found in the garth all in one thatched rick. We have been eating it from then till today; but it is no whit greater nor less." Manawyddan likewise is on record as fisherman, hunter, and farmer. The Mabinogi relates: [39] "He accustomed himself to fish (nota bene!), to hunt the deer in their covert. And then he began to prepare some ground, and he sowed a croft, and a second, and a third. And no wheat in the world ever sprung up better. And the three crofts prospered with perfect growth, and no man ever saw fairer wheat than it." Both Manawyddan and Pryderi, like the Irish Lug, were masters of several trades: saddlery, shield-making, and cobbling shoes. [40] Evidently they were the divine patrons of crafts. There can scarcely be a doubt that Manawyddan, Bran, and Pryderi, though specially connected with the sea, were also lords of the earth.

It is worth adding that the original of the Fisher King, like Merlin and Cuchulinn, is one of those figures concerning whom we have early and specific testimony that he was a god. Cormac

---

[38] *IT*, III, 215.
[39] Guest, *Mabinogion*, ed. Nutt, 51.
[40] *Ibid.*, 46 f.

about 900 wrote [41] that he was "a celebrated merchant who was in the Isle of Mann. He was the best pilot that was in the west of Europe. . . . Therefore the Irish and the Britons called him god of the sea." A later text adds: [42] "He was worshiped by the peoples as a god, because he metamorphosed himself into many shapes." In the nineteenth century the people of the Isle of Man on the eve of St. John the Baptist still carried green meadow grass up to the top of Barule in payment of rent to Mannan-beg-mac-y-Leir.[43] The grandfather of a Manx woman living in 1910 used this prayer: [44] "Little Manannan son of Leirr, who blessed our island, bless us and our boat, going out well, and better coming in, with living and dead (fish) in the boat." And in 1918 Westropp reported that the old sea-god remained "in half-secret belief on the Mayo coast a being of great and dangerous power." [45] Uncanny to think that the Fisher King was still venerated and feared in the twentieth century!

[41] *Cormac's Glossary*, ed. J. O'Donovan, 114.

[42] *RC*, XXIV, 276.

[43] J. Train, *Hist. and Statist. Account of Isle of Man*, II, 120.

[44] W. Y. E. Wentz, *Fairy Faith*, 118. For other Manx traditions *cf.* *ibid.*, 131; A. B. Cook, *Zeus*, I, 301.

[45] *PRIA*, XXXIV, C, 151.

# CHAPTER XIX

## EVALACH, AVALON, AND MORGAN LE FAY

THE approach to the Grail Castle usually lies across or beside a river. But there are a number of passages which place the god's abode in an island out in the sea. These localizations seem to have their basis in a powerful British tradition. Plutarch in his *De Defectu Oraculorum*, as Rhys indicated,[1] writes: "Demetrius further said that of the islands around Britain many lie scattered about uninhabited, of which some are named after deities and heroes. He told us also that, being sent by the emperor with the object of reconnoitring and inspecting, he went to the island which lay nearest to those uninhabited, and found it occupied by few inhabitants, who were, however, sacrosanct and inviolable in the eyes of the Britons."

The Britons were not unlike the Greeks in thus placing the enchanted abodes of the gods in islands of the sea.[2] Beheld in the glamor of distance, surrounded above and below by an expanse of crimson and gold, brooded over by cloudy flames, every island became in the eyes of those on shore an unearthly paradise, the home of their peculiar divinities. The very name of Manawyd or Manawyddan himself is due to the influence of the Welsh name for the Isle of Man, Manaw, with which his Irish prototype Manannan was associated.[3] The Isle of Bardsey was likewise regarded by the Welsh as the place where Merlin had retired to dwell in his glass house,[4] and the Ile de Sein, as late as the year 1810, was the subject of a similar legend among the Bretons.[5] We have already seen how the tiny islet of Grassholm, the westernmost point in Wales, was held to be the site of the marvelous entertainments of the Noble Head, Bran.[6] Rhys has pointed out that the Isle of Lundy off the Devon coast probably owes its Welsh name Ynis Wair to the localization there of the imprisonment of Gwair (alias Gwri).[7] It is perhaps unnecessary

---

[1] Rhys, *Arthurian Legend*, 367 f.
[2] Nutt, *Voyage of Bran*, I, 258–85; *PMLA*, XXXIII, 627.
[3] Loth, *Mab.*², I, 151 note; Thurneysen, *Irische Helden- und Königsage*, 62.
[4] Rhys, *Hib. Lec.*, 155.
[5] A. Plumptre, *Narrative of Three Years' Residence in France*, III, 187.
[6] *Cf.* Chap. XV.          [7] Rhys, *Celtic Folklore*, II, 679.

to remark that we have identified Merlin with Curoi and Celidoine who both betray solar attributes; and the same nature belongs, of course, to the youthful god Gwair or Gwri. It is, therefore, not irrelevant to point out that the Celtic name for St. Michael's Mount was Din Sul, translated as Mons Solis.[8] All these facts point to a powerful belief that the islands not far from the British coast were regarded as the homes of the various gods of the sun.

The land of Sorelois has been identified by Lot with the Sorlingues or Scilly Isles, lying to the west of Land's End.[9] The *Vulgate Lancelot* mentions among the kings of Sorelois Lohoz, his son Gaher, and Galahot,[10] — names in which it is hard not to recognize Welsh Llwch or Lloch, his son Gwair,[11] and a solar epithet. Galahot king of Sorelois suggests strongly identification with Galaad, king of Sarras.[12] This explanation seems all the more plausible when we examine another king of Sarras, Evalach.

In the earlier part of the *Estoire del Saint Graal* we find as lords of Sarras Evalach and his brother-in-law Seraphe, who on conversion took the names Mordrain and Nasciens respectively. We have detected in Evalach, Mordrain, and Nasciens the Avallach, Medrot, and Nasiens of Welsh legend.[13] Avallach is found in the genealogies as the son of Beli, the sun-god.[14]

Now when we are introduced to Evalach in the land of Sarras, we find him enthroned in the temple of the sun. The author of the *Estoire* says [15] that before Mohammedanism was established in Sarras, "this people had no belief, but worshipped all the things that pleased them so that what they worshipped one day, they did not the next. But then they established the sun and the moon and the other planets to worship." When Joseph of Arimathea and his disciples arrived they passed through the city till he came to the temple of the sun, the most beautiful temple in the city.[16] The Saracens held it in greater honor than the rest because it was the temple of the sun, which is the

---

[8] W. J. Rees, *Cambro-British Saints*, 65.

[9] *Étude sur le Lancelot*, 145, note 6.

[10] Sommer, III, 269 f.  Variants of Gaher are Goher, Gloier.

[11] Loth, *Mab.*², I, 276.

[12] Sommer, VI, 196 f.  Sorhaus was probably the intermediate form.

[13] *Cf.* Chap. XV.

[14] Loth, *Mab.*², II, 336.  On Avallach *cf.* ZfSL, XII, 245 ff.

[15] E. Hucher, *Saint Graal*, II, 129.

[16] *Ibid.*, 130.  *Cf.* Potvin, V, 155.

highest of all the planets. In the court of the temple Joseph and
his companions found the aged king Evalach the Unknown, so
called because his birth was a mystery. Later Joseph's son,
Josephe, reveals that Evalach's father was a poor cobbler of
shoes,[17] and though we never in Welsh legend find Beli at that
task, it was for a time the profession of Manawyddan and
Pryderi, and of two other divine personages, Gwydion and
Llew.[18] There seems to have been a Welsh tradition that the
old and young god followed together the craft of shoe-making.
All this points to the divinity of Evalach; his seat in the temple
of the sun, and his rule of Sarras, in which long after Galaad
became king, confirm him as a sun-god.

But we find Avallach connected not only with Sarras or the
Scilly Isles, but also with that one-time island among the fens of
Somerset, Glastonbury, or Ynis Witrin, the Isle of Glass.
On the top of that picturesque cone-shaped hill there rises the
tower of a church, dedicated to St. Michael, who seems here to
have displaced the sun-god just as he did at St. Michael's
Mount. Here ancient tradition, recorded in the *Life of Gildas*,
placed the castle of Melwas, with its "fortifications of reed-beds
and river and marsh." [19]   Melwas' abduction of Guinevere
furnishes so remarkable a parallel to Curoi's abduction of
Blathnat that we may well ascribe to Melwas some likeness to
the solar deity. He was called king of the "aestiva regio," or
Summer Country, apparently a latinization of Welsh "Gwlad
yr Haf," a name of the Other World.[20]  Crestien's description [21]
of the abode of Maheloas, lord of the Isle of Glass, who all
scholars admit is Welsh Melwas, makes it clear that Glastonbury was regarded as a Celtic Paradise. For Crestien's *Ile de
Voirre* is a translation of the Welsh name for Glastonbury, Ynis
Witrin, and he declares that there no thunder is heard, no
lightning strikes, no tempests rage, no toads or serpents exist,
nor is it ever too hot or too cold. At Glastonbury another
tradition placed the abode of Gwynn,[22] the "White One," whom
St. Collen found in the most beautiful castle he had ever seen,
seated in his golden chair, surrounded by musicians, and men

---

[17] Sommer, I, 47.
[18] Loth, *Mab.*², I, 162, 194.
[19] G. Schoepperle, *Tristan and Isolt*, II, 530 f.
[20] Rhys, *Arthurian Legend*, 345.
[21] *Erec*, ed. Foerster, ll. 1946 ff.
[22] Rhys, *Arthurian Legend*, 338 f.

and maidens in the bloom of youth.  Collen, invited to partake
of the most delicious food and drink that his heart could wish,
instead threw holy water over the assemblage, and at once all
vanished.  At Glastonbury, too, tradition placed the Isle of
Avalon.

This name, according to William of Malmesbury, was either
due to the many apples to be found there or to "a certain
Avalloc, who is said to have lived there with his daughters
because of the secrecy of the place." [23]  Rhys also quotes an
anonymous Latin description,[24] which mentions not only the
eternal spring, the abundance of flowers, the absence of age or
disease, but also a royal virgin, most beautiful, surrounded by
her maids.  She bears the wounded Arthur to the hall of King
Avallo, and heals him.  It goes without saying that the relation
of this *regia virgo* to *rex Avallo* is that of daughter to father.
Geoffrey of Monmouth in his *Vita Merlini* gives another description of the fairy isle under the name "Isle of Apples." [25]  He
tells of the nine sisters who dwell there, of whom Morgan is the
fairest.  She teaches them how to use healing herbs, and herself
knows how to change her form and how to fly through the air,
so that when she will she is at Bristol,[26] Chartres, or Pavia.
After the battle of Camlan, the wounded Arthur is brought
across the seas by Telgesinus and Barinthus (in whom Brown
has recognized the mythical bard Taliessin and a sea-god[27]) to
Morgan, who undertakes to cure him if he is left with her long
enough.  De la Rue has justly pointed out [28] how strikingly
this story of nine women, skilled in healing and in shape-shifting,
who live on an island, ministering to those who come, bears to
the account which Pomponius Mela gives [29] of an island Sena off
the coast of Brittany, the modern Sein, which, we have just
seen, modern tradition connects with Merlin.  He speaks of it as
"famous for the oracle of a Gaulish god, whose priestesses,
living in the holiness of perpetual virginity, are said to be nine
in number.  The Gauls call them Senae, and they believe them

---

[23] *Ibid.*, 335.
[24] *Ibid.*; L. A. Paton, *Fairy Mythology*, 46.
[25] Ed. J. J. Parry, *Univ. of Ill. Studies in Lang. and Lit.*, ll. 908–40.
[26] M. Lot informs me personally that he regards this translation of
Bristi as plausible.
[27] *RC*, XXII, 339.
[28] *Essais historiques*, I, 64; L. A. Paton, *op. cit.*, 43 f.
[29] Mela, *De Situ Orbis*, bk. III, ch. 6.

to be endowed with extraordinary gifts, to rouse the seas and the wind by their incantations, to turn themselves into whatsoever animal form they may choose, to cure diseases which among others are incurable, to know what is to come and to foretell it. They are, however, devoted to the service of those voyagers only who have set out on no other errand than to consult them." Since there is no suspicion that Geoffrey is drawing upon Pomponius Mela, one can hardly account for the parallelism except on the theory that these ancient Celtic priestesses came to be regarded as the semidivine daughters of the god, and when the gods were euhemerized into kings, they lived on as the nine daughters of a certain king in Celtic tradition.

Now strangely enough, in the attempts [30] made to explain the name Morgan le Fay, no one seems to have taken the trouble to find out whether Welsh literature supplied us with a daughter of Avallach. One of the triads tells us that she was Modron.[31] She is not represented as a virgin but as the mother of Owein by Urien. If we consult the *Huth Merlin* we find Morgan le Fay the wife of Urien;[32] pretty generally in Arthurian romance we find Urien named as the father of Ivain; and in Malory [33] Morgan is herself called the mother of Ewaine le Blanchmains. Thus as daughter of Avalloc, wife of Urien, mother of Ewayne, Morgan le Fay corresponds exactly to Modron, daughter of Avallach, wife of Urien, and mother of Owein. It is easy to see that the name Modron, being forgotten by the Bretons, was abandoned for Morgan, a similar-sounding man's name. But strangely enough Giraldus Cambrensis speaks of Morganis as "dea quaedam fantastica," "a certain imaginary goddess";[34] and even late in the fourteenth century the author of *Gawain and the Green Knight* speaks of her as "Morgne the goddes." [35] The *Vulgate Lancelot* says that she left human society and dwelt day and night in the forests by the fountains, so that people foolishly called her Morgain *la déesse*.[35a] This is all the

---

[30] Paton, *op. cit.*, 9–12, 148–66, 264–74; *ZfSL*, XLVIII, 82. On Morgan Tud *cf. JEGP*, XXIII, 587.

[31] Loth, *Mab.*², II, 284. Note that tradition assigns to Morgan sisters named Moronoe and Marrion. *Cf.* Paton, *op. cit.*, 50.

[32] Paton, *op. cit.*, 143.

[33] Bk. I, ch. 2.

[34] *Opera*, Rolls ed., IV, 48 f.

[35] Ed. Tolkien, Gordon, l. 2452.

[35a] Paton, *op. cit.*, 165 n.

more significant since Celtic scholars are agreed that Modron is the old Gallo-Roman goddess Matrŏna,[36] who gave her name to the river Marne and to that extent at least was associated with the waters. But of course, she was originally entirely distinct from the nine island priestesses, of whom she later became the chief.

The Welsh made Modron mother not only of Owein but also of Mabon,[37] who goes back to the Apollo Maponos of the Gauls, the latter word meaning "great youth." Now in the German *Lanzelet* there is a Mabuz, who has been equated with the Welsh Mabon,[38] and he is the son of the Lady of the Lake. When one considers how in the last moments of Arthur's earthly life he surrenders first his sword to the lake from which a white arm rises to take it, and how not long after the barge comes and Morgan bears him away, it seems almost certain that Morgan le Fay and the Lady of the Lake were originally the same person. The objection that they are in the later developments of Arthurian romance found opposing each other is of slight value, for we also find Morgan and the Lady of Avalon represented as antagonists,[39] and I imagine there is no one to dispute their original identity.

If our clues have led us aright, both Sarras and Avalon can be identified with islands off the British coast, the Scillies and Glastonbury, and both were held, as Demetrius says, "sacrosanct" because they were thought to be the land of the gods. Arthur's passing to Avalon, as Miss Schoepperle and Cross have proved,[40] is modeled in several respects on the story of the fatal wounding of the Irish hero Fraich and his healing by his goddess kinswomen. And Martin has urged that Arthur lying wounded in Avalon, awaiting the hour of his return, is identical with the Maimed King.[41] None of the accounts of Arthur in Avalon make this very clear, though late Welsh tradition says that Arthur (like so many Maimed Kings) was wounded in the thigh,[42] and Geoffrey in the *Vita Merlini*

---

[36] Rhys, *Hib. Lec.*, 28 f. *Cf.* Robinson's authoritative article on Deae Matres in Hastings' *Encyclopedia of Religion*, IV, 406.

[37] Loth, *Mab.*², I, 322–8.

[38] *Rom.*, 1896, 276.

[39] Paton, *op. cit.*, 52 note 2.

[40] *Vassar Medieval Studies*, 19; *Manly Anniversary Studies*, 284.

[41] *Zur Gralsage*, 31 ff.

[42] Guest, *Mabinogion*, Everyman ed., 316.

describes him lying on a golden bed.[43]    But strangely enough
the legends which the Bretons and Normans planted in Sicily
seem to have preserved the essential details.    Writing in 1212
Gervase of Tilbury reports [44] the local belief that Arthur had
appeared in his time to a groom of the Bishop of Catania, who
had lost his master's horse in the wilds of Etna.    He comes
upon a plain full of all delights, and in a marvelous palace finds
Arthur lying on a royal bed.    Arthur commands the palfrey to
be restored, and tells how in an ancient battle with Modred
and Childeric he was smitten, and because his wounds annually
reopen, he has dwelt there ever since.    Elsewhere Gervase gives
the British version: [45]    "According to the vulgar tradition of the
Bretons Arthur was borne away to the Isle of Avalon (Dava-
lim) in order that his wounds, annually reopening (*recrudes-
centia*), may be cured by the Fay Morgan with her healing
applications."    Now I venture to say that the immortal hero,
whose wounds break out afresh every year, must be like the
Maimed King, in sympathetic tune with the vital forces of the
earth, with the ripening and rotting grain, with the greening
and withering trees, with the waxing and waning solar heat.

Glastonbury certainly can be located on the ordnance map;
Arthur may very plausibly be assigned a place in history; and
the battle of Camlan may, for all we know, have occurred.    But
all three have been woven into the stupendous fabric of Celtic
nature myth.    The battle has become an allegory of the seasons; Arthur has been transformed into an *eniautos daimon*, a
god who is annually wounded or slain and annually revived;
and the Isle of Glastonbury has become the abode of a Maimed
King.

There can be no doubt that the immediate derivation of this
conception of Arthur as an embodiment of the vital forces of
Nature, particularly the sun, is Celtic.    Neither can there be
much doubt that the ultimate derivation is Oriental.[46]    In a
passage which Gaster long since brought forward to prove the
Eastern origin of the Grail story,[47] we hear of an island home of

---

[43] Ll. 934 f.

[44] *Otia Imperialia*, ed. Leibnitz, I, 921.

[45] *Ibid.*, 937.  *Cf.* A. Graf, *Miti, Leggende e Superstizioni*, II, 303.  On
other localizations of the legend *cf.* Nutt, *Studies*, 198; E. S. Hartland,
*Science of Fairytales*, 207–9.

[46] On Oriental features in Celtic *cf.* Patch's discussion, *PMLA*, XXXIII,
612.                                  [47] *Folklore*, II, 60.

the Sun, where the god is seen lying on a couch.  The fourth century romance of Pseudo-Callisthenes recounts how Alexander the Great came to a city on an island, with twelve towers of gold and emerald.  A priest ordered the conqueror to depart.  He next ascended a high mountain, and discovered on the summit fair houses of gold and silver, and a round temple.  "Inside and outside were images of demigods, bacchantes, satyrs and of others initiated in the sacred mysteries. . . .  A couch was placed in the middle of the temple: on this couch lay a man clothed in silk.[48]  I could not see his face, for it was veiled: but I saw strength and greatness.  In the middle of the temple there was a golden chain weighing a hundred pounds, and suspended from it was a transparent wreath; a precious stone which illumined the whole temple took the place of fire."  Alexander was warned to cease opposing the god, and when he was about to feast there with his soldiers, there arose a crash of trumpets, drums, and other musical instr uments.  The whole mountain was covered with smoke as if a heavy storm had broken on them.  In another of the houses Alexander saw an amphora of gold with many figures on it, a golden throne, and a golden vine with seven branches.  Ger vase of Tilbury gives much the same details in his description of the Temple of the Sun in Ethiopia.[49]  Near the confines of Ocean "is the land of the Sun in the form of an island, two hundred stadia in length and of equal breadth. . . .  In this same place are two very similar houses, square, made of gold and cinnamon. . . .  There is the couch of the Sun made of refined gold and ivory, studded with most precious stones, and the splendor of the couch shines throughout the palace."  Here too is a golden vine.  "Next to this building is the house of the priest, páved with gold.  The priest verily lives on frankincense and subsists on balsam; he sleeps under vines on the pavement; he permits entrance to no one, except him who will sojourn at Heliopolis."

Not only do these abodes of the sun-god remind us of Arthur on his golden couch in the isle of Avalon, but also the golden vine and the golden amphora may be the counterparts of the golden tree and the silver kieve,[50] which are commonplaces of the Irish Otherworld palaces.  The jewel-studded couch recalls

[48] The Middle English *Wars of Alexander* says this was the sun-god.
[49] *Otia Imperialia*, ed. F. Liebrecht, 35 f.
[50] *Folklore*, XVII, 143–61.

vividly the couches of Conchobar and the Fisher King which Nitze has already called to our notice. But the most remarkable features are the squareness of the island and the wreath suspended from a golden chain in the middle of the temple. These curious details crop up unmistakably in Celtic descriptions of the Other World which we shall study in the next chapters.

# CHAPTER XX

## KAIR BELLI AND KAER SIDI

In a curious political poem called the *Draco Normannicus*, written by Étienne de Rouen before 1170, we find what purports to be a letter written by King Arthur to Henry II, threatening to return and overwhelm him if he did not cease to molest the Bretons.[1] Arthur's sister Morganis, the deathless "nymph," has healed his wounds with herbs in the sacred isle of Avalon, and has made him immortal.[2] His warlike ardor and prowess have returned and he has become lord of the Antipodes, the lower hemisphere. Half the world acknowledges his sway, and he has the power to return when he wills to the upper world. The passage proves that the Breton belief that Arthur dwelt as king in remote islands beyond the sunset had been interpreted by some learned and realistic mind of the third quarter of the twelfth century in terms of contemporary geographical science. Thus Arthur became King of the western hemisphere, and the Other World became the Antipodes. One may also see why in Crestien's *Erec*, almost exactly contemporary with the *Draco Normannicus*, there appear two brothers, Belin, the dwarf king of the Antipodes, and his giant brother Brien.[3] In Geoffrey of Monmouth's *History*, the rivalry of two kings, Belinus and Brennius, sons of Dunwallo Molmutius, occupies a good deal of space.[4] Welsh tradition mentions both a Beli and a Bran, sons of Dyvnwal Moelmud.[5] The two brothers, Belin and Brien, whom Crestien mentions, would seem to be derived from authentic Celtic tradition. When we remember that Belin goes back to Apollo Bellinus, and that the name Beli occurs in the genealogies as father of Avallach, the solar deity of an Otherworld island, it is not hard to see how he became king of the

[1] *SNPL*, X, 145. *Cf. ibid.* 167.

[2] *Chronicles of Stephen*, etc, Rolls Series, ed. Howlett, ll. 1161 ff.

[3] Ed. W. Foerster, 1890, ll. 1993 ff. In the text Foerster gives the form Bilis, but the MSS. offer more support for the form Belins.

[4] Bk. III, ch. 1–10. *Cf. ZcP*, I, 287.

[5] W. N. Johns, *Historical Traditions and Facts relating to Newport*, I, 16; *Cymmrodor*, IX, 1, p. 174. *Cf. Internat. Cong. of Religions*, III, vol. 2, 237.

Antipodes. His dwarfish stature is a not uncommon supernatural trait in Arthurian romance.[6] But his gigantic brother Brien, whose name must be a Breton substitution for Welsh Bran, could not shrink as easily, for Welsh tradition too explicitly stated that Bran, son of Llyr, was so huge that neither house nor ship could contain him.[7]

Since we have already identified Beli or Belin with King Pelles it should not seem strange that Pelles is called in *Perlesvaus* King of the Low Folk.[8] Nor should it surprise us to find Pelles in the *Vulgate Lancelot* lord of a castle in the Isle of Joy.[9] There we read that his daughter discovers in the garden of Corbenic Lancelot, her beloved, crazed and exhausted. Pelles has him bound and brought to the Palace Adventurous: the Grail exerts its healing virtue and restores his reason. He then tells the king that he wishes to be transported to an island where no one will recognize him, and Pelles prepares for him a castle in an island near by, "which is filled with all good things." There Pelles, his daughter, and Lancelot take up their abode. "Lancelot remained a long time in this castle, he and this damsel who kept him company, and there were damsels with him in great plenty." The island was called the Isle of Joy "because of the damsel who was daughter to King Pelles and the others who were with her, who made the greatest mirth that ever any women made. Nor was there any winter so great that they did not come every day to dance at the pine."

King Pelles' Isle of Joy seems to be not only such a winterless island as those of Maheloas and Avallo, but also to be specifically a land of women such as that depicted in the Chateau Merveil and in its prototype, the island where the Irish Bran sojourned, and to which he doubtless returned. Since in Welsh the sea is called Beli's liquor,[10] it is probable that like Manawyddan and the Welsh Bran, Beli was a god not only of the sun but also of the ocean.

But it is equally clear that Pelles' other castle of Corbenic is situated on the mainland of Logres. According to the testimony of Johannes Cornubiensis, who wrote in the twelfth

---

[6] *Cf.* F. Wohlgemuth, *Riesen und Zwerge;* L. A. Paton, *Fairy Mythology,* 129, and especially ROM, XLVI, 45.

[7] Mabinogi of *Branwen Daughter of Llyr.*

[8] Potvin, I, 2.

[9] Sommer, V, 400–3.

[10] J. Rhys, J. B. Jones, *Welsh People,* 43 note.

century, there was a castle of Beli in Cornwall.[11] "The town (*municipium*) which in our region is called in English Aschbiri and in British Kair Belli, is the Fatale Castrum." This Aschbiri Loth has identified with a circular earthwork in the parish of Gweek St. Mary,[12] placed on a hilltop, several miles inland from the Atlantic, and still called Ashbury Camp.[13] It lies in the center of a region which from early times has been rich in heroic and romantic legend. It commands a magnificent view to the north of Hartland Point, which Ptolemy tantalizingly calls the Headland of Heracles. Beyond, dim across the water, lies Lundy, the island which Rhys conjectured was the place of the mythical captivity of the god Gwair.[14] Southwest, about twelve miles away, invisible beyond the rolling moors, lies Tintagel, also a "Fatale Castrum," for it was called "chastel faé" on account of the tradition that it vanished from sight twice a year.[14a] To the south is Slaughter Bridge, traditional site of the fatal battle of Camlan, and Dozmare Pool, the mere where in popular belief Arthur was borne away by the weeping queens into the sunset.[15] Here at Ashbury Camp the Cornishmen of the twelfth century placed Kair Belli, the Castle of Pelles.

What right have we to equate Kair Belli or Ashbury Camp with the Castle of the Grail? Johannes Cornubiensis says expressly that Kair Belli is the Fatale Castrum, in other words the Faery Castle or the Castle of the Fays.[16] With this we may equate Kaer Sidi, for both Rhys and Gruffydd agree that Kaer Sidi is to be connected with the Irish *Side*,[17] the Irish immortals, who according to *Fiacc's Hymn* [18] were worshipped by the pagan Irish, though later the word lost its meaning of "god" and was used in the sense of fay. Now Kaer Sidi is one of the names of Annwn, where was kept the caldron which would not boil the food of a coward or perjurer, a prototype of the feeding Grail. Thus Ashbury Camp may properly be called the site of the

[11] *RC*, III, 86.
[12] J. Loth, *Contributions à l'étude*, 64.
[13] *Journal of Royal Institution of Cornwall*, X, 233, XV, 113.
[14] J. Rhys, *Celtic Folklore*, II, 679.
[14a] Oxford *Folie Tristan*, ed. Bédier, ll. 131 ff.
[15] W. H. Dickinson, *Arthur in Cornwall*. The best general work on Arthurian topography, though far from scientific, is F. J. Snell's *King Arthur's Country*.
[16] Ducange *sub Fatalis* translates *fatales deae* as fèes.
[17] Rhys, *Celtic Folklore*, II, 678; *Enc. Brit.*, ed. 11, V, 642.
[18] W. Stokes, *Gadelica*, 127, l. 4.

Grail Castle, for as Kair Belli it can be identified with King
Pelles' Castle of Corbenic, and as the Fatale Castrum it can be
identified with Kaer Sidi, where the caldron of the Head of
Annwn abode.

Ashbury was probably only one of several traditional sites of
the Grail Castle in the twelfth century. About them may have
clung such legends as that preserved in *Perlesvaus:* [19] "When it
was fallen into decay, many folk of the lands and islands that
were nighest thereunto marvel them what may be in this manor.
. . . Sundry folk went thither from all the lands, but none
durst never enter there again save two Welsh knights that had
heard tell of it. Full comely knights they were, young and joy-
ous-hearted. So either pledged him to other that he would go
thither by way of gay adventure; but therein remained they of
a long space after, and when again they came forth they led the
life of hermits, and clad them in hair shirts, and went by the
forest, and so ate nought save roots only, and led a right hard
life; yet ever they made as though they were glad, and if that
any should ask whereof they rejoiced in such wise, 'Go,' said
they, to them that asked, 'thither where we have been, and
you shall know the wherefore.'"

It may stick in someone's crop that there is only this indirect
connection through Kair Belli between Beli and the Other
World or its caldron. This is noteworthy because several gods
are mentioned in association with Annwn, — Pwyll, Pryderi,
Manawyd, Hafgan, Arawn, Gwynn, — yet Beli is not among
them; and we have several mentions of Beli, yet none of them
connects him with the caldron. It may relieve this doubt to
recollect how other important links in Welsh mythological
tradition have barely escaped oblivion. The epithet Gwallt
Avwyn, from which all the myriad occurrences of the name
Gawain derive and which must therefore have been fairly
common, is preserved only in a catalogue of heroic names, with
nothing to distinguish it above the rest. The absence of direct
connection between Beli and the caldron castle need not dis-
turb us. If we accept the identification of Kair Belli with Kaer
Sidi, and remember that Pelles had, as well as an inland castle,
a castle in the Isle of Joy, we can feel confident of our position.
For it can be proved beyond the possibility of rejoinder that
Kaer Sidi is identical with an island castle of the Grail described

---

[19] Potvin, I, 347. Tr. Evans, Everyman ed., 378.

in *Perlesvaus*.   Let us examine the pertinent passages in the *Harryings of Annwn*: [20]

> Complete was the captivity of Gwair in Kaer Sidi,
> (Lured thither) through the emissary of Pwyll and Pryderi.
> Before him no one entered into it,
> Into the heavy, dark chain which held the faithful youth.

Then follows the stanza about the pearl-rimmed caldron.   In the next we read:

> In the four-cornered fortress, in quick-door island,
> The dusk and the darkness mingle;
> The sparkling wine is their drink, before their retinue.

And finally:

> Beyond the Fortress of Glass they had not seen Arthur's
> valor.
> Hard it was found to converse with their sentinel.

In the last feature Rhys recognized the tradition recorded by Nennius that three sons of a certain warrior of Spain beheld a glass tower in the middle of the sea and men on the tower, with whom they sought to converse, without receiving any answer.[21]

Other details concerning Kaer Sidi are found in a passage in which the bard conceives himself as having attained that Isle of Joy.[22]

> Perfect is my seat in Kaer Sidi.
> Nor plague nor age harms him who dwells therein.
> Manawyd and Pryderi know it. . . .
> Around its corners ocean's currents flow,
> And above it is the fertile fountain,
> And sweeter than white wine is the drink therein.

Putting together these passages, we have in Kaer Sidi an island castle, four-cornered, where are to be found a fountain, a caldron, a prisoner named Gwair, and a glass tower with a sentry who would not reply to questions.   Its rulers are the older gods Manawyd and Pwyll, and the young god, their stepson and son, respectively, Pryderi.   Now let us turn to the concluding adventures of Perceval in *Perlesvaus*.[23]

---

[20] *Cf.* translations in Skene, *Four Ancient Books*, I, 264 f;  Malory, Everyman ed., I, xxii–xxiv; Rhys, *Celtic Folklore*, II, 679.

[21] Rhys, *Hib. Lec.*, 263 f;  *Mon. Germ. Hist.*, *Auct. Ant.*, XIII, 155.

[22] Rhys, *Arthurian Legend*, 301.

[23] Potvin, I, 327 ff.   Tr. S. Evans, Everyman ed., 357.

Perceval and a pilot sailed far till "they saw a castle and an island of the sea. He asked his pilot if he knew what castle it was. 'Certes,' saith he, 'Not I, for so far have we run that I know not neither the sea nor the stars.' They come nigh the castle, and saw four that sounded bells at the four corners of the town. . . . They issued forth of the ship and went by the side of the sea toward the castle, and therein were the fairest halls and the fairest mansions that any might see ever. He looketh underneath a tree that was tall and broad and seeth the fairest fountain and the clearest that any may devise, and it was all surrounded of rich pillars, and the gravel thereof seemed to be gold and precious stones. Above this fountain were two men sitting, their beards and hair whiter than the driven snow, albeit they seemed young of visage." They welcomed Perceval, saying, "'Marvel not of this that we do, for well knew we the knight that bare this shield tofore you. Many a time we saw him or ever God was crucified.' . . . Perceval looketh beyond the fountain and seeth in a right fair place a round vessel like as it were ivory (*ivoire*), and it was so large that there was a knight within, all armed. He looketh thereinto and seeth the knight, and speaketh unto him many times, but never the more willeth the knight to answer him." Perceval is led to the royal hall, where he and many others all clad in white, set out their cups and wash at a great laver of gold. "The Masters made Perceval sit at the most master-table with themselves. . . . He seeth a chain of gold come down above him loaded with precious stones, and in the midst thereof was a crown of gold. . . . As soon as the Masters saw it descending they opened a great wide pit that was in the midst of the hall. . . . There issued thence the greatest cry and the most dolorous that any heard ever. . . . He seeth that the chain of gold descendeth thither and is there stayed until they have wellnigh eaten, and then draweth itself again into the air and so goeth again aloft." One of the Masters then gives a rather confused explanation: "Yea, be you faithful to the end herein, and you shall have the crown of gold upon your head so soon as you return and so shall you be seated in the throne, and shall be king of an island that is near to this, right plenteous of all things good." But he may not depart from his hosts unless he promises to return as soon as he sees the ship with a red cross on the sail. Perceval promises and sails away the next day, liberates a chained youth, Galobrun, in a neighboring island, and substitutes a certain Gohas, who has imprisoned Galobrun. After sundry adventures, Perceval returns to the Grail Castle on the mainland and dwells there a long time. One day [24] he hears a bell sound loud and high toward the sea, and spies the vessel with the white sail and the cross thereon. Perceval entered it, "and never thereafter did no earthly man know what became of him." But the clear inference is that he, like Bran, returned to his Otherworld island, and in fulfilment of the prediction of the immortal elder, became its king.

Let us first note that the mysterious golden chain with its crown of gold, which descends into the pit and is then withdrawn, does not serve to confine the prisoner in the pit, and therefore cannot be derived from "the heavy dark chain which held the faithful" Gwair. It seems rather analogous to the equally mysterious golden chain which sustained a transparent wreath in the middle of the temple of the Sun as described by Pseudo-Callisthenes, — a description already shown to be closely related to the original of certain Celtic conceptions of the Other World. Somehow this feature must have passed from the Mediterranean into Irish conceptions of the Other World, for it appears in ecclesiasticized form among the legends connected with St. Columba.[24a] The clerics of his household arrived at an island with a fair house in the middle, and were courteously welcomed. "Whilst they were there, a beautiful golden cowl was let down upon the floor of the royal hall. And not one of the folk of the house took it up. . . . They were richly served, and had great cheer that night, and they were given well brewed ale so that they were drunken and merry." The account goes on to say that there were a vast number of men and women there, "praising the King of the Sun." This parallel too is obvious, and renders it certain that all the features in the island visited by Perceval must have their origin in the Welsh conception of Annwn.[25]

For in *Perlesvaus*, it seems, we have the Breton version of Pryderi's entry into his island kingdom, which he was to share, as the Welsh poems seem to imply, with Manawyd or Pwyll. Indeed the two snowy-haired Masters, who yet seemed young of

---

[24] Potvin, I, 347. Everyman, 377.

[24a] O'Donnell, *Life of Colum Cille*, ed. O'Kelleher, Schoepperle, 399 f.

[25] On Annwn *cf. ZcP*, I, 29; *Folklore*, XVIII, 121.

visage, can only be two elder gods, lords of that Kaer Sidi, where neither plague nor age harms him who dwells there. For who does not recognize the island castle with its four corners, its fountain, the drinking, the mysterious prisoner? The knight in his round vessel of ivory who would not answer is unquestionably the sentinel of the glass tower, for the confusion between "de voire" and "d'ivoire" was not only possible but probable, either in oral or written transmission. The name Gwair even seems to be preserved in the names of the two successive prisoners in the neighboring island, for Gohas is an easy development from Gohar, and the youth Galobrun may well have developed from his epithet Gwallt Euryn, through the form Galvariun found on the Modena portal. These prisoners we shall consider more fully in Chapter XXXII.

In *Perlesvaus*, then, we have not only a version of the Beheading Test in which the mythological implications are clearer than in the Irish account, but also a description of Kaer Sidi far fuller than that furnished by the *Harryings of Annwn*. The one essential feature of Kaer Sidi that seems to be missing is the caldron, which we have equated with the Grail. But the French author clearly intimates that when the Grail leaves the inland castle it is transported to Perceval's destination, his island kingdom. For the voice announces to him that "the most holy Graal shall appear herein no more, but within a brief space shall you know well the place where it shall be." If we are right in concluding that Perceval returned to be crowned in his island kingdom, we must believe that the Grail had already preceded him thither. If, moreover, Perceval is that Pryderi who rules over the island where Gwair is enchained, then we may add the Ynis Wair or Lundy Island to the many other islands off the British coast which had a sacred character and were believed to be the blissful dwelling places of the gods.

Lundy is worthy of its traditions. Kingsley, who makes it the scene of the memorable judgment of God upon the Santa Catherina and Amyas Leigh, also gives us a blood-stirring description of the island itself.[26]

"The cyclopean wall of granite cliff which forms the western side of Lundy ends sheer in a precipice of some three hundred feet, topped by a pile of snow-white rock, bespangled with golden lichens. . . . It was a glorious sight upon a glorious day.

[26] *Westward Ho*, ch. XXXIII.

To the northward the glens rushed down toward the cliff, crowned with grey crags, and carpeted with purple heather and green fern; and from their feet stretched away to the westward the sapphire rollers of the vast Atlantic, crowned with a thousand crests of flying foam. On their left hand, some ten miles to the south, stood out against the sky the purple wall of Hartland cliffs, sinking lower and lower as they trended away to the southward along the lonely ironbound shore of Cornwall, until they faded, dim and blue, into the blue horizon forty miles away. The sky was flecked with clouds, which rushed toward them fast upon the roaring south-west wind; and the warm ocean-breeze swept up the cliffs, and whistled through the heather-bells, and howled in cranny and in crag,

Till the pillars and clefts of the granite
Rang like a God-swept lyre."

# CHAPTER XXI

## SONE DE NANSAI

THE description of the island of the immortal elders in *Perlesvaus* reflects, as we have seen, with remarkable fidelity the description of Kaer Sidi in the *Harryings of Annwn;* we found there the four-cornered island fortress, the fountain, the two aged immortals, the silent sentry in the glass tower, the feasting and drinking, and the prisoner. The caldron of the Welsh poem, which we have equated with the feeding Grail, is not there, though it is clearly implied at the close of the *Perlesvaus* that the Grail was to pass to that island where Perceval was to be King.

In the curious romance of *Sone de Nansai*, however, composed in the latter half of the thirteenth century, we have a description of the isle of the immortal elders in which the Grail figures prominently. Singer and Miss Weston have called attention to the importance of this romance for our problem.[1] Its comparatively late date and the strangely untraditional names have been misleading. Its correspondence in a number of features to the *Perlesvaus* and the *Harryings of Annwn* proves its authenticity. In *Sone de Nansai* the Grail abides in an island, with four towers, — apparently at the four corners, — under the guardianship of holy men: we hear of three streams issuing from a rock, and of a great feast.[2] These features, though much less distinctly recognizable than in the *Perlesvaus*, must proceed from the old Welsh tradition of the four-cornered island fortress, of the fountain, of the feasts and wassailing, and of the elder gods. Furthermore, *Sone de Nansai* provides parallels to the *Perlesvaus* on the following points: the hero arrives at the island, is entertained there lavishly, finds besides the two chief holy men a company garbed in white, departs for a time, but returns to be crowned king of the land.[3] On two essential features of Kaer Sidi the *Perlesvaus* and *Sone de Nansai* supplement each other:

---

[1] *Zeitschrift für deutsches Altertum*, XLIV, 327 ff; *Rom*, XLIII, 403 ff.
[2] Ed. M. Goldschmidt, ll. 4339 ff. On Otherworld fountain *cf. PMLA*, XXXIII, 620.
[3] The return is narrated ll. 17017 ff.

the former supplying the mysterious prisoner, and the latter the Grail. There can be little question that *Sone de Nansai* is a document of the highest value for the recovery of the Welsh Grail tradition. Let us look at it more closely.

We learn that Alain, King of Norway, takes Sone into his service, and shows him his land, which, strange to relate, abounds in almond and olive trees, camels, griffins, and so forth.[4] The explanation is not difficult if we identify Alain with Arawn, Head of Annwn,[5] and Norway with Llychlyn, which, according to Rhys, "at first meant the fabulous land beneath the lakes or waves of the sea, but got in the time of the Norsemen's ravages to mean the land of the Fiords or Norway."[6] Alain and Sone came to a plain, the fairest ever seen, manifestly related to the Irish Mag Mell or Plain of Delight. Thence they set out for the island Galoche, which Bruce has correctly interpreted as a misunderstanding of the French "isle galesche," that is, an island of Wales.[7] As they approached Alain sounded a horn, and two monks in a little boat put out from the island, weeping and angry, but on recognizing the king, they welcomed him. They landed, and beheld a most beautiful castle, around which the sea surged. It had four towers on the outer wall, and in the middle a great tower. This central tower was round, a hundred feet in diameter. Within, in the middle there was a fireplace on four gilded columns, which supported a copper flue. Nitze has shown this to be the arrangement described in Crestien's Grail Castle, the central fireplace being an essentially Celtic feature.[8] Here, it is said, he whom God loves would never tire of beholding the marvelous works, and here is there plenty of every good thing. Alain introduces Sone to the company of monks, and all sit down to feast in a walled meadow. Nearby three streams issuing from a rock meet, and where they fall into the sea, all manner of fish gather. Alain and Sone sit at the master dais and banquet so heartily that it may have wearied those who serve. Afterwards and the next morning they attend a solemn mass. Then the abbot tells the history of the institution. He says, "The castle was founded by the holy body

---

[4] Like Bruce I remain unconvinced by Nyrop's theory that the author of *Sone* knew Norway. *Cf.* Bruce, *Evolution*, I, 350 note.

[5] *Cf.* Chap. XV.

[6] Rhys, *Arthurian Legend*, 11.

[7] Bruce, *Evolution*, I, 350 f, note.

[8] *Studies in Honor of A. M. Elliott*, I, 30 ff.

(*cors*) of which you see the holy vessel lying yonder." [9] This muddled statement is, as we shall see in Chapter XXIII, due to the fact that the author has misunderstood the word *cors* which stood in his source; for it was the nominative of *cor*, meaning a drinking horn, and actually referred to the holy vessel or Grail itself. The abbot then tells the story of Joseph of Arimathea's acquisition of the spear and the cup, which fed him during his imprisonment, which shone like the sun, and healed those who touched it. Finally Joseph left Escalone (apparently a confusion of Avalon and Askalon) in a boat alone, became a knight, arrived in Norway, drove out the Saracens, and wedded the daughter of the heathen king. But she, though baptized, remained a heathen at heart, and God punished Joseph for his sin by smiting him sorely in the reins and below, with the result that he always had to lie down. But the good king Joseph had a boat, and right after mass used to go forth to fish, with a boatman to row him whither he liked. Therefore Joseph was called the Fisher King. His realm was called Lorgres, — a clear indication that it was not Norway, but England, for which the Welsh word is Lloegyr and which in Arthurian romance is never far removed from the Other World. During his malady, as we have already read in chapter XVIII, all the reproductive powers of Nature and man were sterile. But finally a knight healed him, and thereafter he had displayed great prowess and confounded the heathen. Before his death he had founded this monastery consisting of an abbot and twelve monks in memory of Our Lord and the twelve apostles.

The abbot then opened a vessel of ivory and took out the Grail, which illumined all the land. He showed also the spear, the blade of which was white, and from which hung a drop of blood. The abbey was well provided with holy bodies (*cors*), and the abbot had served them well. Then there was another long banquet, Alain and Sone again sitting at the master dais. They finally left the island. But the abbot sent after them the sword with which Joseph had guarded the land, and with this weapon Sone slew a giant in single combat.

Long after, when Alain has died, Sone returns with Alain's daughter Odee to be married at Galoche with all ceremony. An archbishop and three bishops officiate, and all are robed in white. After the wedding, the Grail, the spear, a piece of the

[9] Ll. 4557 ff.

cross, and a candle which the angel of the Annunciation had held, are borne in procession, Sone himself carrying the Grail.

We have already concluded that the island of the immortal elders in the *Perlesvaus* is but a partial Christianization of legends concerning Annwn and its lords, the pagan divinities. Is it clear how these dwellers in Annwn became a community of monks? Brown in a penetrating article has shown how many of the pagan Irish *Imrama* or Voyages, such as that of Bran, became Christianized.[10] He quotes from the tenth-century *Imram Snedgusa* an account of a visit to the Other World, in which the supernatural folk of pagan fancy have been replaced by clerics.[11] "And they beheld a great lofty island, and all therein was delightful and hallowed. Good was the King that abode in the island, and he was holy and righteous: and great was his host, and noble was the dwelling of that King, for there were a hundred doors in that house, and an altar at every door, and a priest at every altar offering Christ's body. So the clerics [i.e., Snedgus and his companions] entered that house and each of them [host and guests] blessed the other: and thereafter the whole of that great host, both woman and man, went to communion at the Mass. Then wine is dealt out to them." It is not hard to recognize here a similar development to that in *Sone:* the holiness of the inhabitants of the island, the celebration of Mass, the drinking of wine.

A clearer case is found in the comparison adduced by Brown between the mainly pagan *Voyage of Maelduin* and the Christianized *Navigatio Sancti Brendani,* of the tenth century.[12]

In the *Voyage of Maelduin* we read: "They came to an island with a golden rampart around it. . . . Here they saw a man whose raiment was the hair of his own body. They inquired what sustenance he found, and he told them that in the island was a fountain which yielded whey or water on Friday and on Wednesday, but milk on Sunday, and ale and wine on the greater feasts." In this island they were miraculously fed. "At none there came to every man of them half a cake, and a piece of fish: and they drank their fill of the liquor, which was yielded to them out of the fountain of the island."

In the *Navigatio,* St. Brendan and his companions came to an island where there was a monastery. They were received by the monks, their feet were washed, and they were given mar-

velously white bread, one loaf to each pair, and herbs of wonderful savor. The abbot then said that no man knew the origin
of this food, save that it came of God's charity. Every day the
twenty-four monks received twelve loaves, and on Sundays
and feast-days a loaf apiece. They had been there eighty
years, yet neither age nor feebleness had appeared in their
members. They never lacked for food, and neither cold nor
heat ever overcame them. The lights in the church were miraculously kindled for the services.

The relation of the *Imrama* to *Sone de Nansai* scarcely needs
elaboration. For here without question are parallel developments from the immortal islanders of Celtic mythology into
Christian monastic communities. That such a transformation
took place, no one can doubt, but one may well ask what
specific causes, apart from the general tendency toward Christianization, produced this precise result. In a part of the life of
Patrick which was composed within a generation after the saint's
death,[13] we already find a tendency to confuse the Christian
clergy with the old deities.[14] Patrick and his bishops were
sitting beside a well at sunrise on the slopes of the magic hill of
Cruachan, when two princesses came to wash their hands.
Finding these venerable figures in white mysteriously assembled
there, they asked in alarm: "Whence are ye and whence have
ye come? Are ye of the elves or of the gods?" But the fact
which most clearly accounts for the transformation of the
sacred islands of the gods into the dwellings of monastic communities is the actual occupation of the sacred islands off the
coasts of Britain by Christian monks. Stories told about the
divine inhabitants of these islands were naturally transferred
to the human but still hallowed successors. A good example
is that of Bardsey, an island whither the immortal Merlin was
supposed to have retired to dwell in his glass house, with the
Thirteen Treasures of the Isle of Britain.[15] It became in
Christian times the abode of a group of hermits, who were
called "the pure-souled dwellers of Enlli." [16] We have no
Christianized version of the abode of Merlin in the Isle of
Bardsey, with his Thirteen Treasures, but the picture is not

---

[13] J. B. Bury, *Life of S. Patrick*, 141.
[14] *Tripartite Life*, ed. Stokes, Rolls Series, 99–101.
[15] Rhys, *Hib. Lec.*, 155.
[16] J. E. Lloyd, *Hist. of Wales*, I, 216 f.

unlike that of the Isle Galoche or Welsh island, where dwell the thirteen monks with the Grail, the spear, the sword, and so forth.  In fact, many a hermit, anchorite, and venerable figure in religious garb who crosses our path in Arthurian romance may be legitimately suspected of being a god or goddess in disguise.

Now while the Island of Galoche seems to be a highly Christianized form of the Celtic Other World as described in the *Harryings of Annwn*, yet there is in *Sone de Nansai* another island,[17] which seems to be the most extraordinary composite of Celtic conceptions of the Other World.  After his marriage and coronation in the Isle Galoche, Sone and his queen depart for a visit to a neighboring island, which is said to be so exactly square that no one could tell which side was longer.  The walls are high, wide, and made of crystal.  There were four palaces at the four corners of the walls.  A bowshot away was a great causeway which led to the mainland half a league away.  Connecting the causeway with the island was the Sword Bridge, where many heads were stricken off when Meleagan was lord.  His father was King Baudemagus, and his grandfather Tadus.  In the center of the island was a fountain which welled up through a horn of gilded copper.  And there was also a cemetery, where the names of the buried were inscribed on stones.  While here Sone and his wife were overwhelmed by a terrific tempest.  There was lightning, thunder, and a gale which tore up trees, and drove mountainous waves over the island, so that all who did not take refuge on the walls were drowned.  Sone saved Odee's life.  At last after three days and nights, a thunderbolt fell in the cemetery, tearing open the tomb of Joseph of Arimathea's heathen wife.  Then the sun shone out once more.  But the stench from the opened tomb was not relieved till the body was thrown into the sea.  Sone and his bride returned to Galoche.

First, the four palaces at the four corners of the walls relate this island to Galoche with its four towers upon the walls, to the isle of the immortal elders in *Perlesvaus* with its four-cornered town, and to Kaer Sidi called the Four-cornered Fortress.[18]  Secondly, the fact that the island is so square that no one could tell which side was the longest carries us back to that description of the island of the Sun which Gervase of Tilbury drew from

Oriental sources, for the island is said to be two hundred stadia in length and the same in breadth.[19]   Thirdly, the description of the terrific storm on the sacred island may be a survival of the very ancient British superstition recorded by Plutarch.[20] After mentioning the visit of Demetrius to the sacred islands off the British coast, he adds: "So after his arrival a great disturbance of the atmosphere took place, accompanied by many portents, by the winds bursting forth into hurricanes, and by fiery bolts falling.   When it was over, the islanders said that some one of the mighty had passed away."   The experiences of Demetrius and Sone are similar enough to suggest a connection when we realize that both visit sacred islands off the British coast, both are overwhelmed by a tempest, in both accounts a fiery bolt falls, and the portents are caused by a death or by the dead.   Fourthly, the walls of crystal remind us of Merlin's glass house on the sacred isle of Bardsey, of the Glass Fortress mentioned in the *Harryings of Annwn* and reappearing as a round vessel of ivory in *Perlesvaus*, and of the name Ynis Witrin or Glass Island which the Celts gave to Glastonbury.   Fifthly, the Sword Bridge equates our island once more with the sacred isles of Merlin and of Glastonbury.[21]   In the *Huth Merlin* [22] we read that the enchanter, besides making a Perilous Bed, a testing sword, and a sword set in a block of stone, made a bridge of iron, not half a foot in breadth, connecting the isle with the land.   Before leaving the island he instructed those in the castle that he wished it to be called the Isle of Merlin, and so no one dared to call it otherwise than the Isle of Merlin or the Isle of Marvels.   The Sword Bridge serves also to identify the square island in *Sone* with the famous Otherworld castle in Crestien's *Charette*,[23] to which Meleagant abducted Queen Guinevere.   This castle could be approached either by the Water Bridge or the Sword Bridge, and lay in the land of Gorre, from which no stranger returns.   The author of *Sone* says expressly that the square island was once the dominion of Meleagan and of his father Baudemagus,[24] thus once more equating it with the Otherworld castle in Crestien's *Charette*.

[19] Gervase of Tilbury, *Otia Imperialia*, ed. Liebrecht, 35.

[20] Rhys, *Arthurian Legend*, 368.   *Cf.* S. H. O'Grady, *Silva Godelica*, II, 287.

[21] For an exhaustive treatment of the Sword Bridge *cf. RR*, IV, 166 ff.

[22] *Huth Merlin*, ed. Ulrich, G. Paris, II, 57–60.

[23] Ll. 668 ff.                    [24] Ll. 17138 ff.

Now Meleagan we know is the Melwas who according to the *Life of Gildas*, carried off Guinevere to his castle in the marsh-encircled island of Glastonbury.[25]

Finally, Bruce has shown that the square island in *Sone* bears a marked resemblance to the island of Gundebaldus, described in the thirteenth century Latin romance, *Historia Meriadoci*.[26] Gundebaldus' island is square, lying in the midst of a bog, called the "Land from Which No Man Returns." [27] Four narrow causeways meet in the island, and four castles stand at the points where these causeways touch it. These four castles remind us of the two islands in *Sone*, the island of the immortal elders in *Perlesvaus*, and the Quadrangular Fortress in the *Harryings of Annwn;* but the division of the island by the four causeways meeting in the center may be a reminiscence of the Isle of the Four Precious Walls in the *Voyage of Maelduin*, where four walls of gold, silver, copper, and crystal meet in the center and divide the island into four parts allotted to kings, queens, youths, and maidens respectively.[28] In the center of Gundebaldus' island is a hall of beautiful workmanship, built by the enchanter himself, and surrounded by gardens and streams. When any knight comes to take service under him, the wizard tests him by a joust on the narrow causeway, and has hurled every opponent into the morass. The emperor's daughter, however, provides Meriadoc with a steed stronger than Gundebaldus' own, and the enchanter, falling into his own trap, is swallowed up in the bog. Even though the author of the *Historia Meriadoci* places this island in the Rhine (probably because the story had to do with an emperor and his daughter, and he knew none but the emperor of Germany), yet the names confirm the Celtic origin of the tradition. The wizard Gundebaldus can hardly be other than the wizard Guinebaut of the *Vulgate Merlin*,[29] and Guinebaut Rhys has plausibly identified with Gwynwas, or Gwynn king of Annwn.[30] Gwynn or Gwynwas seems closely connected with Melwas, for Gwynn was like Melwas lord of an Otherworld castle at Glastonbury; [31] and

---

25 *Monumenta Germaniae Historica, chron. min.*, XIII, 109.
26 *Hesperia, Ergänzungsreihe*, II, xxxiv.
27 *Ibid.*, 43 f.
28 P. W. Joyce, *Old Celtic Romances*, 139.
29 Sommer, II, 105 *passim*.
30 Rhys, *Arthurian Legend*, 343 note 1.
31 *Ibid.*, 338 f.

Gwynwas and Melwas appear together as Gunvasius and Malvasius, kings of Orkney and Iceland respectively, in Geoffrey of Monmouth's *History*.[32] The coupling of Gunvasius and Malvasius, the resemblance between the realms of Gundebaldus and Meleagant, both being lands whence no man returns,[33] — these facts seem to have their explanation in the derivation of these names from Gwynwas and Melwas, and in the fact that both Gwynn and Melwas were lords of Otherworld castles localized on the isle of Glastonbury.

The two islands in *Sone de Nansai* are clearly recognizable as variants of the Welsh or Dumnonian dreams of the Other World. They are the realms of Manawyd and Pryderi, of Gwynwas and Melwas; they are the sacred isles visited by Demetrius in the first century. The white-robed gods have given way to white-robed monks, the caldron of plenty to the Grail, but there is no mistaking the original outlines.

[32] Bk. IX, ch. 12. *Cf.* E. Greulich, *Arthursage in der Historia*, 105.
[33] Crestien de Troyes, *Charette*, l. 645.

# CHAPTER XXII

## THE SIEGE PERILOUS

THUS far in our study of the Grail problem we have concentrated our attention on some of the chief persons and places involved. We have seen the Guardians of the Grail assuming more and more distinctly the forms of the Welsh gods, Manawyd, Myrddin, Bran, Avallach, Gwair, Beli, and Llwch; and the Castle of the Grail as distinctly rearing its crystal walls and phantom towers on the islands of Man, Bardsey, Grassholm, Glastonbury, Lundy, at Ashbury Camp, and in the Scilly Isles. It is time now to turn to certain objects associated with the high quest, including the Grail itself. First let us examine the Siege Perilous.

Perhaps few scenes are more familiar to readers of Malory than Galahad's first adventure:[1] "So when the king and all the knights were come from service, the barons espied in the sieges of the Round Table all about, written with golden letters: Here ought he to sit, and he ought to sit here. And thus they went so long till that they came to the Siege Perilous, where they found letters newly written of gold, which said: Four hundred winters and four and fifty accomplished after the passion of our Lord Jesus Christ ought this siege to be fulfilled. . . . So when they were served, and all sieges fulfilled save only the Siege Perilous, anon there befell a marvelous adventure, that all the doors and windows of the palace shut by themself. . . . In the mean while came in a good old man and an ancient, clothed all in white, and there was no knight knew from whence he came. And with him be brought a young knight, both on foot, in red arms, without sword or shield, save a scabbard hanging by his side. And these words he said: Peace be with you, fair lords. Then the old man said unto Arthur: Sir, I bring here a young knight, the which is of king's lineage and of the kindred of Joseph of Abarimathye, whereby the marvels of this court, and of strange realms, shall be fully accomplished. The king was right glad of his words, and said unto the good man: Sir, ye be right welcome, and the young

---

[1] Bk. XIII, ch. 2–4.

knight with you. Then the old man made the young man to
unarm him, and he was in a coat of red sendal, and bare a mantle
upon his shoulder that was furred with ermine, and put that
upon him. And the old knight said unto the young knight:
Sir, followeth me. And anon he led him unto the Siege Perilous,
where beside sat Sir Lancelot, and the good man lift up the
cloth, and found there letters that said thus: This is the siege of
Galahalt the haut prince. Sir, said the old knight, wit ye well
that place is yours. And then he set him down surely in that
siege. . . . Then all the knights of the Round Table marveled
greatly of Sir Galahalt, that he durst sit there in that Siege
Perilous, and was so tender of age, and wist not from whence he
came but all only by God, and said: This is he by whom the
Sangreal shall be enchieved, for there sat never none but he,
but he were mischieved."

Now it is not without significance that Galaad or Galahalt
should wear red arms and a coat of red sendal, for later it is
interpreted as the color of fire: [2] "Just as Our Lord came in the
semblance of fire, so came the knight in vermeil arms, which are
like in color to fire." And it is all the more significant that
Galahot was the baptismal name of Lancelot, and that Lancelot, and Lancelot's prototype, Lug, who we know was of a red
color from evening till morning, and whose face shone as the
sun,[3] should as his first exploit take a seat of special honor in
the royal palace at Tara. In the *Second Battle of Moytura* [4] we
read that the divine youth seeks admittance to the palace, and
by his mastery of many arts obtains it. "'Let him into the
garth,' says Nuada [a euhemerized god]; 'for never before has
man like him entered this fortress.' Then the doorkeeper lets
Lug pass him, and he entered the fortress and sat down in the
sage's seat, for he was a sage in every art." Later Nuada, when
he had "beheld the warrior's many powers, considered whether
he [Samildanach or Summer of Many Arts] could put away
from them the bondage which they suffered from the Fomorians.
So they held a council concerning the warrior. This is the
decision to which Nuada came, to change seats with the warrior.
So Samildanach went to the king's seat, and the king rose up
before him till thirteen days were ended." The significance
of this passage lies mainly in the fact that the Irish considered

---

[2] Sommer, VI, 57.
[3] *Cf.* Chap. IV. *Atlantis,* IV, 161, 163, 177.    [4] *RC*, XII, 79–81.

the occupation of a certain seat a matter of high import, and
that the young god Lug opened his career, like Galahalt and
(as we shall note) Perceval, by taking his place in certain privileged seats.

The solar splendors of the hero are suggested in another version of the adventure of the seat.[5] When Boors had won the victory for King Brangore's party in a tournament, the king and his
daughter clad him in a robe of vermeil samite, led him to a feast
in the meadows, and seated him in a golden chair. "He had
such shame thereof that he became all red, and thus was fairer."
Twelve knights who had fought next best served him, and then
took their seats at the same table of honor. He was given the
choice of damsels for wife, but refused even King Brangore's
daughter. Nevertheless, their union was brought about by
enchantment, and Helain le Blanc was begotten. Though here
the golden seat is the reward, not the test of prowess, the story
is interesting because of the traces of myth. Boors' blushes and
his vermeil robe seem to be realistic interpretations of the
shining of Lug's face and his red color. Of this we may feel
assured when we note another mythic feature rationalized
away. Brangore's name seems derived from Welsh Bran Gawr,
Bran the Giant. And in the Mabinogi we read that at a banquet
given by Bran the guests "were not within a house but under
tents. No house could ever contain Blessed Bran." [6] When the
*Vulgate Lancelot* states that Brangore had the banquet after
the tourney set out in pavilions, we can be certain that this is a
relic of Brangore's descent from the colossal Bran. Yet the
romancer, whose rationalizing tendency Lot has pointed out,
explains the picnic as due to "the heat, which was too great;"
just as he explains Boors' reddening as due to modesty.

The arrival of Galahalt at Arthur's court and his sitting, robed
in flame-colored sendal, on a seat of honor find significant
analogues in the tales of Lug and Boors. But in neither of these
is the element of danger present. For an example of a seat
which tests the hero we must turn back to Arthurian romance,
and in Wirnt von Gravenberg's *Wigalois*, composed about 1205,
we find a highly interesting block of stone which performs this
function.[7] Wigalois, whose name goes back through French

[5] Sommer, IV, 264–70. *Cf. Merveilles de Rigomer*, ed. Foerster, I, 432.
[6] Guest, *Mabinogion*, ed. Nutt, 28.
[7] O. Piper, *Höfisches Epik*, II, 212.

Guiglain, to Irish Cuchulainn, leaves his mother Florie and comes to Arthur's court at Karidol. He sees there (to translate from Piper's résumé) "a square stone, blue and bright as a mirror, with red and yellow stripes. No deceiver could come within six feet of it and lay his hand on it. Wigalois tied his destrier to a linden, and sat upon the stone. Hitherto everyone had been driven back; the King alone had been suffered to sit. Even Gawr in could merely touch it with his hand; the reason was that he had wronged a damsel. When they saw the youth on the stone, they all marveled, and the King bade them welcome him. But the stripling knew nothing of the secret of the stone."

There seems to be authentic Celtic tradition in the fact that the seat is a stone and that before Wigalois only the king had been able to sit on it. "Legend and history both inform us that Irish chiefs were installed in office by being placed on mere undressed flag-stones, on which, however, the impression of two feet was sometimes observable." [8] The Lia Fail, which may mean Stone of Light [9] and which according to tradition was brought from Ireland to Scotland and thence to Westminster, is thus described in an inventory of Edward I: "Una petra magna, super quam Reges Scociae solebant coronari." [10] And in fact the King of Britain, Scotland, and Ireland is still crowned upon a stone. It cannot be said, however, that it now exercises the selective faculty which belonged to the stone in Arthur's court at Karidol.

Galahalt, Boors, Wigalois, — all are thus connected with a seat-taking episode, and all connect themselves in name at least with Gwri or Cuchulinn. But our most significant analogues are found in the stories about Perceval and Pryderi. Let us look at the adventure of the Siege Perilous related in the *Didot Perceval*.[11] There is an empty seat at the Round Table, and Arthur tells Perceval it is reserved for the best knight in the world. Perceval demands the right to sit in it, and in spite of Arthur's warnings finally does so. "As soon as he was seated the stone split beneath him and cried with such anguish that it

---

[8] Wood-Martin, *Traces of the Elder Faiths*, II, 255 f. *Cf. PRIA*, XXXIV, C, 107; *Rev. des études anciennes*, XVII, 193 ff, 202.

[9] G. Henderson, *Survivals in Belief*, 199.

[10] Wood-Martin, *op. cit.*, II, 257.

[11] Weston, *Leg. of Perceval*, II, 20 f. *Cf. ibid.*, 141, for discussion of Gerbert and *Prose Tristan* versions of scene.

seemed to all those who were there that the world would fall
into the abyss, and from the cry which the earth uttered there
issued a great darkness." The voice of Merlin is heard, rebuking
Perceval's audacity, announcing that because of this his grandfather, the Fisher King, has fallen into a great infirmity and
that the enchantments of Britain (which we may assume are
identical with the sterilizing blight which in *Sone de Nansai*
fell upon Lorgres) will not end till the perfect knight ask the
question concerning the use of the Grail in the castle of the
Fisher King, Bron. Long after,[12] Perceval comes to a river, sees
three men in a boat, and is invited by the master, who is the
Fisher King, to go to his castle. After a long ride Perceval
reaches it, only to find the Fisher arrived before him. He sees a
procession, including a damsel with two silver dishes, but fails to
ask the use of the Grail (here distinct from the dishes though
they are doubtless merely a doublet). Seven years later [13] he
returns to the Fisher King's castle, asks the question, thus heals
the king, and becomes on his death guardian of the Grail. At
Arthur's court the stone reunites with a great roar, and the
Enchantments of Britain are ended. It is important to note the
sympathetic relationship which exists between the stone, the
Fisher King, and the fertility of the land.

Now let us look at the Mabinogi of *Manawyddan*.[14] The god,
whom we have already recognized as the original of the Fisher
King, and Pryderi, the original of Perceval, "began a feast at
Narberth, for it was the chief palace. . . . And when they had
ended the first meal that night, while those who served them
ate, they arose and went forth, and proceeded all four [their
wives are included] to the Throne of Narberth, and their retinue
with them. And as they sat thus, behold, a peal of thunder, and
with the violence of the thunderstorm, lo there came a fall of
mist, so thick that not one of them could see the other. And
after the mist it became light all around. And when they looked
towards the place where they were wont to see cattle, and herds
and dwellings, they saw nothing now, neither house nor beast nor
smoke nor fire nor man nor dwelling." When after many adventures which show no resemblance to those in the *Didot
Perceval* except that Pryderi comes to an enchanted palace
containing a golden bowl of rich workmanship,[15] the enchant-

[12] *Ibid.*, 57–60.
[13] *Ibid.*, 81–4.
[14] Ed. Nutt, 45.
[15] *Cf.* Chap. XXXII.

ment is finally ended by Manawyddan.[16] "He rose up and looked forth. And when he looked he saw all the lands tilled, and full of herds and dwellings."

Despite all the differences the essential situation is parallel in the *Didot Perceval* and *Manawyddan*. It will easily be recognized that the French romance is far truer to the primitive conception than the Welsh. For one thing, one can hardly doubt that it is the audacious act of one person in sitting on a certain throne which caused the calamity. This is clear in the French, but in the Welsh the causal connection is not mentioned, four persons are involved instead of one, and for the perilous throne probably local pride has substituted a mound above the palace which was called the Throne or Gorsedd of Narberth.[17] Of this Gorsedd we learn in the Mabinogi of *Pwyll* that "whosoever sits upon it cannot go thence without either receiving wounds or blows, or else seeing a wonder."[18] The author of *Manawyddan*, in order to identify the perilous seat of his original with this local "Throne" of perilous associations has dragged all four persons away from the banquet hall where, by all analogies and the exigencies of the story itself, the seat should have been, and led them scrambling up this mound. Could there be a more striking illustration of the ruthlessness with which the Welsh story-tellers reduced their mythology to chaos, and of the comparative fidelity of the Bretons?

Now while the Welsh offers us the best analogue for the Siege Perilous, Nitze has discovered in the Irish the explanation of the shrieking stone.[19] It is found in a story, *The Champion's Ecstasy*, to which I have already referred in connection with Lug's spear. It runs:[20] "One morning Conn repaired at sunrise to the battlements of the Royal Fortress of Tara, accompanied by his three Druids. . . . While standing in the usual place this morning, Conn happened to tread upon a stone, and immediately the stone shrieked under his feet, so as to be heard all over Tara, and throughout all Bregia, or East Meath." Another text, says the stone cried out "under Conn" and "its heart burst out of it."[21] "Conn then asked his Druids why the stone

---

[16] Ed. Nutt, 57.
[17] Rhys, *Hib. Lec.*, 204 ff.
[18] *Mabinogion*, ed. Nutt, 10.
[19] *Studies in Honor of A. M. Elliott*, I, 42.
[20] O'Curry, *MS. Materials*, 388.
[21] *Eriu*, VIII, 106.

had shrieked, what its name was, and what it said. The Druids took fifty-three days to consider; and at the expiration of that period returned the following answer: 'Fal is the name of the stone; it came from Inis Fail, or the island of Fal; it has shrieked under your royal feet, and the number of shrieks which the stone has given forth, is the number of kings of your seed that will succeed you till the end of time. . . .' Conn stood some time musing on this strange revelation; when suddenly he found himself and his companions enveloped in a mist, so thick that they knew not where they were, so intense was the darkness. They had not continued long in this condition, until they heard the tramp of a horseman approaching them; and immediately a spear was cast three times in succession towards them, coming nearer to them each time. . . . The horseman then came up, saluted Conn, and invited himself and his companions to his house. He led them into a noble plain, where they saw a royal court, into which they entered, and found it occupied by a beautiful and richly dressed princess, with a silver vat full of red ale, and a golden ladle and a golden cup before her. The knight, on entering the palace, showed his guests to appropriate seats, and sat himself in a princely chair at the head of the apartment; and then addressing himself to Conn, said: — 'I wish to inform you that I am not a living knight; I am one of Adam's race who have come back from death; my name is Lugh MacCeithlenn, . . . and the princess whom you have found here on your entrance is the sovereignty of Erinn for ever.'" [22] She subsequently presented him with the silver pail and the golden ladle and cup. The princess then took up the ladle, filled the cup, and said: "Whom shall this cup with the red ale be given to?" The knight answered "Give it to Conn of the Hundred Battles." In other tales in which a woman appears who declares herself to be the Sovereignty of Erin, she becomes, as we shall see in Chap. XXIX, the bride of the hero. We may infer from analogy and logic that this princess, too, who is "the sovereignty of Erinn," goes with the cup to the destined sovereign of Erin. The idea seems to be clearly though somewhat rationalistically expressed in *The Colloquy of the Ancients.*[23] Three sons of the king of Ireland

[22] Lug himself was married to Eriu, the goddess of Ireland. *Folklore*, XXXI, 120.
[23] S. H. O'Grady, *Silva Gadelica*, II, 109–11.

obtain admittance to the Brugh of the Boyne, and Midhir
Yellow-mane commands that they be provided with wives,
"since from wives it is that either fortune or misfortune is
derived." And from their marriages with the three daughters of
Midhir they derived all their wishes — territories and wealth
in the greatest abundance. Though they returned after three
days and nights to the more prosaic world and became kings in
Ireland for thrice fifty years, yet "in virtue of marriage alliance
they returned again to the Tuatha De Danann, and from that
time forth have remained there." Evidently it was a prevalent
belief that marriage with the daughter of the god entailed
not only earthly sovereignty but also immortality. One can
hardly doubt that the climax of Conn's visit to Lug's palace
was union with the Sovereignty of Erin, and that he returned
to her after his earthly reign was over. And it is worth noting
that though we do not know her name we do know those of
other daughters of the Tuatha De Danann. According to
O'Curry Blathnat was a daughter of Mider,[24] and her name
means Little Flower. Her cousin, the daughter of Bodb the
Red, was called Scothniamh or Flower-luster.[25] We shall do
well to remember the conception of a damsel, called the Sovereignty of Erin, who by her embraces confers immortality,
who gives her cup to the hero, and whose floral names may
have some significance.

It can hardly be coincidence that the Mabinogi of *Manawyddan* should furnish originals for certain essential features
of the *Didot Perceval:* the hero who is Perceval's prototype, the
feast, the perilous throne, the roar, the magic cloud, and the
desolation of the Fisher King's land consequent on sitting on a
"throne"; and that the story of the *Champion's Ecstasy* should
furnish precisely the remaining features: the shrieking prophetic stone, which breaks, the meeting with the god who in-
vites to his abode, the lovely princess with her vessel, the hero's
destined acquisition of the vessel and of the kingship. One
could not ask for a neater example of that synchronizing and
harmonizing prescribed as the duty of the Irish *ollamhs* and
carried on, as we have seen, quite as zealously by the inheritors
of their art in Wales and Brittany.

[24] O'Curry, *Manners and Customs*, II, 81. There is doubt, however,
about this reading. *Cf. ITS*, II, 137.
[25] O'Grady, *op. cit.*, II, 203.

There is one characteristic of the Siege Perilous that we have not adequately accounted for; the fact that it brings down upon him who is unworthy to sit in it a fiery fate. Moys is carried away by fiery hands,[26] and Brumant, nephew of Claudas and (like Brumaut, the defender of the bridge of Corbenic) rival of Lancelot, is consumed to ashes by a fire from on high.[27] If, as we have assumed, however, it is the seat destined for the young sun and lightning god when he has shown himself worthy of his dominion over the powers of nature, then we can well understand who and what it is that consumes the audacious pretender with fire. It is the old god with his levin brand.[28] The situation, therefore, is analogous to that in Curoi's fortress, when the three heroes keep vigil three successive nights in the seat of watch and are exposed to the missiles of old Curoi. If the seat of watch in Curoi's castle was confused with that other perilous seat, the Stone of Fal, it would explain not only the lightning which blasts those who sit in the Siege Perilous, but also an unexplained feature of the Marvelous Bed in Chateau Merveil. This Bed without question goes back to the perilous seat of watch, but when Wolfram relates that it cracked under Gawain more loudly than a combination of trumpet blasts and thunder together,[29] we are at a loss to account for it unless we remember that other perilous seat, the Stone of Fal, which roared under the king of Ireland. In Chapter XVII we saw that Wolfram gave a more primitive account of the wheels under the Marvelous Bed than Crestien; here too Wolfram seems to have preserved a detail in a form closer to the Irish. For both Crestien de Troyes and Heinrich von dem Türlin say that the sound which issued from the bed was the clang of bells.[30] There must have been a version of the adventures in the Castle of Marvels which left the quality of the sound and its precise cause somewhat vague, and this version Wolfram follows. It naturally

[26] Sommer, *op. cit.*, I, 248.

[27] *Ibid.*, V, 320.

[28] *Cf.* the myth of Zagreus, son of Zeus and Persephone. As a horned infant he mounted the throne of Zeus, grasping the thunderbolt. The jealous Hera roused the Titans against him, and in spite of Zagreus' many metamorphoses slew him at last in the form of a bull. A. B. Cook, *Zeus*, I, 398.

[29] *Parzival*, sec. 567. On these beds *cf.* A. Hertel, *Verzauberte Örtlichkeiten*, 69.

[30] Crestien de Troyes, *Conte del Graal*, ed. Baist, l. 7663; Heinrich von dem Türlin, *Krone*, l. 20705.

tempted a rationalizer to hang bells under the bed to account for the noise. His version was the source of Crestien and Heinrich. Today one may see in S. Pierre, Caen, a sculptured capital,[31] in the museum at Braunschweig an embroidery, and in numerous museums and collections carved ivories,[32] all of the fourteenth century, which represent vividly the knight lying on the bed, hung below with bells, while arrows and swords rain upon his shield. Little would one suspect, unless the evidence were assembled that these were illustrations of *Bricriu's Feast*, and that the *Ecstasy of the Champion* was responsible for the bells.

Another rationalizer, starting from the tradition, imbedded in Wolfram, that the Bed cracked more loudly than a combination of trumpet blasts and thunder, has literally supplied the bed in *Arthur of Little Britain* with four golden images which successively blow horns that can be heard a mile away.[33] He has also used the traditions concerning the perilous seat of watch in Curoi's castle to supply at the bed's head a golden archer, inscribed: "When this image shooteth, then all this palace shall turn like a wheel." It has been shown [34] that this Perilous Bed in *Arthur of Little Britain* is more primitive by two removes than Crestien's, and therefore represents a *conte* of the first half of the twelfth century. Accordingly it adds much to the powerful arguments of Thurneysen and Webster [35] for Celtic influence on the *Pélerinage Charlemagne* when we note that this poem has drawn upon the same source as *Arthur of Little Britain*. In the *Pélerinage* Hugo's palace contains two copper children holding horns. Whenever the wind blows, it makes the palace turn like the wheel of a cart, and the horns blare like a drum or thunder or a great bell.[36] In fact Hugo himself, Emperor of Constantinople, found plowing with a golden plow, can be no other than the Welsh culture hero Hu Gadarn, "the Strong," who according to a certain triad "taught the Cymry how to plow the earth for the first time, when they were in Gwlad yr Haf, 'the Summer

---

[31] A. Gasté, *Chapiteau de S. Pierre de Caen.*
[32] R. Koechlin, *Ivoires gothiques français*, II, Nos. 1061, 1201, 1281–6, 1290, 1297. *Cf. Art Bulletin*, VI, 111 f.
[33] Berners, *Arthur of Little Britain*, ed. Utterson, 140.
[34] *Cf.* Chap. XVII.
[35] Thurneysen, *Keltoromanisches*, 18; *Englische St.*, XXXVI, 337. On gabs in Arthurian romance *cf.* Bruce, *Evolution*, I, 409.
[36] Ed. Koschwitz, ll. 352 ff.

Country,' the place where Constantinople is now, before they came to the Isle of Britain." [37] So clearly were the characteristics of Hu preserved in Hugo, that the Welsh had no hesitation, when they translated the *Pélerinage*, about restoring to the Emperor the name of Hu Gadarn.[38]

Another curious survival of the tradition of the sun-god's perilous seat may be discovered on St. Michael's Mount in Cornwall. The old Celtic name for the islet was Dinsul or Mount of the Sun.[39] As on Glastonbury Tor, the old divinity has been supplanted by the Archangel.[40] Carew in the 17th century says,[41] "A little without the castle there is a bad seat in a craggy place, called St. Michael's Chair, somewhat danger-ous of access, and therefore holy for the adventure." Halse records another location of the chair: [42] "On the top of the tower of the chapel within the castle in a place of very danger-ous access, is cut in the white cloos a kind of chair, seat, or resting-place for a man, called in Kernawish tongue St. Mighel's Kader, St. Michael's Chair; here it was believed by the Britons was the place of St. Michael's apparition." This rocky seat, regarded as holy because dangerous of access, this dizzy throne where the warrior angel appeared in his panoply may well deserve to be called the Siege Perilous, in more than the obvious sense.

Everything goes to show that the incidents connected with the Siege Perilous have been drawn from various sources. There is a hint of the seat of watch in Curoi's castle. There is a strong resemblance to the sage's or king's seat at Nuada's court, which the youthful Lug occupies at the opening of his career. There is also a clear prototype in the Lia Fail which roared and broke under Conn. Finally the Gorsedd or Throne of Narberth, where Pryderi and Manawyddan sat after their feast, with disastrous consequences to the land, is a garbled form of

[37] Loth, *Mab.*², II, 314.

[38] Stephens (*Lit. of the Kymry*, 428 n.) and Loth (*Mab.*², II, 295 n.) chal-lenge the authenticity of the legends regarding Hu, but their primitive character and abundance prove that they cannot be based on the story of Hugo. The Welsh were not inventing culture-heroes in the fifteenth cen-tury.

[39] W. J. Rees, *Cambro-British Saints*, 65.

[40] On cult of St. Michael in Dumnonia *cf.* W. H. P. Greswell, *Dumnonia*, 52 ff.

[41] R. Carew, *Survey of Cornwall*, ed. 1811, 376 note.

[42] *Ibid.*, 378.

the Siege Perilous.  Accordingly when Robert de Boron says
that it was the seat which Judas occupied at the Last Supper,[43]
he is doing no more than his less pious predecessors had done —
equated it with any chair, throne, couch, or stone which offered
a meaning or led to a story.

[43] *Cf.* L. H. Loomis's article on Round Table, *PMLA*, XLI, 771.

# CHAPTER XXIII

## THE GRAIL AND THE TESTING HORN

IF WE review the chapters thus far devoted to the Grail
tradition we note that we have claimed six Celtic prototypes
for the Grail: 1. the pearl-rimmed caldron of the Head of
Annwn; 2. the Caldron of Britain, of which Manawyd was
perpetual guardian; 3. the caldron of Bran, who was practically
a double of Manawyd; 4. Manannan's cup of truth; 5. the
cup of sovereignty in the palace of Lug; 6. the caldron of
Blathnat. All manner of sacred vessels of the Irish and Welsh
have contributed to the conception of the Grail. It may bring
some order out of this complexity if we recall Gawain's night in
the Palace Adventurous,[1] when the Grail performed three
characteristic functions: first, it healed the desperately wounded
Gawain after his combats;[2] secondly, it provided by magic an
abundance of delicious food;[3] thirdly, it refused food to Gawain
because, in his pride and ignorance, he failed to kneel at its
appearance.[4] These three powers of the Grail are found not only
here but also throughout Arthurian romance. And we may
definitely trace these powers back to their source in one or more
of these Celtic vessels.

First, the Grail is a talisman with healing virtues. Already
we have seen that it appeared in the Palace Adventurous in the
hands of a maiden, to heal the wounds of Gawain after his
combat, and that in the same place it cured Lancelot of his madness.[5] Again, according to Malory,[6] when Ector and Perceval
have wounded each other fatally, "right so there came by the
holy vessel of the Sangreal with all manner of sweetness and
savor, . . . and forthwithal they both were whole of hide and
limb as ever they were in their life days. . . . 'So God me help,'
said Sir Perceval, 'I saw a damozel as me thought all in white,
and a vessel in both her hands, and forthwithal I was whole.'"
In the *Merveilles de Rigomer* [7] Lancelot desperately wounded in

[1] *Cf.* Chap. XVII.
[2] Sommer, IV, 37.
[3] *Ibid.*, 344.
[4] *Ibid.*, 344, 348.
[5] *Cf.* Chap. XX. Sommer, V, 400.
[6] Bk. XI, ch. 14. *Cf.* Potvin, VI, 119 f.
[7] Ed. Foerster, ll. 16954–17018.

227

his struggle with a monster, is laid under a bush of mint. There appears a beautiful damsel in white on a white horse, who has come from far. She brings a powerful ointment in an ivory casket. She dismounts, anoints Lancelot all over, and he is at once healed. Arthur and his folk marvel, conjecturing that she is the Magdalen or our Lady herself. After taking leave, she suddenly vanishes like a white cloud. The author says that this damsel is Lorie de la Roche Florie, Gawain's mistress. Now *Diu Krone, Wigalois*, and the *Livre d'Artus* agree in giving Gawain's mistress the name Florie or Floree, and Wauchier supports this by calling her Lore.[8] The omission of the initial is a common MS. corruption,[9] and we need have little doubt that originally the name of the damsel in white who heals Lancelot with her Grail-like casket was Florie de la Roche. As we have already pointed out, Wolfram names among the damsels of the Grail castle Florie von Lunel. [10] And in Chapter VIII we noted that Lynete and Lyones both possessed vessels of great restorative virtue. All this would seem to confirm our earlier supposition that one of the sources of the Grail was the caldron of Blathnat.[11]

But here we run awkwardly into the fact that nothing related of Blathnat's caldron would suggest that it had curative virtues; on the contrary, it holds the milk of the three cows of Echde, and seems rather to be a symbol of plenty. But in the *Romanic Review* I showed that there are strong reasons to equate Olathnat with Guinevere and Branwen.[12] The abduction and rescue of Winlogee as depicted on the Modena portal agrees point for point with the abduction and rescue of Blathnat. Winlogee we know became in French Guinloie, who like Floree is said to be the *amie* of Gawain,[13] and curiously enough Wolfram von Eschenbach names among the maidens of the Grail castle not only Florie von Lunel but also Garschiloye,[14] whose name may

[8] *Krone*, ed. Scholl, l. 1294 f; Piper, *Höfisches Epik*, II, 211 f; Sommer, VII, 108; Potvin, III, 46.

[9] *MLN*, XXVI, 66 f.

[10] Ed. E. Martin, I, 287. *Cf. Ibid.*, 89. Lunel seems a development from Lunete parallel to the German Garel from hypothetical French Garet.

[11] *Cf.* Chap. XVII.

[12] *RR*, XV, 279 f.

[13] *Ibid.*, 271.

[14] Wolfram, *Parzival*, ed. Martin, 89, 286. The possibility of such corruptions is shown by the development of Crestien's Guiromelans into Gramoflanz.

possibly be a copyist's corruption of Guinloie. Furthermore, Brown has ingeniously proved[15] that the English *Sir Percyvelle* represents Queen Guinevere with a golden cup which must originally have been a talisman of strength. Apparently when the Red Knight stole the cup, Arthur and his knights fell into languishment, which, one infers, was not ended until Gawain returned with the talisman. "The gold cup," Brown concludes, "is an undeveloped grail"; or rather, in my opinion, a faded grail. It would seem, therefore, that Guinevere's cup and Gorschiloye's Grail are sources of vigor, and that both go back to Blathnat's vessel.

Blathnat is the prototype not only of Floree and Guinevere but also of Branwen. For the details let me refer to my article aforementioned. In the caldron of Bran, which Matholwch took away with Branwen as her dowry, we find the healing properties which our extant records do not attribute to the caldron of Blathnat. If a man were slain today and his body were cast into it, on the morrow he would be as well as ever he was at the best, except that he would not regain his speech. [16] Bran himself has been shown to be the original of Bron,[17] and one of the originals of the Fisher King. His sister Branwen corresponds to Blathnat and Guinevere, both of whom we have linked with the Grail. It is natural enough, therefore, to find that in the caldron of Bran and Branwen lies the source, — so far as we can detect with the meager materials we possess, — of the healing powers of the Grail.

The second attribute, that of an inexhaustible provider of food and drink, is very commonly mentioned in the Grail romances, and has been dealt with by Nutt and Brown.[18] As a matter of fact, such vessels of unlimited plenty are familiar in the mythology of many lands. The cornucopia is perhaps the most familiar form, and in the well-known legend belongs to Amalthea, the nurse of Zeus.[19] It is an odd case of parallel development that just as the word *gral* in Germany came to mean a paradise of sensuous pleasures,[20] so the name Horn of

---

[15] *MP*, XXII, 92–5.     [16] Guest, *Mabinogion*, ed. Nutt, 31.

[17] Nitze's article in *Medieval Studies in Memory of Gertrude Schoepperle Loomis*.

[18] Nutt, *Studies*, 184–6; *Kittredge Anniversary Papers*, 239 ff.

[19] P. Saintyves, *Essais de folklore biblique*, 252 ff; Pauly, Wissowa, *Real-encycl.*, I, 1721.

[20] P. S. Barto, *Tannhaüser and the Mountain of Venus*, 9 f.

Amalthea was applied to a sort of richly watered park.[21]  The cornucopia was often borne by Pluto as god of plenty, and we find him depicted thus as he seizes the vegetation goddess Proserpine, or as he follows the winged chariot of Triptolemus accompanied by Demeter and her daughter Kore.[22]  More significant for us is the fact that the cornucopia was also assigned as an emblem to Demeter herself.[23]  The *calathos*, a basket of similar significance, was borne in sacred processions on the heads of virgins.[24]  "When filled with flowers, the *calathos* was a symbol of spring, of Persephone; when filled with ears of wheat, a symbol of the summer and of harvest, an attribute of Demeter."  The cornucopia also played a part in story not unlike that of the Celtic vessels, for Heracles in several stories carries it off,[25] just as Curoi and Cuchulinn carry off the caldron of Echde,[26] as Llwch Lleminawc carries off the caldron of the Head of Annwn,[27] as the Red Knight carries off Guinevere's golden cup in *Sir Percyvelle*.[28]

In Northern Europe, too, similar vessels of plenty are found. Saxo Grammaticus describes an image of the god Suantevit on the island of Rügen, destroyed in 1167, which held in its right hand a horn of metal.[29]  "This the priest, well versed in the ritual, filled once in every year with wine for purposes of divination, for from the condition of the liquid he foretold the measure of plenty the coming year would bring. . . .  While the people were watching outside the door, the priest took the cup from the hand of the image and examined it most carefully.  If aught had been diminished from the quantity of liquid placed in it, it was an omen of scarcity.  If it was still full, there would be a plentiful harvest."

Hucher was the first to point out that the Gallic coinage seemed to represent sacred caldrons, and to connect them, rightly as I believe, with the caldrons of Welsh mythology and with the Grail.[30]  Coins struck more than two centuries before

[21] Pauly, Wissowa, I, 1722.
[22] Daremberg, Saglio, I², 1516.
[23] *Ibid.*, 1517.
[24] *Ibid.*, 1071.
[25] Pauly, Wissowa, I, 1722.
[26] *ZcP*, IX, 194.
[27] Malory, *Morte d'Arthur*, ed. Everyman, I, xxiii.
[28] Ed. Campion, Holthausen, ll. 601 ff.
[29] *Hist., Dan.*, Bk. XIV. *Cf.* J. Machal, *Slavic Mythology*, 279.
[30] E. Hucher, *Saint-Graal*, I, 3 f. *Cf. Rev. d'Auvergne*, XXXVII, 69.

Christ among the Unelles and Baiocasses of Armorica, show caldrons with an indented edge and chains for suspension. Another Gallic coin depicts Mercury on one side and a caldron or bowl on a stand on the reverse.[31] Most interesting of all is a silver piece inscribed with the name Belinos and representing a horn of plenty.[32] Belinos was equated with Apollo, and had a temple at Bayeux.[33] We have seen reason to believe that he is no other than the Welsh Beli or Belin, euhemerized as King of Britain, the father of Avallach.[34] Belin appears in Crestien's *Erec* as lord of the Otherworld isles of the antipodes; [35] Avalloc, according to William of Malmesbury, dwelt at Glastonbury, an Otherworld isle,[36] and in the *Estoire* and MS. B.N. fr. 334 Belin turns up as Pellean, lord of the plenty-giving Grail.[37] Is it coincidence that both Pellean and Belinos should be associated with a vessel of plenty?

In Irish myth similar inexhaustible vessels of food and drink are found. In the Otherworld palace of Labraid described in the *Sickbed of Cuchulinn*,[38]

> "There is a vat there with joyous mead,
> Which is distributed to the household.
> It continues ever, — enduring is the custom, —
> So that it is always constantly full."

Immediately there follows the description of a maiden, golden-haired, accomplished, who excels all the women of Erin. The connection between the vessel of plenty and the goddess seems as clear in Irish as in classical and Arthurian tradition.

The Welsh seem to have been particularly interested in such vessels of the gods. Of the Thirteen Treasures of the Isle of Britain, which according to tradition, Merlin took with him to his glass house on the isle of Bardsey, five were of this kind.[39] There was the *mwys* (a vessel of somewhat indeterminate nature) [40] of Gwyddno Garanhir; if food for one man were put

---

[31] Blanchet, Dieudonné, *Manuel de numismatique* (1912), I, 43.
[32] Blanchet, *Traité des monnaies gauloises*, I, 169.
[33] Holder, *Alt-celtischer Sprachschatz*, sub Belenos.
[34] *Cf.* Chap. XV.
[35] Ll. 1993 ff.
[36] Bruce, *Evolution*, I, 199.
[37] Sommer, I, 290; *PMLA*, XXV, 48 f.
[38] *SNPL*, VIII, 37.
[39] Guest, *Mabinogion*, Everyman ed., 328.
[40] Rhys, *Arthurian Legend*, 312. An old authority translates *mwys* as *vas quoddam*.

into it, when opened it would be found to contain food for a hundred.  There was the horn of Bran Galed; what liquor soever was desired was found therein.  There was the Caldron of Tyrnog, of which we shall presently hear more.  There were the Pan and the Platter of Rhegynydd Ysgolhaig; whatever food was required was found in them.  In *Kilhwch and Olwen* [41] the hero is sent in quest not only of the *mwys* of Gwyddneu Garanhir, but also of the vessel of Llwyr the son of Llwyryon, the horn of Gwlgawd Gogodin, the caldron of Diwrnach of Ireland.  Since Llwyr is probably a variant of Llyr, the father of Manawyddan and Bran, and since the caldron of Diwrnach, as we saw in Chap. IX, is the same as the caldron of the Head of Annwn, there cannot be much doubt that the vessels which Kilhwch was sent for belong among the prototypes of the Grail. As Brueyre said of the many food-providing talismans of folklore: [42] "Under whatever aspect the myth is presented: horn, cup, table perpetually set, food-providing table-cloth, tap from which all sorts of wine are drawn, it is always the symbol of the life-giving and fructifying powers of Nature."

A third property of the Grail is its denial of food to the unworthy.  As we have seen, when Gawain on his unsuccessful visit to Corbenic, failed to kneel before the holy vessel, the place before him remained void, while all the others had a surfeit of food miraculously provided for them.  In Robert de Boron's *Joseph* also the Grail acts as a test of virtue.[43]  Joseph of Arimathea by direction of the Holy Ghost invites the people to sit down at the table.  "Part of the people sit, part do not; the sitters are filled with sweetness and the desire of their heart, the others feel nought.  One of the sitters, named Petrus, asks if they feel nothing, and tells them it is because they are defiled with sin.  The sinners then depart, but Joseph bids them come back day by day.  Thus Joseph detects the sinners, and thus is the vessel first proved."  In this and in other instances that might be cited the Grail denies sustenance to those who do not possess the Christian virtues.  When we turn to its pagan prototypes, we find cups and caldrons which test the heathen virtues.

Among the sources of the Grail we have already noted

---

[41]  Guest, *Mabinogion*, ed. Nutt, 123 f.

[42]  L. Brueyre, *Contes populaires de la Grande Bretagne*, 140.

[43]  Nutt, *Studies*, 64b.

Manannan's Cup of Truth, which would break in pieces if three lies were told, but would reunite if three true sayings were uttered.[44] We learn that "it was used to distinguish between truth and falsehood with the Gael," and that Manannan gave that cup to King Cormac. His Welsh counterpart, Manawyd, we have seen, was perpetual Guardian of the Caldron of Britain, doubtless identical with the Caldron of Tyrnog or Dyrnog, one of the Thirteen Treasures of Britain.[45] Of this caldron it is said that "if meat were put in it to boil for a coward, it would never be boiled, but if meat were put in it for a brave man, it would be boiled forthwith." It is obviously the same as the pearl-rimmed caldron of the Head of Annwn, which would not boil the food of a coward or perjurer. This caldron is associated with Pwyll, the Head of Annwn, and Pryderi, son of Pwyll and step-son of Manawyddan.[46] It is kept, as we know, in a fortress beyond the seas. We also know that Pryderi was the successor of Pwyll as Prince of Dyved; presumably also as sea-god and as keeper of the magic testing caldron beyond the sea.

Let us turn to the story in *Diu Krone*,[47] telling how the King of the Sea, Priure or Privr, sent a magic cup to Arthur's court to test the truth or falsity of the knights and ladies. At Christmastide there rode into Arthur's court a monstrous knight, covered with scales but dressed in the French fashion, riding a steed with eagle's wings and a dolphin's tail. He announced that he had been sent from the King of the Sea, Priure, with a golden cup set with stones and wrought with such wizardry that it would spill the wine over any man who was false and a liar and any woman who had a false heart. If there was one in Arthur's court who could drink from it, the cup would remain with him. Or otherwise, let any knight who desired the cup joust with him for it. Arthur having accepted the conditions, the women first were tested and not one but was convicted of some infidelity or laxity in love. When the knights took their turn, however, the shortcomings they betrayed were by no means confined to sins against love. King Brisaz had failed to aid a damsel in dire distress who had called upon him. Lancelot could not drink because he had once sat in a cart, contrary

[44] *Cf.* Chap. XVIII.
[45] *Cf. Kittredge Anniversary Papers*, 244 note 1.
[46] *Cf.* Chap. XX.
[47] Ll. 918 ff. On testing horns *cf.* Paton, *Fairy Mythology*, 104 ff.

to the customs of knighthood. Parzival was splashed with wine because he had left the question unasked at the "poor fisher's" house. Arthur alone succeeded in emptying the magic cup. The messenger left the talisman at the court, and after overcoming drunken Keii, returned to his master the Sea-King Priure.

The conception of a sea-god, who dwelt in a land of perpetual youth, who possessed a cup which tested the virtues, particularly veracity, and who bestowed that cup on an earthly king, seems to be as clearly distinguishable in *Diu Krone*, written about 1220, as in the *Adventures of Cormac*, which is mentioned in a tenth century list of sagas.[48] Whether Priure is identical with Pryderi in his rôle of sea-god, the reader may judge for himself. The equation of the testing cup with the Grail, however, has not only been hinted at already by Cross,[49] but also is susceptible of proof. The differentiation between the two testing vessels is due, first, to the fact that the one became attached early to a wide-spread story-pattern of chastity tests, of which Cross furnishes certain Irish examples,[50] and secondly to the fact that the other was generally conceived in France as a shallow dish, and called a *graal*, which has the same meaning. Thus both in form and in narrative setting the two vessels diverged. But a little research shows that both at one time were imagined as drinking horns, and were called the Blessed Horn.

In two forms of the chastity test, the *Lai du Cor*,[51] and the *Livre de Caradoc* (inserted in the *Conte del Graal*),[52] the testing vessel is a drinking horn. On the other hand, the ancient Celtic vessel of plenty appears, as we have seen, as the cornucopia of Belinos and the horn of Bran Galed. Twelfth century British folktales of fairy vessels describe them as horns.[53] It is significant that in Arthurian romance we have two Castles of the Horn, in both of which we may detect castles of the Grail.

[48] *PMLA*, XXV, 40.
[49] *MP*, X, 292 note 4. "In connection with these matters [chastity testing talismans] it is important to remember that in certain versions of the story of the Holy Grail, the grail acts as a virtue test."
[50] Analogues in F. Child, *English and Scottish Ballads*, I, 268–71; *MP*, X, 289 ff.
[51] Ed. H. Dörner.
[52] Potvin, III, 217.
[53] Gervase of Tilbury, ed. Liebrecht, 28, 129. For similar tales *cf.* A. W. Moore, *Folklore of Isle of Man*, 41 ff; E. S. Hartland, *Science of Fairy-tales*, 140–60; T. Keightley, *Fairy Mythology*, 295, 299.

One is in the *Vulgate Lancelot*,[54] and of it we learn nothing but that Claudas concentrated his army there, and that when he was defeated, it was bestowed on the husband of the Lady of the Lake. According to Malory this was Pelleas (a form of Pellean), who goes back to the Belinos of the Cornucopia, — call it coincidence if you will. The other Castle of the Horn is found in *Perlesvaus*.[55] This ivory horn blared loudly all day, and a spirit within it uttered oracles and gave his worshippers "such great abundance therewithin of everything they could desire that nought in the world was there whereof they lacked," — a strong hint of its identity with the Grail. The castle itself, moreover, like the Grail Castle in the same romance, has copper men guarding the entrance. Now it would appear that the blaring of the horn is simply due to a mistaken ingenuity on the part of someone who took the horn to be a hunting and not a drinking horn. But the statement that an abundance of everything was to be found within it must be a survival of its original function as a vessel.

Now let us consider the name so frequently applied to the Grail Castle, — Corbenic, which is said to mean "most holy vessel." [56] Is not the original form: li Chastel del Cor Benit, the Castle of the Blessed Horn? The matter is clinched by the fact that the Montpellier MS. containing the Caradoc version of the test, after describing the horn as of ivory, adorned with many sparkling precious stones, announces that this horn (*cor*) is called blessed (*Beneis*).[57] The Grail Castle is therefore rightly called the Castle of the Corbeneit or Corbenit.

In *Sone de Nansai* also we discovered certain cryptic statements which are scarcely comprehensible unless we take them as garbled references to the Grail as a horn. Sone is told that the castle on the Island of Galoche was founded by "the holy *cors*, of which you see the holy vessel yonder." The Grail is taken from a vessel of ivory. The abbey was well provided with holy *cors*, and the abbot had served them well. Put all these statements together, and it is not hard to see that the poet has continually misinterpreted the word *cors* in his source, and does

---

[54] Sommer, V, 339, 356.
[55] Potvin, I, 202 f. The text reads "Li cors de cuivre," and lower on the same page "le cor d'ivoire." S. Evans emended to "tors" and translated "bull."
[56] Sommer, I, 288.                 [57] Potvin, III, 217, l. 15687.

not realize that the holy vessel itself was a *cors* or horn of ivory, for which the castle was founded, and which provided well for the dwellers therein.

While we are dealing with garbled conceptions of the Grail, let us observe another confusion arising from the name applied to the prototype of the Grail, "the caldron of Pen Annwn or the Head of Annwn." [58]    Pen in Welsh, like the word head in English, has two senses, the upper extremity of the body, and the chief of a group. We saw in Chapter XV how this ambiguous meaning combined with the penchant of the old god for decapitation to produce the fantastic story of the Entertaining of the Noble Head. It was also inevitable that some day someone should interpret the phrase "caldron (or vessel) of the Head of Annwn" physiologically. We should not be surprised therefore to find in *Peredur* that the Grail actually had a head in it. In the castle of the second uncle the young hero beholds two maidens, "with a large salver between them, in which was a man's head, surrounded by a profusion of blood." [59]    This severed head was brought into connection with the feud quest, which Nutt detected as one of the strands in the Grail cycle,[60] and of which we shall see an example in the story of Balaain and Garlan. But this, of course, is a late element introduced in order to motivate one of the marvelous adventures of the quest.

Thus the cornucopia of Belinos, the horn of Bran Galed, and numerous horns and caldrons of plenty in Welsh myth and folklore may be added to the prototypes of the Grail. But we have yet to consider one of the most famous Irish vessels of abundance, the caldron of the Dagda, which Brown has put forward as preëminently foreshadowing the sacred vessel of romance. This we shall consider in the next chapter.

[58]  Malory, Everyman ed., I, xxiii.
[59]  Ed. Nutt, 254.
[60]  *Studies*, 181–90.

# CHAPTER XXIV

## THE TREASURES OF THE TUATHA DE

In that solemn scene on which all the mysterious fascination of the Grail Cycle is focused — the scene in which the young knight after long wanderings arrives at the castle of the Maimed King, is welcomed as the expected deliverer, witnesses a strange procession of youths and maidens bearing talismans, and either asks or fails to ask concerning their meaning, with such momentous consequences to the Maimed King and his realm — despite all the diversity of the various accounts, we find that the talismans usually include a broken sword,[1] and a spear bleeding into a cup. In *Diu Krone*, however, and Wolfram von Eschenbach's *Parzival*,[2] instead of the cup the Grail is said to be a stone. In 1888 Nutt first proposed that these talismans correspond to and arose out of the four Treasures of the Tuatha De Danann: the Caldron of the Dagda, the Spear of Lug, the Sword of Lug or Nuada, the Stone of Fal (the Lia Fail).[3] Nutt's theory has been stoutly upheld by Brown,[4] but has not won general acceptance. We ourselves have seen that the spear of Lug or his counterpart Curoi and the Stone of Fal certainly descended into traditions connected with the Quest, and caldrons of plenty akin to the Dagda's certainly contributed to conceptions of the Grail as a feeding vessel. But it is noteworthy that in none of the Irish stories which are concerned with these talismans do we find certain essential elements of the Quest outlined above. There is no Maimed King, lying on a couch awaiting the destined hero. There are no damsels lamenting his infirmity. There is no procession bearing talismans, particularly a spear bleeding into a vessel. There is no question test. Accordingly it behoves us to use caution in determining just how far the Treasures of the Tuatha De can be considered prototypes of the talismans of the Grail Castle.

The Tuatha De Danann or Tribes of the Goddess Dana are a divine race: old men still call the dwellers in ancient raths by

[1] Potvin, V, 143; VI, 257.
[2] *Diu Krone*, l. 29384; *Parzival*, 233.16; 470. 3,11.
[3] Nutt, *Studies*, 184.    [4] *PMLA*, XXV, 34–59.

this name.[5]  They are said to have come from Greece.[6]  They
included the Dagda, their chief, his son, Aengus the Great
Youth, Manannan, Nuada, Ogma the Sun-Faced, Goibniu the
Smith, Mider, and Lug.  Nutt, in his penetrating study of
them, emphasizes their influence on human vitality and agricul-
tural wealth.[7]  They were the first to hold the fair at Carman, a
celebration which in after days ensured to the Leinstermen corn
and milk, men that were royal heroes, tender women, good cheer
in every several house, every fruit like a show, nets full of fish
from waters.[8]  Furthermore, their power was great over the sons
of Mil, immigrants from Spain; for they destroyed the corn and
milk of the sons of Mil till the latter made peace with the Dagda.[9]
Then, thanks to his goodwill, were the sons of Mil able to harvest corn and drink the milk of their cows.

The treasures or jewels of the Tuatha De are mentioned not
only by the seventeenth century historian Keating,[10] but also
in the *Second Battle of Moytura*,[11] which exists in a fifteenth century MS., and must be dated on the evidence of the language
much earlier.  Here is the list: "The Stone of Fal, which was
in Tara.  It used to roar under every king that would take rule
over Ireland. . . .  The Spear that Lugh had. . . .  The Sword
of Nuada.  When it was drawn from its deadly sheath no one
ever escaped from it, and it was irresistible. . . .  The Dagda's
Caldron.  No company ever went from it unthankful."

Taking the last first, let us ask whether the caldron of the
Dagda may be added to the already numerous originals of the
Grail.  The Dagda, whose name may mean Fire of God,[12] is a
divinity of more than one aspect.  The *Fitness of Names* says he
is a "beautiful god of the heathen," [13] and one of his names,
Ruad Rofessa, means "the Red One of Great Knowledge." [14]
These facts seem to support the interpretation that he was a
great solar divinity.  The *Fitness of Names* also calls him "an
earth-god," [15] a term which may indicate that he like Man-

<hr/>

[5] D. Hyde, *Literary History*, 284.

[6] *ITS*, IV, 203.

[7] Meyer, Nutt, *Voyage of Bran*, II, 160–198.

[8] *Ibid.*, 184.

[9] *Ibid.*, 188.

[10] *ITS*, IV, 206.

[11] *RC*, XII, 57 f.  On date *cf. PMLA*, XXV, 36.

[12] *IT*, III, 355.  *Cf.* J. MacNeill, *Celtic Ireland*, 47 f, who translates
"Good God."                                [14] *RC*, XII, 125.

[13] *IT*, III, 355.                        [15] *IT*, III, 355.

annan included agriculture in his sphere or merely that unlike the Christian God who remained remote in the firmament, he trod the earth and dwelt in the Brugh of the Boyne. But the *Second Battle of Moytura* [16] in Rabelaisian vein represents him as a pot-bellied or rather caldron-bellied giant, in a dun tunic which reached to the swelling of his rump, and rough horse-hide brogues. His club could crush bones as hailstones are crushed under the hoofs of horses. Indeed, he seems like a parody of the gigantic Curoi. The epithet Rofessa, "of Great Knowledge," links him curiously with three Welsh divinities who possessed caldrons. Pwyll is called Head of Annwn [17] and as father of Pryderi, dweller in Kaer Sidi, and possessor of the caldron of the Head of Annwn, is clearly connected with Grail tradition. Now Pwyll means "intelligence" or "judgment" [18] and is probably more an epithet than a proper name. The same seems to be true of Gwyddno Garanhir, whose inexhaustible *mwys* or vessel was one of the Thirteen Treasures of Britain. For as Brown pointed out, Gwyddno probably means "the Knowing One," from *gwydd*, "knowledge." [19] Merlin, who retired with the Thirteen Treasures to Bardsey, we have seen described as one "who knows all things." Accordingly it would seem as if in the Dagda, Pwyll, Gwyddno, and Merlin we had similar conceptions of the Omniscient Deity, and it is probably no accident that all four are associated with a vessel of plenty.

It is noteworthy also that the caldron of the Dagda or Echaidh Ollathair, from which no company ever departed unthankful, bears an affinity to the Caire Ainsicen or the Undry Caldron, which is assigned to Eochaidh the Yellow, King of the Picts, from which no party went away unsatisfied.[20] "It would return his own proper share to each, . . . for whatever quantity was put into it there was never boiled of it but what was sufficient for the company according to their grade and rank." The account goes on to say that a caldron of this description was found in other palaces famous in saga, including that of Da Derga.[20a]

---

[16] *RC*, XII, 87–93.

[17] Loth, *Mab.²*, I, 92.

[18] *Kittredge Anniversary Papers*, 243, note 8.

[19] *Ibid.*

[20] *Banquet of Dun na n-Gedh*, ed. J. O'Donovan, 51.

[20a] "Bruighin hu Derga." The reference is certainly to Da Derga's palace, but in the extant text the caldron is not fully described. *RC*, XXII, 307.

This same Palace of Da Derga, which contained a caldron like the Dagda's, also contained a spear much like that of Lug, the Luin of Celtchar, of which we shall have more to say presently. The Caire Ainsicen was also among the legendary possessions of Cormac mac Art, along with Manannan's Cup of Truth. As the latter probably contributed the testing quality of the Grail, the former seems to have contributed its feeding powers.

The Dagda's caldron may also be identical with Blathnat's caldron. It is said that the Dagda's true name was Echaidh Ollathair, Echaidh the All-father.[21] It is quite possible, since Irish systematizers split up Manannan into four separate individuals,[22] and often assumed that the same personage under different epithets should be regarded as several persons,[23] that Echaidh the All-father is identical with the Echaidh or Echde Echbel,[24] from whom Curoi and Cuchulinn stole Blathnat, the three cows, and the copper caldron, as we read in chapter II. In that case, the caldron of the Dagda is the caldron of Echaidh or of Blathnat. And the persistent tradition that associates Lore of Cardoil with a cup, Lorie de la Roche Florie with a healing vessel, Florie von Lunel with the Grail would be amply explained.[25] Just as Florie is Blathnat, so her cup of plenty would be the caldron of Echaidh, who is the Dagda.

Yet the description of Blathnat's caldron and of its most famous employment gives us pause. Echde or Echaidh Echbel "had three marvelous cows who were all speckled and fair. . . . A copper caldron, that was their calf. Sixty sextarii, that was the filling of the caldron from one day to another." [26] This caldron passed together with the maiden Blathnat into the possession first of Cuchulinn and then of Curoi. As will be remembered, Blathnat arranged to betray Curoi to Cuchulinn, and her signal for the attack upon Curoi was to pour the caldron-full of milk down the stream which ran past the Caher Conree and which to this day is called the White Stream, Finnghlais. These barnyard associations hardly harmonize with our conception of the Grail. But one must remember that even the romantic Tristram is immortalized in Welsh tradition as one of

[21] RC, XII,125; ITS, XV, 283.
[22] RC, XXIV,275 f.
[23] MacNeill, op. cit., 61.
[24] In O'Curry, MS. Materials, 584, his cows are referred to as the Three Cows of Echaidh.
[25] Cf. Chaps. II, XXIII.            [26] ZCP, IX, 193.

the three supreme swineherds of the Isle of Britain,[27] and Pryderi, the original of Perceval, distinguished himself in the same pursuit.[28] The *Harryings of Annwn*, which describes the pearl-rimmed caldron, mentions in the next breath a "Speckled Ox with a stout halter and seven score joints in his collar." Manannan, prototype of the Fisher King, possessed besides his Cup of Truth, seven white kine whose milk would satisfy the men of the world.[29] A bovine context is no objection to identifying Blathnat's caldron with a divine vessel of abundance. All the more clear is this when we realize that Echaidh's cows, like Manannan's, were no ordinary cattle. They were surely of the same species as the Glas Gavin or "Gray One of Goibniu," another of the Tuatha De, — a cow which plays a part in modern Irish folktales.[30] Of her we read: "The cow gave milk to every one on her journey each day, — no matter how large the vessels were that people brought or how many times she filled them, there was no lack of milk in Erin while that cow was in it." A similar supernatural cow appears in Breton folklore.[31] Not only did she give milk to sustain four hundred famished workmen, but the more numerous they became, the more milk, butter, and cheese she gave. Clearly it is not inappropriate that a primitive vessel of plenty should take the form of a huge milking caldron, and should be associated with supernaturally exuberant kine. Gradually under the influence of other life-giving talismans and testing vessels and of a different social atmosphere, the caldron of Echaidh and of Blathnat underwent a change in nature and attributes. But it is worth noting that in nearly all its many forms, the caldron of plenty remains associated both with a god and a goddess. We may reasonably believe, then, that the caldron of the Dagda is the caldron of Blathnat. It is therefore one of the prototypes of that vessel which, borne by a maiden through the hall of the Grail castle, supplies the guests with abundance of ambrosial food. But this vessel is not to be confused with the vessel into which the lance bleeds. Neither the Dagda's caldron nor any other vessel of plenty is the source of the vessel, borne by a damsel,

[27] Loth, *Mab.*[2], II, 270.

[28] *Ibid.* I, 81.

[29] *IT*, III, 215.

[30] J. Curtin, *Hero Tales of Ireland*, xlv, 297; W. C. Borlase, *Dolmens*, III, 883.

[31] A. Fouquet, *Légendes, contes et chansons du Morbihan*, 184 f.

into which the spear drips blood and concerning which the hero must ask the momentous question.

The theory that the Stone of Fal,[32] another of the Treasures of the Tuatha De, is the source of the conception of the Grail as a stone, supplied by Wolfram von Eschenbach and Heinrich von dem Türlin, does not seem so absurd after noting the composite and confused nature of the marvelous objects in Arthurian romance. The *Perlesvaus* relates that "the Graal appeared at the sacring of the mass, in five several manners that none ought to tell. . . . King Arthur beheld the changes, the last whereof was the change into a chalice." [33] Wolfram uses the peculiar phrase, "The stone is also called the Grail," implying, as Brown suggests,[34] that Wolfram or his source has combined two objects. Such syncretism we have come to regard as normal, and the details of Wolfram's description bear out a syncretic interpretation. As a shining, food-producing, life-preserving object, borne by a maiden, preserved in the castle of a Maimed King, and adored by his fellowship, Wolfram's vessel can be derived from the various cups and caldrons which we have already studied. But the fact that it is a stone, and that from time to time the names of those destined to belong to the sacred order of Templeisen appear inscribed on it remains unaccounted for except on the hypothesis that it is derived from the Lia Fail, which announced by a cry the destined king of Ireland. We have already discovered that the Lia Fail contributed its roar to the Siege Perilous, and to Wolfram's Marvelous Bed. May it not, through some misunderstanding, have contributed certain features to Wolfram's Grail? That medieval tradition regarding the Grail was muddled is certain.

The feeding vessel in the castle of Corbenic, i.e., of the Blessed Horn, must have been a horn, and yet it is called the grail, which properly means a shallow dish. Obviously there has been confusion of two forms of the vessel of plenty, — a confusion rendered easy by the fact that *graal* was a word fairly common in southern and western France,[35] but comparatively rare and unintelligible elsewhere. If the horn of plenty which fed the dwellers in Corbenic came to be called the Grail, it requires only a slightly greater confusion that a stone associated with the

---

[32] *PRIA*, XXXIV, C, 337–44, 373;  G. Henderson, *Survivals in Belief*, 199.
[33] Potvin, I, 250.
[34] *PMLA*, XXV, 35 note 4.
[35] *MP*, XIII, 683.

vessel of plenty should "also be called the Grail." We have only to imagine that in some lost description of the Otherworld palace there appeared together with the glittering vessel of plenty a stone which was said, rather indefinitely, to announce the name of the successful knight who was to be its guardian. And we have all the elements necessary for Wolfram's curious description of the Grail. It is but another instance, though probably an unintentional one, of that prevailing syncretism in Celtic and Arthurian legend.

Next in importance to the Grail among the talismans of the Grail Castle is the Lance or Spear. In the account which Wauchier gives of Gawain's visit, the hero achieves a partial success by asking concerning the spear, "Whence cometh the blood that floweth in such plenty?" [36] As a result of his asking, the waters flowed again through their channels, and all the woods were turned to verdure: so was the land in part re-peopled.[37] When we try to equate this Bleeding Lance with the Fiery Spear of Lug, we are at once met by the difficulty that the latter is never said to bleed and is never the subject of a question test. Brown, however, has pointed out [38] that in the story of Gawain's nocturnal adventures in the Palace Adventurous of Corbenic, the Grail appears without the Bleeding Spear, but that when later Gawain seats himself on the Marvelous Bed, he hears a terrible roar, and then is smitten with a fiery lance. Now we have seen that these properties of roaring when it strikes and of flaming are those of Lug's spear, the lightning.[39] The lord of the Grail Castle, therefore, who tested Gawain on the Marvelous Bed, was conceived of as possessing the divine weapon, as well as the divine source of food. We have just seen, moreover, that the Palace of Da Derga contained not only the Caire Ainsicen, equivalent of the Dagda's Caldron, but also the Luin of Celtchar, with its bursting flames, which equate it with the Spear of Lug. It is significant that in *Sone de Nansai* there is a Christianized description of the abode of the gods, which is remarkable in that the hero finds there no Maimed King and is subjected to no question test, but nevertheless is shown a Grail, which is recognizable as an ivory horn of plenty,[40] and a spear with a drop of blood on the tip, which

---

[36] Potvin, IV, 4.
[37] *Ibid.*, 7.
[38] *PMLA*, XXV, 24 f.

[39] *Cf.* Chap. IV.
[40] *Cf.* Chap. XXI.

does not, however, bleed into the Grail.  Later, moreover, we
learn that the talismans include a sword, with which Sone slays
a giant.  Here in spite of the fact that a horn is substituted for
the caldron and that the drop of blood on the spear suggests
contamination from another source, nevertheless the talismans
are adequately accounted for as survivals of the Irish vessel of
plenty and the divine spear and sword associated with it.  In
the next chapter, moreover, we shall see even more clearly that
the palace of Pellean in the Balaain story contains a spear the
exact counterpart of the blazing Spear of Pezar, which was
fetched for Lug by the sons of Turenn and which indeed seems
to be Lug's own spear.  Whenever, therefore, in the Grail
romances we observe a spear that blazes or which does not bleed
into a vessel and is not connected with a question test, we shall
be justified in concluding that it derives from the lightning
spears of Irish legend, of which Lug's spear is the representative.

When we come to the Sword of the Grail romances, we enter
a maze of paths and bypaths.  Miss Weston remarks: [41]  "It
is a very elusive and perplexing feature.  It takes upon itself
various forms; it may be a broken sword, the re-welding of
which is an essential condition of achieving the quest; it may
be a 'presentation' sword, given to the hero on his arrival at the
Grail Castle, but a gift of dubious value, as it will break, either
after the first blow, or in an unspecified peril, foreseen, however,
by its original maker.  Or it may be the sword with which
John the Baptist was beheaded; or the sword of Judas Macca-
baeus, gifted with self-acting powers; or a mysterious sword
*as estranges ranges*, which may be identified with the preceding
weapon."

Yet in spite of the complexity of the problem, there seems to
be one fairly constant trait of these many swords: their power
and effectiveness stand in direct relation to the health and
strength of their masters.  When the hero is too young, he
cannot yet wield the sword with full effect.  When he is at the
height of his powers, the sword is invincible.  When he is
wounded, the sword breaks.  He cannot be restored until the
young knight comes who can re-weld the broken blade.  This
I believe to be the clue to the broken sword motif, not the
"feud quest" of which Nutt made so much.[42]  Though Brown

[41] Weston, *Quest of the Holy Grail*, 92.
[42] Nutt, *Studies*, 181–90.

has made an excellent case for the contention that Finn's vengeance upon the murderer of his father influenced the Middle English *Sir Percyvelle*,[43] there is no broken sword involved in the feud. Neither is there any broken sword connected with Peredur's vengeance upon the murderers of his cousin.[44] Only in Manessier's continuations of the *Conte del Graal* is the re-welded sword to be used as an instrument of vengeance.[45] The connection between the shattered weapon and revenge must have been an afterthought.

On the other hand, swords which symbolize the hero's might, which yield themselves only into his hands, break when he is wounded, are restored only by the virtue of the succeeding hero, and whose restoration brings about the healing of the wounded hero, are commonplaces of Arthurian romance. Everyone can recall instances where the young hero is presented with or wins a sword at the outset of his career; for instance, Balaain,[46] Galaad, and Arthur [47] each succeed in drawing a sword from a scabbard or a block of stone and thereby demonstrate their superiority over all those who have failed. In Crestien's account of the visit to the Grail Castle and in *Diu Krone*, the host presents Perceval with a sword destined for him.[48] In all these cases the possession of the sword seems to symbolize the achievement of divine powers.

The Welsh tale of *Peredur* represents the ability to wield the sword and join its fragments as a measure of the young knight's strength.[49] On his first visit to the Grail castle Peredur is told to take a sword and cut through an iron staple. He does so twice, each time severing the staple and breaking the sword, but re-uniting them by merely placing the parts together. On the third trial he fails to re-unite staple and sword. The host blesses him, declares that he has arrived at only two-thirds of his strength, and that when he has attained his full powers he will be peerless. In Wauchier's and Gerbert's continuations of the *Conte del Graal* [50] Perceval's success in re-welding the broken sword is the climax of the quest, the final act which makes him lord of the Grail castle, and presumably coincides with the healing of the Maimed King, and the resto-

[43] *MP*, XVIII, 201.
[44] Loth, *Mab.*², II, 119.
[45] Nutt, *Studies*, 20.
[46] *Huth Merlin*, ed. Ulrich, Paris, I, 216.

[47] Sommer, VI, 10 f; II, 82 f.
[48] Ed. Baist, ll. 3092 ff.
[49] Loth, *Mab.*², II, 63 f.
[50] Potvin, V, 148–50; VI, 258.

ration of the land to fertility. There is not a word in these passages that the sword is to be employed for a vengeful purpose. If the tradition can be relied on, the sword has no connection with a feud quest, but is vitally related to the health of the old god and to the welfare of his domain.

But our particular problem is, does this sword of the Grail romances represent the Sword of Lug or Nuada, one of the Treasures of the Tuatha De? Cook proposed what after all is a natural supposition, that the Sword of Nuada is the lightning.[51] There is no other flashing weapon of the gods that it could be, and several facts reënforce the conjecture. In the *Dream of Rhonabwy* the sword of Arthur is clearly described as the blazing levin. "The similitude of two serpents was upon the sword in gold." [52] When it was drawn from its scabbard, "it seemed as if two flames of fire burst forth from the jaws of the two serpents, and then, so wonderful was the sword, that it was hard for any one to look upon it." Nitze recognized these serpents, somewhat disguised, on the Sword of Strange Hangings which Galaad found in Solomon's Ship.[53] "Its hilt had two sides, and these two sides were of two different beasts. For the first side was of a manner of serpent which frequents Calidoine (Scotland) more than any other land. . . . And the other was of a fish which frequents the River Euphrates and no other water, and this fish is called Ortenax." [54]

The Sword of Strange Hangings is found also in the Dutch *Walewein*, and there Gawain goes in quest of it much as he goes in quest of the Sword of Gurgalain in *Perlesvaus*.[55] Other features connect the Sword of the Strange Hangings with the sword of Gurgalain. The former has a hilt covered with a red cloth, a blade containing letters red as blood, a sheath red as rose leaves, a pommel containing a stone of all colors.[56] The sword of Gurgalain turns bloody at the hour of noon, and the pommel contains a most holy stone which Enax, emperor of Rome, had set there.[57] This Enax is probably the Evax, King of Arabia, who, according to the lapidaries, sent to Nero, emperor of Rome, the

[51] *Folklore*, XVII, 30.
[52] Loth, *Mab.*², I, 363.
[53] *PMLA*, XXIV, 410.
[54] Ed. Pauphilet, 202.
[55] *Folklore*, V, 121.
[56] Ed. Pauphilet, 203; Sommer, VI, 146.
[57] Potvin, I, 74; tr. Evans, Everyman ed., 74.

book on jewels and their properties which formed the basis of later works.[58] Now it is one of the strangest of the vagaries of medieval erudition that somehow this Enax who furnished the pommel-stone for the sword of Gurgalain and who may well in earlier *Perlesvaus* tradition have been emperor of Arabia, has somehow been mixed up with the fish on the hilt of the Sword of Strange Hangings, for that fish haunted the Euphrates and was called Ort*enax!* The sword which Galaad discovered in Solomon's Ship and the sword which Gawain won from Gurgalain must therefore have a common origin.

There are certain features in Gurgalain's sword which are likely to prevent our perceiving that it also, like the Sword of Strange Hangings, is a lightning symbol. But its identification with the weapon with which John the Baptist was beheaded is obviously a Christian interpretation, and even the fact that it turns bloody at noon seems to be an indication of sympathy with its solar master, as we saw in Chapter VI, rather than a part of its essential nature.[59] Gurgalain, we know, is Gwrnach, the Welsh counterpart of old Curoi, and it is more than probable that his weapon, like the axes and spears we have been considering, should turn out to be the lightning.[60] This view is rendered certain by the fact that among the Thirteen Treasures of the Isle of Britain is the sword of Rhydderch Hael: "if any man drew it except himself, it burst into a flame from the cross to the point." This is not only an obvious reference to the storm weapon, but also is the clear source of the phrase concerning the Sword of Gurgalain, that when the King drew it from the scabbard, it came forth all bloody. Thus both the Sword of Strange Hangings and the Sword of Gurgalain can be equated with lightning weapons of Welsh mythology.

Nor is the sword of Gurgalain the only talisman in *Perlesvaus* that finds a counterpart among the Thirteen Treasures of the Isle of Britain. When Gawain returns in triumph with this sword to the Castle of the Fisher King, it is placed in a chapel with other relics. When Gawain is forced to depart,[61] he hears the sweetest voices and the fairest service in the chapel, a form of veneration which recalls vividly the Irish worship of weapons,

[58] *Rom.*, 1909, 57, 271; J. Evans, *Magical Jewels*, 195; Evans, Studer, *Anglo-Norman Lapidaries*, 28.

[59] Potvin, I, 74; tr. Evans, 74.

[60] Loth, *Mab.*², I, 318–21.

[61] Potvin, I, 89 f; tr. Evans, 89 f.

particularly swords.[62]   Besides the sword, these relics adored in the chapel almost certainly included the Grail and a magic chessboard.   It may be coincidence that the Grail of the *Perlesvaus* appeared to Arthur in five several manners, while the Thirteen Treasures of the Isle of Britain included five food-providing talismans.   But it cannot be coincidence that they included a chessboard exactly corresponding to that in *Perlesvaus*.[63]   Gawain during his stay in the castle of the Fisher King beheld a chessboard with an orle of gold full of precious stones, and when he played with the silver pieces, the gold pieces mated him of their own accord twice.   The Thirteen Treasures included the chessboard of Gwendolleu: [64] "when the men were placed upon it, they would play of themselves.   The chessboard was of gold and the men of silver."   We have already noted that Merlin in his glass house in the Isle of Bardsey, surrounded by the Thirteen Treasures of Britain, resembles the holy men of the island Galoche, guarding the holy Grail, Spear, and Sword. But in *Perlesvaus* we actually find in the castle of the Fisher King, encompassed by a river, the clear counterparts of the Sword of Rhydderch and the Chessboard of Gwendolleu, and a Grail which seems to blend in itself five food-providing vessels of the Thirteen Treasures of the Isle of Britain.

Since the sword, chessboard, and changing Grail of the *Perlesvaus* seem to be so clearly foreshadowed in the Thirteen Treasures of Britain, we may feel sure that this Welsh list of talismans lies closer to the sacred talismans of French romance than the Treasures of the Tuatha De.   But even the Welsh list cannot be the immediate source of the surviving Arthurian legends.   The process of euhemerizing has begun.   The sword, which unquestionably goes back through the sword of Gurgalain to that of Gwrnach, is assigned instead to the probably historic character of Rhydderch Hael, whom we have already met as Rodarchus, Merlin's brother-in-law.   The fact that there are five different vessels of plenty shows that the list is a late compilation.   Probably, therefore, the talismans of the Grail Castle are derived from an earlier stage in Welsh tradition than that represented in the list of the Thirteen Treasures, a stage

[62] Hastings, *Enc. of Religion and Ethics*, III, 298;  *RC*, XII, 107.

[63] Potvin, I, 85, 89;  tr. Evans, 85, 89 f.  *Cf.* on chessboard *RR*, IX, 375 f; *Folklore*, V, 121;  Paton, *Fairy Mythology*, 90, 156 f.

[64] Guest, *Mabinogion*, Everyman ed., 328.

when the Irish list of the four Treasures of the Tuatha De still had a marked influence on the legend. Thus we may conclude that, allowing for the modifying influence of the Welsh horn of plenty and other factors, the Caldron of the Dagda did contribute to the feeding Grail; the Spear of Lug to the lance of the Balaain story and of *Sone de Nansai;* the Sword of Lug or Nuada to the Sword of Gurgalain and of the Strange Hangings; the Stone of Fal to Wolfram's conception of the Grail.

But we must not lose sight of the fact that the spear bleeding into the vessel has yet to be accounted for, as well as the question test uniformly linked with this mysterious ritual.

# CHAPTER XXV

## BALAAIN AND GALAAD

THE romances of Balaain and Galaad, as found in the *Huth Merlin* and the *Queste del Saint Graal* describe certain scenes connected with the Grail which have no parallel in the Celtic sources we have examined, but which do correspond closely to situations in the Irish tale of the *Fate of the Children of Turenn.* On the one hand, the *Queste* supplies a spear suspended head downward over a vessel into which it bleeds; on the other, the *Fate of the Children of Turenn* supplies a blazing spear suspended head downward in a caldron of water. The temptation is strong to suppose that here is a solution to the problem of the bleeding spear.

Let us first concentrate our attention on the tale of Balaain.[1] Brown in his fundamental study [2] pointed out not only that certain details, such as the prohibition to enter the royal palace with arms or without a lady, the damsel messenger and guide, the Hospitable Host, the slayer who can be slain only by his own weapon, but also the crisis of the story, the Dolorous Stroke, found analogues in Irish literature. He also pointed out the significant fact that the adventures of Balaain often parallel those of Gawain and are brought to a conclusion by Galaad. Both the Grail quest of Gawain in Wauchier de Denain's part of the *Conte del Graal* [3] and the start of Balaain toward the palace of King Pellean open in the same way.[4] "We find King Arthur in the Balin story, and in Wauchier, Queen Guinevere, in a pavilion pitched beside a meadow. A strange knight passes who refuses at first to return but is persuaded to do so under Balin's (Gawain's) safe conduct, and is presently slain by a mysterious knight who rides invisible. Both Balin and Gawain are urged by the dying knight to take his armor, mount his steed, and undertake the quest. . . . Both stories know the broken sword, and both conclude by an explicit statement that

---

[1] The completest study of the Balin legend is Dr. Vettermann's in *Beiheft ZrP*, LX. The study is more notable for industry than acumen. *Cf.* Miss Hibbard's article in *Medieval Studies in Memory of Gertrude Schoeperle Loomis.*　　　　[3] Potvin, III, 352 ff.
[2] *PMLA*, XXV, 42–56.　　　　[4] *Huth Merlin*, ed. Ulrich, Paris, I, 275 ff.

the kingdom of Llogres was destroyed by the dolorous stroke (in Wauchier of a sword, in the Tale of Balin of a lance) and by a reference to the Waste Kingdom." Brown goes on to point out that Gawain's adventures not only correspond in the points cited to those of Balin but also to those of Galaad. The Galaad Grail scene [5] which we shall presently examine in more detail corresponds likewise to the Gawain Grail scene described by Wauchier.[6] Brown is compelled by the facts to infer: [7] "These relationships will be explained if we suppose that the Tale of Balin and Wauchier's Gawain story represent the introduction and the termination of some lost grail story, which must have been of exceedingly primitive character, and may have been one of the pagan originals to which Chrétien and the other grail writers ultimately go back."

The relationship between the Balaain, Gawain, and Galaad Grail stories is easy to solve if we take each name back as nearly as possible to an earlier form. When we look at the names Balaain, Galvain, and Galaad, realizing that the substitution of initial $B$ for $G$ is a recognized manuscript corruption,[8] and that Galaad is probably a substitution for some form of Galvain,[9] there is hardly any problem left. The correspondence between the stories and the names is only what one would expect when the heroes all derive from Breton Galvagin. The one difficulty — the contrast between the triumphant ending of Galaad as king of Sarras and the tragic death of Balaain in battle with his brother Balaan — is not insurmountable. Certainly there was a tradition of a combat between Gawain and his brother, which could well have given rise to this tragic dénouement. For we read of an encounter between Gawain and Gareth which contains precisely the features of the substituted shield, the recognition, and the lady who comes upon the wounded knights, which are found in the account of Balaain's fight with his brother.[10] And in Manessier's continuation of the Conte del

---

[5] Rom., XXXVI, 573 ff.     [6] Potvin, III, 366–IV, 4.
[7] PMLA, XXV, 51.
[8] Lot, Étude sur le Lancelot, 148 note 8. Cf. Potvin, V, 1. 35172.
[9] Cf. Chap. XVI.
[10] Malory, Bk. VII, ch. 33; Bk. II, ch. 17 f. It is worth noting that not only does Balaan slay a knight that kept an island and take his place, but in Meraugis de Portlesguez (ll. 3170–77) Gawain describes himself as doing the same, and in the Vulgate Lancelot Boors slays the keeper of the Tertre Devee and takes his place. On brother combats cf. Folklore Record, IV, 2, 7; Potter, Sohrab and Rustem, 207.

*Graal,* there is brief mention of a joust between Gauwain and a certain Galiain.[11] Just how there arose a tradition that there were two brothers of practically the same name, both variants of Galvagin, I do not pretend to know. But of its existence there can hardly be a doubt. To terminate this fraternal struggle in a common death seems to have appealed to the tragic instinct of some *conteur* — some victim of Fate like Synge or James Thomson, — and he produced a story which not only stimulated Malory to one of his most powerful renderings, but also inspired Swinburne and Tennyson.

But there are signs enough that originally Balaain's visit to the castle of Pellean or Pelles and his dealing of the Dolorous Stroke, which left the king wounded in both the thighs, is, like the first visit of other Grail Heroes, the prelude to a second visit in which the wound was healed and the disaster ended. The resemblance between certain details in the Galaad quest and others in the Gawain and Balaain quests would therefore fit in perfectly with the hypothesis that all three belonged originally to one long Breton quest of which Galvagin was the hero. The first visit to the Grail Castle ended in disaster and has been preserved with some modifications in the tales of Gawain and Balaain. The second visit to the Grail castle, like the stories of Peredur's and Perceval's second visit, ended in triumph, and that has been preserved, with Christian additions and modifications, in the Galaad quest. Brown has shown[12] how exactly the Galaad visit as narrated in MS. B. N. fr. 343 attaches itself to the story of the earlier Balaain visit. One is the complement of the other. It is no accident, therefore, that both Balaain and Galaad travel with a damsel and fight to prevent her giving her blood, or that Balaain's sword is destined for Galaad; for Galaad is Balaain under a happier star. Pauphilet has shown that, as a character, Galaad is the creation of an author who had found peace and a solution to life's riddle in the cloisters of a Cistercian monastery.[13] No wonder that Galaad, the serene, the invincible, is the antithesis of Balaain, the wretched, the doomed.

The episode of Balaain's Dolorous Stroke runs as follows:[14] After refusing to give up his sword, which the attendants wished to remove, Balaain entered Pellean's court and seated

---

[11] Potvin, l. 39612.

[12] *PMLA,* XXV, 48.

[13] *Études sur la Queste,* 135 ff.

[14] *Huth Merlin,* II, 23.

himself at the banquet. He learned that Garlan, the knight who rode invisible and had slain the knight under his safe-conduct, was serving at the tables. When this Garlan, a red knight with auburn hair, approached, Balaain drew his sword, cut him down, and then thrust into the body the truncheon of Garlan's own spear, with which he had slain Balaain's companion. Garlan's brother, King Pellean himself, attacked Balaain with a wooden beam, and in the struggle Balaain's sword broke. He fled till he came to a chamber, where, on a silver table, was a basin of gold, in which hung a lance, point downward, without any support. A voice told Balaain not to take it; nevertheless, seizing it, he smote Pellean through both thighs. The castle fell in ruins upon them and the land became waste. Two days later Merlin rescued Balaain. The Spanish version definitely identifies the vessel with the Grail,[15] and Malory (who does not mention the vessel) identifies the spear with that of Longinus.

Brown maintained that the essential features in this tale are to be found in the brief summary which is all that is left of a long eleventh-century Irish story.[16] Aengus of the Venomous Spear, to avenge the dishonoring of his sister by the son of Cormac, came to Cormac's palace at Tara. He entered weaponless since it was forbidden to bring a hero's arms into Tara after sunset. But he took down Cormac's own spear, the Crimall or "Bloody," from its rack, and killed his son with it. He also slew the chief of the household (the steward) and put out King Cormac's own eye. After cutting down nine others he escaped. Since no king with a blemish could reign in Ireland, as we know,[17] Cormac yielded the throne to another son, and went into retirement. In all essentials, as Brown proved, this is the story of Balaain's Dolorous Stroke: the vengeance motive, the arrival of the hero at the king's palace, the prohibition against weapons, the slaying of the king's kinsman, the wounding of the king with his own weapon, the disastrous results which were involved, and the survival of the hero. Brown, moreover, noted [18] that this Cormac possessed a Golden Cup of Truth, the gift of Manannan, which "was used to distinguish between truth and

[15] *PMLA*, XXV, 47. On Spanish Grail romances *cf.* W. J. Entwistle, *Arthurian Legend in the Literatures of the Spanish Peninsula.*
[16] *Ibid.*, 53; *MP*, VII, 203; *Senchas Mor*, III, 82–4.
[17] *Cf.* Chap. XVIII.         [18] *PMLA*, XXV, 41.

falsehood with the Gael;" a caldron which would give to every company their suitable food; and Cuchulinn's sword, which shone at night like a candle. Cormac's relation to Manannan, the prototype of the Fisher King, his correspondence in the story above outlined to Pellean, the Maimed King, his possession of a testing cup and a caldron of plenty, a magic sword, and a spear, which is the instrument of a Dolorous Stroke — all show that the traditions that cluster about Cormac mac Art are intimately related to those of the Grail.

Probably because the tale of the blinding of Cormac is such a satisfactory source for Balaain's Dolorous Stroke, Brown failed to point out that another Irish story, *The Fate of the Children of Turenn*,[19] furnishes certain missing points, namely a room, apart from the hall, where over a vessel hangs a spear, head downward. The Spear of Pezar, King of Persia, is one of a series of talismans which the god Lug compels the sons of Turenn to procure for him. Turenn is said to have had another name, Delbaeth, meaning Fire-Shape; his father was Ogma the Sun-faced, and his sons are called three gods of the Tuatha De Danann.[20] Long ago Yeats expressed the opinion that the *Fate of the Children of Turenn* was "an old Grail Quest."[21] Perhaps he had in mind the very analogies that I am about to bring forward.

We first hear[22] of the Irish prototype of Pellean's spear as "the venomed Spear of Pezar King of Persia. Its name is Slaughterer. In time of peace its blazing, fiery head is always kept in a great caldron of water to prevent it from burning down the king's palace; and in time of war the champion who bears it to the battlefield can perform any deed he pleases with it." When the three sons of Turenn after a long voyage arrived at Pezar's palace in quest of the spear, they assumed the rôle of poets and were admitted. Brian sang a brief poem and asked for the spear as his reward. The king replied that after such a presumptuous request Brian was lucky to escape with his life. At once the three brothers drew their swords and began to cut down the courtiers; Brian slew King Pezar himself with the cast of an apple. Finally all were slain or had fled except the three brothers. "Then they went to the room where the spear

[19] *Atlantis*, IV, 158 ff. Free translation in P. W. Joyce, *Old Celtic Romances*, 37 ff.

[20] *ZCP*, XII, 246; *ITS*, IV, 215; *Atlantis*, IV, 170.

[21] W. B. Yeats, *Ideas of Good and Evil*, 227.

[22] Joyce, *op. cit.*, 59.

was kept; and they found it with its head down deep in a great caldron of water, which hissed and bubbled round it. And Brian, seizing it boldly in his hand, drew it forth; after which the three brothers left the palace and went to their coracle." [23] We have only to combine this story with the tale of the blinding of Cormac by Aengus, and practically every feature of Balaain's Dolorous Stroke is accounted for.

Now this spear of Pezar, which Lug required that the sons of Turenn procure for him; which was called the Slaughterer; and whose blazing fiery head was kept in a great caldron of water to prevent it from burning down the king's palace, reminds one strongly of Lug's own spear,[24] of which we read that fire flashed from it, that it tore through and through the ranks of the enemy, never tired of slaying. Lug's spear was that stupendous weapon of the gods, the lightning. The blazing spear of Pezar, procured for Lug, was the same. The caldron in which its head was set, to moderate its fiery nature, is analogous to the cold tubs which were given Cuchulinn, embodiment of the solar heat, in order to bring his temperature down to normal. This vessel is, of course, quite distinct in nature from the caldron of plenty, the prototype of the feeding Grail. Can it be that it provides precisely that other vessel which we need to account for the Grail into which the spear bleeds? To be sure, the weapon which deals the Dolorous Stroke does not bleed into the vessel over which it hangs head downward, but in the version of Galaad's visit to Pellean's castle in MS. B. N. fr. 343, which Brown showed was the proper conclusion to the Balaain visit,[25] what seems to be the same weapon, derived from the spear which the Sons of Turenn fetched for Lug, sheds drops of blood into the vessel over which it hangs. It would seem as if Lug's spear were definitely identified with the bleeding spear.

As we examine the passage,[26] let us note that there are two vessels, one probably the food-providing Grail, and the other the descendant of the cooling caldron. Galaad arrives at Corbenic, enters the rich chamber where King Pellean lies wounded. He sees "the table of silver and the most holy vessel [the feeding Grail] so highly and so fairly adorned as our tale

---

[23] *Ibid.*, 74.

[24] C. Squire, *Mythology of the British Islands* (one edition bears title *Celtic Myth and Legend*), 62 f.

[25] *PMLA*, XXV, 48.     [26] *Ibid.; Rom.*, XXXVI, 575.

has already described. . . . And he sees high above the table of silver the very lance with which the most holy flesh of Jesus Christ was wounded, and it hung marvelously so that mortal man could not see who held it. And know ye that it shed from its point drops of blood which fell thickly into a right rich vessel of silver. But after they had been caught in the vessel no man knew what became of the blood." At the direction of a supernatural voice, Galaad took the vessel containing the blood, and when three drops had fallen upon the wound, the Maimed King arose healed. Lance and vessel of blood were caught up to the skies, but the feeding Grail remained. There is no denying that the lance suspended over the vessel is the same as that found in the Balaain story and that both are analogous to the Blazing Spear of Pezar hanging head downward in a caldron of cooling water.

In Wauchier's continuation of the *Conte del Graal* again the Grail is distinct from the vessel into which the Lance bleeds.[27] During Gawain's entertainment at the Grail Castle, "when all were seated, on every dais bread was set; 'twas the rich Grail that served them, yet no hand held it, but it served them right well, and came and went swiftly amid the knights. . . . Full seven courses had those good knights; well and richly did the Grail serve them. On every dais so soon as the one meat was lifted was the other set, all in great dishes of silver — most fair and fitting was the service." After the repast, Gawain was left alone. "Right suddenly he beheld there a lance, the blade of which was white as snow; 'twas fixed upright at the head of the master-dais, in a rich vessel of silver. . . . From the point of the lance issued a stream of blood, which ran down into the vessel; even unto the brim rose the drops of blood, which fell not save into the silver cup." Throughout Wauchier's narrative there is no confusion of this cup with the food-providing Grail. In *Diu Krone* also the spear sheds three drops of blood, not into the Grail, but into a jeweled salver carried in the procession.[28] All these facts tend to show that the vessel into which the lance bleeds was distinct from the food-providing vessel in origin, and long remained independent.

But the Spanish *Demanda del Sancto Grial* in its version of the Balaain story calls the vessel which stood on the silver

[27] Potvin, III, 367; IV, 1. I quote from J. L. Weston's *Gawain at the Grail Castle*, 21 f.     [28] *Ibid.*, 41.

table and over which the lance was suspended the Holy Grail.[29]
In the *Queste* the lance as it is borne in procession bleeds into a
box, but then it is placed over the Holy Vessel on the silver
table so that the blood flows into it.[30]  In *Perlesvaus* Gawain,
watching the procession, "looketh at the Grail, and it seemed to
him that a chalice was therein, albeit none there was as at this
time, and he seeth the point of the Lance whence the red blood
ran thereinto." [31]  In these three stories the Grail and the vessel
into which the Lance bleeds are united; yet each shows evidence
of soldering.  For the identification made by the Spanish
*Demanda*, since it is not found in Malory, may not be authentic.
The *Queste* represents the Lance at first as bleeding into a vessel
other than the Grail.  *Perlesvaus* in confused fashion implies that
the Grail into which the Lance bleeds was not a chalice and did
not contain a chalice.  Altogether the evidence is conclusive
that the food-providing Grail absorbed an originally distinct
vessel connected with the Bleeding Lance.

Now since on the evidence of MS. B. N. 343 the Bleeding
Lance seems to be identical with the Lance of the Dolorous
Stroke, and so ultimately with the blazing Spear of Pezar
suspended in its caldron of cooling water, must we not conclude
that this caldron of water supplies the vessel we require in
connection with the Bleeding Lance?  In brief, does it not clarify
matters if the blazing spear destined for Lug, hanging over its
cooling caldron, is accepted as the source of the spear bleeding
into the cup, that mysterious and momentous symbol of the
romances of the Grail?

But the theory does not stand examination.  The caldron of
cooling water fails completely to account for the healing of
King Pellean, for the extraordinary sanctity which suffuses the
cup of blood, and for the momentous consequences which attach
to the question concerning its use.  We are forced to believe
that the attribution of bleeding to the lance in MS. B. N. 343
is a false clue, like the drop of blood on the holy spear in *Sone de
Nansai*.  Both features must be due to contamination from
another spear which does bleed.  Our next chapter will be
devoted to following the clues which Miss Weston has provided
for the origin and meaning of this baffling but important element
in the Grail cycle.

[29] *PMLA*, XXV, 47.          [30] Sommer, VI, 189.
[31] Potvin, I, 88;  tr. S. Evans, Everyman ed., 88.

But first let us exhaust the significance of the *Fate of the Children of Turenn* for the romances.  It affords not only an adventure cognate to the Dolorous Stroke in the Balaain story, but also the counterparts for two elements in the Galaad quest: the sister of Perceval; and the long voyage of the three heroes in Solomon's ship.[32]  The Irish story relates that Brian and his two brothers by a ruse obtained from Lug the use of Manannan's coracle, the Wave-Sweeper, and found it waiting for them at the Brugh of the Boyne.[33]  "Eithne [their sister] accompanied them to the port in which the coracle was. . . .  This warrior band pushed their coracle out from the beautiful clear-bayed borders of Erinn."  They used no natural means but spoke to the boat: "We demand of thee, thou Coracle of Manannan, which art under us, to sail to the garden of Hirbeirne."  Later we read [34] that "they went to their ship, and Eithne,[35] the daughter of Turenn, went along with them; and the maiden fell to grief-crying and lamentation. . . .  They went forth upon the tempestuous waves of the green sea; and they were a quarter of a year upon that sea."  Both times they leave Eithne behind: accordingly it must be admitted that the Galaad quest provides no scene precisely corresponding.  Several times the three companions, Galaad, Boors, and Perceval, embark together in a magic ship,[36] but each time but the last Perceval's sister accompanies them on board.  The last time, when they embark without her in Solomon's Ship for the land of Sarras, she has been dead for some time, and her body, afloat on another vessel, meets theirs when they arrive before the island.  Nevertheless, the association of the three heroes in a self-propelling boat, bound on a quest, with a sister who accompanies them to the shore, can hardly have occurred independently to the authors of the Irish tale and French romance.

But how, one may ask, did Manannan's coracle become Solomon's ship?  Pauphilet hints that Marie de France's

[32] For marvelous ships in Arthurian romance *cf.* L. A. Paton, *Fairy Mythology*, 16.

[33] *Atlantis*, IV, 193.

[34] *Ibid.*, 217, 219.

[35] Eithne is a name common in mythological contexts.  It is the name of Lug's and Cormac's mothers, of Cuchulinn's, Conn's, and Conchobar's wives, and of Laeg's sister.  That Eithne should be the name both of a prototype of Perceval's sister and of a wife of Cuchulinn, Gawain's prototype, suggests that there was some intimate connection between Eithne and Florie.                                                [36] Sommer, VI, 143, 163, 192.

lai of *Guigemar* contains an intermediate stage.[37] For the tale tells that the hero finds in a harbor a marvelous vessel of ebony with sails of silk. Under the pavilion of silk there was a rich bed, of cypress and ivory, carved by cunning workmen in the days of King Solomon. This vessel plays a large part in the little romance, and like both Manannan's coracle and Solomon's Ship moves by magic to predestined ends. Now the connection of Guigemar's bed with Solomon is due doubtless to the fame of Solomon's skilled craftsmen.[38] But the author of the *Queste* with his admirable insight seized upon the hint, which he derived probably from an un-Christianized *Queste*, and so Solomon, the builder of the Temple, became the builder of that fantastic barge which symbolized the Church, both of the Old Law and the New.[39]

The importance of the Balaain romance for the study of Grail problems, first emphasized by Brown, can hardly be exaggerated. Its marked kinship to the Galaad and Gawain quests points to the original identity of the three knights. Its connection with certain Irish tales, particularly the *Fate of the Children of Turenn*, is extraordinarily clear. Most significant of all are the indications that the feeding, healing, and virtue-testing vessels of the Celts are not the only sources of the Grail.

[37] *Lais*, ed. Warnke, l. 151 ff.
[38] I Kings, ch. 7, 8.
[39] Pauphilet, *Études sur la Queste*, 150 ff.

# CHAPTER XXVI

## THE MYSTERIES OF THE GRAIL

ONE after another of the features of the Grail legend becomes comprehensible in the light of the theory that it is essentially a seasonal myth containing the following elements: the testing of the young god by the old god; the display of certain talismans representing sometimes the lightning and the fecundity of the earth; the entry of the young god into possession of these talismans, and his marriage to the vegetation goddess. This interpretation harmonizes not only with the details of the various Grail romances but also with that mythologic background which we have seen behind the whole Arthurian cycle.

But it does not explain two vital points. It does not explain why the spear should bleed into the Grail, nor why the failure to ask a question concerning the meaning of Spear and Grail should be particularly emphasized as the source of disaster. Here is the riddle which not only fascinates the layman today but also has baffled the erudite.

As early as 1855 Heinrich noted that what Perceval experienced was "less a series of adventures than a series of initiations." [1] But it remained for Nitze and above all Miss Weston with her article on *The Grail and the Rites of Adonis*, published in 1907, to give this earlier suggestion the weight and fulness of a serious theory.[2] She has followed up her first article in her later books, *The Legend of Sir Perceval*, *The Quest of the Holy Grail*, and *From Ritual to Romance*. Her theory has been attacked on the ground that she based it on the questionable testimony of members of occult orders. She has been able to counter by quoting in its favor some of the most eminent authorities on anthropology and classical myth and ritual.[3] Her book entitled *From Ritual to Romance* Marett has characterized as "scholarly, scientific work through and through." Hartland declared that it "has solved what had been a problem for 700 years." Miss Jane Harrison wrote: "The more I read it,

[1] G. A. Heinrich, *Perceval de Wolfram von Eschenbach*, 128.
[2] *Folklore*, XVIII, 283; *PMLA*, XXIV, 365.
[3] *Bulletin of the Board of Celtic Studies*, II, 176.

the more conviction grows." Cornford went so far as to say that "the argument is self-evident, once stated." In this last opinion I concur. And luckily the evidence is so palpable that one need not be either an initiate or a specialist in primitive religion to feel its force. One may not find so convincing Miss Weston's views on the transmission and later history of the material,[4] but her main thesis, as developed in her books, is amply supported. Here let me merely sum up her reasons for seeing in the question test the survival of an initiation ritual into a fertility cult.

First, several texts inform us that connected with the Grail are secret doctrines. The *Elucidation* prefixed to the *Conte del Graal* speaks of the mysteries of the Grail which, if Master Blihis lie not, none may reveal.[5] In Wauchier's continuation the damsel of the white mule when asked what the Grail is replies: [6] "Sir, this may not be, for I ought not to tell you thereof more. If you were a hundred times my lord, I could not tell more, for this is a matter so sacred, that it may not be uttered by dame, damsel, maid, or virgin, nor by any man who is not an ordained priest or a man of holy life." In the Christianized forms of the legend we meet the same assertion. Here, of course, the idea is related to the esoteric doctrines of the mass. Robert de Boron says in his *Joseph:* "I dare not nor could not tell this unless I had the great book wherein the histories are written by the great clerks; therein the great secrets are written that are called the Graal." [7] Later in the book an angel declares that Bron "is to keep the vessel after Joseph, who must instruct him properly, especially concerning the holy words which God spoke to Joseph in the prison, which are properly called the secrets of the Graal." [8] In the *Didot Perceval* the voice of the Holy Spirit says to Bron: "Our Lord commands thee to teach to Perceval those secret words which he taught Joseph in prison when he delivered the Grail to thee." [9] The tradition of secrecy permeates the cycle.

Secondly, according to Crestien, *Diu Krone*, and certain MSS.

[4] E.g., the early Christianization of the Grail mysteries, Mithraic connections, identification with the Holy Blood at Fécamp.

[5] Potvin, II, 1.

[6] *Ibid.*, IV, 263. *Cf.* Weston, *From Ritual to Romance*, 130 f.

[7] Nutt, *Studies*, 64a.

[8] *Ibid.*, 64c.

[9] Weston, *Leg. of Perceval*, II, 83.

of Pseudo-Wauchier, the Grail is carried by a woman, the spear by a youth or youths.[10]

Thirdly, in the question test the sword does not enter at all, but all the emphasis is on the Spear and Vessel, and the way in which one bleeds into the other is distinctly suggestive of a sexual symbolism.

Fourthly, the language of the question itself as found in Pseudo-Wauchier and *Didot Perceval* lends itself perfectly to a sex initiation. Perceval asked wherefore the Lance bled on its shaft; he failed to ask *for what* the Grail served.[11]

Fifthly, we have already noted that the Maimed King is frequently said to be wounded in or between the thighs. Joseph of Arimathea, according to *Sone de Nansai* as a punishment for marrying a heathen, was wounded by God "in the reins and below." [12] Wolfram's Klinschor is lord of the Chateau Merveil, which we have equated in Chapter XVII with the Grail Castle. Klinschor, then, is a sinister development of the Grail King, and indeed of the Maimed King. For we discover that he has been mutilated by a jealous husband to prevent his enjoying longer the pleasures of love.[13] Anfortas, Wolfram's Grail King, has also been visited by God with a malady because he had taken up arms in the cause of unlawful love: he was smitten with a poisoned spear in the groin.[14] The wound was presumably as appropriate as in the cases of Joseph and Klinschor. Though hidden under the recurrent euphemism of a wound in or between the thighs,[15] the affliction of the Maimed King which had such a powerful sterilizing effect upon land and folk must have been the loss of his reproductive power.

Sixthly, success in the quest, involving the cure of the Maimed King, and his displacement by the youthful hero, brings about not only fertility to the earth but also to birds, beasts, and people. *Sone de Nansai*, which in spite of its Christianization has preserved so many pagan features, not only makes clear the sexual nature of the Grail King's malady, but also tells us, "no child was born of man, no maiden had husband, . . . no bird or beast had young, so sore was the king maimed."

In the presence of these facts, does it require any assurances

---

[10] Weston, *Quest of the Holy Grail*, 141–52.
[11] Potvin, IV, ll. 20352, 20363; Weston, *Leg. of Perceval*, II, 61.
[12] *Sone de Nansai*, l. 4775.
[13] Wolfram v. Eschenbach, *Parzival*, ed. Martin, 657, 9.
[14] *Ibid.*, 479, 12.  [15] Weston, *Quest of the Holy Grail*, 80.

from adepts or occultists to convince us that the question form of the test is a sexual initiation ceremony? [16] Or that the Bleeding Spear and the Grail stand for the male and female principles? Or that the secrets of the Grail were in all probability a solemn doctrine regarding the universal mystery of reproduction and its human application? Perhaps the virginity of the Grail hero, so stressed by late Christian redactors, may be a reminiscence of the virgin state of the initiate in the pagan ceremonial.

Several difficulties remain, but none that cannot be adequately met. How, it may be asked, does it come about that the gods are the actors in what after all is essentially a human ritual? Is it not absurd to conceive of the young god as requiring such instruction or as failing to ask the momentous question? On the contrary, nothing is more familiar to the modern student of religion than the primitive habit of assigning to the god the primacy in those human activities which seem most vital. The modern school of classical mythologists recognizes a tendency not only to make the gods participators in human work and ceremony, but also to invent gods for just such purposes. As Miss Jane Harrison puts it: [17] "We know now that social institutions tend to 'project' mythological figures. Though their aspect as culture heroes was of great importance, the central function of the Kouretes remained that of husbands and potential fathers. On the symbolic performance in ritual of this function depended the fertility and, in general, the luck or fate of the whole community. Primitive ritual is always magical in character: i. e., the worshipper does what he wants done, his rites are those of magical induction: he marries that the land may be fertile, he tends symbolically a holy child that his own children may be nurtured. Then as the religious instinct develops, he projects a daemon leader — a Greatest Kouros, to whom he hands over the functions which he himself performed." In some such way, we may believe that the young god Pry, eri or Gwri became the first initiate, the first to undergo a ritual test on which was supposed to depend the fatness of the crops, the abundance of fish, the number and vigor of the children yet to be born, — all that meant most to the prosperity and the power of the tribe.

[16] On initiation ceremonies, especially their connection with sun-cults, fertility, and ritual marriage, cf. *Folklore*, XXXV, 311 f.
[17] J. Hastings, *Encyclopedia of Religion and Ethics*, VII, 758.

How such a mythical ceremony might become the theme of professional story-tellers is well explained in two passages of Van Gennep's *Rites de Passage*. Speaking of the Eleusinian Mysteries he says: [18] "One knows at least that the initiation included: (a) a journey across a hall divided into dark compartments, each representing a region of Hades: the ascent of a stairway; the arrival in regions brilliantly lighted and the entry into the *megaron* with the exhibition of the sacred objects: (b) a dramatic representation of the abduction of Kore (Persephone), with certain elements unknown to the profane." Testimony exists that among the objects venerated at Eleusis were symbols of both sexes.[19] Later, referring to the *Purgatory of St. Patrick*, Van Gennep says: [20] "These myths and legends may be, in certain cases, only the oral remains of rites of initiation; for it must not be forgotten that, particularly in ceremonies of initiation, the old men, instructors, chiefs of ceremonies, and so forth, recount that which the other members of the social group execute." In fact, it has been urged that not only the legends connected with Lough Derg in Donegal, the site of the *Purgatory of St. Patrick*, but even the Christian ceremonies still observed there contain traces of pagan initiations.[21] One of the legends, *Owain Miles*,[22] relates how a warrior of King Stephen's by the name of Owain resolved as a penance to undergo the terrifying ordeal of Lough Derg. He was locked in the cave, descended into the darkness, found in a twilit hall fifteen men in white with a clerical appearance, who instructed him regarding his journey. After visiting purgatory, he crossed by a sharp bridge, to the Terrestrial Paradise, where Adam and Eve once dwelt. After eating food there he had no desire to return to earth. But being admonished, he started back, passed the fifteen men in white, was told by them what his future was to be, reached the door safely, and when morning came was taken out. In this legend not only does the Earthly Paradise savor of the pagan Other World, but also the whole adventure with its locking up of a solitary man over night in a cave, the instructions of the reverend men in white, the release in the morning seem to hark back to a pagan initiation. In the actual practice of early Christian times, pilgrims who persisted

[18] P. 129.    [19] Dulaure, *Divinités génératrices*, 104 f.
[20] P. 131.    [21] W. Y. E. Wentz, *Fairy Faith in Celtic Countries*, 442–5.
[22] T. Wright, *St. Patrick's Purgatory*, 67 f.

in spite of the warnings of bishop and prior, might descend into the cave after receiving benediction. The door was made fast till the next morning. If the penitent were there, he was taken out. If not, it was understood that he had perished in purgatory, and he was never mentioned again. Christianized stories of the initiation rites of Lough Derg did penetrate into French literature as the legends of St. Patrick's Purgatory. It is not unlikely, therefore, that stories of similar pagan rituals should at an earlier period have reached the Breton *conteurs*, inheritors of the druidic lore of Dumnonia, Wales, and Ireland. For the druids of Gaul we know instructed the youth in secret doctrines,[23] which they themselves received from Britain, and whatever else they taught, they doubtless did not omit certain esoteric matter regarding the cosmic processes of reproduction and the human mystery of generation and birth.

But here I shall be challenged: where is the specific evidence that the sexual aspects of this cycle of legend came from the druids or from any source in the British Isles? The evidence, I grant, is meager, but in the absence of any other immediate source, I think it sufficient. In the first place, we have some hints that in the British Isles worship with a sexual tinge existed. There is the ithyphallic giant cut in the chalk at Cerne Abbas, of unknown date but quite possibly as old as the British period.[24] In the *Life of St. Sampson*[25] we read of Cornishmen worshipping at a certain shrine after the custom of bacchantes by means of a certain play in honor of an abominable image, who declared that thus they were keeping the festival of their ancestors. More precise information as to what the custom of their ancestors probably was we gain from another Celtic territory. At Inverkeithing across the Firth from Edinburgh in Holy Week of the year 1282 a priest compelled the girls of the village to form choral dances, bore phallic emblems on a pole before them, and by lewd gestures and words excited the orgiastic spirit.[26] Highly significant is the fact that he was allowed

<hr>

[23] Caesar, *De Bello Gallico.*

[24] C. Warne, *Ancient Dorset*, 319; J. Sydenham, *Ancient Figure at Cerne*. It is worth noting that the other figure which is cut in the chalk at various places in Southern England is the White Horse, and that the literary evidence of horse worship in the British Isles is abundant. W. Johnson, *Folk Memory*, 320; J. A. Macculloch, *Religion of the Ancient Celts*, 215.

[25] T. Taylor, *Celtic Christianity of Cornwall*, 33.

[26] Kemble, *Saxons in England*, I, 359; *Studies in Philology*, XVII, 40.

to keep his benefice after this performance on the plea that it was the established custom of the country. In other words, it was not a chance outcropping of the licentious spirit, but a survival of pagan spring festivals. In Ireland Patrick testifies that the pagans worshipped idols and foul things (*immunda*).[27] Fergus mac Roich, a predecessor of Conchobar in the kingship of Ireland and foster-father of Cuchulinn, presumably therefore semi-divine, had together with other gigantic features enormous sexual organs.[28] Sexual imagery entered into the myth and ritual of many lands where the sun was adored.[29] The Thracians, when reproached by the Church fathers for their cult of the phallus, replied that it was an emblem of the sun, of the vitalizing influence of the heavenly light on all Nature.[30] Probably the peoples of the British Isles likewise associated their worship of the sun with a reverence for the vital mysteries of reproduction.

In the second place, Macalister has already noted that for the Irish the prosperity of the land depended on the generative function of the divine king.[31] "It is extremely important to notice indications that, in the case of the King of Temair [Tara], the marriage of the king was essential to secure the boon which he was supposed to bring his people. This is probably the reason why the nobles of Erin refused to countenance the unwedded king Eochu Airem and boycotted his assembly; and in the story edited by Mr. Best, under the title of *The Adventures of Art Son of Conn*, the men of Ireland enjoy three harvests of corn annually so long as Conn is wedded to his fitting spouse Eithne Taebfota; but when she dies and he marries in her stead the disreputable Becuma, there 'is neither corn nor milk in Ireland.' The exercise by the king of his martial functions acts sympathetically on the fertility of the land and of the cattle." In other words, there can be little doubt that the Irish would regard the emasculation of their kings as certain to have the same dire effects as the wounding of Joseph of Arimathea or Pellean, and his healing or replacement by a young king as equally certain to restore "the Waste Land."

[27] *Tripartite Life*, ed. W. Stokes, II, 369. *Cf. Folklore*, XXXI, 126.

[28] *Eriu*, IV, 27. As late as 1872 the stone at Tara traditionally identified with the Lia Fail was called the Phallus of Fergus. *Cf. RC*, VI, 200; *PRIA*, XXXIV, C, 337 f.

[29] Dulaure, *op. cit.*, 72, 96.

[30] *Ibid.*, 114.          [31] *PRIA*, XXXIV, C, 325.

In the third place, one of the greatest of ancient Irish festivals, the Lugnasad at Teltown was supposed to celebrate the marriage of the sun-god Lug to the land of Erin. Westropp pointed out:[32] "Oengus after the so-called 'first battle of Magh Tured' made the Lugnasad feast for the marriage of Lug to (the kingdom of) Eriu, when Lug was made king after Nuada. . . . Now Eriu was in some tales a daughter of Umor, and Tailltiu was daughter of Mac Umoir. The solar god Mac Greine, too, had married a goddess (the same or bearing the same name) Eriu." Westropp further shows that the union of the sun-god with the goddess of Erin was deemed an auspicious occasion for human matings not always of a dignified or permanent nature. Teltown marriages were more or less notorious right down into the nineteenth century. Thus we see that one of the great festivals of Ireland centered about the union of Lug with the earth-goddess and the fecundating influence it was presumed to exert.

But the most striking evidence of a phallic element in Irish tradition bears precisely on the point at issue. The spear of Lug itself and the Luin of Celtchar which Brown has equated with it [33] seem upon examination to be a compound of lightning weapon and phallic symbol. The constant elements in the descriptions of these legendary lances are two: first, their fiery destructiveness; second, their periodic assuaging in a caldron of blood or other dark liquid.[34] The latter characteristic is entirely inappropriate in a lightning weapon, but commends itself to me and to others whose attention has been called to it as apt enough in a phallic symbol. There seems to have taken place on Irish soil precisely that confusion of lightning spear and phallic spear

---

[32] *Folklore*, XXXI, 120. *Cf.* Sommer, V, 110.   [33] *PMLA*, XXV, 18–22.

[34] The spear of Lug "was alive, and thirsted so for blood that only by steeping its head in a sleeping draught of pounded poppy leaves could it be kept at rest. When battle was near, it was drawn out; then it roared, and struggled against its thongs; fire flashed from it; and once slipped from the leash, it tore through and through the ranks of the enemy, never tired of slaying." (C. Squire, *Mythology of the British Islands*, 62.) The Luin is thus described in the *Battle of Rosnaree:* "Flood-great streams of fire used to burst out through its sides, and there were four hired soldiers before him with a brazen bright caldron between them filled with blood in which the venomous spear was dipped every hour to quench its venom." Another description reads: "A caldron full of poison is needed to quench it. . . Unless this come to the lance, it flames on its haft and will go through its bearer or the master of the palace." "There is a great boiler in front of them, as big as a calf's caldron, wherein is a black and horrible liquid. Moreover he plunges the lance into that black fluid." (*RC*, XXII, 299)

which did not take place in Arthurian romance till much later. The significant point for us is that the ancient Irish attached a sexual symbolism to lance and caldron.

If this interpretation be correct, the development of the Grail and Lance may be traced as follows. By chance there existed in Irish sacred tradition two spears and two caldrons. There were the mythical spear and caldron of the gods, the first a symbol of the lightning, the second a symbol of the fertility of the earth, akin to the various caldrons and horns of plenty in Celtic and classical mythology. These, together with two other divine talismans, a sword and a stone, were in the possession of the Tuatha De Danann. The stone at least served as a test for the semi-divine kings of Ireland. But none of the talismans were carried in ritual procession, nor were they the subject of a question test. A caldron like that of the Dagda, and a spear which had to be dipped in a caldron, like that of Lug, existed in the palace of Da Derga,[35] but we read of no such use of them as of the talismans in the Grail Castle. The visit of Cormac to Manannan's palace and his receiving the Cup of Truth, prototype of the Grail, are described but there is no testing of Cormac by its means. Likewise the visit of Conn to Lug's palace and his receipt of the Cup of Sovereignty provides no analogy to the Grail test. When Cuchulinn passes the night in Curoi's castle, where the caldron of Blathnat is, the talisman is not even mentioned, and though the young god is tested, it is through no ritual question. Neither is there in any of these stories a wounded god. These facts go to show that the Treasures of the Tuatha De did not belong with the question test or the Maimed King.

But originally distinct from the feeding caldron and lightning spear of the gods were a spear and a caldron which had their origin in a pagan initiation rite, and represented the male and female organs of generation. These tended to take on a sacred character; they became associated with the ritual resuscitation of the maimed or slain representative of the god; they gradually came to be thought of as his possessions. These talismans were presumably borne in ritual procession before the initiate, and on his question concerning their use was supposed to depend the health of the god and prosperity of the tribe.

---

[35] *RC*, XXII, 299, 307; *Banquet of Dun na n-Gedh*, ed. J. O'Donovan, 51.

Both sets of talismans were thus sacred, the possessions of the gods. The spear and vessel of the initiation rite served from the first as a test, and bore a sympathetic relation to the vitality of nature. The Treasures of the Tuatha De, also, so far as we can infer, acquired in the Welsh and Dumnonian stages this function of testers and this connection with the seasons. The caldron will not boil the food of a coward. The sword can be drawn or re-welded only by the young god. To re-weld the sword brings the return of verdure. To sit unworthy in the Siege Perilous is to bring desolation upon the land. To lose the vessel of plenty is the cause of languishment.

Now once both sets of talismans had become divine possessions, which served to test the young hero and which were related mythologically or ritually to the abundance of grain, fruit, milk, and fish, then it was only a matter of time before the inevitable contamination should take place. The scenes in the Grail Castle are a mystifying compound of mythological tests of the power of the young god and ritual tests of a human initiate into a fertility cult.

It is an intriguing task to disentangle the ritual from the mythical elements and to reconstruct the ancient initiation ceremony.[36] We may presume that the youth was of noble blood, a natural successor to the chieftainship, a virgin from whom the functions of sex had been hitherto kept rigorously secret. He was introduced at night to an island sanctuary or a strange palace hall. On a sumptuous couch lay an aged man, groaning with pain. About him women wailed asking how long his agony would endure. Presently, they departed and in complete silence a maiden entered bearing a caldron. After her paced a youth bearing a bleeding lance which he held over the caldron. They stood expectant but silent. If the initiate asked the question: "For what do these things serve?" at once there arose from an invisible audience a great shout of joy. The aged king stepped down from his couch, declaring that his infirmity was healed, that the fertility of the land was assured, and that all the folk owed their welfare to the youth. Thereupon perhaps the aged man revealed the mysteries of nature in

---

[36] Miss Weston has written a charming sketch, reconstructing the Grail rite in *The Quest*, VIII, 127. But she attributed to it a mystical significance for which there seems no warrant in the texts themselves nor in what we know of Irish religion.

the process of reproduction. It was now incumbent upon the youth as chief of the tribe to exercise his generative energies, and there followed a ritual marriage with the damsel of the caldron.[37] It was a ceremony somewhat like this which coalesced with the visits of heroes and Kings to the palaces of Curoi, Lug, and Manannan, with their talismans of plenty and mythical weapons, to form the typical visit to the Grail Castle.

On this interpretation, both mythological and ritual elements have their immediate origin in the British Isles. Of their ultimate origin in the Mediterranean we shall be concerned in Chapter XXVIII. It must be admitted that there is no trace of such a ritual in Irish or Welsh literature. Yet the very nature of the material precluded its publication until its meaning had been lost. To the Christian the whole performance was an abomination of the heathen: to the pagan it was a *secretum secretorum*, a tradition which was passed on orally, to be sure, but was never regarded as fit for any but the most privileged members of the cult. It would be preposterous to expect that the arcana of a secret and discredited order should be written down until the stories had passed into the hands of men who did not realize their true import. The tradition of high significance and extraordinary mystery persisted, and Christian redactors of the Grail legend interpreted it as referring to the hidden meanings of the mass. It has remained for modern scholars, especially Miss Weston and Nitze, to demonstrate that we have here the relics of pagan mysteries.

[37] On ritual marriage *cf. Classical Philology*, XX, 238.

# BOOK FOUR
BRIDES OF THE SUN

# CHAPTER XXVII

## THE GRAIL DAMSELS

THE Grail Kings and Heroes, the Grail Castle, the talismans to be found in it, the very ritual of the Grail have yielded us their meaning. But there is a group of four persons prominent in the Grail Cycle whom we have passed over too briefly, and upon whom we must now concentrate our attention. They are Perceval's sister, his wife, the Grail Messenger, and the Grail Bearer. The materials and inferences which form the first part of this chapter are an original contribution to the subject by Miss Hannah Mallon, who embodied them in a paper prepared under the direction of Miss Peebles, and has generously allowed me to incorporate them in this book.

What of Perceval's sister? [1] Though Crestien never mentions her, two of his continuators, Wauchier and Gerbert, do. Wauchier tells how Perceval after a ten years' absence returns to his native country. On entering his mother's house he meets a damsel, remarkably beautiful and richly clad, whom he recognizes as his sister. Thinking him a stranger, she tells him of her brother, at whose departure ten years before their mother died. When Perceval discloses his identity, she is overjoyed. Together they set forth for their uncle's hermitage. On the way Perceval slays a knight who offers violence to his sister. They spend the night with their uncle, and the next day he rebukes Perceval for having slain the knight on the previous day. After receiving good advice from his uncle, Perceval returns with his sister to his home, and there he stays for three days. Then he departs, in spite of the entreaties of his sister. This is the last we hear of her in Wauchier.

Gerbert relates how Perceval, on coming to his sister's castle, overcomes Modret, who is attacking her; sends him to Arthur's court as prisoner; and then proceeds with his sister to the Castle of the Maidens, a nunnery, and there leaves her. Here he meets his cousin, the lady of the castle, who tells him of his mother and of the Grail.

[1] On Perceval's sister *cf.* Weston, *Leg. of Perceval*, II, 169.

273

The *Didot Perceval* recounts the same episode. When he returns to his father's house, the hero finds there a sister and a kinswoman. The sister fails to recognize him; she speaks to him of her brother, who had gone to Arthur's court, and of their mother, who had died of grief. Perceval reveals his identity, whereupon his sister tells him of the Holy Grail and inspires him with the resolve not to rest until he has found it. Together they visit their hermit uncle, who gives the hero more information concerning the sacred vessel. When, on the morrow, Perceval and his sister ride forth, they meet a knight who challenges them. At first Perceval, absorbed in thought, gives him no heed; then, warned by his sister to beware the attacker, he overcomes and slays him. The next day he leaves his sister, promising to return as soon as he may.

The incident of the sister is similar in these three accounts. It is not difficult to recognize another version of the episode in *Peredur*, although here many of the details prove different and the sister has become a foster-sister. On leaving his uncle's castle, Peredur comes upon a beautiful woman with a corpse by her side. At once she recognizes Peredur, and, having re- vealed herself as his foster-sister, heaps curses upon him for having been the cause of their mother's death. The knight by her side, she informs her brother, was her wedded husband, slain by a savage knight of the forest. Peredur assists her in burying the body; then he seeks the slayer, overcomes him, and forces him to marry his foster-sister.

Without doubt, the foster-sister of Peredur corresponds to the sister in the continuators of Crestien and in the *Didot Perceval*. Like that figure, she informs her brother of his guilt in leaving his mother, whose grief at her son's departure caused her death. The incident of the attacking knight contains a new element, since here he has slain the sis- ter's husband.

In the *Perlesvaus* and the *Queste* Perceval's sister plays a larger rôle. "And the Good Knight had one sister that hight Dindrane," [2] is the first mention of her in *Perlesvaus*. Gawain, on his journey to the Grail Castle stops at Camelot, the abode of Perceval's sister and mother, and finds them in great distress because of the departure of Perceval, whose return they anx- iously desire. Gawain overcomes the Lord of the Moors, who is

---

[2] Potvin, I, 3. Alternative forms Dandrane, 3 note, Dandrenor, 145.

attacking the castle, and restores to the Widow Lady her lands. When later he arrives at the Grail Castle, he again sees Dindrane. Here he learns that she is the Fisher King's niece; that she has once more been plundered of her land and disinherited "in such wise that never can she have it again save through her brother only, whom she goeth to seek." Henceforth, throughout the greater part of the book, she wanders in search of Perceval, encountering many an adventure on the way. Finally Perceval, coming upon her in the forest as she is praying, learns her identity and offers her his services but without revealing his name. She, in turn, after an adventurous visit to the Chapel Perilous, recognizes her brother, to whom she presents a piece of the altar cloth from the Chapel Perilous to help him in his battle against their oppressors. Having freed his lands, Perceval again departs on adventures. When one day he learns that his sister has been carried off from Camelot by Aristot, a savage knight who intends to marry her and then cut off her head on the day of the New Year, "sith that such was his custom," he hastens to her rescue. Eagerly he overcomes Aristot, smites off his head, and delivers Dindrane. Though her brother wishes to see her happily married, she announces that none will she ever marry save God alone, and until her death lives a holy life as a nun.

In the *Queste*, Perceval's sister appears. Galaad is led by a damsel to a boat, where Boors and Perceval await him. The maiden exhorts the three knights to enter another ship, known as Solomon's Ship; then, revealing herself as Perceval's sister, she proceeds to explain the mysteries of that strange vessel. She takes the Sword of the Strange Hangings, whose history she has related, and replaces its poor hangings with others made from her own hair, which she had cut off on the day Galaad was knighted at Arthur's court. When she and the three knights have embarked in Solomon's Ship and sailed to a far country, they arrive at the castle of a leprous lady, who can be cured only by a dish of the blood of a virgin. Perceval's sister offers her blood, heals the lady, but sacrifices her own life. In accordance with her wish, her body is set adrift in a barge, and eventually arrives in the land of Sarras at the same time as the three companions. There she is buried.

It will be observed that the rôle of Perceval's Sister consists of three main elements. (1) She is a lady attacked by a wicked knight and rescued by her brother. (2) She is, in addition, the companion of the hero's childhood, and in this capacity her chief significance lies in the knowledge of his early life and her relation to the Widow Lady, their mother. (3) Finally, she is a damsel connected in some way with the Grail or with Perceval's quest for the Grail.

She appears in the first of these rôles, as a lady attacked by a hostile knight, in most of the versions of the legend: in Wauchier, Gerbert, *Didot Perceval*, *Peredur*, and *Perlesvaus*. One recalls that in the accounts in which Perceval is given a wife (Crestien, Wolfram, *Sir Percyvelle*), the central episode connected with that lady is the attack upon her by a hostile knight and her rescue by Perceval. The general pattern of her story is as follows: Perceval comes to her castle, finds her besieged by oppressors, rescues her from her foes, and secures her love. When he has remained with her for some time, he departs, either to seek his mother or to find the Grail. After many adventures, he returns once again to his lady. A point which cannot fail to strike the student of the Perceval story as significant, is that in the versions of the legend in which Perceval's wife plays a leading rôle (Crestien, Wolfram, *Sir Percyvelle*) he has no sister, whereas in those in which the sister becomes prominent (*Queste*, *Perlesvaus*) he has no wife. When this evidence is combined with the fact that the same episode is related of both personages, one is led to the hypothesis that the sister is in some sense identical with the wife. Whether as wife or sister, she serves as a guardian to the hero, his informant, and at times the controller of his destiny; and proves the lady of greatest importance in his career, with the possible exception of the Widow Lady, his mother.

It must not be considered improbable that a sister should take the place of a wife or *vice versa*. Not to speak of the confusion of wife and sister in mythology and in stories among primitive peoples, where the wife is often also the sister,[3] this substitution occurs in almost all forms of literature. Gummere has shown examples of it in old ballads.[4] In medieval romance also, there are instances of the interchanging of sister and lady.[5] Furthermore, as the religious side became dominant

---

[3] *Folklore*, XXXI, 127.
[4] Gummere, *Popular Ballad*, 182.
[5] L. A. Paton, *Fairy Mythology*, 136; *MLN*, 1903, 166.

and the legends more and more ecclesiasticized, it would be natural for episodes in which the wife appeared to be suppressed. Miss Weston has remarked on this fact: [6] "The hero became the champion of Christianity, *le nouvel loi,* and Holy Church, and as such displayed the qualities most approved by the religious views of the time; he became not merely chaste but an ascetic celibate, and any connection with women was dropped altogether." In this final stage the wife has vanished, but the sister remains as an ascetic, like the hero himself.

It is especially in Wauchier, Gerbert, the *Didot Perceval,* and *Peredur,* that Perceval's sister appears in her second function: the companion of the hero's enfances and his informant concerning his mother's grief at his departure. Since this element appears essential to her character, it is impossible to ignore certain figures who play analogous rôles. Of these, the most obvious parallel is Perceval's cousin in Crestien, who bears a striking resemblance to the foster-sister of *Peredur.* Bruce gives the following summary of her appearance.[7] After leaving the Grail Castle, Perceval "proceeds on his way and comes to an oak, beneath which there is a girl sitting who is holding a dead knight in her arms and lamenting over him. She asks him where he has passed the night, and, on learning it, tells him the fisher who had directed him to the castle and his host were one and the same person. Wounded by a spear-thrust through both thighs, his only solace is in fishing, whence he is called the Fisher King. She asks Perceval whether he had seen the bleeding lance, the Grail, and the silver plate, and whether he had asked their meaning. He replies no. She asks him his name and, according to the strange statement of Crestien's poem, he answers rightly that it was Percevaus li Galois, although he really did not know his name and this was a mere guess. She replies that it ought to have been Perceval the Caitiff, for had he asked concerning what he saw, the good king would have been made whole again, and great good would have sprung therefrom. She tells him too that he has been guilty of his mother's death, for she died of grief after he left her; moreover, that she herself is his cousin and had been brought up with him. Perceval offers to avenge the death of her lover upon his slayer. She warns him, however, about the sword which he wears and

<hr />

[6] Weston, *op. cit.,* I, 118.
[7] *Evolution,* I, 227.

which one of the nieces of his host at the Grail Castle had sent
him the evening before." The similarity of this figure to the
foster-sister of *Peredur* is too evident to justify any hesitation
in acknowledging them as the same character.

In Wolfram von Eschenbach's *Parzival*, which so closely
resembles Crestien's version, the corresponding figure is Sigune,
whom Parzival meets as she is mourning for her dead husband.
In reply to her inquiries as to his name, Parzival answers that he
knows it not; that he has always been called *Bon Fils*, *Cher Fils*,
*Beau Fils;* whereupon she recognizes him and tells him his
name and lineage. The knight meets Sigune a second time,
after his visit to the Grail Castle. On learning where he has
been, and that he did not ask the question, she rebukes him,
heaping curses upon his head. A third time Parzival encounters
her. Though years have elapsed, she still bemoans her dead
husband. Now she is fed from the Grail by the Grail Messenger,
Kundrie. This time she forgoes her anger against Parzival and
directs him to the Grail. At her death, Parzival has her buried
beside her lover.

Obviously, Sigune and the cousin german of Crestien's poem
are fundamentally the same character as the foster-sister of
*Peredur*. Like her, they are connected with the hero's mother
and his childhood, and play an explanatory and reproving rôle.
The episode of the lover, who is killed by a wicked knight, and
whom Perceval desires to avenge, is similar to that in *Peredur*,
and recalls the incident told of Perceval's sister in Wauchier,
Gerbert, *Didot Perceval*, and *Perlesvaus*, where a wicked knight
who attempts to abduct her is slain by Perceval.

The identification of these two characters with Perceval's
sister establishes an important fact: that she is definitely to be
connected with the Holy Grail. Sigune and the cousin german
of Crestien give information and advice to Perceval concerning
the Fisher King, the Grail Castle, or the Grail itself. ·This adds
new significance to the sister's position in the *Queste* and *Perlesvaus*, where her intimate knowledge of the Grail Castle and its
mysteries is emphasized. In *Perlesvaus* it is she, always a
saintly maid, "souded in virginity," who goes in search of the
hero to spur him on to seek the Grail and thus bring about the
healing of the Fisher King and the redemption of the land from
war. As the Fisher King's niece and an inmate of the Grail
Castle, she is constantly associated in our minds with holiness,

if not definitely with the Grail.  In the *Queste* she appears as a holy maid, niece of Pelles, the Grail King, and daughter of Pellean, who we have seen is in some accounts a Grail King also. She aids the questers in their search and leads them to the Grail Castle.

These facts seem to indicate that Perceval's sister is related to a group of characters known as Grail Messengers.  They too seek the hero and, finding him, give him information concerning the Grail and upbraid him roundly for his neglect of duty, his failure to accomplish his task.  It is through their words that he is fired to set forth on his quest again.

In Crestien the Grail Messenger is a loathly damsel,[8] with rat-like eyes, long ears, and a beard, who comes on a yellow mule to Arthur's court, and curses Perceval for having omitted to ask concerning the Lance and the Grail.  Had he put the question, the king would have been healed, but now ladies will be widowed, maidens orphaned, and lands alienated.  Perceval swears that he will rest no two nights in the same place till he has learnt concerning the Grail and the Lance.

In *Perlesvaus* the rôle of Grail Messenger is likewise filled by a Loathly Damsel, who appears at Arthur's court, tells him of the languishment of the Fisher King, caused by Perceval's failure to ask the question, and reproaches Arthur for his inactivity.  Immediately after leaving the court, she is joined by Gawain and starts him on the way to the Grail Castle, to succor the Fisher King.  Now it is interesting to note, that not only does the Loathly Damsel of *Perlesvaus* behave at Arthur's court much like Crestien's Loathly Damsel and spur on the secondary hero, Gawain, to the relief of the languishing king, but we also learn later that she is herself the Grail Bearer and that she keeps her arm in a sling because she would not permit it to hold anything less sacred.  Furthermore, she rides a snow-white mule, and her head-dress is studded with precious stones that flamed like fire. With strong dramatic effect she lifts the head-dress, "and showeth the King and Queen and knights in the hall her head all bald without hair. 'Sir,' saith she, 'my head was right seemly garnished of hair plaited in rich tresses of gold at such time as the knight came to the hostel of the rich King Fisherman, but I became bald for that he made not the demand, nor never again shall I have my hair until such time as a knight shall go thither

---

[8] On the Loathly Lady *cf*. Weston, *op. cit.*, II, 187.

that shall ask the question better than did he, or the knight that shall achieve the Graal.'" [9]

In *Peredur* a damsel, riding on a yellow mule, appears at Arthur's court. She is as black as pitch, her face is long, her nostrils wide, her teeth yellow and long, and one black eye is sunken in her head. Her back is crooked, her stomach protrudes, and her legs are huge. Angrily she upbraids Peredur for neglecting to put the question to the Lame King concerning the Bleeding Spear and other marvels. If he had done so the King would have been restored. But now he will have to endure battles and conflicts, his knights will perish, wives will be widowed, and maidens will be left portionless. When finally Peredur arrives the second time at the Castle of Marvels and sees the Lame King, a yellow-haired youth enters and reveals himself as identical with the black damsel who chid him at Arthur's court, with various damsels who had shared in his adventures, and also with the youth who came bearing the bloody head in the salver and the lance that streamed with blood. There seems to be here some mistake, for we know that the overwhelming weight of tradition makes the Grail Bearer not a youth but a maiden, and it seems irregular that it should be a youth who transformed himself on so many occasions into female form. Now the Old French words for youth and damsel differ only by a letter: *damoisel* and *damoisele*. If we suppose that the *e* was omitted or worn away in a much thumbed MS. or more probably that the light sound was not caught by the ear, then we have an easy explanation for the yellow-haired youth who is identical with the Loathly Damsel. For it is really a beautiful maiden, the hag transformed, who greets Peredur on his second and successful visit to the Castle of Wonders.

Wolfram von Eschenbach describes the Grail Messenger much as Crestien does, though the correspondence is not precise. He gives her the name made famous by Wagner, Kundrie. Nutt made long since two penetrating observations: [10] "There is nothing in Wolfram . . . to show that the fortunes of the loathly damsel (Wagner's Kundry) are in any way bound up with the success of the Quest. But we have seen that the Celtic folktales represent the loathly damsel as the real protagonist of the story. She cannot be freed unless the hero do his task."

[9] St. Ciaran restored the lost hair of one of Oenach's two wives. S. H. O'Grady, *Silva Gadelica*, II, 77 f.          [10] *Studies*, 254 note.

Elsewhere he remarks:[11] "Besides his Kundrie la Sorcière (the loathly damsel) he has Kundrie la Belle, whom I take to be the loathly damsel released from the transforming spell." The latter, moreover, is the sister of Gawain,[12] whom we have proved identical with Perceval. A French form of the name Kundrie la Surziere Miss Weston has discovered in the *sorchiere* Gondree, mentioned in Gerbert's *Roman de la Violette*,[13] — a name which in turn suggests connection with the name of Perceval's sister in *Perlesvaus*, Dindrane or Dandrane. Both Gondree and Dindrane may be corruptions of the name Keindrech or Ceindrych, which is applied to Peredur's sister in a Welsh triad.[14]

In these four Grail Messengers, all more or less repulsive in appearance, we have figures who come from the land of the Grail to seek Perceval, who denounce him for past shortcomings, tell of the state of the Fisher King, and urge the young hero on to the relief of King and land. In the *Queste* the Grail Messenger has completely disappeared, but the function of Perceval's sister is so similar that the two must have been originally one. Even in the other versions we find traces of such a development. The *Didot Perceval* makes no mention of a Grail Messenger, but here Perceval's sister, though she behaves like the same character in Wauchier and Gerbert in other respects, differs in that she loses no opportunity to speak of the Grail and its mysteries. In *Peredur*, Crestien's continuators, *Perlesvaus*, and Wolfram, where a Grail Messenger appears, the sister does not speak of the Grail, and her reproaches concern only the neglect of his mother. We may conclude that the Grail Messenger and Perceval's sister are one.

Miss Mallon has thus demonstrated the highly significant thesis that Perceval's sister and cousin, Perceval's wife, and the Grail Messenger are one and the same. *Peredur* and *Perlesvaus*, moreover, explicitly state that Grail Messenger and Grail Bearer are identical. All these figures, therefore, may be regarded as differing aspects and activities of the same mythological figure. Now at the very outset of our investigation we discovered signs that Blathnat with her caldron was, as her name implied, a flower maiden, a vegetation goddess. We have

[11] *Ibid.*, 263 note.
[12] Wolfram, ed. Martin, II, 278.
[13] Weston, *Leg. of Perceval*, I, 122.
[14] Loth, *Mab.*², II, 284.

since had reason to believe that Blathnat with her caldron was a prototype of the Grail Bearer. Now nothing is more astonishing than to observe how Perceval's wife, Perceval's sister, the Loathly Damsel betray in one way or another connections with the flowers or vegetation.

Perceval's wife, throughout the *Conte del Graal*, is called Blanchefleur. Perceval's sister, we have observed, seems to correspond to Gawain's love Floree, for she is the mistress, in Platonic fashion, of Galaad, who is a sublimated Gawain; and if we accept the tradition of the *Didot Perceval*, Robert de Boron's *Joseph*, and *Perlesvaus*, which make her the daughter of Alain le Gros, she would certainly be identical with Floree, who according to the *Livre d'Artus* was the daughter of Alain.[15] Moreover, Perceval's sister in *Perlesvaus* is the heroine of an abduction episode which, though the parallel is not close, reminds us of the abduction of Blathnat, the flower goddess. In the *Queste*, as we have noted, Perceval's sister cuts off her hair on the day when Galaad is knighted at Arthur's court. The fact has no meaning until we bring it into relation with the far more significant statement of the Grail Messenger in *Perlesvaus*, that she had lost her hair when the Grail hero had failed to ask the question, when the Fisher King had fallen into languishment, and when all the lands had begun to suffer sorrow and warfare. Now we know by this time that the true effect of the Maimed King's languishment was the sterilizing of the land, the blight of winter or famine. When the Grail Messenger (who is also the Grail Bearer) tells us that her tresses fell off in sympathy with the King's infirmity, we need have no hesitation in saying that they represent the falling leaves and withering flowers. And when she foretells that she will have her hair again when the Grail Hero shall ask the question, she refers of course to the bursting buds and shooting stalks of reawakened earth. If we could rewrite the *Queste*, Perceval's sister would then declare that her tresses instead of being cut off when Galaad received the stroke of knighthood, fell off when Balaain dealt the Dolorous Stroke. Perceval's sister in the *Queste* and *Perlesvaus* is clearly a flower maiden, identical with Floree and ultimately going back to Blathnat.

The Grail Messenger of *Perlesvaus* we have already seen is in sympathetic accord with nature, and by inference wears her

[15] Sommer, VII, 108.

loathly aspect only during the desolate seasons of the year. Curiously enough Wauchier tells us that a hideous woman corresponding closely to the description of the Grail Messenger was named Rosette la Blonde,[16] and both he and the *Didot Perceval* make the challenging assertion that she was the most beautiful woman in the world. Both the name and the contradictory statements regarding her appearance are in perfect harmony with the conception which we have formed of the vegetation goddess.

The Grail Messenger, we have seen, is the Grail Bearer. In Chapter XXIII we have seen how many are the links between the Grail Bearer and the many goddesses who in Welsh and Irish tradition are associated more or less closely with magical vats, cups, and caldrons. We need not recapitulate except to remind ourselves that Florie von Lunel is the name of one of Wolfram's Grail maidens, and that Lorie de la Roche Florie plays the rôle of healer in exactly the same fashion as a Grail Bearer. Altogether the case is complete that Grail Bearer, Grail Messenger, Perceval's Wife, and Perceval's Sister are identical, and are but variant names of a vegetation goddess known centuries before in Wales and Ireland.

We can most clearly equate her with Blodeuwedd and Blathnat. But Nitze pointed out that Fand, the wife of Manannan, seems to foreshadow the Grail Damsel in some of her manifold activities. For it is Fand who seeks out the hero, Cuchulinn, and goads him on to visit her Otherworld home across the seas, to deliver it from its foes and to become her consort [17] It is a land which bands of women frequent, and "there is a vat there, with joyous mead, which is distributed to the household. It continues ever, — enduring is the custom, — so that it is always constantly full." We have but to blend Fand [18] with Blathnat, and we have most of the activities of the Grail Damsel accounted for; just as we have seen that the stories of Manannan and Curoi account for most of the traditions regarding the Grail

[16] *Cf.* Gifflet's *amie* Rose Espanie in *Bel Inconnu.*

[17] A. H. Leahy, *Heroic Romances of Ireland*, I, 59–61. Nitze in *Studies in Honor of A. M. Elliott*, I, 47 f was the first to call attention to the connection.

[18] Fand's companion as messenger goddess is the green-clad Liban. Another Liban is said to ride in a chariot drawn by two stags. L. A. Paton, *Fairy Mythology*, 10. Noteworthy is the fact that in *Perlesvaus* the Grail Messenger is accompanied by a chariot drawn by three white harts. Potvin, I, 27; tr. Evans, 25.

Castle. Now still another mistress of Cuchulinn's, as Nutt pointed out, was Lebarcham,[19] the famous messenger of the Ultonian cycle, who could wander over all Ireland in a day; and Nutt also called attention to the significant fact that Lebarcham resembled the Grail Messenger in being an exceedingly hideous creature. His conclusion that Cuchulinn, "counterpart of Perceval in his youthful feats, was also the hero of some such adventure as forms the staple of Perceval's Grail Quest," seems more than warranted. It becomes indeed a certainty when one notes that Lebarcham is a female satirist, whom no one could refuse because of her sharp tongue[20]— a proclivity which clearly connects her with the Grail Messenger and other guiding damsels of romance. If, therefore, we blend the three loves of Cuchulinn, — Blathnat, Fand, and Lebarcham, — we have a prototype for the various loves of the Grail hero in all their essential phases and forms.

The Grail Bearer, moreover, like Merlin and Morgan le Fay, can produce explicit testimony to her divinity. In *Diu Krone*, which we have often found a valuable guide to primitive meanings, speaks of her as "die gotinne wolgetân." [21] In spite of centuries of Christianization, in spite of the corruptions produced by successive translation into several languages, the secret will out. The figures from whom the Grail Damsels derive are goddesses.

[19] *Academy*, XLI, 425. On Lebarcham *cf. RC*, VIII, 55; XXIV, 273.
[20] *IT*, I, 71.
[21] L. 29622.

# CHAPTER XXVIII

## THE GODDESSES OF SAMOTHRACE

"THERE is an island near Britain where they offer sacrifices to Demeter and Kore like those in Samothrace." [1] This Strabo, about 30 A.D., records as one of the more trustworthy stories of the traveler Artemidorus, who flourished about 100 B.C. We might be inclined to dismiss the story if we had not already realized that the statements of Plutarch and Pomponius Mela regarding the supernatural beliefs of the inhabitants of the western world were amply confirmed. And the tradition recorded by Strabo is backed up by a combination of facts that is nothing less than uncanny.

First, there are abundant indications of a close relationship between the British Isles and the Hellenic world in early times. We have already observed in the preceding chapters many mythological concepts common to the Irish and the Greeks: the divine Father reborn in the divine Son, the fusion of sun-god and storm-god, the lightning represented as ax and forked spear, the one-eyed sun-god, the priesthood of Nemi, the *eniautos daimon*, the divine Kingship. Rhys and D'Arbois de Jubainville have been struck by resemblances in the heroic legends; Gilbert Murray notes the analogous development of Homeric and Arthurian traditions.[2] Nutt, after a profound study of the conception of the Other World and the doctrine of rebirth, announced as his conclusion that "Irish mythic legend shows in both cases the closest affinity with what is apparently the most archaic, the most primitive stratum of Greek myth." [3] Archaeology tells the same story. The earliest British coinage is derived directly from the gold stater of Philip II of Macedon (382–336 B.C.); [4] and the labyrinth design on Cretan coins made between 200 and 67 B.C. is reproduced on a carved stone in the

[1] Strabo, *Geography*, Bk. IV, ch. 4, sec. 6.
[2] Rhys, *Arthurian Legend*, 184 ff; D'Arbois de Jubainville, *Cours*, VI; Murray, *Rise of the Greek Epic*,[1] 100.
[3] Meyer, Nutt, *Voyage of Bran*, II, 133.
[4] J. Evans, *Coins of Ancient Britain*, 47.

Wicklow Mountains, the Klondike of the ancient world.[5]   An
old mariner's guide of Massalia (modern Marseilles), dating from
the end of the sixth century B.C. has been embodied in the late
Roman work of Avienus, and tells of the traffic between Tartessos, the Biblical Tarshish, in southwestern Spain, and the
people of the Breton peninsula, and between them and Ireland.[6]
So there is a new fascination in Arnold's magic lines of the
grave Tyrian trader, who

> day and night held on indignantly
> O'er the blue Midland waters with the gale
> > Betwixt the Syrtes and soft Sicily,
> > > To where the Atlantic raves
> Outside the western straits; and unbent sails
> > There, where down cloudy cliffs, through sheets of foam,
> > > Shy traffickers, the dark Iberians come;
> And on the beach undid his corded bales.

For to him and his Greek rivals, "the young light-hearted masters of the waves," must be due that close kinship which exists
between Irish and Greek life and legend.

At the beginning of this study, the abduction of Guinevere,
seized while she was out in the meadows according to the
versions of *Durmart* and Malory, reminded us strongly of the
rape of Persephone while plucking flowers in the field of Enna.
We have just observed, too, that Perceval's sister is the heroine
of an abduction story.   The abduction of Persephone was
performed in the Eleusinian mysteries, the most celebrated of
all the Hellenic initiation cults.   Next in renown to the rites of
Eleusis were those of the Cabeiroi at Samothrace.[7]   Now though
we have no direct statement that the rape of Persephone was
enacted in these mysteries, yet there is testimony that the
search for the earth goddess after her abduction formed part of
the Samothracian festivals.[8]   The abduction itself must also
have been included.   And we may be fairly sure that any cult of
Demeter and Kore which resembled that of Samothrace would
retain this feature, even though it were found as far away as
"an island near Britain."   There may, therefore, be a reason

[5] *Journ. Roy. Soc. Ant. Ireland*, 1923, 177.

[6] Avienus, *Ora Maritima*, ed. Schulten, ll. 94–114; *Abhandlungen aus
dem Gebiet der Auslandskunde* (Hamburgische Universität), VIII, 67.

[7] Daremberg, Saglio, *Dictionnaire*, I², 763.

[8] Hastings, *Encyclopedia of Religion and Ethics*, VII, 632;   Conze,
*Untersuchungen*, I, 43; Pauly, Wissowa, X, 1428 f.

why the abduction story of Blathnat and its derivatives should be among the most firmly established traditions of Celtic and Arthurian legend.

What clinches the connection is the fact that the beloved of the sun hero (Gawain, Gareth) is, like Persephone, both vegetation and moon goddess. The goddess of the moon from the very earliest times has also been the power that could blast or bring to luxuriant ripeness all green things.[9] Thus we find combined under one name such diverse figures as the queen and huntress, chaste and fair, seated in her silver chair, and the many-breasted Diana of the Ephesians, embodiment of fecundity. The vegetation goddesses, Hecate, Demeter, Persephone, had also their lunar aspects. Plutarch, for example, says:[10] "One Demeter is in the earth, lady and mistress of that which is on the earth, and the other is in the moon, and is called by those who live in the moon, Kore or Persephone." We have noted that the original tradition made Gareth the lover of Lynete,[11] and Crestien de Troyes makes Gawain, who is of course Gareth under another name, lover of Lunete, and says expressly that she was the moon.[12] We are already familiar with the tradition which represented Gawain as the lover of Florie.[13] Lunete, moreover, like Lorie de la Roche Florie, is called a fay, her name assuming the corrupt form Felinet.[14] Probably her Welsh progenitor is Arianrhod, "Silver Wheel," a name which suggested to Lessmann a lunar nature.[15] Is it coincidence that both in classical and Arthurian mythology the mistress of vegetation, heroine of an abduction story and the object of a mystery-cult, should be equated with the goddess of the moon?

The vegetation goddess who is the prototype of so many damsels of Arthurian romance must have been notorious for her shapeshifting. There is a consistent tradition which tells of her transformation from a hideous animal-faced, mis-shapen hag into a golden-haired paragon of loveliness. In that ancient and exquisite Homeric *Hymn to Demeter* of the seventh century B.C. we find that Demeter assumed and put off the form of a withered crone.[16]

[9] J. G. Frazer, *Adonis, Attis, Osiris*, II, 131–9; Meyer, Nutt, *op. cit.*, II, 224 f.
[10] *De Facie Lunae*, LXX.
[11] *Cf.* Chap. VII.
[12] *Ivain*, l. 2398.
[13] *Cf.* Chap. II.
[14] Warnatsch, *Mantel*, 75.
[15] *Mitra*, I, 161 n. 4.
[16] J. Harrison, *Mythology*, 86.

Then as she spake — the goddess cast away her stature old
And changed her shape in wondrous wise, and beauty manifold
She breathed around.  From forth her robe a perfumed fragrance shed
That makes the heart to yearn.  Her golden hair about her
head
Streamed, and her flesh celestial through the goodly chambers
glowed —
Like lightning fire from forth the halls, straightway the goddess strode.

Though Strabo refers to the goddesses whose rites, celebrated
in an island near Britain, resembled those of Samothrace as
Demeter and Kore, it is more than possible that they were
blended with the rites of another goddess, sometimes equated
with Persephone, also worshipped at Samothrace, Hecate.[17]  We
read in a classical source that "In Samothrace there were mysteries of the Korybantes and of Hecate." [18]  In the Cave of
Zerynthos, "it is said that they worshipped Hecate with orgies
and performed initiation rites to her and sacrificed dogs." [19]
Now one of the peculiarities of Hecate was her power of taking
on hideous forms.  She became "a dog, or a woman with a dog's
head, or a lioness, mare, cow, gigantic old woman, with serpents
in her hair, her legs ending in a dragon's tail." [20]  Elsewhere,
however, we learn that her shape was that of Demeter, "the
fair goddess of fruits." [21]  In her ability to take on both a hideous
and a radiantly beautiful form, the Grail Messenger or Grail
Bearer corresponds closely to Hecate-Demeter, worshipped at
Samothrace.

Another point on which the goddess of Samothrace and the
goddess who appears in the Grail romances agree, is that they
are messengers or guides to the Other World.  Hecate is called
*aggelos* or *hegemone*.[22]  She is thought of as the guide of the
spirits of the dead to her under-world realm.  The resemblance
between the Greek and Irish conceptions of that Other World

---

[17] Daremberg, Saglio, I², 761; III¹, 47; Strabo, Bk. X, 472.
[18] Schol, Arist., *Pax*.
[19] *Ibid.*
[20] Daremberg, Saglio, III¹, 49; Pauly, Wissowa, VII, 2774.
[21] Farnell, *Cults of the Greek States*, II, 512.
[22] *Ibid.*, II, 516 f; Daremberg, Saglio, III¹, 46 f.

has been conclusively demonstrated in Nutt's extended study.[23] And it has been remarked how often in Irish legend the goddess summons and sometimes leads the hero to the land of immortals.[24]

It may be objected that in the Irish and Arthurian stories the goddess does not seem to be leading the soul of a dead hero but rather a very much alive demigod or god to her palace of delights, often to be her spouse. Cuchulinn is not a ghost but a god. To be sure, the analogy would fall flat if we had not already observed the tendency to attribute to the gods rôles that were essentially human. If the young man required an initiation into the mysteries of reproduction, so did the young god. If Hecate was imagined as the messenger and guide who led the soul of the hero to the abode of the elder divinities, it is only a step to the Loathly Damsel or Perceval's sister, who urge the young god on to the Fisher King's Castle, to be tested and prove himself a worthy successor.

Another strange parallel exists between the myths of Samothrace and of the British Isles. Among the gods celebrated in the mysteries of the Cabeiroi, indeed their reputed founder, was Iasion, son of Zeus.[25] Ovid represents the youth as a huntsman on Cretan Ida. Demeter lived retired in the forests near by, but the land was fruitless. She saw the young huntsman, fell in love with him, and satisfied her passion. Thereafter the crops were plentiful.[26] But the *Odyssey* relates that Zeus (here regarded as the jealous husband of Demeter) was not unaware when the goddess with the fair tresses mingled in love with Iasion on a thrice-tilled field, and slew him with a stroke of the blazing levin.[27]

If we cast back to the second chapter, we may remember how in the *Mabinogion* Blodeuwedd became infatuated with the young huntsman Gronw and enjoyed his love during her husband's absence. Perhaps the similar stories of the two vegetation goddesses may be due to coincidence. But what are we to make of the fact that when Lyones, identical with Lynete,[28] and therefore also vegetation goddess, is interrupted when about to enjoy the embraces of the young Gareth, by a knight brand-

---

[23] Meyer, Nutt. *op. cit.*, I.        [24] *Ibid.*, 159.
[25] Daremberg, Saglio, I², 764; Pauly, Wissowa, IX, 755.
[26] Pauly, Wissowa, IX, 754.
[27] *Odyssey*, V, 125–9.
[28] *Cf.* Chap. VIII.

ishing a great ax, in whom we have detected old Curoi with the lightning? What are we to say when we find that in the *Chevalier à l'Epée* a host whose behavior identifies him with various Arthurian developments of old Curoi, sends Gawain, the young Curoi, to bed with his daughter (though the analogues make it clear that she should be the old god's wife); when we note that all who have previously slept with the damsel have been slain by a magic sword which darts from its sheath, and that Gawain is twice slightly wounded by it? [29] What are we to make of the fact that in *Diu Krone* Gawain is lured by Amurfina to her bed, and when he is about to mate with her, a magic sword hanging over them darts down and encircles the knight,[30] and that later Amurfina appears, as we saw in Chapter XII, as the presumptive spouse of Gansguoter, Curoi himself? Does it not seem as if in these stories of Gareth and Gawain we had romanticized versions of the story of Iasion? Especially when we consider that in two cases at least the women are clearly identifiable as goddesses of vegetation or the moon, and that in every case the husband who interrupts or prevents her embraces is the lord of the thunderbolt?

By a strange coincidence, not only the mythical elements of the Grail legend, but also the ritual elements confused with them are accounted for by the cults of Samothrace, for they seem to supply the prototype of the Grail Bearer. The Great Earth-Mother was worshipped at Samothrace not only as Demeter and Hecate, but also as Cybele, whose original cult center was in Asia Minor.[31] It is known that in her mysteries a priestess bore on her head a *krater* (the very word from which the word Grail is ultimately derived), usually called the *kernos*, to each side of which a lamp was attached [32] — a reminder of the candles which nearly always attended the Grail Bearer. The contents of the *kernos* are supposed by the best scholars to have been of a distinctly sexual nature.[33]

Now this association of the Grail Bearer with the mysteries of Cybele is supremely significant since it is with the cult of Cybele and Attis, her consort, that Miss Weston long since connected the Grail initiation rite.[34] We hear of the image of the

[29] *Chevalier à l'Epée*, ed. Armstrong, ll. 513 ff.
[30] Heinrich von dem Türlin, *Krone*, ll. 7932 ff.
[31] Pauly, Wissowa, X, 1427.          [33] Hepding, *Attis*, 191 f.
[32] *Ibid.*, XI, 325.          [34] *From Ritual to Romance*, 139.

mutilated god placed on a couch, of lamentations by night about the bier, of the bringing in of a light, the anointing of the weepers by the priest, and a pronouncement that all should rejoice because the god is healed and their salvation has come.[35] There is good reason to infer that the god too was anointed to bring about his renewed vitality.[36] We hear also of a ritual feast at the beginning of the ceremony and of a ritual marriage of the initiate with the goddess at the end.[37] If we combine the myths about Demeter and Iasion with the mysteries of Cybele and Attis, we can explain an incredible number of features in the Grail legends. Nothing, as Miss Weston points out to me, was more characteristic of the mystery-religions than their tendency to syncretism. Of such a process the Grail tradition seems to be the ultimate and exquisite flowering.

The report preserved by Strabo that in an island near Britain sacrifices were offered to Demeter and Kore like those of Samothrace finds an incredible amount of corroboration in Arthurian romance. For the corresponding divinity, who must have sprung from ancient mythological roots which ran deep in the soil of the British Isles, and whom we can trace back to Wales and Ireland, shares six characteristics with the Greek goddesses. She is the heroine of a seasonal abduction story. She is mistress both of moon and vegetation. She transforms herself from the most hideous animal-like forms to radiant beauty. She is a guide to the Other World. She embraces a youthful god with the knowledge of her husband, who interrupts them with his lightning stroke. Finally she is associated with a cult in which a priestess bears a vessel adorned with lights in an initiation ceremony, intimately connected with the healing of a maimed god.

The significance of these correspondences may well be challenged on the ground that the Irish goddesses we have equated with the Grail damsels do not represent exactly intermediate stages between the Grail damsels and the classic goddesses. But we have already seen why the priestess of Cybele does not find a counterpart in Irish story; the Celtic initiation rites never were committed to writing. Moreover, there is good reason why we do not find plainly recognizable descendants of Hecate, Persephone, and Demeter in Irish saga, since we know that the Ulster cycle probably preserves only adulterated forms of those

[35] Pauly, Wissowa, XI, 2274.    [36] *Ibid.*, 2275.    [37] *Ibid.*

myths of Southern Ireland which were the sources of Welsh and Arthurian romance. Yet even as it is, the Ulster cycle furnishes in Lebarcham, the hideous guiding goddess, the beloved of the sun-god, a figure which relates Hecate to the Grail Messenger; and in Blathnat, the vegetation goddess, the heroine of an abduction story and the possessor of vessels of plenty, a figure which relates Demeter and Persephone to the Grail Damsel and Perceval's Sister. We may feel sure that the lost mythology of southern Ireland would have shown a far completer correspondence.

There is other evidence for such a connection. Macalister says: [38] "It is quite clear that the Celtic incomers [the tall blondes of whom classical historians speak] took over much from the religion of their pre-Celtic predecessors. It was natural that they should do so; for the aborigines would know how the gods of the land should be worshipped; we have already . . . spoken of the awe with which people in pagan times enter a strange country before they discover how its spiritual inhabitants should be propitiated." Peake refers to the race which has given Wales, Scotland, and Ireland the majority of their small brunette inhabitants as the Mediterranean race.[39] And Macalister asserts that there is "a general similarity between the legends of Partholon, Nemed, and the Fir Bolg, close enough to justify us in regarding them as variants of one and the same group of tales — namely, the tales that the aboriginal, pre-Celtic people of the country told about their own beginnings." [40] Now it is a singular fact that many of the Irish traditions concerning the origins of the races which at one time or another inhabited the island carry us to Greece or more specifically Thrace. Partholon, if we may believe Keating, came from Migdonia (possibly Macedonia), sailed through the Mediterranean, and settled in western Munster.[41] Nemed, the next colonist, was the son of Agnoman, said to be "a Scythian Greek," whatever that may mean.[42] Even the certainly mythical folk, the Tuatha De Danann, came from the northern islands of Greece.[43] The Fir Bolg came from Thrace.[44] The historic

---

[38] R. A. S. Macalister, *Ireland in Pre-Celtic Times*, 293.

[39] H. Peake, *Bronze Age and the Celtic World*, 28.

[40] *PRIA*, XXXIV, C, 295.

[41] *ITS*, IV, 159.

[42] *Leabhar Gabhala*, ed. J. MacNeill, R. A. S. Macalister, I, 73, 81.

[43] *Ibid.*, 143.         [44] *ITS*, IV, 235.

Cruithnigh or Picts are said to have come from Thrace.[45] The Scots according to legend were originally settled on the Pactolus in Asia Minor, set out to conquer Thrace, were driven by storms through the Straits of Gibraltar, and up to Ireland.[46] Obviously such traditions cannot be taken at their face value, and only a specialist in the complicated problem of Irish ethnology would dare to interpret them. Nevertheless, considering the ample evidence of intercourse between Ireland and the Mediterranean, and the extraordinarily complete case for the transmission of the religious cults of Samothrace to an island near Britain, one cannot pooh-pooh lightly the persistence of legends deriving certain non-Celtic peoples of Erin from Greece and particularly from a part of Greece so close to Samothrace. Where there is so much smoke, there must be some fire.

Now whereas the classical mythology accounts so largely for the goddesses of Celtic legend, it does not so adequately account for the gods. Lug, Ogma,[47] Goibniu we know were Celtic divinities. The existence of many Eochus, Echaids, Ech-cenns, Marcs, and certain rites points strongly to a worship of horse gods which was perhaps Celtic, certainly not Mediterranean.[48] Manannan seems to have originated as the local god of the sacred isle of Man. Nevertheless, there is reason to believe that other cults besides the Samothracian were carried by merchants or colonists into the Atlantic isles. Ptolemy called Hartland Point the Headland of Heracles,[49] and we find Ercoil turning up as a rival of Cuchulinn's in *Bricriu's Feast*.[50] He shows no signs of being a figure introduced after a recent reading of the classics, but has every appearance of being a well established and familiar hero of myth. Knowing as we do that there existed a powerful cult of Heracles in the neighborhood of the Columns which bear his name,[51] we need not be surprised that it was carried up to the British Isles. From Southern Spain, too, the worship of Kronos [52] seems to have spread to the islands of the Atlantic, where it is witnessed by Plutarch.[53] Dalton has urged

---

[45] *ITS*, VIII, 109, 113.
[46] *Irish Arch. Soc. Pub.*, XI, 225 note a;   Colgan, *Acta Sanctorum*, 494.
[47] *IT*, *Tain Bo Cualnge*, xxx f.
[48] *Cf.* Chap. XXVI, n. 24.
[49] J. Rhys, *Arthurian Legend*, 362
[50] *ITS*, II, 85–9. *Cf. Gött. Gel. Anz.*, 1890, 496.
[51] Pauly, Wissowa, VII, 448.      [52] *Ibid.*
[53] *De Facie Lunae*, XXVI; *Defectu Oraculorum*, XVIII.

the identity of Kronos with the Irish Cromm Cruaich,[54] who
is said to have been " an everlasting monster that is in Greece,"
and the god of every folk that colonized Ireland.[55]  It is worth
noting that King Tigernmas, who Keating says established the
worship of Cromm, was reputed the descendant of Eiremon,
who came from Spain.[56]  And in a later chapter we shall see
clear traces in Welsh and Arthurian legend of the myth of
Kronos as a god imprisoned on a North Atlantic island.  Beside
the cult of Kronos in Southern Spain, we find in Tartessos that
of the Curetes,[57] who worshipped the son of Kronos, Zeus, under
the title of Kouros.[58]  It was brought thither from its center
in Crete, probably at a time when the Cretans were the great
seafaring folk of the Mediterranean.[59]  A hymn of the Curetes
reveals them in ritual dance, "designed to stimulate the reproductive energies of Nature, to bring into being fruitful fields,
and vineyards, plenteous increase in the flocks and herds, and
to people the cities with youthful citizens." [60]  Miss Weston
maintains that in such dances as these originated the morris
dance and sword dance still surviving in the British Isles.[61]  In
Zeus the Curetes worshipped a god who was familiar both as
the venerable lord of the thunder and as a youthful leader of
their ritual dances.  As the one, he wielded the double-ax; [62]
as the other he doubtless had, as Murray expresses it, a touch
of the sun in him.[63]  Is it not possible that together with Kronos
and Heracles he voyaged up to Ireland, and Zeus Kouros settled
down as Curoi King of Munster?

Whether or not the Cretan cult of the Curetes reached Ireland
and gave us Curoi mac Daire, as the worship of Kronos seems
to have survived into the nineteenth century as the worship of
Cromm Dubh,[64] yet there can be no doubt of the contribution
made to the Grail Legend by the Samothracian goddesses.  An
initiate into their mysteries might witness a performance of
Wagner's *Parsifal* and feel that among all the appalling riddles of
modern life here was at last something that in part he could

[54] *PRIA*, XXXVI, C, 59 note 3; *Breifny Antiq. Soc. Journal.* II. 66.
[55] *PRIA*, XXXVI, C, 65 f.
[56] *ITS*, VIII, 49, 79, 121, 123.          [57] Pauly, Wissowa, XI, 2206.
[58] *Ibid.*, 2205; Hastings, *Encyclopedia*, *sub* Kouretes.
[59] Strabo, Bk. X, ch. 4, sec. 17.
[60] Weston, *From Ritual to Romance*, 83.
[61] *Ibid.*, 88 ff.                          [63] *Ibid.*, 186 ff.
[62] A. B. Cook, *Zeus*, I, 606 ff.          [64] *PRIA*, XXXVI, C, 49 ff.

comprehend. For Wagner not only expresses through word and act and a music more eerie and magical than was ever before heard on earth his mystic philosophy; he has also interwoven with it a drama of the divinities whose life is in the warm sun and the green earth. Does not one hear in the Prelude the mourning and anguish of a wintry forest? Is not the Good Friday Spell a yearning lyric of spring? Is not that the old god lying wracked with pain? These sacred talismans, are they not symbols of the red life blood and of the silver-bladed lightning, symbols which acknowledge the young god as their master? Even more uncanny is the treatment of Kundrie. Simrock seems to have furnished the clues,[65] but Wagner by a kind of miracle has resurrected the old Goddess of the Earth and its fruits, much as the old mythologies conceived her. She is not only the Loathly Messenger of tradition, but she also appears transformed into a seductive enchantress in Klingsor's garden. She dwells among flower maidens, who sing to the young god: "We here abide through sunlight and summer  If thou wilt not fondle and cherish, we swiftly must wither and perish." Just as in the authentic tradition of Demeter and Iasion, she tempts the young hero, and the old god, her master, breaks in upon them and hurls his lightning spear. Our hypothetical initiate into the ancient mysteries would be startled to find enacted within a few steps of the colossal and baffling unintelligibility of twentieth century Broadway a spectacle in which he could recognize, though the coincidences are partly accidental, the love of Demeter for Iasion, the founder of the mysteries of the Cabeiroi at Samothrace?

[65] Wolfram von Eschenbach, *Parzival*, tr. Simrock, 345 f.

# CHAPTER XXIX

## THE HAG TRANSFORMED

THE mysterious Loathly Damsel of Arthurian romance, who is transformed into a paragon of golden-tressed loveliness, can claim descent from the shape-shifting Demeter and Hecate. The transformation of Demeter into a radiant young goddess may derive its meaning from the fact that the young Kore or Persephone was always regarded as the younger self of Demeter. The metamorphosis of Demeter as related in the *Homeric Hymn* may refer, then, to the power of all green things to renew their life and beauty with the return of spring. But no classical myth, so far as I know, recounts this transformation of the goddess under circumstances which reveal its seasonal significance. Curiously enough, however, Irish legend, which usually conceals its connections with the powers and processes of Nature more completely than the Greek, provides several stories of the transformation of a hideous hag which can be recognized as charming allegories of the sere fields and forests bursting into beauty at the kiss and warm embrace of the young sun. In several of the versions the hero is a Lugaid son of Daire. Now in Chap. V we noted that Lugaid is practically a variant form of the name Lug, the sun-god, and we are well aware that another sun-god, Curoi, was traditionally a son of Daire. The solar suggestions of the name Lugaid son of Daire must have been strong. In the *Fitness of Names* we read: [1] "This is why Daire gave the name of Lugaid to each of his [five] sons. Because it had been foretold to him that a son of his would obtain the sovereignty of Erin and that Lugaid would be his name. Then said Daire to his druid: 'Which of my sons will take the kingdom after me?' The druid replied: 'A fawn with a golden lustre upon it will come into the assembly, and the son that shall catch the fawn is he that will take the kingdom after thee.' Thereafter the fawn entered the assembly, and the men of Erin, together with Daire's sons, pursued it till they reached Ben Etair. A magical mist is set between them (Daire's

---

[1] *IT*, III, 319 ff. *Cf. ITS*, VIII, 149.

sons) and the (rest of the) men of Erin. Thence on after the
fawn went Daire's sons to Dal Moscorb in Leinster, and Lugaid
Laigde caught the fawn. . . . Thereafter they hunt in the
wilderness. A great snow fell upon them, so that it was a labor
to hold their weapons. One of them goes to look for a house,
and he finds a wonderful house with a great fire therein, and ale,
and abundance of food, and silvern dishes, and a bed of white
bronze. Inside he discovers a huge old woman, wearing a frontlet (?), and her spears of teeth outside her head, and great, old,
foul, faded things upon her. [She refuses to give him shelter
unless he lie with her, but he spurns her and departs: three
brothers do likewise.] At last went Lugaid Laigde. . . . 'I
will sleep alone with thee,' says Lugaid. The hag entered the
bed and Lugaid followed her. It seemed to him that the radiance of her face was the sun rising in the month of May. A
purple, bordered gown she wore, and she had beautifully colored
hair. Her fragrance was likened unto an odorous herb-garden.
Then he mingled in love with her. 'Auspicious is thy journey,'
quoth she. 'I am the sovereignty, and the kingship of Erin
will be obtained by thee.' Lugaid went to his brothers and
brings them to the house, and there they get the freshest of
food and the oldest of ale, and self-moving drinking horns
pouring out to them. . . . Thus were Daire's sons on the
morrow: on a level, houseless plain — with their hounds asleep,
fastened to their spears."

In the metrical *Dindsenchas of Carn Mail* we have much the
same story.[2] The number of Daire's sons is confused. The
fawn is said to be a familiar of Daire. The four sons meet it
near Tara and kill it. As they sat before a fire in a house where
they were resting, a hag approached, ugly and bald. "High
she was as any mast, larger than a sleeping hut her ear, blacker
her face than any visage, larger her front tooth than a square of
a chess-board. Larger than a basketful of ears of wheat each
fist; larger than a rock in a wall each of her rough black knees.
She was one continuous belly, without ribs, without separation.
A rugged, hilly, thick block head was upon her like a furzy
mountain. She endeavored to excite their passions and threat-
ened to transform them into monsters if one of them would not
lie with her. Lughaidh Laidhe consented. But as the fire
darkened, she assumed a form of wondrous beauty; ruddy were

[2] *Miscellany of the Celtic Soc.*, 1849, 69–75.

her cheeks, round her breasts; three sunbeams shone in each
of her eyes, and when she removed the purple garment, the
house was lighted by her fair skin. She said: 'With me the
arch-kings lie. I am the majestic, slender damsel, the Sovereignty of Alba and Eire.'"

In certain other versions the hero is Niall of the Nine Hostages.[3] According to the *Exploits of the Sons of Eochaid Mug-
medon*,[4] the five brothers were camping beside the lakes of
Erne after slaying a boar. Fiachna went to seek water from a
fountain, but was struck with terror by a sorceress on its brink.
"A mouth she had into which a hound would fit; the spiked
tooth-fence about her head was more hideous than all the
goblins of Erin." When she asked for a kiss, Fiachna fled.
Three brothers in succession were frightened away. At last
Niall went, and beheld that hideous shape, thin-shanked, gray-
headed, bushy-browed. Thrice nine rows of long teeth had she.
As it were a flash (?) from a mountain-side in the month of March,
even so blazed her bitter eyes. Niall accepted her conditions.
He placed his lips upon her lips, and warmly clasped her sturdy
waist. "When he looked up from beneath his cloak, though
fair be the sun from the dome of heaven, that maiden's beauty
was lovelier far. Blooming her countenance in hue as the crimson lichen of Leinster crags, clear like crystal was her throat,
her locks were like Bregon's buttercups. A mantle about her,
matchless, green; a border it had of refined gold." She then
told Niall of his destined reign in Tara.

Far be it from me to deny that Niall of the Nine Hostages and
Lugaid Laigde were historic kings. But the context makes it
clear that they have fallen heir to the functions of the sun-god.
The transformation of an allegorical figure of the Sovereignty of
Erin by the embraces of the future king is destitute of meaning,
except such forced moralizing as we find in the Niall versions,
to the effect that the kingship is loathsome at the outset but
happy in the ending. But once see in the monstrous hag that
primeval figure of the Earth, "Lady and Mistress of that which
is on the earth," whom we have detected as the destined bride
of the sun-gods both in Irish and Arthurian legend, and as the
Loathly Damsel of the Grail romances; then her transformation
suddenly glows in the imagination with the magic of poetry.
Surely there are signs enough that the embodiment of the Sover-

[3] S. H. O'Grady, *Silva Gadelica*, II, 368.          [4] *Eriu*, IV, 101–7.

eignty of Erin is really the embodiment of green Ireland, which renews its beauty every spring under the warm rays of the new sun. Her glance before her metamorphosis is like a flash (?) from a mountain-side in the month of *March;* after the change the radiance of her face was the sun rising in the month of *May.* Before, she is a huge, black, bald, shapeless mass.[5] Afterwards, her countenance blooms like the crimson lichen, her locks are like Bregon's buttercups, she wears a green mantle, and her fragrance is like that of an odorous herb-garden. Such a personification of landscape is thoroughly Irish. Finn, hearing some verses about "a bright-faced queen, with couch of crystal and robe of green," says: "I understand the sense of that poem also. The queen you saw is the River Boyne. . . . Her couch of crystal is the sandy bed of the river; and her robe of green the grassy plain of Bregia." [5a]

One may easily find precise and minute correspondences between the hideous hags of these Irish tales and the Loathly Damsels of Arthurian romance; baldness or sparse stringy hair, blackness, long tusks, etc. It is significant that in two points the version found in the *Fitness of Names* affords additional resemblances to the Grail stories, for in the marvelous house where the hideous hag seems to dwell, there are self-moving drinking-horns which serve the brothers, and when they wake on the morrow they find themselves, like Cormac and Gawain, outdoors, and behold not a sign of the house where they have gone to rest. In this version we may surmise the shining fawn is probably the goddess, luring the hero to her abode.

It was Stokes who first suggested [6] and Maynadier who most completely elaborated [7] the thesis that these Irish stories lie at the root of a number of English poems: Chaucer's *Wife of Bath's Tale*, Gower's Florent in the *Confessio Amantis*, the *Marriage of Sir Gawain, Dame Ragnell*, the ballad of *King Henry*. All these except the last, in my opinion, go back in their earlier stages to a common French original. For they show more or less clearly the same deformation of the Irish concept that the

---

[5] Descriptions of the mythical carlin in Highland folktales mention "gnarled brushwood on her head like the clawed-up wood of the aspen root," and assert that "her head bristled dark and gray, like scrubwood before hoar." A. Nutt, *Studies*, 167.

[5a] P. W. Joyce, *Old Celtic Romances*[2], 187. *Cf. Prose Edda*, tr. Brodeur, 3.

[6] *Academy*, Apr. 23, 1892.

[7] *Wife of Bath's Tale.*

lady was the Sovereignty. Just as that concept was itself an attempt to give a euhemeristic meaning to a tale which had lost among Christians its mythological value, so in turn when the story had been adopted into the Arthurian cycle, the euhemeristic significance of the hag's declaration that she was the Sovereignty had faded completely and demanded reinterpretation. A *conteur* casting about for some way to inject sense into his story, naturally thought of the desire of some women for "sovereignty," for having their own way, and refashioned the whole plot to lead up to this dénouement. Now in all the English stories, though the details of the preparation differ, the climax is always the same: the hero yields the sovereignty to the loathly hag, and thus brings about her transformation. Moreover, it is noteworthy that none of the English versions introduce the motif of the rival brothers which is found in all the old Irish forms of the legend. On the other hand, in the *Marriage of Sir Gawain*, in *Dame Ragnell*, and in the modern Irish folktale of *Bioultach* the hag has a brother, who like her is at first repulsive to view but later, we may infer, undergoes a transformation into a fair knight.

Now this parallel is important because the brother in the English poems and the Irish folktale can be identified with the Turk in the *Turk and Gawain*, and the Turk is already known to us as a development of Curoi.[8] Maynadier pointed out the fact that the brother of the hag in *Dame Ragnell* bears the same name as the Turk, namely Gromer,[9] and the statement that he, like his sister, was witched by their stepmother into a foul shape, justifies the belief that, like his sister, he was also released from the spell. At any rate, we read that Gromer was forgiven by Arthur, and in Malory a Gromer, Gromer's son, is numbered among knights friendly to Gawain.[10] The implications are that Gromer, brother of Dame Ragnell, like Gromer, the Turk, is disenchanted at the end of the story. And Gromer, the Turk, is a short man in gray, who plays the part of helpful companion in Gawain's journey to slay the King of Man; thus identifying himself clearly with Curoi, the man in gray who plays the part of helpful companion in Cuchulinn's voyage to carry off the daughter of the King of the Men of Falga.

Now Bioultach, in the modern Irish folktale, is accompanied and aided on his journey to slay the Bocaw More by a ragged

[8] *Cf.* Chap. X.    [9] *Wife of Bath's Tale*, 148.    [10] Malory, Bk. XX, ch. 2.

green man. Green, as we have learned, is often a misinterpretation of the ambiguous word *glas*, which also means gray.[11] It is no surprise, therefore, to learn that this helpful companion in green, after the giant has been destroyed, becomes, like the Turk, a handsome youth. Nor to learn that he, like the Gromer of *Dame Ragnell*, is brother of the hideous carlin. The unavoidable conclusion is that the monstrous brother of the hideous hag goes back to the common source of *Bioultach*, the *Turk and Gawain*, and *Dame Ragnell*, and that source can hardly be anything else than an ancient Irish myth in which the brother was the shape-shifting man in gray, Curoi. His relationship to the goddess of vegetation in *Bioultach* and *Dame Ragnell* is fraternal, not conjugal, — a change perhaps caused by the impossibility of preserving the decencies and a natural motivation if he is to be on good terms with the young hero who wins the goddess for his bride.

*Dame Ragnell* ends with a naïve bit of humor. The author was doubtless aware that Gawain, like his prototype Cuchulinn, was involved in numerous amours with ladies of different names. With true Anglo-Saxon delicacy he remarks that Gawen was wedded oft in his days;[12] and in order to make room for his other wives, cuts short Dame Ragnell's life five years after her marriage. But he adds consolingly that she was the dearest wife Gawen ever had. Perhaps there is a better consolation in the fact that most of his other loves, Floree, Lorie de la Roche Florie, Lore, Lunete, the guiding damsel, Orgueilleuse de Logres, Guinalorete, Guinloie, reveal in one way or another that they are but different manifestations, different names for the same primeval divinity, whose power is felt in the mysterious influences of the moon, and whose beauty in the golden gorse and yellow fields of wheat. She has always borne many names: Isis, Europa, Artemis, Rhea, Demeter, Hecate, Persephone, Diana; one might go on indefinitely. Gawain was no light of love, for in spite of his many marriages, it was the same goddess he loved.

[11] *Cf*. Chaps. V, X.                [12] Ed. L. Sumner, l. 832.

# CHAPTER XXX

## PROSERPINE AND FEBUS

THE circumstantial evidence convicting the damsels of Arthurian romance and their Irish forerunners of being reincarnations of the goddess Persephone herself is overwhelming. But there is more. The romance of *Arthur of Little Britain* which though late has already been demonstrated in Chapter XVII to contain masses of authentic Breton tradition, bears direct witness to their identity with the classical goddess.

In his altogether too little known study of *Sir Orfeo*, published in 1888,[1] Kittredge proved beyond a shadow of doubt that this English version of a Breton lai consisted of the story of Orpheus refashioned with delicate art to conform to Celtic conceptions of the Other World, particularly as found in the Irish saga of the *Wooing of Etain*. Kittredge explains the phenomenon in these words: "The Armorican minstrels picked up good stories wherever they could find them, and nothing is more likely than that, in their wanderings, they heard somebody tell the tale of Orpheus and Eurydice. . . . It was a subject for popular poetry — or, at least, for the lightest style of monkish verse — as early as the tenth century, . . . and it may have reached Breton ears in some *cantilena* similar to that *De Narcisso* mentioned by Peter Cantor in the twelfth century as performed by a strolling musician. Our Breton harper, however, probably got the story by word of mouth and in no very accurate shape; and, in making it over into a lay, he must inevitably have changed the story still further to make it square with his own beliefs and traditions and those of his auditors."

The important point for us to note is that probably as early as the twelfth century the Breton heirs of Celtic paganism were equating their own mythical motifs with those of classical paganism. Eurydice takes the rôle of Etain; Pluto has been transformed into Mider; the drear land of the shades has become the typical Otherworld castle of Breton romance. In brief, the nimble-minded Bretons recognized in the mythology of Greece, which reached them as a more or less dead tradition,

[1] *American Journal of Philology*, VII, 176.

a similarity in certain points to their own half living faith. One result was the altogether charming and vivid *Lai of Sir Orfeo*.

Another astonishing result is to be found in the romance of *Arthur of Little Britain*. The heroine is Florence, daughter of the King of Sorolois, whose relation to the magician Steven corresponds so closely to that of Amurfina to Gansguoter. Now both Steven and Gansguoter are unquestionably descendants of Curoi,[2] and the statement that Florence loved the magician Steven right well [3] may be derived ultimately from the Irish tradition that Blathnat loved "the wizard and enchanter Curoi mac Daire." [4] Florence, like Florie, is marked as a representative of Blathnat.

Now in many of the traditions surrounding the old god, defender of the Otherworld castle in which the goddess abides, the old god has been degraded into the position of a servant or unsuccessful suitor of the lady. For example, Malgiers le Gris in the *Bel Inconnu* is a scorned wooer; Gansguoter is represented in *Diu Krone* as the servant of Amurfina; some scholars have taken Esclados the Red in *Ivain* to be in origin not the consort but the inferior of Laudine.[5] In other words, the goddess has been exalted at the expense of the old god. Now this very process has transformed Florence not only into the mistress of the wizard Steven but also into the mistress of the whirling castle, the Perilous Bed, and so forth. The goddess of the flowers has attained dominion over the old god's castle. This fact attains supreme significance when we are informed that she had been bequeathed this castle of Porte Noire by Proserpine herself. More than that, Florence herself according to the romance was a reincarnation of Proserpine, chief of the four queens of the faery.

Immediately after her birth Florence had been placed beside a fountain on the Mount Perilous, where the four queens walked every night.[6] Presently they appeared, crowned, with great torches and lights before them. Proserpine takes the infant under her special favor and declares: "First, I will that this

---

[2] *Cf.* Chaps. XII, XVII.

[3] Berners, *Arthur of Little Britain*, 49.

[4] *ZCP*, IX, 193.

[5] *SNPL*, VIII, 49 f.

[6] *Arthur of Little Britain*, 46 f. On this incident *cf.* Paton, *Fairy Mythology*, 193 n., 234; Layamon, *Brut*, ll. 34143 ff. On confusion of Matres with Parcae *cf.* Hastings, *Encycl. of Relig.*, IV, 409.

child be named Florence, and that she shall be flower of beauty of all other creatures as long as ever she shall live. And properly I will she shall resemble to me both in face, in body, in countenance, in going and coming; and in all other things so like that whosoever see us both together shall not consider nor discern the one from the other." She also bestows on her the castle of the Porte Noire, and a pavilion containing an image of the queen herself.

Later the romance describes this image in some detail, — a description which of course applies equally to Proserpine and Florence.[7] It wears a crown of six branches, and a vesture of green samite, straight girt with a lace of gold. It held between the hands a chaplet of silk wrought full subtly of fresh flowers. Not only does this garland of flowers furnish another sign of the nature of Florence, but the green silk vesture, adorned with gold, is an even more striking feature. For in the last chapter the transformed hag wore in one version a mantle "matchless, green; . . . a silken thread that secured it well, a border it had of refined gold."[8]   A similar description of Flower-luster, daughter of Bodhb the Red, and one of the Tuatha De Danann, is given in the *Colloquy of the Ancients*, where she appears as a lone woman in mantle of green, with a glittering plate of yellow gold on her forehead.[9]

Unluckily we have no description of Blathnat, but there is no figure in Irish legend whom Blathnat so closely resembles as Etain. The parallels between their abduction tales are numerous.[10] Etain's flower-like nature betrays itself in her name which seems to mean "gorse,"[11] the golden, honey-sweet bloom that covers so many of the green mountains and moors of Ireland, and also in the fact that when she languishes she is restored by Aengus, who places her in a glass sun-chamber and feeds her on the fragrance of flowers.[12] Of Etain we have an exquisite description in the *Destruction of Da Derga's Hostel*.[13] Eochaid Feidlech discovers her beside a fountain. "A kirtle she wore, long, hooded, hard-smooth, of green silk, with red embroidery of gold. . . . The sun kept shining upon her, so that the glistening of the gold against the sun from the green silk was manifest

[7] *Ibid.*, 156.
[8] *Eriu*, IV, 105.    [10] *RR*, XV, 278 f.
[9] O'Grady, *Silva Gadelica*, II, 202 f.    [11] *Eriu*, I, 117 note.
[12] A. H. Leahy, *Heroic Romances of Ireland*, 7 f.
[13] *RC*, XXII, 14 ff.

to men. . . . The hue of that hair seemed to them like the flower of the iris in summer. . . . Red as the fox-glove were the clear-beautiful cheeks. Blue as a hyacinth were the eyes. Red as rowan-berries the lips. . . . The bright radiance of the moon was in her noble face."

Here, then, in Etain we have both flower maiden and moon maiden. Such Blathnat must have been also. And the re-appearance of the type in Florence and Proserpine is fully explained. We are driven to the conclusion that there must have come through to the Breton *conteur* who furnished the ground-work for *Arthur of Little Britain*, not merely the information that one of his chief characters was a pagan goddess, just as Morgan le Fay and the Grail Bearer were known for god-desses by Giraldus Cambrensis and Heinrich von dem Türlin, but also the specific information that she was goddess of the flowers. On the basis of this information he quite naturally drew upon his stock of classical mythology to identify and desig-nate her as Proserpine. We may indulge a supercilious smile to discover the ancient divinity disguised as a queen of faery, walking by night on the Mount Perilous, and described as "a fresh young lady and a fair without comparison," [14] but after all the triumph is with the medieval author, for he anticipated modern scholarship by at least five hundred years. He in turn was making the same identification of the gods of the barbari-ans with the figures of the classic pantheon which Aelfric early in the eleventh century made.[15] The abbot of Eynsham, after referring to the worship of sun, moon, stars, fire, and water in ancient times, says that Jove "among certain nations was called Thor, most beloved of the Danish people"; Mercury he equates with Odin, Venus with Frigg. Equally natural was it for the romancer, whose audience by the thirteenth century had forgotten their ancestral deities altogether, and had become familiarized with the Olympians through the rising popularity of Latin literature and its French adaptations, to call his flower goddess by a name which all would recognize.

Other neglected sources of genuine Celtic tradition, the com-pilation of Rusticien de Pise and *Palamedes*, show that a similar equation of Celtic sun-gods with Phoebus Apollo took place among the Breton *conteurs*. In the former romance we read

[14] *Arthur of Little Britain*, 44.
[15] A. S. Cook, C. Tinker, *Select Translations from Old English Prose*. 186.

that the huge old knight Branor le Brun, in whom it is possible
to detect Bran once more, "belongs to the mighty lineage of
those of Brun, of which many books speak; of this lineage was
the celebrated Phebus." [16]  In *Palamedes* we learn more of these
Breton traditions of Phebus.  Guiron, the hero, was a grandson
of Febus le Fort, who descended from Clovis, and who left
his lands in order to conquer others in remote regions.[17]  Later
in the romance Brehus (Malory's Breuse sans Pitié) was entrapped by a damsel in a cavern.[18]  There he discovered the
body of Febus lying in state, his huge weapons showing that they
belonged to a time long past.  A letter in his grasp related that
these very hands had dealt destruction in one day to the realms
of Norgalles, Gaules, and Norbellande, for he had dealt one
hundred and fifty blows and with each had slain a man.  "Febus
was my name, and it was given me for good cause, for just as
Febus gives light to this world, so was I certes light and splendor
of all mortal chivalry so long as I could bear sword."  In another chamber lay Febus' wife, the daughter of the king of
Norbellande, for whose love he had died.  In still another
chamber were the tombs of Febus' four sons: their names are
given in very corrupt forms but it seems possible that Lannor or
Laimor may go back through Lambor to Lug's epithet, Lamfada, Matus through Mabus to Mabon, Enaoc through Evaloc
to Avallach.  A fifth son, whose name is not given, is still alive,
and meets Brehus in another chamber, clad in a ragged white
robe.  His hair reaches his waist, and his beard to his knees,
but still he is larger than Brehus, and cannot believe that knights
so puny as Brehus can compare with the men of old.  When
Brehus mentions the fact that the greatest knight of the
world has been in prison for ten years, the old man recognizes
him at once as his grandson, Guiron le Courtois.  Afterwards
two old men appear, who likewise dwell in the cavern, clad in
torn white robes.  One of them is son of the first old man and
father of Guiron, and he demonstrates his strength by lifting
in one hand a huge boulder.  Brehus departs after promising
not to disclose to any but Guiron what he has seen.

Certain features of this late romance seem to stamp it as

---

[16] E. Löseth, *Tristan en prose*, 428.

[17] *Ibid.*, 437.

[18] *Ibid.*, 460 f.  Since the French text is unpublished, I have used not
only Löseth's résumé but also Lord Vernon's *Febusso e Breusso* (Florence,
1847), cxvi–clxx, to supply details from the Italian translation.

genuine Celtic tradition. First, the names of three of Febus' sons, as we have noted, seem to be corruptions of Lamfada, Mabon, and Avallach, all solar names or epithets. Secondly, the name Guiron appears sometimes as Guron in the romance,[19] and very naturally suggests the Welsh name Gwron. Now Gwron is mentioned in a triad together with Plenydd, whose name means "shining," among the three original bards of the Isle of Britain; [20] oddly enough the *Palamedes* says not only that Guiron was a musician and composed the *Lai des Deux Amants*, but also that his son Galinan le Noir was an excellent musician.[21] Since such accomplishments are by no means common among heroes of French romance, one can hardly attribute to accident the resemblance between Guron and Gwron. Thirdly, we find the same notion that the men of old were much larger than the Britons of later days in the Welsh *Dream of Rhonabwy*,[22] where Arthur exclaims: "It pitieth me that men of such stature as these should have this island in their keeping, after the men that guarded it of yore." Fourthly, the conception of the gods as old men in white, dwelling apart from the world, we have discovered in *Sone de Nansai* and *Perlesvaus*, in contexts which had every appearance of reposing on Welsh tradition. Fifthly, the cavern as an abode of the departed god or deified hero is attested not only in the Breton legends of Arthur in Etna but also in the Welsh folktale of the sleeping warriors of Craig-y-Ddinas.[23] Finally, the Dolorous Stroke dealt by the sun-god himself is already familiar to us through the story of Balaain.

Someone may be tempted to urge that the author of *Palamedes* need not have drawn upon a tradition which essentially reproduces an old Welsh myth, but might have collected his various motifs from intermediate sources. If this episode is a late mixture, then the compiler has been very skillful in forging a thoroughly Celtic situation and nomenclature. But the fact that tells most decisively against such an hypothesis is the part played by Febus. Can anyone suggest a passage in Ovid or Virgil which would lead the romancer to depict Phoebus Apollo as lying, a huge knight with his armor beside him, in a cavern?

[19] Löseth, 441 note.     [20] Loth, *Mab.*², II, 315.
[21] Löseth, 459, 462 f.     *Cf. ZfSL*, XLVII, 73; *Studi Romanzi*, XIV, 150.
[22] Loth, *Mab.*², I, 356.
[23] E. S. Hartland, *Science of Fairy Tales*, 207–9. *Cf.* Nutt, *Studies*, 198.

Is there anything suggestive of classical inspiration in the episode?  On the other hand, postulate that the source of the episode was ultimately Welsh, that it made quite clear that the dead warrior was a god of the sun, that it passed into the hands of a Breton or French *conteur*, who knew only one sun-god, namely Phoebus; and there is no more problem.

The same mental processes must account for the various passages in Arthurian romance, collected by Miss Paton,[24] in which the fay Niniane is associated with Diane in such a way as to suggest that she was a counterpart of the classical goddess. Particularly noteworthy is the application to Diane in the *Huth Merlin*,[25] of the Blodeuwedd story, which we studied in Chapter II.  Diane dwells with Faunus in a beautiful palace; but falls in love with Felix, whom she found hunting.  She resolves that Faunus must die, and when he comes in from the chase to take a bath in an enchanted tomb, she first drains it of its healing waters and then fills it with boiling lead.  Felix, however, when told of her deed, cuts off her head.  The version of the Blodeuwedd story which came down into French romance must have contained explicit statements that its heroine was a goddess of the forest.

If, therefore, modern scholars have failed to recognize in some of the figures of the *Matière de Bretagne* the goddess of the flowers and forests or the divinity of day, it is not for lack of explicit statements.  The failure is due entirely to the prevalent obsession that any romance dated after 1200 was a mere *rifacimento* from a few early French romances preserved to us, and could not contain any new authentic materials from Celtic heathendom.  The composers of *Sir Orfeo*, of *Arthur of Little of Britain*, and of *Palamedes*, had a keener insight into the meaning of their tales than many who have dogmatized on the subject since.

[24] Paton, *op. cit.*, 228 ff.          [25] II, 145–9.

# BOOK FIVE

## FROM IRISH AND WELSH GODS TO A BRITISH CHIEFTAIN

# CHAPTER XXXI

## KNIGHTS OF THE SWAN

THE preceding chapters have made increasingly secure two fundamental positions: the presence of mythical meanings in even the least promising parts of the *Matière de Bretagne;* and the illumination which classical mythology casts on those meanings. In this and the next chapter we shall perceive that classical analogues throw light on the meaning of two great themes of medieval story: the coming and departure of the swan-drawn knight, and the imprisonment of the hero in a western isle. Both of these themes can be shown to have their more immediate origin in Wales or Ireland, but both are without significance until one looks up their Hellenic parallels. Then all becomes luminous with a new beauty.

Thanks to Wagner, there are few legends of the Middle Ages more familiar than that of the Swan Knight.[1] We all know how Lohengrin [2] arrives in a boat drawn by a white swan, at the opportune moment to rescue the Lady Elsa from a hated suitor; how he weds her on condition she ask no question concerning his name and origin; how, when her curiosity overcomes her prudence, the strange knight departs, telling her that he is the son of Parzival, and leaving for her his ring, and for his two sons a horn and a sword; how the boat drawn by the swan, his brother, bears him away; and how from him was descended Godfrey de Bouillon, the hero of the First Crusade.

From early times this legend has been localized on the Rhine, at Mainz, Cleves, and Nymwegen. Gui de Bazoches, who about 1175 refers to the tradition, speaks of Godfrey as "the descendant of that faery (?) knight whom a white swan guided through the shallows of the Rhine." [3] And with one significant exception all the later stories of a knight who comes to court in a boat drawn by a swan are attached to the same general neighborhood. This fact and the vague resemblance between the Swan Knight story and that of the Danish hero Scyld, who

---

[1] The most complete discussion (with bibliography) of the Swan Knight Legend is found in L. A. Hibbard, *Medieval Romance in England,* 239.
[2] R. Jaffray, *Two Knights of the Swan,* 13.     [3] *Ibid.,* 4.

arrived a helpless infant in an oarless boat, became king, reigned long, and after his death was consigned again to the waves, has suggested a Teutonic origin for the story.[4] But such data after all are slender props for a theory, and can appeal only to those whose attention is focused on Teutonic tradition.

As early as 1892 Lot showed that the story of the swan children, which is usually attached to that of the Swan Knight, bore a marked resemblance to the Irish legend of the children of the god Lir.[5] In 1913 Poisson argued for the Celtic origin of the whole tradition, and I shall later develop some of his points.[6]

Now one of the most telling facts in favor of Celtic origin, though mentioned by Jaffray,[7] has hardly entered into the debate. In Pseudo-Wauchier's continuation of the *Conte del Graal*, which may be dated between 1180 and 1190, we find the figure of the Swan Knight in a setting which every reader of the preceding pages will recognize as thoroughly characteristic of the *Matière de Bretagne* and which contains no hint that the author had ever heard of the associations with the lower Rhine region or Godfrey de Bouillon. Here in brief is the story.[8]

The hero, whose name the MSS. supply in nearly every variation — Karaheus, Geresches, Gaheries, Gaharies, Guerehes — comes to an empty, enchanted castle, finds three rich beds in one chamber, and another still richer in the next chamber. He sees from the window a dwarf with a silver hanap entering a tent. Gaheries follows him and finds within a huge, wounded knight in purple raiment, lying on a bed. The dwarf holds before him the hanap containing almond milk and bread, and a beautiful damsel feeds him with a spoon. When Gaheries greets him, the gigantic knight orders him removed and his wounds bleed. Presently there enters on horseback a "Petit Chevalier," very fair but rising only half a foot above the saddle, so small is he. He forces a combat on Gaheries, overthrows him, and sets his foot on his neck. Nevertheless, he grants Gaheries a year's respite on condition that he return at the end of that time and choose between fighting again, having his head cut off, or becoming a weaver. Gaheries agrees, is mocked by the damsels and chess-players who now occupy the formerly deserted castle, and rides away to Tintagel.

---

[4] *JEGP*, XIX, 190 ff; A. Olrik, *Heroic Legends of Denmark*, 413 ff.
[5] *Rom.*, XXI, 62.          [7] Jaffray, *op. cit.*, 21.
[6] *RC*, 1913, 191.          [8] Potvin, IV, ll. 21135 ff.

There he learns that a swan has drawn thither in a boat the body of a knight. He later draws out from the body the truncheon of a spear with which the fatal blow had been dealt, and finds on it a beautiful, gleaming blade. This he places on one of his own shafts, and when he departs at Easter to keep his engagement, carries it with him. Gaheries meets and slays the Petit Chevalier and his lord, who is apparently the huge wounded knight of his previous adventure. A maiden in silk, adorned with silver flowers, comes and looks at the spear-head with which Gaheries has slain the gigantic knight, identifies it as the same with which her lover was killed, and declares that now Gaheries has killed her lover's slayer with his own weapon. Gaheries accompanies the damsel across the seas to a castle, where he is served with cups of fine gold. He spends the night there, only to find himself the next morning at Arthur's court in the very boat drawn by the swan in which the dead knight had arrived. The damsel, who has come with Gaheries, now reveals that the slain knight was King Brangemuer of the isle where no mortal dwells, and that when his body returns thither, a great marvel will betide. Arthur and his court then send away the body of Brangemuer in the swan-drawn boat.

Does the context of Gaheries' appearance in a boat drawn by a swan indicate whether or not the motif is of Celtic origin? Surely the hostile dwarf encountered in the Other World, the arrangement for a return combat at the end of a year, the theme of vengeance carried out by means of the very weapon with which a knight has been killed, are distinctive and familiar features of the *Matière de Bretagne*. Surer signs of the fundamentally Celtic nature of the whole adventure can be detected in the wounded Knight in purple fed from a goblet by a beautiful damsel. He can be no other than a Maimed King fed by a Grail Damsel. But which of the Maimed Kings? His huge stature and his lying in a tent point to Bran, who was so large that no house could contain him and who therefore feasted in tents.[9] We know, furthermore, that Crestien couples the gigantic Bran with the dwarf king Belin.[10] We need not hesitate to identify Belin with the Petit Chevalier. Everything goes to prove that the adventure embodies authentic tradition. Since in Pseudo-Wauchier's account there is not a trace of non-Celtic sources in the circumstances surrounding the swan-drawn boat,

---

[9] *Cf.* Chap. XXII.                    [10] *Cf.* Chap. XX.

and since the Irish were familiar with the notion of gods in the shape of swans, we may take that picturesque feature also to be Celtic.

A study of the names of the Swan Knight tends to confirm this supposition. We have already identified Gaheries with Welsh Gware or Gwri, the original of Gawain and Gareth. In the Icelandic *Karlamagnus Saga* the Swan Knight is called Geirarth,[11] in the Danish folkbook, Gerard.[12] The name Elyas or Helyas can claim to come from as far as Ireland. Poisson proposed that the name was due to a confusion between the Greek Helios, the sun, and the Biblical Elias (Elijah),[13] — a confusion which has been noted by scholars in many fields.[14] The suggestion derives plausibility from the fact that Irish monks of the Dark Ages were familiar with Greek at a time when no one else in the West was,[15] and that St. Patrick himself certainly associated Elias with the sun. He relates in his *Confession*[16] that he dreamed one night that a huge stone fell upon him. He cried out, "Helias, Helias!" and behold, he saw a sun rising, which shone upon him and removed the weight altogether. We must agree with the editor who comments,[17] "There can be no doubt that . . . the name was chiefly associated in his mind on this occasion with the sun (Helios)." It seems not improbable that the name Helyas, as that of an ancestor of Galaad and as that of the Swan Knight, was bestowed by some Celt who regarded it as an appropriate name for the sun-god.

Furthermore, though it may be coincidence, it is nevertheless a curious coincidence that the Grail King Helyas is said to be the son of Alain li Gros,[18] while the Swan Knight Lohengrin is the son of Parzival, who in certain French romances is the son of Alain li Gros. Again it is a curious coincidence that the Swan Knight Helyas is represented as the grandson of Pieron King of Lislefort,[19] while the Swan Knight Lohengrin is the son of Parzival, king according to French tradition of an Otherworld isle. For the identity of Pieron with Parzival, far-fetched though

---

[11] *Karlamagnus Saga*, ed. C. R. Unger, 42.
[12] C. Pedersen, *Danske Skrifter*, V, 12.     [13] *RC*, 1913, 194.
[14] P. Saintyves, *Saints successeurs des dieux*, 379; J. C. Lawson, *Modern Greek Folklore*, 44.
[15] D'Arbois de Jubainville, *Cours*, I, 381.     [17] *Ibid.*, 288.
[16] *PRIA*, XXV, C, 241.     [18] Sommer, VI, 97.
[19] Jaffray, *op. cit.*, 73. *Chevalier au Cygne*, ed. Reiffenberg, 5, gives Pietre and Piron also.

it may seem, is not unlikely in view of the probable identity of
the sea-king Priure with Perceval.[20] It may not, therefore, be too
bold to suggest the possibility that the name Lohengrin itself
and the name of the Swan Knight's father, Lothaire, in MS.
B. N. 12558,[21] are corrupt derivations from Welsh Llwch or
Lloch, and that the names of their brides, Elsa and Elioxe,[22]
are substitutions for Elaine, who is in French tradition so
constantly connected with the French counterparts of Llwch,
— with Loth as daughter, and with Lancelot as mistress. This
suggestion is corroborated by the general parallelism between the
loves of Lohengrin and Elsa and that of Lancelot and Elaine,
the daughter of Pelles. In both the hero leaves his lady; in
both their offspring is destined to high emprise. It seems
plausible that these two famous romances are cognate growths
from the loves of Llwch and Elen.

It is, moreover, uncanny, when we remember that King
Priure possessed a magic drinking horn, that Pieron's grandson
Helyas should also be given by his father a magic hunting horn,[23]
and that Parzival's son, Lohengrin, should likewise possess a
magic horn, which he leaves with his son when he departs.[24]
These horns may seem to be a far cry from the Celtic caldron
of plenty from which they would theoretically derive. Yet we
have already seen that the caldron was absorbed by a horn of
plenty, that the Grail Castle did become the Castle of the Horn,
and that the horn is described in *Perlesvaus* not as a vessel,
but as a blast-horn.[25]

Moreover, the ring which Lohengrin leaves in the possession
of Elsa, the mother of his son, has its exact counterpart in
Irish legends. Cuchulinn before leaving Aife pregnant with
his son Conlai gave her a thumb-ring for his son. Even more
striking is the fact, cited in this connection by Cross,[26] that
King Elotha, son of Delbaeth (Fire-Shape), a glorious figure,
with golden hair and golden raiment, comes over the sea in a
magic bark, lies with Eri, also a daughter of Delbaeth, and
before parting, gives her his ring.[27] That Elotha, son of Fire-

---

[20] *Cf.* Chap. XXIII.     [21] Jaffray, *op. cit.*, 37 f.     [22] *Ibid.*, 13, 37.
[23] *Chevalier au Cygne*, ed. Reiffenberg, 98: "Homs qui le sonnera . . .
ne puet avoir anoy ne damage pesant." Probably a confused form of the
Cor Beneis.     [25] *Cf.* Chap. XXIII.
[24] *Ibid.*, lvii.     [26] *RC*, XXXI, 466 f.
[27] *RC*, XII, 61 ff. It is noteworthy that elsewhere Lug is the mate of
Eriu, the goddess personifying Ireland.

Shape, the golden King, has transmitted some of his solar characteristics to the Swan Knight seems probable, for the *Chanson d'Antioche* relates that when the latter arrived in his boat, "his head shone more brightly than peacock's feather." [28]

The swan, too, seems to have been regarded by the Irish as a natural form for the god to take.[29] The goddesses Fand and Liban and the Children of Lir assumed that shape. And in the *Voyage of Bran* [30] Manannan the son of Lir predicts that his own son, Mongan, will take, among other animal forms, that of a fair-white swan. It is perhaps an echo of Mongan's statement in O'Donnell's *Life of Colum Cille* [31] that "in especial he knows the thrice fifty islands that are westward from Erin in the sea," that the Swan Knight Helyas should have his home in Lislefort.

Poisson pointed out what is perhaps the most significant analogue to the coming of the Swan Knight, namely the return of Apollo from the land of the Hyperboreans to Delphi in a chariot drawn by swans. The land of the Hyperboreans, which was later identified with Britain, was at first but a joyous Other World lying to the north of Greece. "Neither sickness nor dread old age comes near that holy tribe; they dwell without labor or warfare." [32] Miss Macurdy expresses the general belief of classical scholars when she says [33] that the underlying thought behind the myth was the sojourn of Apollo in the northern land of bliss during the winter months, and "his return to Delphi in the month Bysios, which marked the revival of nature in the spring." Perhaps the medieval legends of the Swan Knight may have had the same significance. If only we could be sure that his bride corresponded to the typical earth or vegetation goddesses of Arthurian romance, then the solution would be simple. The Swan Knight from Lislefort or the Grail Castle would then be the sun coming from his winter abode. Like Apollo he comes drawn by a swan. He wins his bride, the goddess of the flowers and grain, and begets on her a rebirth of himself, the new sun. But there must be a reason for

---

[28] Jaffray, *op. cit.*, 6; *Rom*, XXX, 407.

[29] W. G. Wood-Martin, *Traces of the Elder Faiths*, II, 146.

[30] Meyer, Nutt, *Voyage of Bran*, I, 26.

[31] M. O'Donnell, *Life of Colum Cille*, ed. O'Kelleher, Schoepperle, sec. 87.

[32] G. Macurdy, *Troy and Paeonia*, 197.

[33] *Ibid.*, 199. *Cf.* Déchelette, *Manuel*, II, 444.

his departure, and the mystery of his identity offers the required pretext. He departs, leaving the horn and sword, symbols of fertility and might, and predicting the splendor of his reborn self.

Granted that some of these points of resemblance are due to accident; granted that many of them are inexact. But the sum total forms an impressive bulk of evidence. The theory that in origin the legend of the Swan Knight was part of the *Matière de Bretagne* explains far more than any other provenance. Nor is it hard to understand how it came to form the ancestral tradition of the House of Bouillon. For the twelfth century shows other attempts to connect the Breton *contes* with the Crusades and with certain great families. The story of Gahmuret Anschevin, Parzival's father, incorporated in Wolfram von Eschenbach's poem, is on the face of it an attempt to give the material a certain contemporary interest and to glorify the House of Anjou. And when we recall the Breton *conteur* at Bari in the train of Robert Curthose on the way to the Conquest of Jerusalem by Godfrey de Bouillon, it is not hard to imagine that other *conteurs*, engaged in the same or later expeditions to the Holy Land, should have seen fit to connect their romances with the House of Bouillon. Did not their stories prophesy again and again the coming of the perfect knight, the great warrior, who was to be crowned in some mysterious far-off land? Did not Godfrey, whose achievements finally elevated him to rank with Arthur and Charlemagne as one of the Nine Worthies of the World, fit the description? At any rate, the figure of the Swan Knight, which occurs but once in Arthurian romance proper, became definitely established as the ancestor of the House of Bouillon: the many versions of his story owe scarcely more than their outline and some names to their Celtic originals, and for the rest draw upon other legendary materials or upon contemporary courtly life.

Though the solar explanation of the Swan Knight legend may seem plausible, one may object with reason that in the absence of any intermediate Welsh swan stories between the Irish and the Arthurian, it is rash to assume a Celtic origin or a mythological meaning for the legends of Lohengrin and Helyas. But we have already seen that though there is not a trace of specific solar attributes in Gwri, Pryderi, or Peredur, yet their Arthurian counterpart, Perceval, turns up with the sun on his shield. And there is another striking illustration where a solar symbol skips all the intermediate extant literary stages between the Irish sagas and a German romance. Yet there it is, a golden wheel, emblazoned on the shield of Wigalois, whose name can be traced back definitely to that of Cuchulinn himself.

Cuchulinn's association with a wheel is confined to an episode in the *Wooing of Emer*.[34] As a boy he meets on his journey to the Land of Scathach a brave youth, who gives him a wheel and an apple,[35] and tells him to run across the Perilous Plain as fast as the wheel rolls before him or he will stick in his tracks. Cuchulinn does so and eventually reaches the Land of Scathach. Now the wheel has been a common method of conceiving or representing the sun, which it resembles in being circular and in moving. Gaidoz notes [36] that "'the wheel of the sun,' 'the wheel of Phoebus,' 'the wheel which flies on high' are familiar expressions in Latin poetry. . . . Later among the barbarous inhabitants of the Scandinavian North we find analogous expressions: in the *Eddas* the sun is called 'the shining wheel,' 'the fair wheel,' and in certain runic calendars the 25th of December, the day of the winter solstice, is represented by a wheel." Gaidoz, moreover, rightly interpreted the wheel borne by a number of statues of Gallic gods as solar symbols, and the helmets of Gallic warriors were sometimes adorned with the wheel as a crest. At Caerleon on Usk there is a monument of a man carrying a wheel in both hands, a wheel at his left foot, and the swastika, another solar symbol, at his right foot. In Ireland one finds the wheel not only combined in the familiar way with the cross to form the so-called Celtic cross, but also mounted above the cross as a combination of the emblems of pagan and Christian deity.[37] In the *Destruction of Da Derga's Hostel*, King Conaire, who is described with the attributes of the sun-god, wears embroidered on the front of his mantle a large golden wheel reaching from his chin to his navel.[38] Even twelfth-century Christians, like Durandus and the author of the *Kaiserchronik*, were perfectly familiar with the solar connotations of the wheel.[39] We can hardly doubt that the mys-

[34] E. Hull, *Cuchulinn Saga*, 74.

[35] Rolleston, *Myths and Legends*, 187 note, suggests that this youth is his father Lug.

[36] Gaidoz, *Le dieu gaulois du soleil*, 9.

[37] J. F. M. ffrench, *Prehistoric Faith and Worship*, 50, 64.

[38] *RC*, XXII, 202 f.    [39] J. Grimm, *Teut. Myth.*, tr. Stallybrass, II, 620.

terious wheel which Cuchulinn followed across the Plain of
Ill-Luck was the sun of which he was himself the embodiment.[40]

Now Cuchulinn became, as we know, Guiglain. The nominative ending -s gave either Guiglains or Guiglais. The
parallel between the romances of Guiglain and Wigalois are so
close that there can be no doubt that the latter name is a
corruption of Guiglais due to a false association with the French
word meaning Welsh, galois. Accordingly when we read that
Wigalois, the descendant of Cuchulinn, bears as the cognizance
on his shield a gold wheel on a black ground and was known as
the Knight with the Wheel,[41] we must admit that here is a solar
attribute which has survived through all the stages of transmission from Irish through Welsh, Breton, and French, to
German. There is not a trace of the solar wheel in the extant
romances of Wales or France, yet the lost versions, whose
number we can never reckon, must have contained this feature.
And so likewise we may properly believe that the divine swan
"whose fame endures forever because he drew by a golden chain
a panoplied knight in a boat," [42] must have been glimpsed in
the waters of the Usk, the cove of Tintagel, and the lower
reaches of the Loire before he finally came to port in the Rhine.

[40] Macalister (*PRIA*, XXXIV, C, 345 ff) has some interesting material
on a divine wheel. I do not believe, however, that the reference was to a
bull roarer, but agree with Rhys and Sayce that the Roth Fail is the sun.
*Cf.* Rhys, *Hibbert Lectures*, 210 ff; *Cymmrodor*, X, 215 ff. *Cf.* the amateur-
ish but interesting H. C. Levis, *British King Who Tried to Fly*.

[41] O. Piper, *Höfisches Epik*, II, 213.

[42] Jaffray, *op. cit.*, 60; *Rom.*, XXXIV, 209.

# CHAPTER XXXII

## THE CAPTIVE GOD

ANOTHER basic myth traceable in Arthurian romance is that
of the god imprisoned in a western isle. This too, as Rhys was
the first to suggest, finds its ultimate explanation in classical
legend. Already in our studies of the Grail heroes and of Kaer
Sidi we have observed several knights enchained or imprisoned
who seem to have their original in the Welsh Gwair. Let me
repeat the lines from the *Harryings of Annwn:* [1]

Complete was the captivity of Gwair in Kaer Sidi,
(Lured thither) through the emissary of Pwyll and Pryderi.
Before him no one entered into it,
Into the heavy, dark chain which held the faithful youth.

Then after several lines which do not concern us, the poem
continues:

The Head of Annwn's caldron, what is it like?
A rim of pearls it has around its edge;
It boils not the food of a coward or perjurer(?).

In one of the most penetrating studies ever made of Celtic
literature Gruffydd has shown how we find the same captive
god under several names: Gwair, Pryderi, and Mabon.[2] The
circumstances of the captivity differ greatly in the various
versions; nevertheless the conclusion seems warranted that
they are all variants of the same fundamental myth. Of the
captivity of Mabon, the Great Youth, whom we have traced
back to Apollo Maponos, let me say that the triad which states
that he was one of the famous prisoners of the Isle of Britain
released by Goreu [3] seems to have left its impress on Arthurian
romance. For Mabon's name has been recognized in the solar

---

[1] J. Rhys, *Celtic Folklore*, II, 679; *RC*, XXXIII, 460; Malory, Everyman ed., I, xxiii; C. Squire, *Mythology of the British Islands*, 319. J. A.
Macculoch in *Mythology of All Races*, III, 192, speaks of Gweir as "lured
there through the messenger of Pwyll and Pryderi."

[2] *RC*, XXXIII, 452–61.

[3] Loth, *Mab.²*, II, 267 f.

hero Mabonagrain,[4] held by his plighted word in the enchanted
island of everlasting spring; and the name of his deliverer,
Erec, is a corruption of Gwri, and so corresponds to Goreu.[5]

The imprisonment of Pryderi is another analogue brought
forward by Gruffydd. In Chapter XVIII we saw how as a
result of Pryderi's sitting on the "Throne" of Narberth the land
of Dyved became desolate. The Mabinogi goes on to relate
that when he was hunting with his step-father Manawyddan
near Narberth, he started a pure white boar.[6] They pursued it
till it entered a vast and lofty castle newly built in a place where
they had never before seen stone or building. In spite of Manawyddan's warnings Pryderi entered the mysterious castle,
but could see within neither man nor beast. In the middle of
the floor was a well, inclosed with marble, and on the margin a
golden goblet, and chains going upward to the sky, and he could
see no end to them. Lured by the rich workmanship of the
goblet, he grasped it, and at once his hands became fast to it,
and his feet to the marble slab. His mother Rhiannon, seeking
her son, was likewise held prisoner by the goblet and slab.
When it became night, there came a thunder and a fall of mist,
and the castle and its prisoners vanished. After a while,[7]
Manawyddan became, as we know, a wheat-grower, but the
ears were carried away by armies of mice. He finally caught a
pregnant she-mouse, and was about to hang it on the "Throne"
of Narberth, when there appeared in succession a poor scholar,
a priest, and a bishop, to intercede for it. Manawyddan would
not free the mouse till the bishop had promised to free Pryderi
and Rhiannon, to remove the enchantment from Dyved, and
to tell his name and purpose. The shape-shifter revealed
himself as Llwyd, the "Gray One," who had wrought these
spells in order to revenge himself for the trick which Pryderi's
father, Pwyll, had played on Llwyd's friend, Gwawl.

Now certain points in this story should not need elucidation.
First, Llwyd, the Gray One, must be like Glewlwyd Gavaelvawr, "The Gray Champion of the Mighty Grasp," and like
Arawn, who is clad in gray and rides a gray horse,[8] a shape-
shifting lord of Annwn. Secondly, it is clear that the pure
white boar which entices Pryderi into the enchanted castle where

[4] *RC*, XXXIII, 456; *Rom*, XXV, 284.    [5] *Cf.* Chaps. IX, XIII.
[6] Loth, *op. cit.*, I, 159–61. On white boars, *cf. Rom*, XXX, 14.
[7] *Ibid.*, 163–70.    [8] *Ibid.*, 84.

he becomes a prisoner, is Llwyd himself in one of his shapes or at least his emissary. Thirdly, the endless chain dangling from the sky is identical with the chain descending from above into the great pit, described in *Perlesvaus*.

Whence and why has the goblet this adhesive quality? Now apparently the bard who gave these legends their present shape was attempting to make Llwyd's revenge correspond to Pwyll's offense. He was applying the Dantesque and Gilbertian principle of making the punishment fit the crime. Let us see what Pwyll's crime had been.[9] Pwyll was feasting as Rhiannon's affianced bridegroom at her father's house when Gwawl entered, a tall, auburn-haired youth of royal bearing. By the conventional device of the rash promise, Gwawl obtains from Pwyll the right to Rhiannon, but not till a year later. Pwyll, in turn, enters the nuptial feast of Gwawl, disguised as a beggar, and asks to have his little bag filled. It proves to have an unlimited capacity for food. When finally Gwawl steps into it himself, at once he is tied up in it. Pwyll's men rush in, throw Gwawl's attendants into prison, and beat the man in the bag till he is glad to give up his right to Rhiannon and get off with his life. It seems clear that a parallelism, which would have been at once apparent to Welshmen, who associated goblets in faery castles with vessels of plenty, was intended here. Just as Gwawl was entrapped by a bag which would hold endless supplies of food, so Pryderi had to be caught by the well-known goblet which supplied endless potations. Both bag and goblet are forms of that favorite talisman of Welsh tradition, represented by the *mwys* of Gwyddno, the horn of Bran, the caldron of Dyrnog, and both are related to the Grail. The captivity of Pryderi is a pendant to the captivity of Gwawl.

It is worth noting that the name Gwawl means "light," [10] and that its bearer is a tall, auburn-haired youth. Since the other prisoners of Welsh mythology, Mabon, Pryderi, and Gwair, are known to originate in sun-gods, is it not possible that Gwawl himself is a sun-god, and his name an intentional substitution for Gwair? Perhaps, but the identity is none too clear and the circumstances of the imprisonment as different as they could be. Yet after all, we can feel sure that the goblet of Pryderi's captivity corresponds to the caldron of Gwair's

---

[9] *Ibid.*, 98–103.
[10] Guest, *Mab.*, ed. Nutt, 374.

captivity; and that like the captivity of Mabon they are stories of the imprisonment of the sun-god.

What does it all mean? Again we may find our clue in those Greek legends to which Milton refers when he speaks of those deities "who with Saturn old Fled over Adria to the Hesperian fields, And o'er the Celtic roamed the utmost isles." We know from various sources that Kronos after his overthrow fled to the western Mediterranean; Hesiod relates that "Zeus the father decreed for certain of the heroes a stead at the world's end, far off from mortals"; and an early interpolation adds: "where reigneth Kronos." [11] "There they dwell evermore, with minds untroubled, by the waves of ocean deep, in the isles of the blessed." Plutarch adds to the passage about the isles near Britain, which our previous study has abundantly corroborated, the more precise information that in a certain island "Kronos is imprisoned with Briareus keeping guard over him as he sleeps; for, as they put it, sleep is the bond forged for Kronos." [12] Plutarch also has a much more elaborate description of this island five days' sail west of Britain, and of the god in a deep cave, ministered to by subordinate daimons, destined by Zeus to perpetual sleep instead of to chains.[13] This Greek tradition would be no more intelligible than the Welsh were it not for another tradition recorded by Plutarch: [14] "Those who dwell in the west account and call the winter Kronos, and the Summer Aphrodite, and the Spring Persephone, and from Kronos and Aphrodite all things take their birth. And the Phrygians think that in the winter the god is asleep, and that in the summer he is awake, and they celebrate to him Bacchic revels, which in winter are Goings to Sleep, and in summer Wakings-up. The Paphlagonians allege that in winter the god is bound down and imprisoned and in spring aroused and set free again." From all this it becomes clear that Kronos, king of the blessed isles, is but another form of the god of Life and Light; that he corresponds to Apollo in the land of the Hyperboreans; that his sleep and captivity are but variant concepts of the dormant or latent condition of Nature in winter; and that the tradition of his periodic release, though largely supplanted by the legend of his

[11] Hesiod, *Works and Days*, ll. 167–9. *Cf.* A. B. Cook, *Zeus*, II, 695.
[12] Rhys, *Arth. Leg.*, 368; Plutarch, *Defectu Oraculorum*, sec. 18.
[13] Plutarch, *Facie in Orbe Lunae*, sec. 26.
[14] J. Harrison, *Themis*, 179; Plutarch, *Iside et Osiride*, 69.

perpetual overthrow and banishment by the new god Zeus, was still current.  The same interpretation may be applied to the captivity of the Welsh sun-gods, and derives some confirmation from the fact that the release of Pryderi coincides with the removal of the enchantment from Dyved.  Indeed, if the story of Pryderi's captivity had not been contaminated by the story of Pryderi's sitting on the Throne of Narberth, we should probably find that in the former tale, the blighting of the land began as soon as he and his mother were trapped in the castle of the golden goblet and there came a thunder and a fall of mist. For in the latter tale a peal of thunder and a fall of mist, and in the *Didot Perceval* the roaring of the Siege Perilous and the great darkness are signals of the desolating enchantment.   In other words, the Mabinogi of *Manawyddan* has combined two accounts of the wasting of the land, of which the first attributes the disaster to the presumption of the young sun-god in sitting prematurely in the divine seat, and the second to the imprisonment of the god.

Since the captivity and the slumber of the god in his western isle amount to the same thing, the seasonal meaning of the concept seems clearly preserved by the fourteenth century poet, Davydd ab Gwillym, who speaks of the summer as going to Annwn to rest for the winter.[15]  Hafgan, "Summer Light," was one of the Kings of Annwn, and Annwn is but one name for the isle where Gwair, another sun-god, was imprisoned.

Another name was Kaer Sidi.  Anwyl suggested that this was the name of the castle in which Pryderi of the Golden Hair was imprisoned.[16]  We saw in Chapter XX that the remarkable similarity of Kaer Sidi to the isle of the immortal elders in *Perlesvaus* justifies our assuming that the mysterious captive in the pit was Gwair.  We have also seen that Perceval goes on to another island, where he liberates a chained youth, Galobrun, and substitutes for him a certain Gohas del Chastel de la Baleine. The name Gohas could easily be derived from Gwair through the intermediate form Gohar, and the name Galobrun from Gware's epithet Gwallt Euryn through the intermediate form Galvariun, found on the Modena sculpture.  Embedded in the *Perlesvaus*, therefore, are three variants of the imprisonment of Gwair: first, the nameless prisoner in the isle of the immortal

[15] *International Congress of Religions*, III, vol. 2, 239.
[16] *ZCP*, II, 130.

elders; second, Galobrun in his island near by; and third, Gohas, whose character seems to be suggested by the traditions of the older Curoi or Gwrnach. Gohas' curious title, "del Chastel de la Baleine," has probably nothing to do with whales, but since we know that Kair Belli was another name for Kaer Sidi and that Belli had a variant form Belin, Gohas del Chastel de la Baleine may be the equivalent of Gwair of Kaer Sidi. It seems plausible that some Welsh or Breton composer, knowing as separate traditions the imprisonment of Goha(r)s and that of Galobrun, and identifying one with the elder god and the other with the younger, concocted the story of Perceval's intervention to account for the replacement of one by the other.

We have noted in Chapter IX that in *Kilhwch and Olwen* there is a quartet of Gwairs, all equipped with different epithets but of course the same mythical figure. Two of them are said to be sons of Llwch Llawwynnyawc from the other side of the raging sea. And in these we have recognized little Curoi and his father Lugh Loinnbheimionach from beyond St. George's Channel, as well as Gaeres and his father King Lot. Now in the *Vulgate Lancelot* we learn that Galahaut won the land of Sorelois from King Gaher or Goher, son of King Lohoz.[17] In Lohoz we may properly see Welsh Llwch or its variant Lloch; in Gaher or Goher, Llwch's son Gwair. And the statement that Galahaut adopted Gaher's daughter seems the usual attempt to explain the fact that Gaher and Galahaut were both said to be father to the same woman; of which fact the real explanation was that Gaher and Galahaut were identical, just as were Gaeres and Galvain. Whatever the derivation of Galahaut, the name seems to be another corruption of a Welsh epithet attached to Gwair.

Once having detected in Galahaut, King of Sorelois, the divine Gwair, prisoner and king in the Scilly Isles, we seem to have the key to the story of Galaad's end in the highly Christianized *Queste del Saint Graal.*[18] For like Perceval in *Perlesvaus*, Galaad after achieving the adventures of the Grail in the mainland castle sails out to sea to become king of an island, whither the Grail is transferred. There in the island city of Sarras, Galaad is first imprisoned and then crowned. The king who imprisons him is called Escorant, and in a variant version Eschoharz is

---

[17] Sommer, III, 269.      [18] *Ibid.*, VI, 194–7.

the name of a lame beggar, who is healed by carrying the table on which the Grail rested.[19] Sommer had noted the coincidence in names, but he did not perceive that if we put the two traditions together we seem to have a version of the healing of the Maimed King which has been recast on the model of a Biblical miracle; and that the king's name was Eschoharz. Stripped of the prefix Es-, the same that has made Escalibor from Calibor, we have Choharz, in whom we may easily recognize King Goha(r)s. And the imprisonment of Galaad by Choharz in the isle of Sarras seems to be a variant of King Goha(r)s' imprisonment of Galobrun in a solitary isle. The miraculous feeding of the imprisoned Galaad by the Grail corresponds to the feeding of the imprisoned Galobrun by the daughter of a sick knight, in other words, by a Grail Damsel. And the succession of Galaad to the island kingdom of Choharz or Escorant finds parallels in the succession of Galobrun to Goha(r)s, and of Galahaut to Goher. Despite all the confusion and the discrepancies of detail, these various stories of captives who become kings and kings who become captives, seem to be based on the Welsh tradition of the god Gwair, to whom we can assign the epithet Gwallt Euryn, and whose captivity in an island where the Head of Annwn kept his caldron, was a familiar theme.

It would be strange if Gawain, the most famous representative of Gwair or Gwri did not figure in Arthurian romance as the captive on an island and was not connected somehow with miraculous feeding like Galobrun and Galaad. In fact, there are several such traditions.

One of them is found in the *Lanzelet* of Ulrich von Zatzikhoven (1195–1200), and is a good example of the combination of stories.[20] The enchanter Malduc undertook to recover the stolen Guinevere from Falerin on condition that Gawain and Erec, who had slain Falerin's father and brother, were surrendered to him. The conditions were accepted, the queen was rescued, but in spite of her intercession Malduc threw his two foes into a tower in the midst of the Misty Lake, and left them to starve. But some of Arthur's knights headed by Lanzelet were not content to let them remain there, and accompanied by Esealt, who grew a span every month and was already taller than a tower though only seventeen, they came to the lake. They leapt into the water, but Esealt saved them from drowning

[19] *Ibid.*, 194.          [20] O. Piper, *Höfisches Epik*, II, 191–3.

and finally cast them over the walls of Malduc's castle. They slew the enchanter and his folk. His beautiful daughter, however, who was next to Femurgan in wisdom and who had saved the lives of Gawain and Erec, was spared.[21] She rode out with the two heroes and entered Arthur's service.[22]

One could hardly find a better example of that harmonizing and synchronizing which the Celtic story-teller felt to be his duty, for here are three plots interwoven. First, there is the abduction of Guinevere, a theme which apparently had its origin in the abduction of Blathnat by Curoi. Secondly, there is the imprisonment of Erec and Gawain, whose names we know are based on the Welsh Gwri Gwallt Avwyn, and whose story reminds us of Galobrun's imprisonment in an island, fed by a Grail Damsel. Finally, there is the release of the damsel and the slaying of her father, — incidents which in more than one respect seem based on an Irish tradition of the abduction of Blathnat from her father Mider.[23] First of all, the fact that the daughter of Mardoc corresponds to a Grail Damsel and that she enters the service of Arthur links her up with Lore of Cardoil, who entered Arthur's service as cup-bearer.[24] And Lore we know is descended from Blathnat through Floree.[25] Malduc, I have suggested in the *Romanic Review*,[26] goes back through the forms Mardoc and Medrot to Mider — a conclusion confirmed by the fact that one tradition makes Blathnat the daughter of Mider. But what seems to clinch these identifications is the fact that Esealt seems to perform here a part closely analogous to that of Cuchulinn when he was carrying off an unnamed "daughter of the king," who may be safely identified with Blathnat, daughter of Mider. In the *Phantom Chariot of Cuchulinn* the Ulster hero boasts: [27]

> The caldron was given
> By the daughter of the king.
> After we had come upon the ocean, . . .
> The crew of my currach was drowned
> By the fierce storm.
> After this I floated them,

[21] Ulrich v. Zatzikhoven, *Lanzelet*, ed. Hahn, ll. 7172–87, 7630–39.
[22] Ll. 7676–81.
[23] O'Curry, *Manners and Customs*, III, 80.
[24] Sommer, III, 272.    [26] *RR*, XV, 282.
[25] *Cf.* Chap. II.    [27] E. Hull, *Cuchulinn Saga*, 283 ff.

> Though it was a sharp danger,
> Nine men upon each of my hands,
> Thirty on my head,
> Eight upon my two sides
> Clung to my body.
> Thus I swam the ocean
> Until I reached the harbor.

Not only does this sound like the feat of Esealt, but even Esealt's age, seventeen, is a significant one in Cuchulinn's life, for he was seventeen at the Cattle-Raid of Cualnge.[28]  Finally, Lot detected in the name Esealt a MS. corruption of Galehalt,[29] and Galehalt or Galahaut we have already concluded goes back through a Welsh solar epithet to Cuchulinn.  The three figures, Malduc, his daughter, and Esealt, can be shown on various grounds to correspond to Mider, his daughter Blathnat, and Cuchulinn, and their story in *Lanzelet* bears clear marks of its Irish derivation.

In spite of its contamination with other Celtic stories, we can easily perceive in *Lanzelet* the same captivity motif.  The Tertre Devee episode in the *Vulgate Lancelot* offers another illustration.[30]  Again the hero is Lancelot.  He comes to an abbey and finds the shields of many captive knights including that of Gawain.  He ascends the hill to deliver them.  The prisoners warn him, but he fights their captor.  Lancelot recognizes that his opponent's sword is that of Galahaut, asks who he is, and learns that it is Boors.  The two are at once reconciled.  Boors tells how he had come there three months before, had slain the lord of the hill, Clochides, and was obliged to take his place, slaying all who essayed the adventure, but had merely imprisoned the knights of the Round Table.  He makes what seems to be an absurd excuse for holding Gawain and the others in prison: that he did not know them because they would not reveal their names.  Of course, being vanquished, Boors freed his captives, and obtained their pardon.  The authentic archaism of this story is shown not only by the fact, pointed out by Lot, that Boors is here playing the rôle of the Priest of Nemi,[31] but also by the very lameness of his excuse

[28] *Ibid.*, lix.
[29] F. Lot, *Étude sur le Lancelot*, 168.
[30] Sommer, V, 236–42.
[31] Lot, *op. cit.*, 447.  *Cf.* Chap. VII.

for imprisoning Gawain. For it was surely not the young Boors who imprisoned Gawain in the Tertre Devee but the old Boors or Gohors, corresponding to Goha(r)s of the *Perlesvaus*, who imprisoned Galobrun. The romancer, being more familiar with the younger Boors, Lancelot's cousin, has been forced to invent some explanation for his treatment of his fellows of the Table Round. The impossible excuse that he did not recognize them because they would not tell their names betrays the desperate shifts to which a *remanieur* was driven who did not know that fundamental axiom of Arthurian romance, that there were two Curois, two Gwris, two Boors, etc. ; one the young and gracious hero, the other, the old and often cruel giant.

Still another version of the imprisonment of Gawain and his liberation by Lancelot is found in the story of the Dolorous Dungeon (Douloureuse Chartre) in the *Vulgate Lancelot*.[32] We have seen clearly that Bran is brother of Manawyddan and appears in the *Didot Perceval* as Bron, predecessor of Perceval in the lordship of the Grail; in other words, he must have been closely associated in Welsh tradition with Kaer Sidi, the Otherworld island of Manawyddan and Pryderi. Bron, moreover, in the *Didot Perceval* is lord of a castle beside a river. It should not surprise us, therefore, to find that the lord of the Dolorous Dungeon, a castle in the midst of the River Humber (Hombre),[33] is a certain Brandus des Illes, whose name easily resolves itself into Bran Dus des Illes, "Duke of the Isles." When we read that he sent a vavasour to entice thither Gawain and his companions, we are naturally reminded of that mysterious "emissary of Pwyll and Pryderi," because of whom Gwair was taken captive in an island. The romance relates that no sooner have Gawain and his fellows been ferried over to the castle and have disarmed themselves than they are overpowered and dragged to the dungeon. Lancelot hears of a damsel who mourns for Gawain and his companions, and by her guidance is able to attack single-handed a troop of knights from the Dolorous Dungeon. Later Lancelot again attacks Brandus and his knights, drags him from his horse, rides over him, and forces him finally to yield. All his prisoners are then sent as Lancelot's to Arthur and Guinevere.

[32] Sommer, III, 158–69.
[33] Is not Hombre a misunderstanding of Ombre, the Land of Shadow, corresponding to the Irish Land of *Scath?*

The theme of Lancelot's deliverance of Gawain from prison, we may remember, was one of the first stories studied in this book, namely the Dolorous Tower episode, which was an ingenious fusion of the Gawain imprisonment and rescue with the Guinevere abduction and rescue motifs. The fact that there are three accounts of Lancelot's liberation of Gawain in the *Vulgate Lancelot*, and one in the German *Lanzelet*, seems to attest the existence of a tradition in which Llwch Lleminawc was the rescuer of Gwair or Gwri. There is no direct statement to that effect, but in the *Harryings of Annwn*, Llwch Lleminawc plays a prominent part in carrying off the caldron from the island of Gwair's captivity.

> The shining sword of Llwch was lifted to it,
> And in the hand of Lleminawc it was left.

Macculloch suggests that the object of the expedition [34] was not only the seizure of the caldron but also the release of Gwair.[35] It is likely therefore that a principal part in the rescue of Gwair would be attributed to Llwch. The *Perlesvaus*, moreover, whose authenticity as representing Welsh tradition seems abundantly demonstrated, points to the existence of another variant which made Perceval's original, Pryderi, the rescuer of Gwair Gwallt Euryn, instead of his captor, as he is represented in the *Harryings of Annwn*. Certainly the names of the young god's captors are many, of his rescuers more than one, but so far as Arthurian romance is concerned, the most famous of captives, — Gawain, Galaad, and Galobrun, — seem to be direct descendants of Gwair. And since we know that Gwair was the sun, we can hardly doubt that his imprisonment in a western isle possessed the same meaning as the Paphlagonian myth of the binding of Kronos, who shared with Gwair a solar nature. Both legends dramatize the annual restriction and restoration of the great life-giving luminary.

[34] *Cf.* note 1.
[35] *Mythology of All Races*, III, 192.

# CHAPTER XXXIII

## THE KINSHIP OF GAWAIN, POPE GREGORY
## AND MORDRED

ONE of the strangest freaks in the development of Arthurian romance is the part which the captivity of Gwri-Gwair played in causing the story of the birth and youth of Gawain to fall into the pattern of a pious legend, very similar to that told of Gregory the Great. All the accounts of Gawain's early life that have survived, instead of conforming to the more pagan and romantic types which we should expect from the descendant of Gwri, bear the impress of an ecclesiastic's mind. Geoffrey of Monmouth says that Gawain was sent by his uncle, Arthur, "to be brought up as a page in the service of Pope Sulpicius, from whom he had received arms." [1] The *Enfances Gauvain*,[2] *De Ortu Walwanii*,[3] and *Perlesvaus*,[4] also bring the child to Rome and make him a protégé of the Pope; the *Ridder metter Mouwen*,[5] a Dutch variant of the same story, relates how the hero was educated in a cloister to be a clerk.

Gawain's story, as we have said, approximates in its early parts the pious legend of Pope Gregory. He is the child of a clandestine union between Lot and Arthur's sister. He is handed over by his mother, with a sum of money and a rich cloth, to others to be disposed of. A fisherman discovers and fosters him. Finally he is delivered up to the Pope and trained in knighthood.

Quite diverse views have been expressed concerning the relationship between the Gregory and Gawain legends. Bruce's assumption that the Gregory legend existed quite independently of the romances, and after the middle of the twelfth century was transferred in part to Gawain, has much in its favor and seems generally accepted.[6] On the other hand, Sparnaay has pointed out numerous analogies to the motifs of the Gregory legend in

---

[1] Bk. IX, ch. 11.
[2] *Rom.*, XXXIX, 1 ff.
[3] Ed. J. D. Bruce.
[4] Potvin, I, 252 ff.
[5] *Histoire littéraire*, XXX, 122.
[6] *Historia Meriadoci and De Ortu Walwanii*, ed. Bruce, xli-lii.

the romances which have no ecclesiastical coloring, and has reached the conclusion that the Gregory legend is a pious adaptation of an Arthurian romance.[7] The latter theory we shall find is nearer the truth, but by no means the whole truth.

The evidence produced in this chapter shows, first, that features of the Gregory legend are associated not only with Gawain (Walwanius), but also with Galobrun, Girardo, and Albanus, and that therefore the legend must have been first attached to Gwri before it spread to heroes whose names are recognizably corruptions of Gwri and his epithets. Secondly, that the presence of two Celtic traits in the Gregory legend proves that it also was derived from that of Gwri, and not vice versa. Thirdly, that this Gwri legend in turn originated as a pious Coptic tale, and was fastened to Gwri because of certain resemblances it bore to a pagan myth of Gwri's birth, upbringing, and later captivity. Finally, that the story of Mordred's birth preserves substantially the outlines of the pagan myth of Gwri, before it was influenced by the Coptic tale of King Armenios. (Consult Chart C.)

First, let us observe how features of the Gregory legend appear in tales of heroes whom we may suspect of being derived from Gwri. We have already noted their occurrence in the Gawain *enfances*. Let us examine, moreover, in detail the story of Galobrun's captivity and deliverance which we glanced at in the last chapter. *Perlesvaus* relates [8] that when Perceval leaves the isle of the immortal elders, he sails away till he reaches another island, and finds a poverty-stricken widow and her two daughters. He learns that she is his aunt, and that her son Galobrun, son of Galobrutus, is held in prison by Gohas del Chastel de la Baleine. Perceval divulges his relationship and cheers the distressed ladies. On the morrow "he roweth until that he is come under a rock, wherein was a cave at top, round and narrow and secure like as it were a little house. . . . He is come forth of the ship and goeth up the little path until he cometh into the little house. He findeth within one of the comeliest knights in the world. He had a ring at his feet and a collar at his neck, with a chain, whereof the other end was fixed by a staple into a great ledge of the rock." Galobrun says that he has been kept alive by food sent him by the daughter of the

---

[7] H. Sparnaay, *Verschmelzung legendarischer und weltlicher Motive in der Poesie des Mittelalters*, 52.          [8] Potvin, I, 332 ff.

Sick Knight, and that he cannot be released without the key which Gohas has in his keeping. Perceval departs, kills a dragon, who had swallowed the key, frees the daughter of the Sick Knight from the assault of Gohas, forces Gohas to go back to the rock where Galobrun is confined, and releases the youth. Galobrun then chains Gohas in his place, who "never thereafter ate nor drank." Perceval then returns with Galobrun and the damsel to their land, and has all King Gohas' folk swear allegiance to Galobrun and his sister. "He sojourned there so long as it pleased him, and then departed and took leave of the damsel and Galobrun, that thanked him much for the lands that he had again through him."

We have already detected in this narrative certain well-known Celtic traditions: two versions of the imprisonment of Gwair in a remote island, the feeding of the captive by the daughter of the Maimed King, and his rescue. We may add to the Celtic features the fact that Galobrun has practically the same name as his father Galobrutus,[9] and that it may be derived easily through Breton Galvariun from Welsh Gwallt Euryn. But there are signs that like the Gawain *enfances* the Galobrun captivity is somehow related to the Gregory legend. From the *Gesta Romanorum*[10] we learn that Gregory, discovering that he was the child of incest and the unwitting partner in incest, took the garb of a pilgrim and was taken by a fisherman to a fitting place for the expiation of his guilt. It was "a huge rock, having chains at its feet, which, without a key, could not be unloosed. After the fisherman had undone them, he cast the keys into the sea, and returned home. The pilgrim remained in that place seventeen years." Then on the death of the pope, a voice from heaven commanded that a man named Gregory be sought out and appointed the vicar of God. The messengers sent to find the unknown at last came to the fisherman's house, learned of the penance of Gregory, and when the keys were miraculously recovered from the belly of a fish, set out for the rock. They found the solitary prisoner, unchained him, and brought him back to Rome, where he became pope.

Now these keys swallowed by the fish and recovered at the right moment to release a captive from a solitary rock in the ocean too singularly resemble the key swallowed by the dragon and recovered in order to release a captive from a solitary rock

---

[9] *Ibid.*, 333 f.            [10] Ed. Oesterley, 399 ff.

in the ocean to escape our attention. And the fact that dragons swallowing keys are not a commonplace of Celtic myth, whereas fish swallowing keys are a commonplace of hagiology derived from the East, makes it clear that the Galobrun story has been influenced directly or indirectly by a pious legend which contained the episode of the fish which swallowed the keys. This episode is found in the very legend of Pope Gregory which stands in such close relationship to the Gawain *enfances*. Since we know that the names Galobrun and Gawain represent the epithets of Welsh Gwri, we can hardly escape the conclusion that the connection between the Gregory legend and those of Gawain and Galobrun must go back to a period in Welsh or Dumnonian tradition before the epithets Gwallt Avwyn and Gwallt Euryn split off from Gwri.

There is still other evidence that this pious tale was attached to the Welsh god. The heroes of two analogues of the Gregory legend are named Girardo and Albanus.[11] Both these versions differ from the Gregory legend in that the original incest is between father and daughter, there is no trace of the captivity episode, and immediately after the second incest has been revealed, mother and son enter on a life of penance. The legends of Girardo and Albanus, therefore, form one branch of this story, just as those of Gregorius and Walwanius form another. The correspondence in names is certainly more than fortuitous, especially since we know that Gregorius and Walwanius derive from Welsh Gwri Gwallt Avwyn. We have seen Gwri or Gware become Gerard the Swan Knight;[12] why should he not become Girardo? Gwallt Avwyn does become Galvan; in MS. transmission the initial letter is often dropped.[13] What more natural, then, than to attach a legend of the holy man Alvan to St. Alban? There seems no other way to explain the fact that the same tale in whole or in part reappears in the stories of Girardo, Walwanius, Albanus, and Galobrun, than to infer that all are offshoots from a legend of Gwri Gwallt Avwyn or Gwallt Euryn, and were propagated by Bretons either as romances of the knights Galvain and Galobrun, or as saintly legends of Girardo and Albanus.

One might be tempted to suppose that the legend of illegiti-

[11] L. Constans, *Légende d'Oedipe*, 115, 118.
[12] *Cf.* Chap. XXXI.
[13] J. D. Bruce, *Evolution*, I, 33; *MLN*, XXVI, 66 f.

mate birth, exposure, fosterage by a fisherman, enchainment on
an island, and deliverance must have evolved first as a legend of
Pope Gregory and then because of the similarity of names been
transferred to Gwri. But facts point in the other direction.
The legend was attached to Gwri before it was transferred to
Gregory. In the first place, Sparnaay has shown that the
Gregory legend cannot be traced back further than the late
twelfth century; [14] whereas the evidence of Geoffrey of Monmouth attests the connection of Gawain with Rome and his
upbringing by Pope Sulpicius as early as 1136. And this, we
know, implies the existence of an ecclesiasticized Gwri legend
even earlier. Though these facts by no means prove the priority
of the Gwri over the Gregory version, at least they put the
burden of proof on the other side.

In the second place, the internal evidence of the Gregory
legend itself betrays in two details the influence of pagan
traditions about Gwri. These are the naming of Gregory after
his foster-father, and the placing of rich cloths in the cradle with
the exposed infant. It is highly significant that these do not
appear in the Coptic tale of King Armenios, which was the ultimate source of the Gregory legend.[15] That it is the source,
not the derivative, accords with the known influence of Coptic
manuscripts on Irish illumination and on Western art,[16] whereas
there are no signs of similar influence from the West on the
Copts. Accordingly we may assume that the Coptic legend
preceded and was the direct or indirect source of the Gregory
legend. Almost every feature of the latter is accounted for
by the Oriental tale except the two features which we have
mentioned, and to which we shall recur later. In order that
anyone familiar with the legend of Pope Gregory may judge for
himself, here is a summary of the Coptic tale.

King Armenios of Tarsus and his wife, dying at the same time,
left a son, John, and a daughter. John was so inconsolable that
the courtiers deliberately tried to restore him by a banquet.
Intoxicated as a result, he forced his sister, and when she became

---

[14] Sparnaay, *op. cit.*, 24.

[15] E. Amélineau, *Contes et romans de l'Egypte chrétienne*, I, 174–89.
Summarized by R. Köhler, *Kleinere Schriften*, II, 182.

[16] Prof. G. L. Hamilton kindly refers me to the *Journal of the Royal Soc.
of Ant.*, IV, 128–39, 147–51 for instances of Coptic and Eastern influence on
Irish art and literature. *Cf.* Boswell, *Irish Precursors of Dante*, 114 ff;
W. Stokes, *Ireland and the Celtic Church*, 169 ff.

pregnant reproached her.  He learned from her the truth and
went into a monastery to expiate his sin.  When her time came,
she placed the child in a cradle with three tablets, one of ivory
disclosing his incestuous birth, one of silver for the expenses of
his upbringing, one of gold for the boy when he should come of
age.  (Note the absence of any rich clothing.)  She had the
cradle placed on a river, where it was caught in a fisher's net.
The boy, first committed to an abbot, was returned by him to
the fisher with the tablet of silver, and well brought up.  He
learned from the fisher's sons that he was not their brother, and
though advised by the fisher to become a monk, decided to
become a knight.  By selling the gold tablet he was able to buy
horse, spear, sword and armor.  Before departing he learned
from the fisher the secret of his birth.  By chance he came to
his native city, and took prisoner a king who was besieging it.
The queen, his mother, in gratitude to the handsome stranger,
lost no time in offering him her hand, and they were married.
The young husband, however, was known to weep secretly;
a spy discovered the ivory tablet and brought it to the queen.
She thus learned that she had been united to her son, and told
him so.  He at once fled, and finding himself on the sea-shore,
exchanged clothes with a fisher, had himself chained, threw the
key into the sea, and was transported to an island.  There,
eating only grass, he lived for years.  At last, the patriarch
dying without leaving a worthy successor, the king sent messengers to search for one.  By the Lord's guidance they came
to the fisherman's home, and when they learned that the fish
which was being served up to them miraculously contained the
key of the chain which bound the penitent on his isle, they
demanded to be taken out to see this holy man.  They found him
in prayer, took him back, and he was consecrated patriarch
forthwith.  His mother meantime had passed through a serious
illness which left her shortsighted.  Hearing of the sanctity of
the new patriarch, she came to ask his prayers for her cure.
They proved at once efficacious.  Before his mother departed,
the patriarch revealed himself and clothed her in a religious
habit.  Both lived saintly lives thereafter, and God, because they
had committed their monstrous sins in ignorance, pardoned
them.

No one familiar with the Gregory legend needs to have demonstrated the closeness of the parallel.  It is perfectly clear that

the tale of King Armenios has not a single peculiarly Celtic trait and therefore could not be derived from a Gwri legend. On the other hand, it is also clear that the Coptic tale did not supply the name Gregory, the naming of Gregory after his foster-father, or the rich apparel which is placed in his cradle. The first of these features seems to be borrowed from the Gwri legend, because we have no evidence that the Gregory legend existed until after the ecclesiasticized Gwri legend had already existed for some years. The second and third features corroborate the supposition, for we have good reason to believe that they were embodied in one form of the pagan Gwri birth-story, were preserved in the story as remodeled under the influence of the Coptic tale and were thence carried over into the Gregory legend. The fact that Gregory is named after his foster-father, just as young Gawain in the *Enfances* and *Perlesvaus* is named after his temporary fosterer, and just as Galobrun bears the name his father bore in the corrupt form Galobrutus, proves that all three traditions go back to Gwri, when it is taken into consideration that one of the cardinal hypotheses of this book is that according to one tradition young Gwri, like young Curoi, had a father of the same name. I do not doubt that the naming of a child after his father or foster-father is fairly common: yet in this case the odds are certainly in favor of the derivation of this feature from the pagan myth of Gwri.

The third feature in the Gregory legend which goes back to Celtic myth is the silk garment embroidered with gold which finds a place with the exposed infant. This rich garment occurs in the stories of the exposure of Gawain in *De Ortu, Perlesvaus*, and *Enfances*. Fortunately we do not have to argue that it was derived from any hypothetical Gwri myth; for it is mentioned with marked emphasis in the version of Gwri's birth we actually possess.[17] Teirnyon finds the infant boy, wrapped round in a mantle of satin. When he brings the child to his wife, she asks, "What sort of garments are there upon the boy?" "A mantle of satin," said he. Here there can be no question of contamination from the outside. The tales of Gawain's half brother Mordred,[18] and of Fiachu Fer-mara,[19] both begotten in incest, both exposed on the sea, also contain the feature of the rich robe. Since, therefore, three of the elements in the Gregory legend

[17] Loth, *Mab.*², I, 110.     [18] See below.     [19] *PRIA*, XXXIV, C, 311 f.

which are not accounted for by the tale of King Armenios are accounted for by Celtic traditions of Gwri, we must conclude that the Coptic tale was first attached to Gwri, and to that attachment the Gregory legend owes these details.

But why this singular attachment of a pious tale to a mythological hero? We have come to see that the scientific principle of causation is operative among the phenomena of Celtic and Arthurian story to a far greater extent than has hitherto been recognized. The maddest fancies of *file* and *conteur* are not due to motiveless and meaningless caprice, as so many eminent scholars have been inclined to believe. The fault is with ourselves, with our profound ignorance of so much that must have been taken for granted, with our exaggerated skepticism regarding every utterance of medieval story-tellers regarding themselves or their work, and with our frequent failure to understand the play of their minds and imaginations. Just as scientists like Huxley have had to admit that, given Catholic premises, the logical inferences of Aquinas and other medieval theologians are as accurate and as cogent as those of any modern philosopher, so let us not accuse the medieval story-teller of inconsequence or absurdity until we have at least made an attempt to discover his motive or his reason. It is not likely that a Cymric bard would have resolved out of sheer irrational whim to fasten to Gwri Gwallt Avwyn the revolting tale of John the son of Armenios. What led him to do it?

It was probably the presence in the Gwri legend of motifs which he found better arranged and motivated in the legend of Armenios. The tradition of Gwri-Gwair's captivity has survived in Arthurian forms which show how it might have perplexed a rational bard. But the similar chaining of the Coptic penitent on an island of the sea was to a good Catholic not only a comprehensible but even a laudable proceeding. Furthermore, Gwri's birth, as narrated in the Mabinogi of *Pwyll*, was accompanied by his mother's disgrace, thus remotely resembling the birth of the Coptic hero. Again, we have reason to believe that there were other versions of Gwri's infancy closer to that of the Coptic hero than the extant account.

For we have the testimony of three excellent Celtists, Anwyl, Gruffydd and Baudis,[20] to the effect that the account in *Pwyll* bears every indication that it is but one version, and that a

[20] *Folklore*, XXVII, 50; *RC*, XXXIII, 455; *ZCP*, I, 288.

corrupt one, of the legend. We are obliged to infer from other sources what some of the other and more authentic versions must have been. Now one of the points made in the Mabinogi of *Pwyll* is that Gwri was born during the night before May 1.[21] He therein resembles and tends to coalesce with Mordred, the brother of his Arthurian counterpart Gawain. Now the story of Mordred's birth was recognized by Bruce as containing several elements in common with the stories of the birth of Gawain and Gregory.[22] But it is highly significant that the story of Mordred's birth does not have the ecclesiastical smack of the Gawain and Gregory legends; it seems uninfluenced by the edifying Coptic tale. We may properly regard it as a natural outgrowth of Celtic tradition.

In Malory [23] we read first that King Lot's wife came to Caerleon, richly bisene, with her four sons: Gawain, Gaheris, Agravain, and Gareth. "For she was a passing fair lady, wherefore the king cast great love unto her, and desired to lie by her; so they were agreed, and he begat upon her Mordred, and she was his sister on his mother's side Igraine. So there she rested her a month, and at the last departed. . . . But all this time King Arthur knew not that King Lot's wife was his sister." Later [24] we read: "Then King Arthur let send for all the children born on May-day, begotten of lords and born of ladies; for Merlin told King Arthur that he should destroy him should be born on May-day, wherefore he sent for them all, upon pain of death; and so there were found many lords' sons, and all were sent unto the king, and so was Mordred sent by King Lot's wife, and all were put in a ship to the sea, and some were four weeks weeks old and some less. And so by fortune the ship drove unto a castle, and was all to-riven, and destroyed the most part, save that Mordred was cast up, and a good man found him, and nourished him till he was fourteen year old, and then he brought him to the court." The *Huth Merlin* supplies the additional details [25] that the infant Mordrec was borne from the wrecked ship in his cradle to the shore, and was discovered by a fisherman out in his boat. Mordrec's name was revealed by a paper in the cradle, his high extraction by the rich apparel; and the fisherman took the infant to his lord. A famous figure

[21] Loth, Mab.², I, 109.
[22] *Historia Meriadoci*, ed. J. D. Bruce, xli.
[25] *Huth Merlin*, ed. Paris, Ulrich, I, 204 ff.
[23] Bk. I, ch. 19.
[24] Ch. 28.

in Welsh legend, Taliessin, who according to Nutt "succeeded to the attributes of a far older, a prehistoric, a mythic singer," [26] is the subject of a similar birth story.[27] Born for the second time by the hag Caridwen, Taliessin was wrapped in a leather bag and cast into the sea on the twenty-ninth day of April. Elphin, the son of that Gwyddno Garanhir who possessed the food-supplying *mwys*, went to draw his salmon weir on May eve, and found the bag. When someone opened it, he exclaimed, "Behold a radiant brow!" "Radiant brow" is in Welsh Taliessin, and thus from his shining forehead this supernatural child derived his name. Elphin brings him up until he is thirteen, and then takes him to his uncle's court at Christmas time, where he triumphs over all the bards.

Now from the Mordred and Taliessin stories it is evident that the Welsh connected the story of exposure on the sea and discovery by a fisherman with the supernatural child born on May Eve. And therefore it is highly probable that there was a version of the birth of Gwri, born on May Eve, with such a tale of exposure and discovery by a fisherman. When we combine this feature with other known features of his story, we have four correspondences of a general nature between the mythic legend of Gwri and the Oriental tale of King Armenios: the disgrace which his mother incurs at his birth; his exposure on the sea; his discovery by a fisherman; his subsequent chaining upon an island. Now we have no reason to believe that these resemblances between the Celtic and the Coptic legends were other than very general. Except in so far as they were due to a common very ancient source, they were accidental. But they sufficed to inspire some Welsh clerk with the notion that here was a very edifying form of the adventures of the great Welsh hero, Gwri, which, whether originally applicable to him or not, should be applied to him without further delay. His story gained such authority that not only are all the Gawain *enfances* modeled upon it, not only does the Galobrun captivity show plainly its influence in the key-swallowing dragon, but also it inspired the next ingenious development. For this name of the saintly penitent raised to high ecclesiastical office, Gurius or Gorius, could only be Pope Gregorius himself. There is certainly a poetic justice if not a Divine Providence in the fact that Pope Gregory, the hardened punster, should be the victim of this

[26] *Mabinogion*, ed. Nutt, 356.  [27] *Ibid.*, 297.

more or less deliberate confusion of names. Who does not know how when Gregory was confronted by certain Anglian slaves in the market-place of Rome he perpetrated that triple iniquity:[28] "Non Angli, sed angeli. . . . Bene Deiri; de ira eruti. . . . Alleluia in Aelli regis provincia oportet cantari." Perhaps the only defect in the adaptation of the punishment to Gregory's triple crime is the fact that his legend is blotted by only two cases of incest. There should be three.

The legend of Pope Gregory, then, seems to be a pious tale from the Orient, modified only slightly by the confusion with Gwri; the Gawain *enfances* are myths of Gwri almost entirely remodeled through the influence of the Oriental tale; the *enfances* of Mordred are probably unadulterated Celtic tradition.

For this last statement there is other support besides the analogue of Taliessin. An Irish story relates[29] that Fiachu Fer-mara (Man of the Sea) "was begotten by Oengus on his own daughter, when drunken, and that Oengus was so much ashamed of what he had done that he put the infant adrift on the sea with a purple royal robe and a gold pin upon him. The child was rescued by a fisherman, who gave him the name Fer-mara, 'Man of the Sea,' in commemoration of the event." Here we have compacted five features of the Mordred *enfances* : the incestuous union, the exposure of the child on the sea, the rich clothing, the discovery by a fisherman, and the naming by him. Other features of the Mordred story echo Irish motifs. The prophecy that Mordred should slay his father recalls the prophecies that Lug should slay his grandfather Balor,[30] and that Noine's birth should coincide with the death of his grandfather Dare.[31] The fact that Mordred is the offspring of brother and sister,[32] and also the opponent of his father in battle recalls the tale of Eochaid Bres, who was the offspring of the son and daughter of Delbaeth, and the unwitting opponent of his father in sword-play.[33] The legend of Mordred is saturated with Celtic lore.

---

[28] Bede, *Eccl. Hist.*, Bk. II, ch. 1.     [29] *Cf.* note 19.

[30] *Cf.* H. Lessmann, *Die Kyros-sage in Europa*, 13; *Mitra*, I, 171; J. Curtin, *Hero Tales of Ireland*, 296; Rhys, *Arthurian Legend*, 21. Finn also slays his grandfather. *Cf. RC*, II, 86 ff; J. Curtin, *Myths and Folklore*, 204 f.

[31] *ZCP*, XII, 332.

[32] On the incest motif in general *cf.* O. Rank, *Inzest Motiv in Dichtung und Sage;* Roscher, *Ausführliches Lex.*, III[1], 743; in Irish life and literature *cf. Folklore*, XXXI, 127.

[33] *RC*, XII, 61, 73.

The parallelism between the birth-tales of Mordred and Gawain can be extended to many other points in their history, and in the history of their cognates. Not only is Arthur the father of Mordred, but according to Malory he is also father of a certain Borre,[34] whom without much difficulty we can trace back through hypothetical Gorre to Gwri. Likewise, Mordred, Boors and Gasozein (a corruption of Garravain) are abductors of Guinevere.[35] Mardoc is a lover of Guinevere,[36] and Gawain also, under her other name of Guinloie.[37] Both Mordred and Gawain have their onomastic counterparts among the kings associated with the Grail: Mordrain or Mordrach, Galaad, the son of Joseph of Arimathea, Galaad, King of Sarras, and Galaphes. Just as Gawain is descended from the Irish Curoi and Cuchulinn, so Mordred, as we saw in Chapter II, and Mardoc, as we saw in the last chapter, go back to the god Mider. As the destined slayer of his father, Mordred seems to have inherited such a tradition as made Lug the destined slayer of his grandfather. A May-day child, he resembles Gwri of the golden hair and Taliessin of the shining brow.

Doubt there can be none that Mordred, the descendant of Mider of the Tuatha De Danann, was in origin a god as resplendent as Cuchulinn himself. Here is the description of Mider from the *Wooing of Etain* : [38] "The tunic that the warrior wore was purple in color, his hair was of a golden yellow, and of such length that it reached to the edge of his shoulders. The eyes of the young warrior were lustrous and grey; in the one hand he held a five-pointed spear, in the other a shield with a white central boss, and with gems of gold upon it." In Welsh tradition, Medrot still has his amiable side.[39] But it was inevitable as soon as he fell heir to the tradition of the incestuous birth and was made the destined slayer of his father, Arthur, that his character should be more and more darkened. As Arthur increased, Mordred decreased in valor and good-fame. It was not enough that the traitor himself should die, but his sons, too, must perish by the sword. Mider, the light god,

[34] Bk. I, ch. 17.
[35] Sommer, IV, 301; Crestien, *Erec*, l. 1710; O. Piper, *Höfisches Epik*, II, 265, 274. The successive forms are Garravain d'Estrangot, Gasoain d'Estrangot, Gasozein de Dragoz.     [36] *Cf.* Chap. I.
[37] *Chevalier as Deus Espees*, ll. 91–3.
[38] A. H. Leahy, *Heroic Romances of Ireland*, I, 27.
[39] Loth, *Mab.²*, II, 289.

because of his traditional opposition to Arthur, shared the fate of those pagan divinities whose worship was opposed to that of Christ. The glorious Apollo became the frightful fiend Apollin; the solar Osiris appears in Milton's hell. So in the French romances the once resplendent Mider has been degraded into the arch-traitor Mordred.

# CHAPTER XXXIV

## THE GODS AND GEOFFREY OF MONMOUTH

THE two general theories which have been so frequently proposed in this book to account for the phenomena of Arthurian romance, namely the mythological origin and the Breton transmission of these stories, also account for much in that epoch-making pseudo-history published by Geoffrey of Monmouth early in 1136,[1] the work which supplied Arthur with a pedigree going back to Aeneas and made him victorious over the legions of Rome itself. There is nothing new in maintaining that Geoffrey drew for his Arthurian materials on Breton sources or that he introduced figures from Welsh mythology.

Geoffrey himself declares that the deeds of Arthur and his successors were pleasantly rehearsed from memory in the traditions of many peoples as though they had been written down, but that he could find no authoritative mention of them in books until Walter Archdeacon of Oxford offered him a most ancient book in the "British" language which supplied the missing information.[2] At the end of his *History* Geoffrey again refers to his source as that book in the "British" speech which Walter did convey hither out of "Britannia," which he has taken pains to translate into Latin.[3] That Geoffrey meant Brittany by "Britannia" is proved by his statement in Bk. V, ch. 12: "Armoricum regnum quod nunc Britannia dicitur." Here is certainly direct testimony to the Breton derivation of the material.

Zimmer has shown that some of the names in Geoffrey confirm his statement.[4] And we have already observed certain names which cannot have been derived directly from Welsh but only through the Breton tradition. Most obvious is the case of Gawain, whose name Geoffrey cites in the following forms: Walvanus, Walgannus, Walganius, Walguainus, and Walgainus. These beyond question are closer to Breton Galvaginus than to Welsh Gwalchmai, or rather Gwallt Avwyn. Instead of Welsh Avallach Geoffrey gives Avallon(is), the reg-

[1] *Speculum*, I, 155.
[2] Bk. I, ch. 1.
[3] Cf. *ZfSL*, XII[1], 256.
[4] *Ibid.*, 231 ff.

ular French form.[5]  Modredus is likewise not a Welsh, but a
Cornish form.[6]  Lot occurs neither in the Welsh form Lloch
from which M. Loth derives it,[7] nor in the form Lleu or Llew
with which the Welsh versions equate it,[8] but in the regular
form of the French romances.  Caliburnus, Arthur's sword, is
hardly recognizable as the Welsh Caletvwlch, but is close to the
French Calibourne, Escalibourne.[9]  In his *Vita Merlini* Geoffrey refers to the enchantress who heals the dying Arthur as
Morgen or Morgan,[10] not under her Welsh name of Modron.
These facts, together with a few others we shall presently consider, make it clear that in the main Geoffrey knew Celtic tradition in its Breton forms.  The list in Bk. IX, ch. 12, which
includes Peredur map Elidur, may repose on a highly corrupted
Welsh document, but the rest of the Arthurian nomenclature
tends to verify his testimony that he was drawing upon a very
ancient book brought from Brittany.

Nor is the contention that Geoffrey incorporated myth in
his book a novelty.  Fletcher suggested that Arthur's conquest
of Ireland reposed on ancient Welsh myths, and that Ireland
has taken the place of the Other World.[11]  The conquest of
Scandinavian countries, according to Rhys, is due to the changed
meaning of the word Llychlyn, which once meant the Other
World.[12]  With both these suggestions we may well agree.
Furthermore Fletcher states:[13]  "It has been demonstrated
with certainty or with a very high degree of probability, that
Geoffrey must have found in Celtic myth or tradition the
characters, and at least in part the outlines, for his stories of
King Bladud, . . . Guanius and Melga. . . .  There is no
clear evidence to show, for instance, whether he was the first to
represent the Celtic gods Melwas and Gwynwas in the rôle of
the foreign ravagers Melga and Guanius. . . .  Certainly
mythical in origin is the idea of Modred's abduction of Guene-
vere. . . .  Lud is undoubtedly an ancient mythological figure,
identical with 'Ludd of the Silver Hand' of Welsh literature."
King Leir has been identified with the Welsh Llyr father of
Bran, and Cordeila, his daughter, with Kreiddylat the daughter

[5] Gottfried von Monmouth, ed. San Marte, 374.
[6] *ZfSL*, XII,[1] 254.          [8] Gottfried, 379 f.
[7] *RC*, XVI, 84.               [9] Sommer, Index vol., 34.
[10] Ed. J. J. Parry, *Univ. of Ill. Studies in Lang. and Lit.*, X, 9.
[11] *SNPL*, X, 83 f.            [12] Rhys, *Arth. Leg.*, 11.
[13] *SNPL*, X, 85 f, 94, 68.

of Lludd:[14] an identification reënforced by the fact that two versions of the same triad interchange Lludd and Llyr.[15] Such a transformation of gods into kings was natural enough not only because of the euhemeristic tendency which develops where-ever a mythology has lost its hold, but also because the genealo-gies of the Welsh chiefs and kings, whose importance Giraldus attests,[16] often carried the line back to a mythical figure. Just as the first ancestor of Alfred the Great is Wotan himself, and as the claim of practically all the Irish was, according to MacNeill,[17] descent from Lug, so Welsh pedigrees go back to Beli and Anna.[18] It was logical enough to conclude that Beli was a king. And when historians were put to desperate shifts, as Nennius and Gildas testify, to collect any information what-soever about the kings of the Britons, these lists would naturally be made the most of.

One of the most interesting of the mythological stories is that of Brennius and Bellinus, the two sons of Dunwallo Molmutius, unquestionably the traditional lawgiver of Wales, Dyfnwal Moelmud. Henry of Huntingdon, in his résumé of what was probably an early stage of Geoffrey's *History*, substitutes Brennus for Brennius,[19] and the *Brut Tysylio* and *Brut Gruffydd ap Arthur* give Bran and Bely.[20] Gwynedd or Northwest Wales was called the Land of Beli, and Northeastern Wales the Land of Bran.[21] Crestien, as we saw in Chapter XX, knows the gi-gantic Brien and the dwarf Belin as brothers. There is no doubt that, though the names of Beli and Bran were given to human beings,[22] Geoffrey's story goes back to myths of the gods Bran and Belin. In fact, he introduces Beli again as Heli (the Welsh versions read Bely)[23] the father of Lud, Cassibelaunus, and Nennius, thus identifying him with Beli Mawr, who is repre-sented in the *Story of Lludd and Llevelys* as the father of Lludd, Caswallawn, and Nynyaw.

But what are we to make of it when we realize that Geoffrey's Brennius is also the Gallic chieftain of history, who actually in

---

[14] Loth, *Mab.*², I, 284, 331.
[15] *Ibid.*, II, 273.
[16] Ed. Dimock, VI, 167.
[17] J. MacNeill, *Celtic Ireland*, 57.
[18] *Cymmrodor*, VIII, 84–6.
[19] *Chronicles of Stephen*, ed. R. Howlett, IV, 69.
[20] *ZfSL*, XII¹, 232. *Cf. ZCP*, I, 287.
[21] *International Congress for History of Religions*, III, vol. 2, 237.
[22] *Beiheft ZrPh.*, LX, 200 ff; *ZfSL*, XIV, 172.
[23] Gottfried, 250. *Cf.* J. A. Macculloch, *Rel. Anc. Celts*, 112 f.

390 B.C. sacked Rome and who is the reputed author of that oft re-echoed phrase "Vae victis!" It is manifestly a case of the same procedure as we detected in the compounding of Nennius' Ambrosius.[24] In both cases a mythological figure floating in the clouds of tradition has been consciously equated with a solid figure of earth who happened to have the same or a similar name, and so has found his way into history. The result in the tale of Brennius and Bellinus was even more fortunate than in that of Ambrosius, for it demonstrated the superiority of British to Roman arms and added another precedent to that of Maximus for Arthur's claim to tribute from Rome. The confusion of the Welsh fairy lady Elen, daughter of Coel, with the Empress Helena, mother of Constantine,[25] found not only in Geoffrey but also in the *Dream of Maxen Wledig*, exemplifies the same procedure and constitutes another claim on the Roman empire.

Even the two emperors whom Geoffrey sets up in order that Arthur may knock them down are Welsh gods. It is not only that Lucius and Leo recall the names Llwch and Llew, but a number of facts prove the identity. Llwch we know is derived from Irish Lug Lamfada, "of the Long Arm"; and Llew must also be descended from Lug since his epithet Llaw Gyffes, means, according to Rhys, the same thing.[26] Moreover, Llwch has been shown to be the original form of Lot, the father of Modred, but Welsh tradition by making Llew the father of Medrod,[27] equates Llew with Lot. Again, where Geoffrey mentions Lot and his brothers, the Welsh versions mention Lleu in Lot's place.[28] These identifications of Lot and Llew are easily explicable on the ground that the Welsh naturally confused the two derivatives from Lug, — Llwch and Llew. The very same fact explains why Geoffrey is never quite sure whether Lucius or Leo is emperor of Rome, or both.[29] His source probably used the names indiscriminately.

We have a curious check on the derivation of Lucius from

[24] *Cf.* Chap. XIV.

[25] Baring-Gould, Fisher, *Legends of Brit. Saints*, III, 255 ff; Rhys, *Hib. Lec.*, 161–7. *Cf.* the case of Anna; Baring-Gould, Fisher, I, 164 f; Rhys, J. B. Jones, *Welsh People*, 42.

[26] Rhys, *Hib. Lec.*, 237. In a triad (Loth, *Mabinogion*, II, 254, note 5) Llew is one of the three crimson-stained ones of the Isle of Britain. *Cf.* Chap. IV, where Lug is said to have a red color on him from evening to morning.          [28] Gottfried, 379 f. *Cf. Speculum*, I, 344 ff.

[27] Loth, *op. cit.*, II, 289.          [29] *SNPL*, X, 85 note 2.

Llwch.   In Chap.  IX we found that Llwch Lleminawc and
Llenlleawc of Ireland brandished a sword in different versions
of Arthur's expedition for the Otherworld caldron.   The implication was that both names were derived from Lugh Loinbheim-
ionach of Ireland.   There is, therefore, good reason to suppose
that Llwch might be referred to as Llwch Gwyddel, or, in Latin,
Lucius Hibernus.   Now the Rev. Acton Griscom informs me
that the best MS. authority calls Arthur's antagonist Lucius
Hiberus, and since $n$ is constantly indicated in MSS. by a dash
over the preceding letter, nothing could be easier than for
Hibernus to become Hiberus.

Another check is supplied by the fact that Llwch Llenlleawc
of Ireland survived in later tradition not only as Lucius Hiberus,
but also as Lanceor the King of Ireland's son.   We discovered in
Chapter XXV the derivation of the Gareth and Balaain stories
from a common tradition.   When, therefore, we observe that
Lanceor in the latter story starts in pursuit of the young hero and
jousts with him just as Lancelot does in the former,[30] it is patent
that Lancelot and Lanceor are variants of the same name.   It
seems equally patent that the repeated qualification of Lanceor
as the Irish knight must be a survival of the name Llenlleawc
Gwyddel.

Furthermore, the war between Arthur and Lucius seems to
be based on the same tradition which in the *Huth Merlin* represents Arthur in conflict with Lot [31] and in the *Mort Artu*, with
Lancelot.[32]   For all three stories would be explained by a lost
Welsh tradition of a war between Arthur and Llwch Llenlleawc,
of which Layamon suggests the existence.[33]   Be it noted that
the wars with Lucius and Lancelot are both fought in Gaul
(probably a substitution for Guallia), and that both wars are
terminated for the same reason — the treachery of Modred.
Be it also noted that in these two conflicts Gawain plays the
principal part, which in the war with Lot is assigned to Balaain,
identical with Gawain.   Furthermore, in the final battle with
Lucius much is made of the division of his army into twelve
battalions, each with its senatorial or royal commander, while
in the army of Lot there are twelve kings.   In short, there is
enough resemblance between the wars of Lucius, Lot, and
Lancelot to confirm the belief that all repose on a common Welsh

---

[30] *Huth Merlin*, ed. Paris, Ulrich, I, 225 ff.     [32] Sommer, VI, 294 ff.
[31] *Ibid.*                                          [33] *SNPL*, X, 163.

legend of a great struggle between Arthur and Llwch, in which Gwri was Arthur's chief support,[34] and in which Llwch and his twelve subordinate kings were defeated and slain.

Another important derivation is that of the name Hider or Hiderus, filius Nu. Both Welsh *Bruts* recognize, as well as all modern scholars, that this is Edern son of Nudd.[35] The French usually render the name Yder or Ydier fis Nu. Since the Modena sculpture furnishes the Breton form Isdernus, still retaining the *n*, it is clear that Geoffrey employs a form far closer to the French than the Welsh. Not only does the name Hiderus support the Breton derivation of Geoffrey's material, but it also affords one more proof of mythological origin. Welsh Nudd is also the father of Gwynn, who is said to rule over the "devils" in Annwn, and fights, as we know, every first of May with Gwythyr for the hand of Kreiddylat. There is little doubt that both Gwynn and Nudd are supernatural figures, and since Gwynn is also said to be son of the Firmament (Nwyvre),[36] Nudd is probably a sky god. The name of his son Edern seems clearly to go back through the recorded forms Etern, Aetern,[37] to Aeternus, probably derived from Latin inscriptions to the gods, where it is found as a divine epithet.[38] "Hider filius Nu" may therefore be interpreted "The Eternal One, son of the Firmament."

That there are more fragments of British myth buried in the tales of Brutus, Corineus, Ludhudibras or Rudhudibras, Bladud, and Locrinus seems plausible, but let the task of excavation rest for some other scholar, better equipped or more inspired. At least, the burden of proof is upon those who maintain that Geoffrey excavated his materials largely from his own brain.

[34] A modern Irish folktale describes a combat between Cuculin and Lug. *Cf.* J. Curtin, *Myths and Folklore of Ireland*, 309.

[35] Gottfried, 406.

[36] *Ibid.*, I, 262.

[37] *Ibid.*, II, 329, 348.

[38] Cook, *Zeus*, I, 608 note 7.

# CHAPTER XXXV

## ARTHUR MAB UTER

As THIS study of the nature and origin of the Arthurian legend draws to a close, we may well ask: "What of Arthur himself? If most of his knights are gods of sun and storm, if his wife is the leading lady in a nature myth, if his son Mordred plays the part of the Irish god Mider, and if Arthur in Avalon is but another form of the Maimed King, embodiment of the enfeebled forces of Nature awaiting the spring, must we give up the historic Arthur? Was Arthur from the beginning a god?"

Rhys endeavored to connect Arthur with the Irish mythological figure Airem, and with the root *ar-* meaning to plow, with the implication that Arthur originated as an agrarian deity.[1] Singer has urged that Nennius' explanation of the name as "the terrible bear" (Welsh *arth* = bear) suffices to relate Arthur to a Bernese bear-goddess Artio and to make him a bear-god.[2] Malone has woven a most ingenious case for the identity of Arthur with the Welsh god Uthyr, and for the derivation of his name from that of his divine father.[3] None of these derivations convince me that Arthur was originally a god. There is nothing in the legends to identify him with a plowman or a bear, divine or otherwise; and Malone, whose argument for regarding his name as a corruption of Uthyr was far more complete and careful than the case for the other theories, has shifted his support to the derivation from the Roman name Artorius.[4] And this after all, in view of the fact that some Welsh proper names are of Latin derivation (for example, Custennin from Constantine) seems the most satisfactory explanation. The name Arthur is not recognizably mythological.

Neither are his activities when we first hear of them from the ninth century historian Nennius. During that period of desperate struggle between Celt and Anglo-Saxon for the possession

---

[1] Rhys, *Arthurian Legend*, 39 ff.

[2] S. Singer, *Die Artussage.*

[3] *JEGP*, XXIII, 463. *Cf. RC*, XLII, 306 ff.

[4] *MP*, XXII, 367–74. I do not accept the identification with L. Artorius Cassus, prefect of the Sixth Victrix in the second century.

of Britain, early in the fifth century, in the oft-quoted words,
"Arthur fought against them in those days, together with the
kings of the Britons, but he himself was a battle-chief." [5]
His twelve victories are named. In the last, on Mount Badon,
he is said to have struck down 960 men single-handed. To be
sure, this feat must be exaggerated, to say the least, and Bede
makes the British leader at the Badonic Mount Vortigern.
There is no disputing the dubious nature of Nennius' account
of Arthur. But the essential point is this: in spite of the fact
that Nennius had no scruples against the admission of the
fantastic and the supernatural into his chronicle, there is not a
single mythological trait in his treatment of Arthur. Here is no
bear-god, genius of the plow, or solar hero. The *Mirabilia*
attached to Nennius's *History*,[6] though they affirm that Arthur's hound Cabal left his print in a stone during the hunt of
the mythological boar Troit, and that Arthur slew his son
Amir, do not show more than that Arthur was beginning to be
associated with marvels. If his origin was in myth, the earliest
clear evidence for the contention must be sought in the Modena
sculpture, which reposes on a tale told in the winter of 1096–7.
In sum, the facts point toward a historic Arthur, of Roman
name and at least partly Roman blood, who identified himself
with the cause of the Britons and early in the sixth century
united them against the Saxon invaders in a succession of
victories.

The probabilities are that Arthur began his career in history,
extended his conquests into the realm of Welsh, Dumnonian and
Breton myth, and completed his triumph by achieving the
sovereignty of European romance. He is comparable rather to
Alexander the Great and Theodoric than to King Lear or St.
Dionysius. Welsh literature affords in the legend of *Maxen
Wledig* [7] a fairly close analogy to what we have concluded was
the development of the Arthurian legend. In both a historic
warrior lives on in the tales told by the ancients around the
fire-side; in both he has become the hero of a legend which takes
him into the Other World, marries him to a supernatural bride,
and surrounds him with mythic figures. We have already seen
how the venerable lord carving chessmen in his castle, clearly a
Welsh god, has made his way not only into the *Dream of Maxen*

[5] *Mon. Germ. Hist., Auct. Ant.*, XIII, 199 note 1.
[6] *Ibid.*, 217.  [7] Loth. *Mab.*², I, 211.

but also into Arthurian romance. Likewise his daughter Helen, in her vest of white silk and her crown and girdle of gold, though clearly a lady of Faery, becomes in the *Dream* the bride of Maxen, and enters the Arthurian cycle as Elaine the daughter of Pelles, though in Welsh she is the daughter not of Beli, but of Beli's successor as ruler of Britain.

Malone's article is of value not only in raising the issue of the relation between Arthur and Uther, but also in pointing out that Uther existed independently as a Welsh god. His name means "The Wonderful," and Uthyr Ben, "the Wonderful Chief," Uthyr Pendragon, "the Wonderful Chief Sovereign." [8] As Malone asserts, this title "is meant to mark Uthyr as over-god." The *Death-Song of Uthyr Pendragon* represents him as belted with a rainbow, riding above the storm of battle.[9] Geoffrey of Monmouth's account of Uther's invasion of Ireland to bring away the stones which he set up at Stonehenge, Malone interprets plausibly as a version of the mythical harrying of Annwn, usually attributed to Arthur and his heroes.[10]

His relationship to Arthur is best explained, however, by Guest, who [11] proposed that it arose from a misunderstanding of the gloss found in Nennius, which asserts that he was called "mab uter," that is, "filius horribilis." The fact is that the phrase can have any one of three meanings: "the terrible son," "the marvelous or admirable youth," or "the son of Uter." Miss Schoepperle settled the matter by adducing an exact analogy from the Irish.[12] Meyer proved that the father who is assigned to Cuchulinn in certain stories, Soalte, owes his existence to just such a misunderstanding.[13] For in Irish "mac Soalte" may mean either "well nurtured youth" or "son of Soalte." In Arthur's case, the confusion was much more likely since Uthyr already existed as a divine name or title. As soon as Arthur began to emerge out of the misty past as a glorious superhuman champion, the interpretation of *mab uter* as "son of Uthyr" was almost inevitable.

The descriptive phrase, *mab uter*, may mean more than the

[8] *JEGP*, XXIII, 463, 472;  E. Greulich, *Arthursage in der Historia Regum Britanniae*, 23.

[9] Skene, *Four Ancient Books*, I, 297.  *Cf. JEGP*, XXIII, 469 ff.

[10] *JEGP*, XXIII, 470.

[11] *Origines Celticae*, II, 159.  *Cf. RC*, XLII, 306 ff.

[12] *Vassar Medieval Studies*, 4 f.

[13] K. Meyer, *Miscellanea Hibernica*, 9–11.

glossator supposed when he explains that Arthur was called the terrible son "because from his boyhood up he was cruel." It may mean "the marvelous or admirable youth," [14] and in that case it probably sets the youthful Arthur in a class of young Celtic gods, just as his lying wounded in Avalon places him with the venerable deities. In the *Hymn of St. Columba* the author protests that he does not adore "a *youth*, nor chance, nor woman." [15] Evidently he refers to the worship of youthful gods, of whom Cuchulinn may possibly have been, and Aengus In Mac Oc, the Young Son, was surely one.[16] In Gaul we have Apollo Maponos, and in Welsh Mabon, the Great Youth.[17] Welsh, too, is Melwas, the abductor of Guinevere, whose name both Rhys and Zimmer derive from *maelgwas*, the Prince Youth.[18] The glossator of Nennius, who inserted the phrase *mab uter*, may therefore have preserved for us one of the earliest signs of the apotheosis of Arthur, his inclusion among the Great Youths.[19]

Arthur, we may conclude, was both man and god. Neither the account of his exhumation at Glastonbury nor the solid oak of the Round Table at Winchester proves as convincing to us as they did to good Caxton. But Nennius' account, in spite of all that may be said against it, sounds far more like confused and perhaps exaggerated history than myth. It was a singular trick of fate that this obscure leader of a temporary resurgence of the Britons should have become not only the perpetual embodiment of the British hope, but also should have become the central figure of the accumulated mythology of a thousand years.

The myths of certain islands lying in the eastern Mediterranean, the mystery cults of the Cabeiroi and Curetes, of Cybele and Demeter, seem to have been carried on one of those waves of colonization out beyond the Pillars of Hercules to Tartessos or Gades. Thence they were carried by traders to Armorica and the Sacred Isle, or by settlers, perhaps the Iverni of Ptolemy,[20] and were firmly planted in Southern Ireland. Here

[14] *JEGP*, XXIII, 463.

[15] *Miscellany of Irish Archaeological Soc.*, I, 6, l. 65.

[16] J. A. Macculloch, *Religion of the Ancient Celts*, 81.

[17] *Ibid.*, 123.

[18] W. Foerster, *Karrenritter und Wilhelmsleben* (1899), xxxviii; J. Rhys, *Arthurian Legend*, 51.

[19] Late indications of the apotheosis of Arthur are his association with the heavens by Gavin Douglas, *Eneados*, III, 85, and Lydgate, *Troy Book*, C 3.

[20] *Mitteilungen der Anthropologischen Gesellschaft in Wien*, XXXIX, 107.

probably the conquering Goidels found them, absorbed them, and amalgamated them with the mythology of Lug and Manannan, the worship of the horse and the stag, the cult of the sacred caldron, stone, sword, and spear. From Southern Ireland the new mythology spread to South Wales and Dumnonia, and mingled again with the worship of Brythonic and Romano-British divinities, with the legends of Myrddin, Drystan, and Peredur, and with the glorified memories of Arthur. The astounding fact about the whole process is the distinctness with which the original outlines of myth and ritual can be detected in French romances of the twelfth and thirteenth century, — myth and ritual which may have left the shores of Samothrace and Crete perhaps two thousand years before. The tradition must have been guarded from the beginning to almost the end by a priestly caste, who made it their pride to convey from generation to generation, with due allowance for embroidery and harmonizing, the essential form of their sacred heritage. Periodically there was an enlargement of the pattern or a new distribution of divine names. In the last Breton and French stages the pagan matter was purged of its wilder licenses of fancy and morals, and adapted to the taste of a courtly and nominally Christian society. But the medieval respect for tradition still forced the retention of so much of the pagan material, and thanks to the activity and talent of the Breton *conteurs*, so large a body of the mythico-heroic legend of Arthur has been preserved, that if one grasps the right clues, he may unravel the tangled skein. Rhys, Gaston Paris, Martin, Nutt, Miss Weston, Nitze, and Gruffydd have made the greatest contributions to the elucidations of the mythical patterns in the Arthurian cycle. May this book serve to show how fruitful will ultimately be the study of scholars who bring to it a knowledge of one or more of these subjects: 1. the vast literature of the Arthurian cycle in all languages; 2. the ancient literature of Ireland and Wales; 3. the religion of the Celts in Ireland, Britain, and Gaul; 4. the myth and ritual of the Hellenic world as interpreted by Murray, Cook, Miss Harrison, Miss Macurdy, and others of the same school; 5. the testimony of classical authors regarding the beliefs and practices of the inhabitants of the western world; 6. the ethnology of the British Isles and its relation to ancient trade routes and archaeological evidence; 7. the modern folklore of Ireland, the

Scotch Highlands, and Brittany. When all these sources have been drawn upon, it will be possible to reconstruct, not indeed a chronicle of the British Isles before the coming of Caesar, but a fairly complete conception of the inhabitants, their origin, their contacts with the rest of the world, their priests and kings, their fundamental beliefs regarding Nature and her ways, the character and functions of their multitudinous gods. The last hundred years which by means of the newspaper, the moving picture, the factory, the "tripper," have brought about the extinction of a pagan culture which had existed in the "Celtic fringe," in Ireland, and in Brittany for over two thousand years, have made some amends by making accessible to all the pertinent records and by providing the scientific apparatus for their interpretation. The task is one upon which not only Irishman and Briton may unite, but also the scholars of all the many lands who received and cultivated the *Matière de Bretagne*. Classicist and medievalist, archaeologist and ethnologist, students of folklore and mythology, all have their contributions to make toward the elucidation of that primitive culture of the western isles whose resurgence in the romances of the Round Table supplied to medieval Europe the same sort of imaginative stimulus that the Homeric tradition had supplied to the Hellenic world two thousand years before.

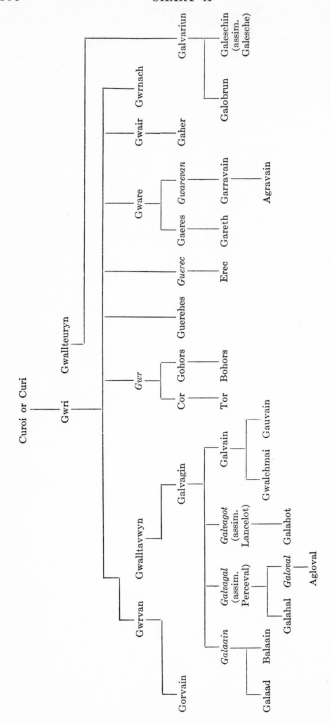

TABLE OF DERIVATIONS FROM CUROI

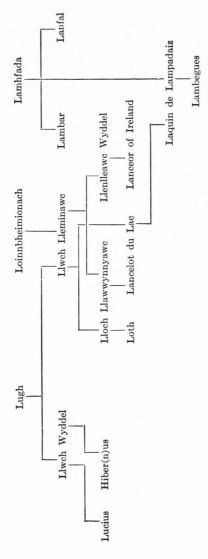

TABLE OF DERIVATIONS FROM LUG

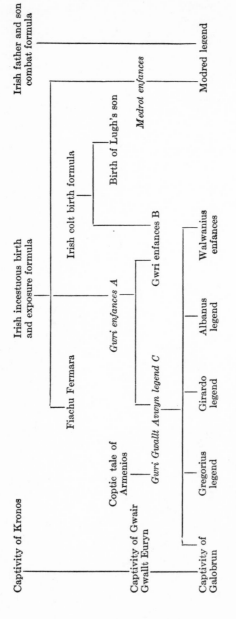

N. B.  Gwri enfances A = Pagan myth as inferred.
       Gwri enfances B = Pagan myth extant in *Pwyll*.
       Gwri legend C = A contaminated by Coptic tale.
       **Italics** indicate hypothetical versions.

# LIST OF WELSH NAMES AND ARTHURIAN DERIVATES

*(Not included in charts)*

| | |
|---|---|
| Anna (wife of Beli) | Anna (wife of Lot) |
| Arawn | Alain le Gros |
| Arianrhod | Lunete (?) |
| Avallach | Evalach, Avalloc, Avallo |
| Bedwyr | Bedivere, Beduerus |
| Beli Mawr | Bellinor, Pellinor |
| Bel(l)i | Pelle(s) |
| Belin | Belin, Pellean, Pelleas |
| Blodeuwedd | Florie, Lore |
| Bran | Bron, Ban, Brian, Bran-dus |
| Bran Gawr * | Brangorre |
| Bran Mabon * | Bandemagus |
| Branwen | Bringvain |
| Caledvwlch | Caliburnus |
| Cath Paluc | Chapalu |
| Ceindrech | Cundrie |
| Don | Do |
| Edern ab Nudd | Isdernus, Ydier filz Nu, Hiderus |
| Essyllt | Iseut, Ysolt |
| Gilvaethwy ab Don | Giflet filz Do |
| Gwenhwyvar | Guenievre, Guinemar, Guanhumara Winlogee, Guinloie, Guinelorete |
| Gwri or Gware Don * | Giri fils Do, Carrado, Garadue, Cardu-ino |
| Gwynwas | Guinebaus, Gundebaldus, Gunvasius |
| Helen | Elaine |
| Kadwr | Cador |
| Kae Hir | Kaherdin (assimilated to Kaardin) |
| Kei | Che, Kai, Cajus |
| Llew | Lyonel |
| Mabon | Mabon, Mabuz, Mabon-agrain |
| Manawyddan | Manaal |
| March | Mark |
| Medrot | Modred, Mordrain Mardoc, Madoc, Mador, Malduc, Malgiers |
| Melwas | Maheloas, Melians, Meleagans, Malvasius |
| Modron | Morgan, Morgawse |
| Myrddin | Merlin |
| Nasiens | Nasciens |
| Owain | Evein, Ivain, Eventus |
| Peredur | Perceval, Perlesvaus |
| Pryderi | Priure, Pierre, Petrus |
| Rhiannon | Niniane |
| Rhitta | Ryons, Ritho |
| Trystan | Tristan |
| Twrch Trwyth | Tortain |
| Urien | Urien, Uen-t-res |
| Uthyr | Uther |

The * indicates unrecorded compounds.

# LIST OF ABBREVIATIONS

*Archiv: Archiv für das Studium der neueren Sprachen.*

Bruce, *Evolution:* J. D. Bruce, *Evolution of Arthurian Romance, Hesperia, Ergänzungsreihe,* IX.

*IT: Irische Texte,* ed. W. Stokes, E. Windisch.

*ITS: Irish Texts Society.*

Loth, *Mab.*[2]: Joseph Loth, *Les Mabinogion,* ed. 1913.

*MLN: Modern Language Notes.*

*MLR: Modern Language Review.*

*MP: Modern Philology.*

Nutt, *Studies:* A. Nutt, *Studies on the Legend of the Holy Grail.*

Potvin: C. Potvin, *Perceval le Gallois.*

*PMLA, Publications of the Modern Language Association of America.*

*PRIA, Proceedings of the Royal Irish Academy.*

*RC: Revue Celtique.*

Rhys, *Hib. Lec.:* John Rhys, *Lectures on the Growth of Celtic Heathendom, Hibbert Lectures,* 1887.

*Rom: Romania.*

*RR: Romanic Review.*

Sommer: H. O. Sommer, *Vulgate Version of the Arthurian Romances.*

*SNPL: Studies and Notes in Philology and Literature.*

*ZCP: Zeitschrift für celtische Philologie.*

*ZfSL: Zeitschrift für französische Sprache und Literatur.*

*ZrP: Zeitschrift für romanische Philologie*

# INDEX OF NAMES